W9-AWW-569

How to Do Everything
iPod® & iTunes®

Fourth Edition

WITHDRAWN
From the
Mishawaka-Penn-Harris Public Library

Mishawaka - Penn Public Library
Mishawaka, Indiana

GAYLORD M

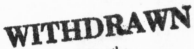

About the Author

Guy Hart-Davis is the author of more than 40 computer books, including *CNET Do-It-Yourself iPod Projects, How to Do Everything with Microsoft Office Word 2007,* and *How to Do Everything with Microsoft Office Excel 2007.*

About the Technical Editors

Marc Campbell is a technology author, graphic designer, and instructor. His popular books on computer topics have appeared around the world in eight languages.

Brandon Jones is the founder of iKaput.com, one of the leading iPod repair companies on the Web. His latest business venture is Sync, bringing iPod repair, accessories, and exchange to a mall near you (synctogo.com).

How to Do Everything
iPod® & iTunes®

Fourth Edition

Guy Hart-Davis

04/08

**Mishawaka-Penn-Harris
Public Library
Mishawaka, Indiana**

New York   Chicago   San Francisco   Lisbon
London   Madrid   Mexico City   Milan   New Delhi
San Juan   Seoul   Singapore   Sydney   Toronto

The **McGraw·Hill** Companies

Cataloging-in-Publication Data is on file with the Library of Congress

McGraw-Hill books are available at special quantity discounts to use as premiums and sales promotions, or for use in corporate training programs. To contact a representative, please visit the Contact Us pages at www.mhprofessional.com.

How to Do Everything: iPod® & iTunes®, Fourth Edition

Copyright © 2008 by The McGraw-Hill Companies. All rights reserved. Printed in the United States of America. Except as permitted under the Copyright Act of 1976, no part of this publication may be reproduced or distributed in any form or by any means, or stored in a database or retrieval system, without the prior written permission of publisher, with the exception that the program listings may be entered, stored, and executed in a computer system, but they may not be reproduced for publication.

1 2 3 4 5 6 7 8 9 0   DOC DOC   0 1 9 8 7

ISBN   978-0-07-226387-9
MHID   0-07-226387-3

Sponsoring Editor
  Megg Morin
Editorial Supervisor
  Janet Walden
Project Manager
  Vasundhara Sawhney,
  International Typesetting
  and Composition
Acquisitions Coordinator
  Carly Stapleton

Technical Editors
  Marc Campbell
  Brandon Jones
Copy Editor
  Bill McManus
Proofreader
  Manish Tiwari
Indexer
  Valerie Perry
Production Supervisor
  Jean Bodeaux

Composition
  International Typesetting
  and Composition
Illustration
  International Typesetting
  and Composition
Art Director, Cover
  Jeff Weeks
Cover Designer
  Pattie Lee

Cover image used by permission from Apple Inc.

Information has been obtained by McGraw-Hill from sources believed to be reliable. However, because of the possibility of human or mechanical error by our sources, McGraw-Hill, or others, McGraw-Hill does not guarantee the accuracy, adequacy, or completeness of any information and is not responsible for any errors or omissions or the results obtained from the use of such information.

This book is dedicated to the people who gave us MP3, AAC, Apple Lossless Encoding, the various iPods, and the iPhone.

Contents at a Glance

Contents

Acknowledgments

I'd like to thank the following people for their help with this book:

- Megg Morin for developing the book and relaying hardware as necessary
- Carly Stapleton for handling the acquisitions end of the book
- Marc Campbell and Brandon Jones for reviewing the manuscript for technical accuracy and contributing many helpful suggestions
- Bill McManus for editing the manuscript
- Vasundhara Sawhney for coordinating the production of the book
- Janet Walden for assisting with the production of the book
- International Typesetting and Composition for laying out the pages
- Valerie Perry for creating the index
- Roger Stewart for lurking in the background, pulling strings as required

Introduction

iPods are the best portable music players available. Small enough to fit easily into a hand or a pocket, an iPod classic can hold the contents of your entire CD collection in compressed audio files, your entire photo collection, and enough hours of video to keep you entertained for a week or more. An iPod nano holds much less but is correspondingly smaller and cuter. And an iPod shuffle, the tiniest of the lot, not only holds enough music to keep you listening all day but also has enough battery life to play it all.

And just when mobile phones were starting to mount a serious challenge to the iPod family's dominance of the portable player market, Apple released the iPhone, which packs in not only a full set of mobile phone features but also a video-capable iPod driven by a touch screen.

Apple then followed up with the iPod touch, a widescreen iPod that uses a touch screen like the iPhone's but doesn't have the phone features.

Whichever model of iPod or iPhone you have, you can download a dozen CDs' worth of music from your computer to it in less than a minute, and you can recharge the iPod or iPhone quickly either from a power outlet or from your computer. And whether you use Windows or Mac OS X, you can enjoy music on your computer with iTunes, the best all-round jukebox and music-management application available.

But you can also do more … much more.

This book shows you how to get the most out of your iPod or iPhone.

What Does This Book Cover?

Chapter 1, "Choose an iPod or iPhone and Get Your Computer Ready to Work with It," explains what the iPods and iPhone are and what they do; how to distinguish the current models from each other; and how their capabilities differ. The chapter then suggests how to choose the model that's best for you and shows you how to get your PC or Mac ready to work with it.

Chapter 2, "Configure iTunes and Load the iPod or iPhone," runs you through the steps of installing iTunes on your PC or Mac and connecting the iPod or iPhone for the first time. The chapter then shows you how to start creating your library and how to load the iPod or iPhone with songs—and then disconnect it safely.

Chapter 3, "Listen to Music on an iPod or iPhone," shows you how to connect your speakers or headphones to the iPod or iPhone, how to use its controls, and how to use its main features.

Chapter 4, "Extend the iPod's or iPhone's Capabilities with Hardware Accessories," discusses the various types of accessories available for the iPod and iPhone, from mainstream accessories (such as cases and stands) to more esoteric accessories (wait and see).

Chapter 5, "Use an iPod or iPhone as Your Home Stereo or Car Stereo," discusses how to connect the iPod or iPhone to your home stereo or car stereo.

Chapter 6, "Create Audio Files, Edit Them, and Tag Them," shows you how to use iTunes and other tools to build a library packed with high-quality, accurately tagged song files. You'll learn how to choose the best location to store your library, how to configure iTunes to get exactly the audio quality you need, and how to work with compressed audio in ways that iTunes itself can't manage. You'll also learn how to convert other audio file types to MP3, AAC, Apple Lossless Encoding, WAV, or AIFF so you can play them on your iPod or iPhone, how to create audio files from cassettes or vinyl records, and how to save audio streams to disk so you can listen to them later.

Chapter 7, "Buy and Download Songs, Videos, and More," explains your options for buying song and video files online. The chapter starts by covering what digital rights management (DRM) is and what it means for computer users. It then discusses what the iTunes Store is, how to set up an account, how to find music and videos by browsing and searching, and how to buy and download music and videos. The chapter also discusses other online music stores that you may want to examine (although the song files most of the stores sell aren't directly compatible with the iPod or the iPhone) and points you to sites where you can find free (and legal) songs online.

Chapter 8, "Burn CDs and DVDs from iTunes," shows you how to use the features built into iTunes to burn CDs and DVDs. You'll learn the basics of burning and the differences between audio CDs, MP3 CDs, and data CDs and data DVDs; learn to configure iTunes for burning discs; and learn how to troubleshoot problems you encounter when burning discs.

Chapter 9, "Make the Most of iTunes," shows you how to make the most of iTunes for playing back music—with or without graphical visual effects. You'll learn how to use audio features such as the graphical equalizer, crossfading, and Sound Enhancer; and you'll find out how to control iTunes both via keyboard shortcuts and via the iTunes widget on Mac OS X.

Chapter 10, "Manage Your Library with iTunes," explains how to browse, mix, and import and export music; how to share music with others and access the music others are sharing; and how to tune into podcasts. You'll also learn how to move your library from one folder to another, remove duplicate items from your library, and even use multiple libraries on the same computer.

Chapter 11, "Put Your Contacts and Calendars on the iPod," covers how to put your contact information and calendars on the iPod classic or iPod nano so that you can carry them with you and view them whenever you need to. This chapter does not cover putting contacts on the iPhone; Chapter 19 does.

Chapter 12, "Put Text and Books on the iPod," shows you how to put text other than contacts and calendar information on the iPod. This chapter starts by discussing the limitations of the iPod as a text-display device and mentioning the types of text best suited to the iPod. Then it explains how to use the iPod's built-in Notes feature before going on to cover a variety of third-party utilities for putting text on your iPod.

Chapter 13, "Put Photos and Videos on the iPod or iPhone," shows you how to synchronize photos from your computer with the iPod or iPhone. You'll learn how to fine-tune the synchronization of photos and video files, view photos or videos on your iPod or on a connected TV, and configure and view a slideshow. You'll also learn how to create video files that will play on the iPod or iPhone, and how to get photos from the iPhone's camera to your computer.

Chapter 14, "Use Multiple iPods or iPhones, Multiple Computers, or Both," explains how to synchronize several iPods or iPhones with the same computer and shows you how to load an iPod from multiple computers. The chapter walks you through the processes of moving an iPod or iPhone from Mac OS X to Windows or the other direction and shows you how to change the computer to which your iPod is linked.

Chapter 15, "Recover Your Songs and Videos from an iPod or iPhone," shows you how to transfer files from the iPod's or iPhone's library to your computer—for example, to recover songs from the iPod after the hard disk on your computer fails.

Chapter 16, "Use the iPod with Software Other Than iTunes," explains why you might want to use software other than iTunes to control the iPod, and it gives examples of several Windows applications that are viable alternatives to iTunes. On the Mac, iTunes rules almost unchallenged, but Clutter provides a wonderful super-graphical interface that makes iTunes even easier to use. At this writing, these programs do not work with the iPhone or iPod touch.

Chapter 17, "Use the iPod as an External Drive or Backup Device," shows you how to use an iPod as an external drive for backup and portable storage. If your computer is a Mac, you can even boot from a hard drive–based iPod for security or to recover from disaster. Along the way, you'll learn how to enable disk mode on an iPod and transfer files to or from an iPod. You'll also learn how to use iPhone Drive to store files on an iPod from a Mac.

Chapter 18, "Troubleshoot the iPod, iPhone, and iTunes," discusses how to troubleshoot the iPod, the iPhone, and iTunes when things go wrong. You'll learn how to avoid making the iPod or iPhone unhappy, how to approach the troubleshooting process in the right way, and how to perform essential troubleshooting maneuvers. Plus, you'll find solutions for problems that occur frequently on the iPod, on the iPhone, and in iTunes.

Chapter 19, "Make Phone Calls with the iPhone," shows you how to make calls with the iPhone, including conference calls. You'll also learn how to receive calls, how to get your messages with Visual Voicemail, and how to sync your contacts to the iPhone from your computer.

Chapter 20, "Connect the iPhone or iPod touch to Wireless Networks, Send E-mail, and Surf the Web," takes you through the iPhone's most compelling features after telephony, music and video, and photos. If you have a wireless network, you'll almost certainly want to connect the iPhone to it so that you can browse the Web, and send and receive e-mail, at full speed rather than relying on the cell-phone network. This chapter also shows you how to create text notes using the iPhone's built-in Notes program. The information about wireless networks and surfing the Web also applies to the iPod touch.

On the purple-shaded pages, you'll find a Special Project that explains how to use the diagnostic tests built into the iPod classic and the iPod nano to identify problems.

Conventions Used in This Book

To make its meaning clear without using far more words than necessary, this book uses a number of conventions, four of which are worth mentioning here:

- Note, Tip, and Caution paragraphs highlight information to draw it to your notice.

- The pipe character or vertical bar denotes choosing an item from a menu. For example, "choose File | Open" means that you should click the File menu and select the Open item on it. Use the keyboard, mouse, or a combination of the two as you wish.

- The ⌘ symbol represents the Command key on the Mac—the key that bears the Apple symbol and the quad-infinity mark on most Mac keyboards.

- Most check boxes have two states: *selected* (with a check mark in them) and *cleared* (without a check mark in them). This book tells you to *select* a check box or *clear* a check box rather than "click to place a check mark in the box" or "click to remove the check mark from the box." (Often, you'll be verifying the state of the check box, so it may already have the required setting—in which case, you don't need to click at all.) Some check boxes have a third state as well, in which they're selected but dimmed and unavailable. This state is usually used for options that apply to only part of the current situation.

Part I

Enjoy Audio with an iPod or iPhone and iTunes

Chapter 1

Choose an iPod or iPhone and Get Your Computer Ready to Work with It

How to...

- Understand what iPods are and what they do
- Understand what the iPhone is
- Distinguish the different types of current iPods
- Identify earlier iPod models (if you have one)
- Choose the right iPod or iPhone for your needs
- Get your PC or Mac ready to work with an iPod or iPhone

If you don't already have an iPod or iPhone, you'll need to beg, borrow, or buy one before you can make the most of this book. This chapter tells you about the iPhone and the iPods available at this writing, and shows you how to distinguish among earlier models in case you have one of those rather than a current model. The chapter then suggests how to choose the one that will best suit your needs. Finally, it shows you how to get your PC or Mac ready to work with an iPod or iPhone.

If you're already the proud owner of an iPod or iPhone, you may prefer to skip directly to Chapter 2, which shows you how to get up and running with it.

What Are iPods and iPhones?

iPod is the umbrella term for the wildly popular portable music players built by Apple Inc. At this writing, there are four main families of iPod: the regular, full-sized iPod, which is now called the iPod classic; the iPod touch, which has a large, touch-sensitive screen; the tiny iPod nano; and the even tinier iPod shuffle. Then there's the iPhone, which has an iPod built into it. Figure 1-1 shows examples of the iPod classic, the iPod touch, the iPod nano, the iPod shuffle, and the iPhone.

Apart from these current models, Apple has also produced—and discontinued—five earlier generations of regular iPod, two earlier generations of the iPod nano, one earlier generation of the iPod shuffle, and one generation of the iPod mini, a medium-sized iPod built around a miniature hard disk (technically, a Microdrive). You'll meet these older models briefly later in this chapter.

All current iPods connect to your PC or Mac via USB, enabling you to transfer files quickly to the player.

NOTE   *The early generations of iPods used FireWire connections only before switching to USB. You can also use a FireWire connection to charge the iPhone or any iPod except the iPod shuffle, but not to transfer files to them. A FireWire connection is useful only if you happen to have a FireWire-to-Dock Connector cable left over from an earlier iPod.*

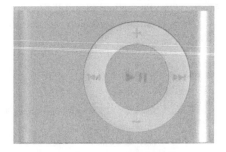

FIGURE 1-1   iPods come in four basic types and the iPhone: the iPod classic, the iPod touch, the iPhone, the iPod nano, and the iPod shuffle. The iPhone includes iPod features along with cell-phone features and wireless networking.

The iPhone and What It Does

The iPhone (see Figure 1-2) is a cell phone that plays music and video (like an iPod, discussed next) along with an impressive list of other features. The iPhone's capabilities include:

- Making phone calls, including conference calls
- Checking your voicemail messages either in the order received or out of order
- Connecting to the Internet via a wireless network connection

FIGURE 1-2 The iPhone includes full iPod functionality—along with normal cell-phone capabilities, mail, and web browsing.

Did you know?

The Advantages and Disadvantages of Flash Memory

Except for the iPod classic, which uses a hard drive, all iPods and the iPhone use flash memory chips for storage.

Flash memory has two main advantages:

- Flash memory is shockproof, so the iPod won't skip unless you damage it badly enough to prevent it from playing.

- Flash memory uses far less power than a hard disk—around 1/30 of the amount a hard drive takes—so the iPod or iPhone requires a smaller battery than it would otherwise need.

The disadvantage of flash memory is that it is still much more expensive per gigabyte than hard disks. This is why there is such a vast difference in capacity between the iPod classic (80GB or 160GB) and the next-most capacious iPod, the iPod touch (8GB or 16GB).

- Browsing the Web with the Safari browser
- Sending and receiving e-mail messages via your existing e-mail account
- Taking pictures with the built-in camera—and sending them immediately via e-mail if you so wish
- Watching videos from YouTube
- Getting maps, weather reports, stock quotes, and more

The iPod classic and What It Does

The iPod classic is the sixth generation of regular iPod. The iPod classic is a portable music and video player with a huge capacity, a rechargeable battery good for 8 to 15 hours of music playback (less if you watch a lot of video), and easy-to-use controls.

The iPod classic is built around the type of hard drive used in small laptop computers and comes in different capacities—at this writing, up to 160GB. (The capacity is engraved on the back of the iPod.) So far, as hard-disk manufacturers have released higher-capacity hard disks, Apple has continued to release higher-capacity iPods, so the maximum capacity seems certain to rise. The more space on the iPod's hard disk, the more songs, video, or other data you can carry on it.

The iPod classic (see Figure 1-3) has a 2.5-inch color screen with a resolution of 320×240 pixels, which is called Quarter VGA resolution, or QVGA for short. (VGA resolution is 640×480 pixels.) The screen can display videos, photos, and album covers as well as the iPod's menus, information about the song that's currently playing, and text-based items, such as your contacts, calendars, and notes.

Below the screen is a control device called the Click wheel. The Click wheel has four buttons built into it, which you click by pressing the wheel so that it tilts slightly in the required direction. You drag your finger around the surface of the Click wheel to scroll through items such as menus. You press the Select button or Center button, in the middle of the Click wheel, to access the item you've selected by scrolling.

At the bottom of the iPod is a narrow, wide port called the Dock Connector port, which is used to connect the iPod to your computer or to accessories (such as a dock or a charger). At the top is a headphone socket and a Hold switch that you slide to put the iPod on hold (which locks all its controls) or to take it off hold again.

The iPod classic doubles as a contact database, calendar, and notebook, enabling you to carry around not only all your music but your vital information as well. You can also put other textual information on an iPod so you can carry that information with you and view it on the iPod's screen.

With extra hardware, you can extend an iPod's capabilities even further. For example, with a custom microphone, you can record audio directly onto it. With a custom media reader, you can transfer digital photos to the iPod's hard disk directly from a digital camera without using a computer. This capability can make an iPod a great travel companion for a digital camera—especially a camera that takes high-resolution photos.

If music, contacts, calendar, notes, and other text aren't enough for you, you can also use an iPod as an external hard disk for your PC or Mac. An iPod provides an easy and convenient means of backing up your data, storing files, and transporting files from one computer to another.

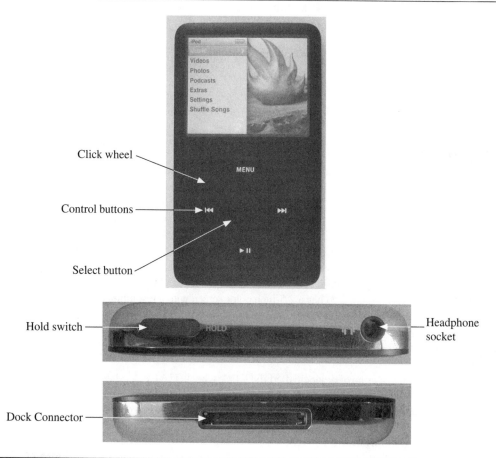

Click wheel

Control buttons

Select button

Hold switch

Headphone socket

Dock Connector

FIGURE 1-3   The front, top, and bottom of an iPod classic

And because the iPod is ultra-portable, you can take those files with you wherever you go, which can be great for school, work, and even play.

The iPod supports various audio formats, including Advanced Audio Coding (AAC), MP3 (including Audible.com's Audible files, an audiobook format), Apple Lossless Encoding, WAV, and AIFF. Although the iPod doesn't support other formats—such as Microsoft's Windows Media Audio (WMA), RealNetworks' RealAudio, and the open-source audio format Ogg Vorbis—at this writing, you can convert audio files in those formats to AAC, MP3, or another supported format easily enough so that you can put those files on the iPod.

The iPod contains a relatively small operating system (OS) that lets it function on its own—for example, for playing back music and videos, displaying contact information, and so on. The OS also lets the iPod know when it's been connected to a computer, at which point the OS hands over control to the computer so you can manage it from there.

The iPod is designed to communicate seamlessly with iTunes, which runs on both Windows and the Mac. If you prefer, you can use the iPod with other software as well on either operating system (Chapter 16 discusses some of the applications you can use). If you use an iPod with iTunes, you can buy songs or videos from the iTunes Store, download them to your computer, and play them either on your computer or the iPod.

NOTE   *The iPod discussed in this section is the sixth generation of regular ipod. For brief details on the first five generations, see the section "Older iPods That Apple Has Now Discontinued," later in this chapter. Because you're most likely to have one of the current iPods if you're reading this book, the book concentrates on the latest iPod models and mentions the earlier models only at key points.*

Did you know?

Why the iPod's or iPhone's Capacity Appears to Be Less Than Advertised

One hundred sixty gigabytes is a huge amount of music—around 40,000 four-minute songs at the iPod's default audio quality, or enough for about 55 days' solid listening. It's also a decent amount of video: about 1000 hours at the compression rate the iTunes Store uses. But unfortunately, you don't actually get the amount of hard disk space that's written on the iPod.

There are two reasons for this. First, you lose some hard-disk space to the iPod's operating system (OS—the software that enables it to function) and the file allocation table that records which file is stored where on the disk. This happens on all hard disks that contain operating systems, and costs you only a few megabytes altogether.

Second, the hard-drive capacities on iPods are measured in "marketing gigabytes" rather than in real gigabytes. A real gigabyte is 1,024 megabytes, a megabyte is 1,024 kilobytes, and a kilobyte is 1,024 bytes. That makes 1,073,741,824 bytes ($1,024 \times 1,024 \times 1,024$ bytes) in a real gigabyte. By contrast, a marketing gigabyte has a flat billion bytes ($1,000 \times 1,000 \times 1,000$ bytes)—a difference of 7.4 percent.

So an iPod will actually hold 7.4 percent less data than its listed drive size suggests (and minus a bit more for the OS and file allocation table). You can see why marketing folks choose to use marketing megabytes and gigabytes rather than real megabytes and gigabytes—the numbers are more impressive. But customers tend to be disappointed when they discover that the real capacity of a device is substantially less than the device's packaging and literature promised.

The same discrepancy applies to the other iPods and the iPhone—and is perhaps even more painful because of the much lower capacities of these devices.

The iPod touch and What It Does

The iPod touch (see Figure 1-4) resembles an iPhone without the phone and the camera. Like the iPhone, the iPod touch has a large, touch-sensitive screen that you use to control most of its functions, from playing back songs and videos to surfing the Web via a wireless network.

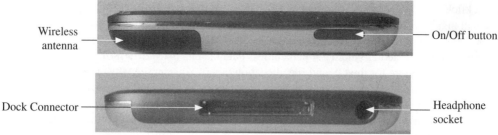

FIGURE 1-4   The iPod touch resembles the iPhone but is marginally smaller and substantially slimmer.

The iPod touch has only two buttons—an on/off button on the top, and the Home button below the screen. Unlike the iPhone, the iPod touch does not have a built-in speaker, so you listen to audio through headphones or external speakers.

At this writing, the iPod touch has some limitations that you might not expect. For example, even though the iPod touch can connect to the Internet via wireless networks, it has no Mail program. Likewise, it has no Notes program, and while you can create new contacts on the iPod touch, you cannot create new calendar appointments. However, Apple may respond to user feedback by adding such missing features—or even other features—via firmware updates, so if you're considering buying an iPod touch, check the latest features list first.

The iPod nano and What It Does

The iPod nano is tiny—smaller than a credit card and thinner than a pencil—and has a relatively modest capacity: at this writing, 4GB and 8GB models are available, but higher-capacity models are likely to be released before long.

The iPod nano (see Figure 1-5) comes in several colors and has a similar layout to the iPod classic, with a screen at the top of the front, the main control buttons built into the Click wheel, and a Dock Connector port on the bottom. The only major difference in layout is that the headphone socket and Hold switch are on the bottom of the iPod nano rather than on the top.

Despite its diminutive size, the iPod nano can play back video as well as songs, and can even output that video to a TV. The iPod nano can also display photos and album art on its screen or on a TV. The iPod nano's capacity is engraved on the back.

The iPod shuffle and What It Does

The iPod shuffle is the smallest and least expensive iPod, costing $79 and holding 1GB at this writing. This is the second-generation iPod shuffle, the one with a metal case and a clip for attaching the player to your clothing—about the size of a wristwatch without a strap. The first-generation iPod shuffle is a white plastic device about the shape and size of a traditional packet of gum.

The iPod shuffle has no screen and two play modes, either playing back an existing playlist in order or "shuffling" the songs into a random order—hence its name. To change from playlist mode to shuffle mode, you move one of the two switches on the bottom of the player.

The iPod shuffle (see Figure 1-6) has only five buttons: Play/Pause, Previous Track and Next Track, and Volume Up and Volume Down. The buttons are laid out in a circular arrangement. Though limited and small, the controls are easy to use, even without looking.

Because the iPod shuffle has no screen, the only way you can navigate through your playlist is by using the Previous button and Next button and listening to the song that plays. The shuffle mode makes a virtue out of this limitation by offering to mix up the songs for you.

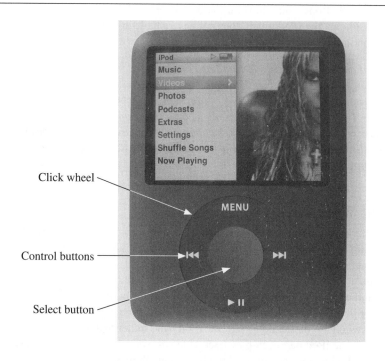

Click wheel

Control buttons

Select button

Dock Connector

Hold switch

Headphone socket

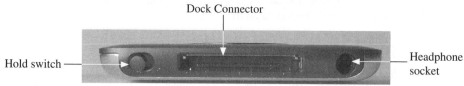

FIGURE 1-5   The iPod nano is very small and contains flash memory rather than a hard disk. Its controls and ports are similar to those on a regular iPod, but its headphone socket is on the bottom rather than the top.

The iPod shuffle is great for exercise or extreme activities that would threaten a larger iPod. But it's also great if you often get new music and want to focus your listening on it without being distracted by your existing collection, or if you want to force yourself to listen to artists or albums that you normally neglect.

Because of the iPod shuffle's limitations, much of what you'll read in the rest of this book doesn't apply to it. For example, you can't put your contacts, your calendar, or notes on the iPod shuffle, because it has no way to display them to you; likewise, you can't watch video on it. The iPod shuffle doesn't use equalizations, but it does support the Start Time and End Time options in iTunes, which allow you to skip part of the beginning or end of a track.

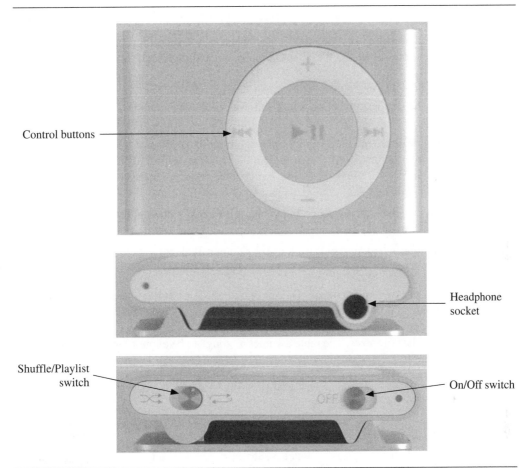

Control buttons

Headphone socket

Shuffle/Playlist switch

On/Off switch

FIGURE 1-6   The iPod shuffle clips onto your clothing.

But the iPod shuffle isn't only for playing music. You can also use the iPod shuffle as a portable disk, and because of its diminutive size, the iPod shuffle is a great way to take your key documents with you.

Troubleshooting the iPod shuffle is usually more straightforward than troubleshooting the regular iPods and the iPod nano because there are fewer things to go wrong with the iPod shuffle. There's also no screen for displaying diagnostic information.

The second-generation iPod shuffle plays AAC, MP3, WAV, AIFF, and Audible.com files, but it can't play Apple Lossless Encoder files. The first-generation iPod shuffle can't play AIFF files or Apple Lossless Encoder files.

Choose the iPod or iPhone That's Best for You

By ruthlessly discontinuing earlier iPod models even when they were selling strongly, Apple has made the process of choosing among the different iPods pretty straightforward:

- If you need a mobile phone that includes an iPod, buy an iPhone.
- If you need the smallest player possible, or a player for active pursuits, get an iPod shuffle.
- If you want the cutest medium-capacity player, go for an iPod nano. The iPod nano is great for smaller libraries, or for carrying only the newest or most exciting songs and videos in your colossal library with you, but its lower capacity makes it a poor value alongside the iPod classic.
- If you want to carry as many songs and videos as possible with you, buy the highest-capacity iPod classic model available.
- If you want to watch videos and surf the Web on your iPod, but you don't want to pay for an iPhone contract, get an iPod touch.

Table 1-1 shows you how much music you can fit onto the current iPod models at widely used compression ratios for music. For spoken audio (such as audio books, plays, or talk radio), you can use lower compression ratios (such as 64 Kbps or even 32 Kbps) and still get acceptable sound with much smaller file sizes. The table assumes a "song" to be about four minutes long and rounds the figures to the nearest sensible point. The table doesn't show less widely used compression ratios such as 224 Kbps or 256 Kbps. (For 256 Kbps, halve the 128 Kbps numbers.)

iPod Nominal Capacity	iPod Real Capacity	128 Kbps		160 Kbps		320 Kbps		Apple Lossless Encoder[1]	
		Hours	Songs	Hours	Songs	Hours	Songs	Hours	Songs
1GB	1GB	17	250	14	200	8	100	n/a[2]	n/a
4GB	3.7GB	67	1,000	54	800	27	400	10	143
8GB	7.5GB	135	2,000	110	1,600	55	800	20	290
16GB	15.2GB	270	4,000	220	3,200	110	1,600	40	590
30GB	27.9GB	500	7,500	400	6,000	200	3,000	71	1,075
80GB	75GB	1,350	20,000	1,100	16,000	550	8,000	190	1,850
160GB	155GB	2,700	40,000	2,200	32,000	1,100	16,000	380	3,900

[1]Apple Lossless Encoder encoding rates vary; these figures are approximations.

[2]The iPod shuffle cannot play Apple Lossless Encoder files.

TABLE 1-1   iPod Capacities at Widely Used Compression Ratios

Did you know?

Audio Formats That the iPods and the iPhone Support

At this writing, the iPods and the iPhone support five audio formats: AAC, MP3 (including Audible.com's AA format), WAV, AIFF, and Apple Lossless Encoder.

iPods and the iPhone don't support some major formats, such as the following:

- Windows Media Audio (WMA), Microsoft's proprietary format. WMA has built-in digital rights management (DRM) capabilities and is used by several of the largest online music stores (such as Napster 2.0). iTunes can convert unprotected WMA files into AAC files to add them to your music library.

- RealAudio, the RealNetworks format in which much audio is streamed across the Internet and other networks.

- Ogg Vorbis, an open-source audio format intended to provide royalty-free competition to MP3.

- Free Lossless Audio Codec (FLAC), the open-source format that uses lossless compression to provide high audio quality (similar to that of Apple Lossless Encoding).

Because you can convert audio files from one format to another, and because the MP3 format is very widely used, this limitation isn't too painful. But if your entire music library is in, say, WMA or Ogg format, you'll have to do some work before you can use it on an iPod. Worse, if your songs are in another compressed format, you'll lose some audio quality when you convert them to AAC or MP3.

The iPod shuffle supports AAC, MP3 (including AA), AIFF, and WAV, but not Apple Lossless Encoder.

NOTE *The iPod refers to tracks as "songs," so this book does the same. Even if the tracks you're listening to aren't music, the iPod considers them to be songs. Similarly, the iPod and this book refer to "artists" rather than "singers," "bands," or other terms.*

Get Your PC or Mac Ready to Work with an iPod or iPhone

If your PC or Mac is a recent model, it probably is ready to work with whichever new iPod you choose. If it's older, or if it's a budget model, or if you've picked up an older iPod, you may need to add new components.

How to ... Buy an iPod or iPhone for Less Than Full Price

If you're reluctant to pay full price for an iPod or iPhone, consider these alternatives:

- **Buy a refurbished iPod or iPhone from Apple**   Apple sells refurbished iPods and iPhones at a discount—sometimes up to a third off the normal price. To find them, search the Apple store (http://store.apple.com) for **refurbished iPod** or **refurbished iPhone**. These iPods and iPhones have a one-year limited warranty, which you should read before buying one (look for a link to the warranty on any page that offers a refurbished iPod). You can also buy AppleCare to extend the coverage, although this is typically worthwhile only for the most expensive models.

- **Buy a reconditioned iPod or iPhone from another vendor**   eBay and other sites have reconditioned iPods and iPhones. However, you will not normally get a warranty, and it may be hard to determine the quality of the reconditioning.

- **Grab an old iPod when a relative or sibling upgrades**   At this writing, you'll be lucky to get an iPhone this way—but when someone you know buys an iPhone or a new iPod, you might want to get in line for their existing device.

Here are the requirements for an iPod classic, an iPod touch, an iPod nano, an iPod shuffle, or an iPhone:

- A PC running Windows Vista (Home Premium, Business, Ultimate, or Enterprise Edition) or either Windows XP Home Edition or Windows XP Professional with Service Pack 2, or a Mac running Mac OS X 10.4.10 (Tiger) or Mac OS X 10.5 (Leopard).

- A USB port. It's best to have a high-power USB 2.0 port, although you can scrape by with a USB 1.x port if you're prepared to be patient. The USB port must deliver enough power to recharge the iPod or iPhone. If your keyboard has a built-in USB port (as many Apple keyboards do), chances are that it doesn't deliver enough power for recharging.

- An optical drive (a CD drive or a DVD drive) if you want to be able to rip songs from CDs to put on the iPod or iPhone.

- A CD burner if you want to burn CDs from iTunes, or a DVD burner if you want to be able to burn both DVDs and CDs. (Most modern optical drives include burning capabilities.)

How Much Faster USB 2.0 Is Than USB 1.x

The terms USB 1.x and USB 2.0 don't suggest a great difference, but USB 2.0 is up to 40 times faster than USB 1.x. USB 1.x has a top speed of 12 megabits per second (Mbps), which translates to a maximum transfer of about 1.5MB of data per second; USB 2.0 has a top speed of 480 Mbps, which gives a data transfer rate of about 60MB per second. So loading an iPod via a USB 2.0 port will go far faster than via a USB 1.x port. The difference is most painful when you're loading a regular iPod, but you'll feel the pinch of USB 1.x even with the lower capacity of an iPod shuffle or an iPod nano.

Get Your PC Ready to Work with an iPod

If you bought your PC in 2003 or later, it most likely has everything you need to start using an iPod or iPhone and iTunes:

- A USB 2.0 port
- Windows Vista (Home Premium, Business, Ultimate, or Enterprise Edition) or Windows XP (either Home Edition or Professional) with Service Pack 2. (If you don't yet have Service Pack 2, you can download it from the Microsoft website for free.)
- A 500-MHz or faster processor (you can get away with a slower processor, but it won't be much fun).
- 512MB RAM (for Windows Vista) or 128MB RAM (for Windows XP). Much more RAM is much better.
- Enough hard-disk space to contain your library, on either an internal hard disk or an external hard disk.
- A CD or DVD burner.

If your PC can't meet those specifications, read the following sections to learn about possible upgrades.

Add USB 2.0 if Necessary

Most PCs manufactured in 2003 or later include one or more USB 2.0 ports—some have a half-dozen or more USB ports. If your PC has one or more, you're all set. If your computer has only USB 1.x, you can add USB 2.0 by installing a PCI card in a desktop PC or by inserting a PC Card in a laptop PC.

If you don't know whether your computer's USB ports are USB 1.*x* or USB 2.0, simply plug in the iPod or iPhone and set it up. Either iTunes or Windows itself will warn you if the device is using a USB 1.*x* port rather than a USB 2.0 port. The Windows warning is usually a notification-area pop-up saying "HI-SPEED USB Device Plugged into non-HI-SPEED USB Hub" or "This USB device can perform faster if you connect it to a Hi-Speed USB 2.0 port," while the iTunes warning is an easy-to-understand message box.

Check Your Operating System Version

Make sure your PC is running Windows Vista or Windows XP with Service Pack 2. If you're in doubt about which version of Windows your computer is running, press WINDOWS KEY–BREAK, and then look at the System window (on Windows Vista; see Figure 1-7) or the General tab of the System dialog box (on Windows XP; see Figure 1-8). If you don't have one of these versions of Windows, upgrade to one of them. Windows XP is probably a better bet for an older computer because Windows Vista requires powerful hardware, but you may have to search on the Internet for a copy of Windows XP, because vendors are now pushing Windows Vista instead.

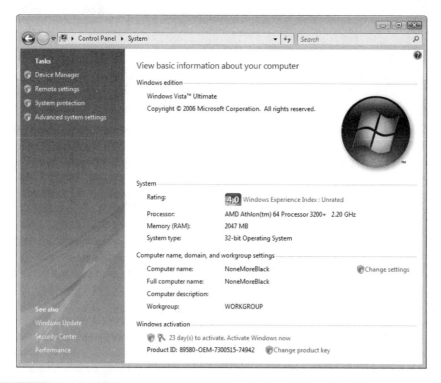

FIGURE 1-7   In Windows Vista, the System window shows which version of Windows you're using and tells you how much RAM the computer contains.

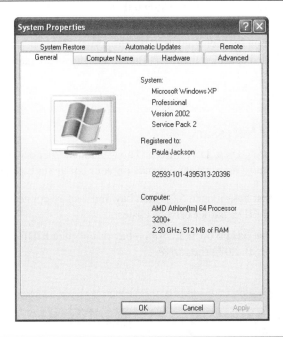

FIGURE 1-8 The readouts on the General tab of the System Properties dialog box typically include the version of Windows and the amount of RAM in your PC. For Windows XP, details of the current service pack also appear.

NOTE *Apple doesn't support using versions of Windows other than Windows Vista and Windows XP with Service Pack 2 for current iPods and the iPhone. But you may be able to use an iPod with Windows 98 Second Edition, Windows Me, or Windows 2000 Professional if you get third-party software such as Anapod Explorer (www.redchairsoftware.com). Chapter 16 discusses Anapod Explorer and other third-party software for controlling iPods. At this writing, there are no third-party programs for controlling the iPhone.*

Check Memory and Disk Space

If you don't know how much memory your computer has, check it. As in the previous section, press WINDOWS KEY–BREAK, and then look at the System window (on Windows Vista) or the General tab of the System dialog box (on Windows XP).

To check disk space, follow these steps:

1. Open a Windows Explorer window to display all the drives on your computer:

   ■ **Windows Vista**   Choose Start | Computer.

   ■ **Windows XP**   Choose Start | My Computer.

2. Right-click the drive you want to check, and then choose Properties from the shortcut menu to display the Properties dialog box for the drive.

3. Look at the readout on the General tab of the Properties dialog box to see the amount of free space and used space on the drive. Figure 1-9 shows an example using Windows Vista.

4. Click the OK button to close the Properties dialog box.

Add a Burner Drive if Necessary

If you want to be able to burn CDs or DVDs from iTunes, add a burner drive to your computer. Which drive technology is most appropriate depends on your computer type and configuration:

- For a desktop PC that has an open 5.25-inch bay and a spare connector on an EIDE channel, an internal EIDE burner drive is easiest.

- For a desktop PC that has no open 5.25-inch bay or no spare EIDE connector, or for a portable PC, get a USB 2.0 burner drive.

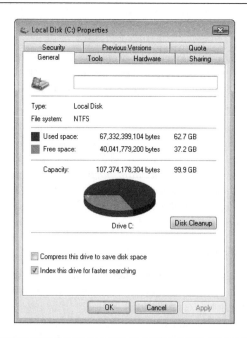

FIGURE 1-9 The General tab of the Properties dialog box for a drive shows you how much space has been used and how much remains free.

Because USB 1.x is relatively slow, USB 1.x CD recorders can manage only 4 × burning speeds. Therefore, you'll probably want to use USB 1.x only when you must—for example, if you have a USB 1.x drive available and can't afford to upgrade.

Get Your Mac Ready to Work with an iPod or iPhone

If you bought your Mac in 2004 or later, chances are it's already all set to work with an iPod or iPhone: It has one or more USB 2.0 ports, Mac OS X (Tiger or Leopard) with iTunes, plenty of disk space and memory, and a CD or DVD burner drive as well.

But if you have an earlier Mac, it may lack a USB 2.0 port; that means you'll either need to add a USB 2.0 port or suffer slow USB 1.x transfer speeds instead. And if your Mac doesn't have a CD or DVD burner drive, you may need to add a burner drive to get the best out of iTunes.

Add USB 2.0 if Necessary

If your Mac lacks a USB 2.0 port, add one or more USB 2.0 ports:

- **Desktop Mac**   Insert a PCI card in a vacant slot.
- **Laptop Mac**   Insert a PC Card.

If you have an iPod shuffle and your Mac has only a USB 1.x port, you probably don't need to upgrade, because the USB 1.x port will fill an iPod shuffle in a tolerably short time.

Check Your Operating System Version

Make sure your version of Mac OS is advanced enough to work with the iPod. You need Mac OS X 10.4.10 (Tiger with updates) or 10.5 (Leopard) to use current iPods or the iPhone. Upgrade if necessary, or use Software Update (choose Apple | Software Update) to download the latest point releases. If you're not sure which version of Mac OS X you have, choose Apple | About This Mac to display the About This Mac window. Then look at the Version readout.

Apple frequently adds new features to iTunes, the iPods, and the iPhone. To get the latest features and to make sure that iTunes and the iPod or iPhone work as well as possible, keep Mac OS X, iTunes, and the device up to date. To check for updates, choose Apple | Software Update.

Check Disk Space and Memory

Make sure your Mac has enough disk space and memory to serve the iPod or iPhone adequately.

In most cases, memory shouldn't be an issue: If your Mac can run Mac OS X and conventional applications at a speed you can tolerate without sedation, it should be able to handle the iPod or iPhone. Technically, Tiger requires a minimum of 256MB and Leopard requires a minimum of 512MB, but you'll get far better performance with 1GB or more.

Disk space is more likely to be an issue if you will want to keep many thousands of songs and videos in your library. The best situation is to have enough space on your hard drive to

How to ... Check the Speed of Your Mac's USB Ports

If you're not sure of the speed of your Mac's USB ports, check them like this:

1. Choose Apple | About This Mac to display the About This Mac dialog box.

2. Click the More Info button to launch the System Profiler utility, which displays more detailed information about the Mac.

3. Expand the Hardware entry in the Contents pane if it's collapsed. Then click the USB item to display its contents.

4. Select one of the USB Bus items in the USB Device Tree pane and check the Speed readout in the lower pane, as shown here. If the readout says "Up to 12 Mb/sec," it's USB 1.x. If the readout says "Up to 480 Mb/sec," it's USB 2.0.

5. Press ⌘-Q or choose System Profiler | Quit System Profiler to close System Profiler.

contain your entire library, both at its current size and at whatever size you expect it to grow to within the lifetime of your Mac. That way, you can easily synchronize your entire library with the iPod or iPhone (if your library fits on the device) or just whichever part of your library you want to take around with you for the time being.

How to ...   # Connect an Older iPod via FireWire

If you have a first- or second-generation iPod, you'll need to connect it to your computer via FireWire rather than via USB.

If your computer is a Mac, this shouldn't be a problem, because all Macs for the last several years include one or more FireWire ports. If you have an older Mac that doesn't have FireWire, add a PCI card (for a desktop Mac) or a PC Card (for a PowerBook). Make sure the card is compatible with the version of Mac OS X you're using, and then install the card and any drivers needed to make it work.

If your computer is a PC, it's less likely to have a FireWire port, because FireWire isn't part of the standard PC specification. But you can add one or more FireWire ports easily enough by inserting a PCI card (in a desktop PC) or a PC Card (in a laptop PC).

On a PC that has built-in FireWire, there's one more thing to watch out for. FireWire ports and cables come in two basic types: four-pin and six-pin. Four-pin ports are more compact than six-pin ports, so they're easier to build into laptops. Six-pin cables supply power to the FireWire devices via the cable, whereas four-pin cables don't supply power. Six-pin cables can recharge an iPod, whereas four-pin cables cannot.

If your PC or Mac does have a FireWire port, you can use the port to charge a current iPod or an iPhone, but not to transfer data to it.

For example, to fill a 160GB iPod with music and video, you'll need 160GB of hard-disk space to devote to your library. Recent desktop Macs have hard disks large enough to spare 160GB without serious hardship, but if you have an older desktop Mac or a laptop Mac, you may not be able to spare that much space.

If you have a desktop Mac, you should be able to add another hard drive without undue effort. Typically, the least expensive option will be to add another EIDE hard drive or SCSI drive (depending on the configuration of your Mac) to the inside of your Mac. Alternatively, you can go for an external FireWire, USB, or SCSI drive (if your Mac has SCSI).

If you have a laptop Mac, an iMac, an eMac, or a Mac mini, your best bet is probably to add an external FireWire or USB hard drive. Upgrading the internal hard drive on these Macs tends to be prohibitively expensive—and you have to transfer or reinstall the operating system, your applications, and all your data after the upgrade.

Add a Burner Drive if Necessary

If your Mac doesn't have a CD or DVD burner, you may want to add one so you can burn CDs or DVDs from iTunes and other applications.

For a desktop Mac that has a full-sized drive bay free, an internal CD-R drive is the least expensive option. Alternatively, turn to one of the alternatives that suit both desktop Macs and portables: external FireWire, USB, or SCSI recordable CD drives.

Chapter 2

Configure iTunes and Load the iPod or iPhone

How to...

- Identify the different components included with the iPod or iPhone
- Set up the iPod or iPhone and connect it to your PC or Mac
- Install iTunes
- Activate the iPhone
- Start creating your library from existing files and CDs
- Load music onto the iPod or iPhone

In this chapter, you'll unpack the iPod or iPhone (if you haven't already done so), give it an initial full charge if it needs one, and connect it to your PC or Mac. You'll install iTunes if you don't already have it installed. Then you'll start creating your library from any existing digital audio and video files you have and from your audio CDs. Finally, you'll load your library—or parts of it—onto the iPod or iPhone.

This chapter discusses how to proceed on both Windows and the Mac. Most of the way, the process is the same for both operating systems. Where they differ, the chapter presents Windows first and then the Mac, so you'll need to skip past the sections that cover the operating system that you're not using.

Unpack the iPod or iPhone

The different models of iPod and iPhone ship with different components and accessories, but most have the following basics:

- The iPod or iPhone itself.
- A pair of ear-bud headphones. The iPhone headphones include a control button, which the other headphones don't.
- A USB cable for attaching the iPod or iPhone to your computer.
- Booklets containing basic instructions and technical information.

The iPhone also includes a power adapter. This is built to accept AC input from 100 to 240 volts, so with the right adapters, you can use it to power the iPhone most of the way around the world.

TIP   *The Apple Store (http://store.apple.com) sells a World Travel Adapter Kit for the iPod. You can also get clumsier but less expensive adapters at RadioShack or any competent electronics store.*

The iPhone and the iPod shuffle also include a dock on which to stand, charge, and load the device. You can buy docks for other iPods, such as the iPod classic and the iPod nano, from the Apple Store (http://store.apple.com) and many other sources. The iPod classic, the iPod touch, and the iPod nano include adapters for docks that meet the Apple iPod Universal Dock specification, a standard design that works with these iPods and several earlier models.

Install iTunes if It's Not Already Installed

Before you connect the iPod or iPhone, you need to install iTunes on your computer—unless you have it installed already, as is likely on a Mac. The process is a little different on Windows and on the Mac, so the next two sections discuss the operating systems separately.

Install iTunes on Your PC

To install iTunes on your PC, follow these steps:

1. Open your browser, go to the iTunes Download page on the Apple website (www.apple .com/itunes/download/), and then download the latest version of iTunes.

2. If Internet Explorer displays a File Download – Security Warning dialog box like the one shown here, verify that the name is iTunesSetup.exe. Then click the Run button.

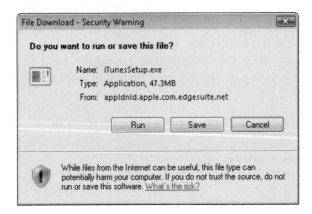

3. If Internet Explorer displays an Internet Explorer – Security Warning dialog box like the one shown here, verify that the program name is iTunes and the publisher is Apple Computer, Inc. Then click the Run button.

4. On the Welcome To The iTunes Installer screen, click the Next button.

5. On the License Agreement screen, read the license agreement, select the I Accept The Terms In The License Agreement option button if you want to proceed, and then click the Next button.

6. On the Choose iTunes + QuickTime Installer Options screen (see Figure 2-1), choose installation options:

■ **Add iTunes And QuickTime Shortcuts To My Desktop** Select this check box only if you need shortcuts on your desktop. The installation routine creates shortcuts on your Start menu anyway. The Start menu is usually the easiest way to launch iTunes.

■ **Use iTunes As The Default Player For Audio Files** Select this check box if you plan to use iTunes as your main audio player. If you plan to use iTunes only for iPod synchronization and use another player (for example, Windows Media Player) for music, don't make iTunes the default player. iTunes associates itself with the AAC, MP3, Apple Lossless Encoding, AIFF, and WAV file extensions.

■ **Automatically Update iTunes, QuickTime And Other Apple Software** Select this check box if you want iTunes, QuickTime, and other Apple programs to check for updates and prompt you to install them. Having the latest version of iTunes is usually helpful, as you get any bug fixes and new features that Apple has included.

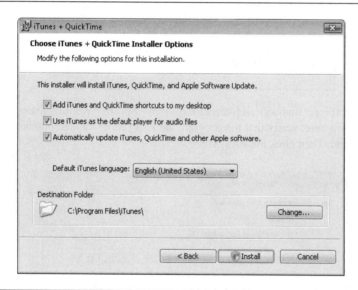

FIGURE 2-1   Choose whether to create shortcuts for iTunes and QuickTime on your Desktop, use iTunes as the default audio player, and update iTunes and QuickTime automatically.

7. The installer displays the iTunes + QuickTime screen while it installs iTunes and QuickTime. On Windows XP, you need take no action until the Congratulations screen appears, telling you that iTunes and QuickTime have been successfully installed. However, on Windows Vista, you must go through several User Account Control prompts for different components of the iTunes installation (unless you've turned User Account Control off).

CAUTION   *On Windows Vista, the User Account Control prompts may get stuck behind the iTunes + QuickTime screen. Look at the taskbar now and then to see if there's a flashing User Account Control prompt that you need to deal with before the installation can continue.*

8. When the Congratulations screen appears, select the Open iTunes After The Installer Exits check box if you want to run iTunes immediately. Then click the Finish button.

Configure iTunes the First Time You Run It

After installing iTunes, you must configure it.

If you allowed the installer to run iTunes, the program now opens. If not, choose Start | iTunes | iTunes when you're ready to start running iTunes. The iTunes Setup Assistant starts, and walks you through the setup process.

During the setup process, you make the following decisions:

■ **Whether to have iTunes scan your Music folder or My Music folder for any music files so that it can add them to your library**   Scanning now is usually a good idea (see Figure 2-2), but you may prefer to add files manually later (see "Add Existing Song Files to Your Library," later in this chapter). Select the Add MP3 And AAC Files check box if you want to find files of these types and add them to the library. Select the Add WMA Files check box if you want iTunes to find unprotected WMA files and create AAC files from them.

■ **Whether to let iTunes keep your music folder organized**   On the Keep iTunes Music Folder Organized screen (see Figure 2-3), decide whether to let iTunes rename files for you. See the sidebar "Decide Whether to Let iTunes Organize Your Music Folder" for details on this decision.

■ **Whether to have iTunes take you directly to the iTunes Music Store so that you can start spending money there**   Select the No, Take Me To My iTunes Library option button if you'd rather build up your library from your CDs and existing audio files first. For most people, this is the better option, as you can always buy songs from the iTunes Store later.

Once you've finished the iTunes Setup Assistant, the iTunes window appears.

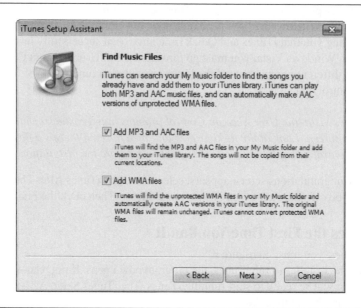

FIGURE 2-2   iTunes offers to scan your Music folder or My Music folder for AAC and MP3 files. You can also have iTunes create AAC files from any WMA files you have.

How to ...   Decide Whether to Convert Your WMA Files to AAC Files

Converting your unprotected WMA files to AAC files is usually a good idea. WMA files can be protected with digital rights management (DRM) restrictions that control which computers can play the files. iTunes can't convert protected WMA files to AAC files.

Technically, the AAC files you end up with contain all the flaws of the original WMA files plus any flaws that the AAC encoding introduces. This is because all "lossy" audio formats lose audio quality, introducing flaws into the resulting audio files.

In practice, however, if the WMA files sound great to you, the AAC files will probably sound at least acceptable—and you can play them on the iPod, which you cannot do with the WMA files.

In any case, the conversion process leaves the original WMA files untouched, so if you don't like the resulting AAC files, you can simply delete them. One thing to bear in mind is that the AAC files will probably take up around the same amount of space on your computer's hard disk as the WMA files, so you should make sure you have plenty of free space before you convert the files.

FIGURE 2-3   iTunes can automatically rename song files and folders for you to keep your
library in apple-pie order.

NOTE   *If your computer is connected to the Internet, iTunes checks to see if an updated version
is available. If one is available, iTunes prompts you to download it (which may take a
few minutes, depending on the speed of your Internet connection) and install it. Usually,
after updating iTunes, you'll need to run through the iTunes Setup Assistant again. You
may also need to restart your PC.*

Connect the iPod to Your PC

Next, connect the iPod to your PC and, if necessary, "restore" it to change it from Macintosh
formatting to PC formatting. Follow these steps:

1. Connect the USB end of the iPod's cable to your computer, and then connect the other
end to the iPod. iTunes displays the following message box, telling you that the iPod is
Macintosh-formatted and that you must restore the iPod before you can use it on Windows.

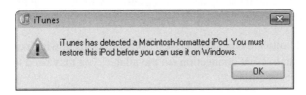

2. Click the OK button to close the message box, and then click the Restore button. iTunes displays a confirmation message box, as shown here.

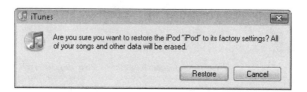

3. Click the Restore button. iTunes formats the iPod's hard disk or flash memory, reinstalls its operating system, and then displays a message box telling you it has done so, as shown here.

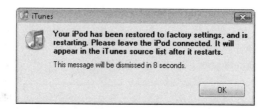

4. Either click the OK button or simply allow iTunes to complete the countdown and dismiss the message box itself.

iTunes may tell you that the iPod's software isn't up to date and prompt you to update it. Doing so is almost always a good idea.

Install or Update iTunes on the Mac

If you have a Mac running Mac OS X, you most likely have iTunes installed already, because iTunes is included in a default installation of Mac OS X.

Even if you explicitly exclude iTunes from the installation, Software Update offers you each updated version of iTunes that becomes available, so you need to refuse the updates manually or tell Software Update to ignore them. (To tell Software Update to ignore updates, select the iTunes item in the list, and then press ⌘-BACKSPACE or choose Update | Ignore Update.)

Get and Install the Latest Version of iTunes

If you've managed to refuse all these updates, the easiest way to install the latest version of iTunes is to use Software Update:

1. Choose Apple | Software Update to launch Software Update, which checks automatically for updates. (If an Internet connection isn't available, you may need to establish one.)

How to ...   Decide Whether to Let iTunes Organize Your Music Folder

Take a moment to think about the Keep iTunes Music Folder Organized setting, because it decides whether you or iTunes controls the organization of your library.

If you turn this feature on, iTunes stores a song in a file named after the track number (if you choose to include it). iTunes places the song in a folder named after the album; this folder is stored within a folder named after the artist, which is placed in your iTunes Music folder.

For example, if you rip the album *Icky Thump* by The White Stripes, iTunes stores the fourth song as \The White Stripes\Icky Thump\04 Conquest.aac on Windows or as /The White Stripes/Icky Thump/04 Conquest.aac on Mac OS X. If you then edit the artist field in the tag to "White Stripes" instead of "The White Stripes," iTunes changes the name of the artist folder to "White Stripes" as well.

This automatic renaming is nice and logical for iTunes, but you may dislike the way folder and file names change when you edit the tags. If so, turn off the Keep iTunes Music Folder Organized feature. You can change this setting at any time on the General subtab of the Advanced tab in the iTunes dialog box (in Windows) or the Preferences dialog box (on the Mac), but it's least confusing to make a choice at the beginning and then stick with it.

2. If Software Update doesn't turn up a version of iTunes that you can install, choose Software Update | Reset Ignored Updates. Software Update then checks automatically for the latest versions of updates you've ignored and presents the list.

3. Make sure the iTunes check box is selected, and then click the Install Items button. Follow through the update process, entering your password in the Authenticate dialog box and accepting the license agreements.

4. Restart your Mac when Software Update prompts you to do so. iTunes Setup then runs automatically (see the next section).

Set Up iTunes if You Haven't Already Done So

If you haven't used iTunes before, or if you've just installed it, follow the steps in the iTunes Setup Assistant to configure iTunes.

If the iTunes Setup Assistant isn't running yet, click the iTunes icon on the Dock. If there's no iTunes icon on the Dock, choose Go | Applications from the Finder menu (or press ⌘-SHIFT-A) to open your Applications folder, and then double-click the iTunes icon.

During the setup process, you make the following decisions:

- **Whether to use iTunes for Internet audio content** If you accept the default setting (leaving the Yes, Use iTunes For Internet Audio Content option button selected, as shown in Figure 2-4), iTunes becomes the helper application for audio you access through your web browser (for example, Safari). This is normally a good idea unless you prefer to use another music player.

- **Whether to have iTunes scan your Home folder for any music files so that it can add them to your library** Scanning now is usually a good idea (see Figure 2-5), but you may prefer to add files manually later (see "Add Existing Song Files to Your Library," later in this chapter).

- **Whether to have iTunes take you directly to the iTunes Music Store so that you can start spending money there** Select the No, Take Me To My iTunes Library option button if you'd rather build up your library from your CDs and existing audio files first. For most people, this is the better option, as you can always buy songs from the iTunes Store later.

During setup, iTunes also displays an information screen telling you that it can download album artwork when you add songs to your library and that you need to sign into the iTunes Store to use this feature.

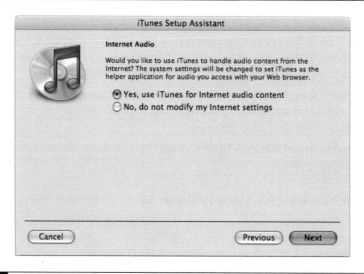

FIGURE 2-4   Choose whether to use iTunes for Internet audio content.

FIGURE 2-5 iTunes offers to scan your Home folder for AAC and MP3 files. If your files are in other folders, you can add them manually later.

NOTE   *iTunes requires QuickTime for some of its features to work. The iTunes Setup Assistant may prompt you to use Software Update (choose Apple | Software Update) to install the latest version of QuickTime so that all the iTunes features work.*

Now connect the USB end of the iPod's cable to your computer, and then connect the other end to the iPod.

Complete the iPod Setup Assistant

After you install iTunes and connect the iPod, iTunes displays the iPod Setup Assistant (see Figure 2-6). Follow these steps to set up the iPod:

1. In the text box called The Name Of My iPod Is, you can change the name that iTunes has suggested for the iPod—for example, Max's iPod.

2. If the iPod has enough space to store your entire library, and you want to synchronize all items in your library with the iPod, select the Automatically Sync Songs And Videos To My iPod check. If you want to update the iPod manually from the start, clear this check box.

3. If you want to synchronize photos automatically with the iPod, select the Automatically Sync Photos To My iPod check box. In the Sync Photos From drop-down list, select the source of the photos—for example, your Pictures folder on Windows Vista, your My Pictures folder on Windows XP, or your Pictures folder on the Mac.

4. Click the OK button to close the iPod Setup Assistant and apply your choices to the iPod.

FIGURE 2-6 The iPod Setup Assistant lets you name the iPod, choose whether to update it automatically from the start, and decide whether to synchronize pictures.

Activate the iPhone

Before you can use the iPhone—even as an iPod or a calculator—you must activate it. Activation involves signing up for a two-year contract with AT&T using a major credit card.

To activate the iPhone, follow these steps:

1. Install iTunes as described earlier in this chapter.

2. Connect the iPhone's dock to your computer via the USB cable, and then insert the iPhone into the dock. You may have to press it down firmly to make the connection. When the connection is made, the iPhone chirps at you and displays information on its screen. iTunes adds the iPhone to the Devices list in the Source pane and displays the Welcome To Your New iPhone screen (see Figure 2-7).

3. Click the Continue button. iTunes displays the Are You A New Or Existing AT&T (Cingular) Wireless Customer? screen (see Figure 2-8).

4. Select the appropriate option button—for example, select the Activate One iPhone Now option button if you're not an existing AT&T customer—and then click the Continue button. iTunes displays the Transfer Your Mobile Number screen (see Figure 2-9).

FIGURE 2-7   You must activate the iPhone with an AT&T account before you can do anything with the device.

5. If you're transferring your mobile number, select the Transfer Existing Mobile Number Information check box, type the details in the text boxes, and then click the Continue button. If you're not transferring a number, simply click the Continue button. iTunes displays the Select Your Monthly AT&T Plan screen (see Figure 2-10).

6. Select the plan you want, and decide whether to upgrade to more SMS text messages per month. Click the Continue button, and then work your way through the billing and account details.

7. When you reach the Completing Activation screen, click the Continue button. iTunes activates the iPhone, and then displays the Set Up Your iPhone screen (see Figure 2-11).

8. In the Name text box, change the suggested name for the iPhone if necessary.

9. If you want to synchronize your contacts, calendars, e-mail accounts, and Safari bookmarks automatically, select the Automatically Sync Contacts, Calendars, Email Accounts, And Bookmarks check box. If you prefer to sync only some items, clear this check box.

10. Click the Done button. The iPhone is now ready for use.

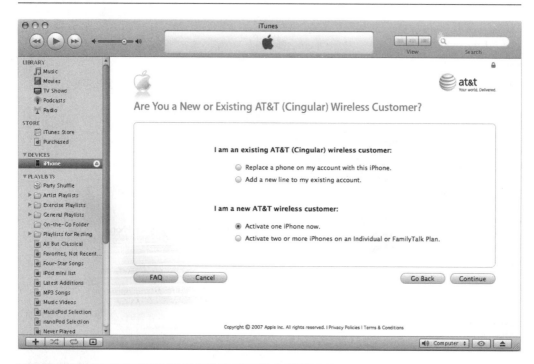

FIGURE 2-8   If you are an existing AT&T Wireless customer, you can use the iPhone to replace your existing phone or add a new line to your account.

How to ...
Activate the iPhone if AT&T's System Doesn't Like Your Credit Rating

If AT&T's system judges your credit rating too poor for you to qualify for a standard two-year contract, you have two options.

First, you can go to an AT&T store in person and discuss your options.

Second, you can sign up for a prepaid plan. This is called GoPhone and is a reasonable option. Because a GoPhone contract is month-by-month, you can cancel it at any time. However, it works out to be more expensive than a standard contract and provides fewer features. For example, you cannot add international roaming to a GoPhone contract.

Technically, there's a third option as well: You can start the activation process again from the beginning. But anecdotal evidence suggests that, unless you approach the process using a different identity, you're likely to get the same result.

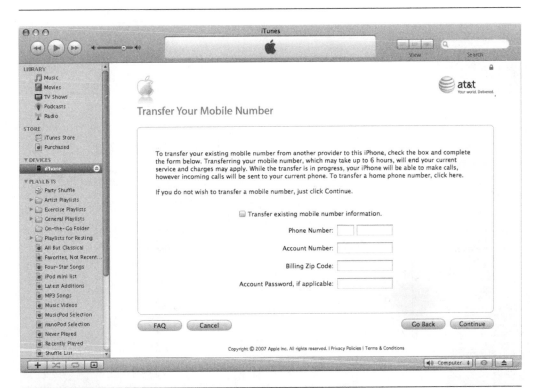

FIGURE 2-9   If you're transferring an existing mobile number to the iPhone, complete the information on the Transfer Your Mobile Number screen.

NOTE   *Hackers have devised various ways of bypassing iPhone activation so that they can use the nonphone features of their iPhones. To learn more about this topic, search for* **iPhone activation hack** *on the Internet.*

Start Creating Your Library

Before you can add any songs to the iPod or iPhone, you must add them to your library. This section gets you started with the basics of adding songs to your library either from CDs or from existing digital audio files. Chapters 6 and 10 cover this topic in far greater depth, discussing how to plan, create, and manage an effective library for iTunes, an iPod or iPhone, and your household.

Add Existing Song Files to Your Library

While setting up iTunes, you probably let iTunes add song files automatically to your library from your Music folder (on Windows Vista), your My Music folder (on Windows XP), or your Home folder (on the Mac). You can quickly add further songs to your library from other folders—but before you do, check whether iTunes is set to copy the songs to your music folder.

FIGURE 2-10 On the Select Your Monthly AT&T Plan screen, decide how much you want to spend. Click the More Minutes link if you need more calling time than these plans show.

Decide Whether to Copy All Song Files to Your Library

The ideal setup is to store all your songs within your Music folder (on Windows Vista), your My Music folder (on Windows XP), or your Home folder (on the Mac). Typically, this folder is on your computer's hard drive (or on its primary hard drive, if it has more than one hard drive).

That means your hard drive must have enough space for all your songs, videos, and other items (for example, podcasts), not to mention the operating system, your applications, and all your other files (for example, documents, pictures, and video files). For a modest-sized library,

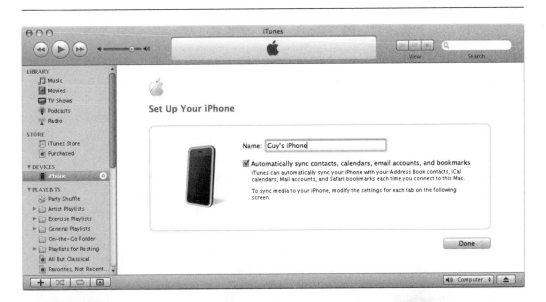

FIGURE 2-11   On the Set Up Your iPhone screen, name the iPhone and choose whether to synchronize your contacts, calendars, e-mail accounts, and bookmarks automatically.

this is easy enough. But for the kind of library that most music enthusiasts accumulate over the years, it means your computer must have a huge hard drive. Most modern desktop computers do, but at this writing laptop hard drives are limited to 200GB—and most laptops have hard drives that are far smaller than this.

TIP   *Another possibility is to store your entire library on a server or on an external disk. See Chapter 10 for a discussion of this option.*

If your computer does have a huge hard drive, all is well. But if it doesn't, you'll have to either make do with only some of the songs and videos you want or store some of the files on other drives or other computers. You can tell iTunes to store references to where files are located rather than store a copy of each file in the library folder on your hard drive.

NOTE   *Even if your computer has enough hard drive space for all your songs, you may prefer not to store them in your Music folder, My Music folder, or Home folder so that you can more easily share them through the file system with other members of your household. iTunes' Sharing features (discussed in Chapter 10) enable you to share even files stored in your private folders, but they limit other users to playing the songs (rather than adding them to their music libraries) and work only when iTunes is running. For more flexibility, you may prefer to store shared songs on a server or in a folder that all members of your household can access.*

To control whether iTunes copies song files or merely stores references to where the song files are, follow these steps:

1. Display the iTunes dialog box or the Preferences dialog box:

   ■ In Windows, choose Edit | Preferences or press CTRL-COMMA or CTRL-Y to display the iTunes dialog box.

   ■ On the Mac, choose iTunes | Preferences or press ⌘-COMMA or ⌘-Y to display the Preferences dialog box.

2. Click the Advanced tab to display its contents.

3. Select the Copy Files To iTunes Music Folder When Adding To Library check box if you want to copy the files (see Figure 2-12). Otherwise, clear this check box.

4. Click the OK button to close the dialog box.

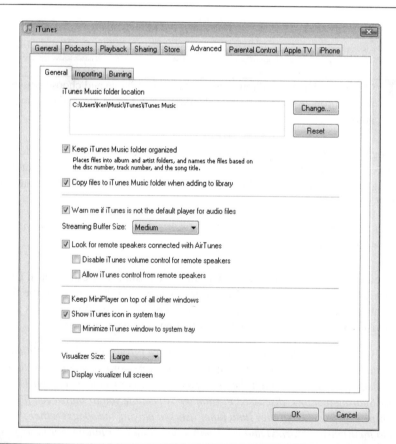

FIGURE 2-12   Clear the Copy Files To iTunes Music Folder When Adding To Library check box if you don't want to store a copy of each song file on your hard disk.

Storing references is great when you have too little space free on your hard disk to accommodate your colossal library. For example, if you have a laptop whose hard disk is bulging at the seams, you might choose to store in your library only references to songs located on an external hard disk rather than trying to import a copy of each song. However, you won't be able to play any song stored on the external hard disk when your laptop isn't connected to it.

Add Songs to Your Library

To add songs to your library, follow these steps:

- In Windows, to add a folder of songs, choose File | Add Folder To Library. In the Browse For Folder dialog box, navigate to and select the folder you want to add. Click the OK button, and iTunes either copies the song files to your library (if you selected the Copy Files To iTunes Music Folder When Adding To Library check box) or adds references to the song files (if you cleared this check box).

- In Windows, to add a single file, choose File | Add File To Library or press CTRL-O. In the Add To Library dialog box, navigate to and select the file you want to add. Click the OK button, and iTunes adds it.

- On the Mac, choose File | Add To Library or press ⌘-O. In the Add To Library dialog box, navigate to and select the folder or the file you want to add and then click the Choose button to add the folder or file.

Copy CDs to Your Library

The other way to add your existing digital music to your library is to copy it from CD. iTunes makes the process as straightforward as can be, but you should first verify that the iTunes settings for importing music are suitable.

Check iTunes' Settings for Importing Music

Follow these steps to check iTunes' settings for importing music:

1. Display the iTunes dialog box or the Preferences dialog box:
   - In Windows, choose Edit | Preferences or press CTRL-COMMA or CTRL-Y to display the iTunes dialog box.
   - On the Mac, choose iTunes | Preferences or press ⌘-COMMA or ⌘-Y to display the Preferences dialog box.

2. Click the Advanced tab, and then click the Importing subtab to display its contents (see Figure 2-13).

3. In the On CD Insert drop-down list, choose the action you want iTunes to take when you insert a CD: Show CD, Begin Playing, Ask To Import CD, Import CD, or Import CD And Eject. When you're building your library, Show CD is usually the best choice, as it gives you the chance to scan the CD information for errors that you need to correct before you import the CD.

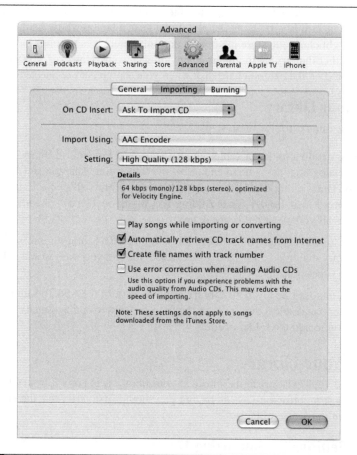

FIGURE 2-13 Before importing music, make sure that iTunes is configured with suitable settings.

4. Verify that AAC Encoder is selected in the Import Using drop-down list.

5. In the Setting drop-down list, choose High Quality if you want good audio quality with a compact file size—for example, if you have an iPod shuffle or a low-capacity iPod nano or iPhone. Choose Higher Quality if you're prepared to use twice as much disk space to improve the audio quality.

6. Clear the Play Songs While Importing Or Converting check box if you want to import the songs from your CDs, or convert them from other file formats, as quickly as possible.

7. Click the OK button to close the dialog box.

iTunes can store the music extracted from CDs in several different formats, including Advanced Audio Coding (AAC, the default), MP3, and Apple Lossless Encoder. Chapter 6 discusses the pros and cons of the various formats and how to choose between them. For the moment, this book assumes that you are using AAC.

Add a CD to Your Library

To add a CD to your library, follow these steps:

1. Start iTunes if it's not already running.

2. Insert the CD in your computer's optical drive (CD drive or DVD drive). iTunes loads the CD and displays an entry for it in the Source pane. If an Internet connection is available, iTunes retrieves the CD's information and displays it (see Figure 2-14).

3. Look at the CD's information and make sure that it is correct. If not, click twice (with a pause between the clicks) on the piece of information you want to change, type the correction, and then press ENTER (Windows) or RETURN (Mac).

TIP *You can also change CD or song information in other ways. See Chapters 6 and 9 for the details.*

4. Click the Import CD button. iTunes extracts the audio from the CD, converts it to the format you chose, and saves the files to your library.

FIGURE 2-14   Load a CD, check that the data is correct, and then click the Import CD button to import its songs into your library.

Check That the Songs You've Added Sound Okay

After adding the first CD, click the Library item in the Source pane, double-click the first song you imported from the CD, and listen to it to make sure there are no obvious defects (such as clicks or pauses) in the sound. If you have time, listen to several songs, or even the entire CD.

If the songs sound fine, you probably don't need to use error correction on your CD drive. But if you do hear defects, turn on error correction and copy the CD again. Here's how:

1. Display the iTunes dialog box or the Preferences dialog box:

   ■ In Windows, choose Edit | Preferences or press CTRL-COMMA or CTRL-Y to display the iTunes dialog box.

   ■ On the Mac, choose iTunes | Preferences or press ⌘-COMMA or ⌘-Y to display the Preferences dialog box.

2. Click the Advanced tab, and then click the Importing subtab to display its contents.

3. Select the Use Error Correction When Reading Audio CDs check box.

4. Click the OK button to close the dialog box.

In your library, click the first song that you ripped from the CD, hold down SHIFT, and click the last song from the CD to select all the songs. Press DELETE or BACKSPACE on your keyboard, click the Yes button in the confirmation dialog box, and then click the Yes button in the dialog box that asks whether you want to move the files from your music folder to the Recycle Bin (on Windows) or the Trash (on the Mac).

Click the CD's entry in the Source pane, and then click the Import CD button to import the songs again. Check the results and make sure they're satisfactory before you import any more CDs.

Load the iPod or iPhone with Music

If you chose to let iTunes update the iPod or iPhone automatically, iTunes performs the first update after you connect the iPod. If your library will fit on the iPod, iTunes copies all the songs to the iPod (see Figure 2-15). All you need to do is wait until the songs have been copied and then disconnect it (see "Eject and Disconnect the iPod," later in this chapter).

Load Only Some Songs from Your Library on an iPod or iPhone

If your library is larger than the capacity of the iPod or iPhone, iTunes warns you of the problem (see Figure 2-16). Click the Yes button to let iTunes put an automatic selection of songs on the iPod or iPhone; iTunes creates a playlist named *device's name* Selection (where *device's name* is the name you've given the iPod or iPhone), assigns a selection of songs to it, and copies them to the iPod or iPhone. Click the No button if you want to make the selection yourself.

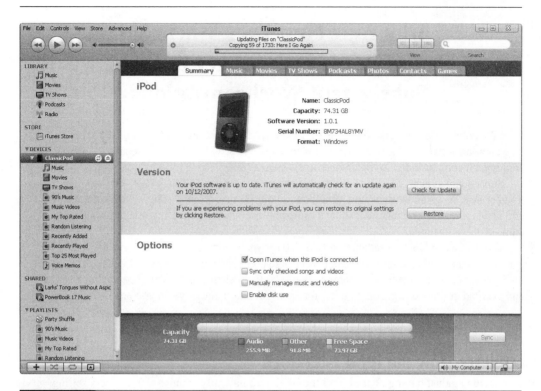

FIGURE 2-15   iTunes copies the songs in your library to the iPod or iPhone.

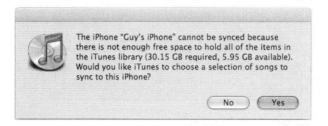

FIGURE 2-16   If your library is too large to fit on the iPod or iPhone, decide whether to let iTunes choose a selection of songs for it automatically.

Did you know?

Why Your First-Ever Synchronization May Take Much Longer than Subsequent Synchronizations

USB 2.0 connections are fast, but your first-ever synchronization of an iPod or iPhone may take an hour or two if your library contains many songs or videos. This is because iTunes copies each song or video to the device.

Subsequent synchronizations will be much quicker, because iTunes will need only to transfer new songs and videos you've added to your library, remove songs you've deleted, and update the data on items whose tags (information such as the artist name and song name) you've changed.

If you're using USB 1.x rather than USB 2.0 to synchronize an iPod or iPhone, the first synchronization will take several hours if your library contains many songs and videos. You might plan to perform the first synchronization sometime when you can leave your computer and the iPod or iPhone to get on with it—for example, overnight, or when you head out to work.

Configure How the iPod Is Loaded

If you decide against having iTunes load the iPod automatically, change the device's settings as follows:

1. Click the iPod's entry in the Source pane.

2. On the Summary tab, select the Manually Manage Music And Videos check box. iTunes displays a confirmation message box, as shown here.

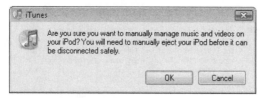

3. Click the OK button to close the message box.

4. Click each of the other tabs in turn, and choose the items you want to sync. For example, here's how to choose settings on the Music tab:

   ■ Select the Sync Music check box.

■ Select the All Songs And Playlists option button to synchronize your entire library. Select the Include Music Videos check box if you want to include music videos with the songs.

■ Select the Selected Playlists Only option button if you want to synchronize the iPod with the playlists whose check boxes you select in the list box. This is a good choice when the iPod doesn't have enough capacity to hold your entire library.

5. Click the Apply button.

Load Music on the iPod Manually

If you decided against automatic updating of either your entire library or iTunes' automatic selection from it, you need to load the iPod manually. You can perform either of the following actions:

■ Connect the iPod to your computer, wait until its entry appears in the Source pane, and then drag songs, artists, albums, or playlists to its entry. When you drop the items, iTunes copies the songs to the iPod, which takes a few seconds.

■ Create a playlist for the iPod by choosing File | New Playlist, typing the name in the text box, and then pressing ENTER (Windows) or RETURN (Mac). Drag songs, albums, or artists to the playlist to add them. When you're ready to load the playlist, connect the iPod to your computer, wait until its entry appears in the Source pane, and then drag the playlist to the entry. iTunes then copies the songs to the iPod all at once.

TIP *To force iTunes to copy to an iPod any song files that lack the tag information the iPod normally requires, add the songs to a playlist. Doing so can save you time over retagging many files manually and can be useful in a pinch. (In the long term, you'll probably want to make sure all your song files are tagged properly.)*

Connect and Load the iPod shuffle

Because the iPod shuffle is different from the regular iPod, the iPod touch, the iPod nano, and the iPhone, connecting it and loading it are different too.

Connect the iPod shuffle

To connect a second-generation iPod shuffle, connect its dock to a high-power USB port on your computer, and then impale the iPod shuffle's headphone port on the connector in the dock. To connect a first-generation iPod shuffle, plug it directly into a USB port. (If the USB port is inaccessible, use an extension cable or a hub.)

The iPod shuffle is formatted with the FAT32 file system for use with both PCs and Macs, so the iPod Software doesn't need to reformat it the first time you connect it to a PC.

Load the iPod shuffle

As the iPod shuffle doesn't have enough capacity to hold any but the most modest library, iTunes includes a feature called Autofill for loading the iPod shuffle. Autofill lets you tell iTunes to fill the iPod shuffle to capacity with songs from either your library or a specified playlist. You can also load an iPod shuffle manually if you prefer.

Configure the iPod shuffle

Before you load the iPod shuffle for the first time, check that it is correctly configured:

1. Click the iPod shuffle's entry in the Source pane to display its screens. Click the Settings tab if it isn't already displayed (see Figure 2-17).

2. Select the Convert Higher Bit Rate Songs To 128 Kbps AAC check box if you want to get as many songs as possible on the iPod shuffle.

> **NOTE** *Converting songs to 128 Kbps has two benefits: It prevents higher-bitrate songs from sneaking onto the iPod shuffle and hogging its limited space, and it enables you to load songs in formats that the iPod shuffle doesn't support (for example, Apple Lossless Encoder). The drawbacks are that the conversion slows down the loading process a bit and reduces sound quality somewhat.*

3. If you want to be able to store data on the iPod shuffle as well as songs, select the Enable Disk Use check box. iTunes displays a message box warning you that you will need to eject the iPod manually, as shown here.

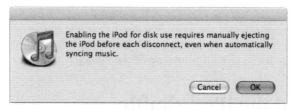

4. Click the OK button to dismiss the message box.

5. Drag the slider along the More Songs–More Data axis so that it shows the amount of space you want to reserve for data.

6. Click the Apply button to apply the changes.

Load the iPod shuffle Using Autofill

The easiest way to load an iPod shuffle is to use Autofill:

1. Connect the iPod shuffle to your computer and wait for iTunes to add its entry to the Source pane.

2. Click the iPod shuffle's entry in the Source pane to display the iPod shuffle's contents (see Figure 2-18).

FIGURE 2-17   On the iPod shuffle, you can make iTunes convert higher-bitrate songs to 128 Kbps, and you can specify the amount of space you want to reserve for data.

FIGURE 2-18 Autofill is the fast-and-easy way to fill an iPod shuffle with songs chosen by iTunes either from your entire library or from a specific playlist.

The first time you use Autofill, configure it:

1. In the Autofill From drop-down list, select the Music entry if you want iTunes to choose songs from your entire library. Choose a playlist if you want to confine the selection to just that playlist.

2. Select the Choose Items Randomly check box if you want a random selection on the iPod shuffle. Clear this check box if you want iTunes to choose from your chosen playlist (or your library) in order, starting from the first song and using all the available space.

3. Select the Replace All Items When Autofilling check box if you want iTunes to remove the songs that are currently on the iPod shuffle. Clear this check box if you want to keep the existing songs.

4. Select the Choose Higher Rated Items More Often check box if you want iTunes to prefer the songs you've given a higher rating.

How to ... Keep the iPod shuffle Loaded with Your New Music

If you want to load an iPod shuffle with the latest music you've added to your library, use the Recently Added Smart Playlist that iTunes automatically creates.

Check that the iPod shuffle is set up to use the Recently Added Smart Playlist by following these steps:

1. Connect the iPod shuffle to your computer.
2. Click the iPod shuffle's entry in the Source pane, and then click the Contents tab to display the iPod shuffle's contents. The Autofill pane appears at the bottom of the contents area.
3. Make sure that Recently Added is selected in the Autofill From drop-down list.

Next, check that the Recently Added Smart Playlist is set to track songs added during a suitably long period of time. The default setting is two weeks. If you add music frequently, you may need to specify a shorter interval; if you seldom add music, you may need a longer interval. You can choose among days, weeks, and months.

Right-click the Recently Added item in the Source pane, and then choose Edit Smart Playlist from the shortcut menu to display the Smart Playlist dialog box. Check the condition, change it if necessary, and then click the OK button to close the dialog box.

Once you've configured Autofill, follow these steps to load songs on the iPod shuffle:

1. Click the iPod shuffle's entry in the Source pane.
2. Click the Autofill button to load a new selection of songs. Wait until the display shows that the update is complete, and then check the list for songs you don't want to hear. If you find any, select them, and press the Delete button to remove them. You can then either add replacement songs manually or clear the Replace All Songs When Autofilling check box and click the Autofill button again to fill up the remaining space with other songs.
3. When you're satisfied with the selection iTunes has loaded, disconnect the iPod shuffle. (See the section "Eject and Disconnect the iPod," later in this chapter, for more details.)

TIP

With its limited capacity, the iPod shuffle is a great target for a well-thought-out Smart Playlist. See the section "Automatically Create Smart Playlists Based on Your Ratings and Preferences" in Chapter 10 for details on Smart Playlists. See the nearby sidebar, "Keep the iPod shuffle Loaded with Your New Music," for a way to use Smart Playlists to put the latest songs you've acquired onto the iPod shuffle.

Load an iPod shuffle Manually

Instead of using Autofill, you can load an iPod shuffle manually. The most direct way is to connect the iPod shuffle to your computer, wait until the iPod shuffle's entry appears in the Source pane, and then drag songs, artists, albums, or playlists to its entry. iTunes copies the songs to the iPod shuffle when you drop them.

Another option is to create a playlist for the iPod shuffle and then drag songs to the playlist. When you're ready to load the playlist, connect the iPod shuffle to your computer, wait until the iPod shuffle's entry appears in the Source pane, and then drag the playlist to the entry. iTunes then copies the songs to the iPod shuffle all at once.

Eject and Disconnect the iPod

When iTunes has finished loading songs onto the iPod, you can disconnect it unless you're using it in disk mode (or you need to continue recharging its battery). iTunes displays the message "iPod update is complete. OK to disconnect." The iPod displays the message "OK to disconnect." When you see this message, you can unplug the iPod from the cable or from your computer.

If you're using disk mode, however, iTunes doesn't prepare the iPod for disconnection after it finishes loading songs. Instead, it leaves the iPod mounted on your computer as a disk so that you can transfer files to and from it manually. When the iPod is in disk mode like this, it displays the "Do not disconnect" message. In Mac OS X, an icon for the iPod appears on the desktop unless you have specifically chosen to exclude it (see the "Prevent the iPod from Appearing on the Desktop in Mac OS X" sidebar).

How to ...
Prevent the iPod from Appearing on the Desktop in Mac OS X

When the iPod is mounted in disk mode, it appears on the Mac OS X desktop by default. You can prevent it from appearing, but doing so also prevents CDs and DVDs from appearing. Here's how:

1. Click the Finder button on the toolbar, or click the desktop.
2. Choose Finder | Preferences to display the Finder Preferences window.
3. Click the General tab if it isn't already displayed.
4. Clear the CDs, DVDs, And iPods check box.
5. Click the Close button on the window, or choose File | Close Window or press ⌘-w, to close the window.

NOTE *At this writing, the iPhone and iPod touch have no disk mode, so you can safely remove either at any time it is not showing the Sync In Progress screen. When the iPhone or iPod touch is showing this screen, you can drag your finger across the slider at the bottom of the screen to cancel the sync—for example, if you receive a phone call while the sync is running on the iPhone.*

TIP *If you forget to eject the iPod or iPhone before you log out of Mac OS X, you shouldn't need to log back in to eject the device. If it's an iPod classic or an iPod nano, make sure that the screen is displaying the "OK to disconnect" message, and then disconnect the iPod. If it's an iPod shuffle, make sure that the amber light isn't blinking. If it's an iPhone or iPod touch, make sure it's not displaying the Sync In Progress screen.*

You can eject the iPod in any of the following ways (see Figure 2-19 on the next page):

- Click the Eject button that appears next to the device's entry in the Source pane.
- Right-click the device's entry in the Source pane and then click the Eject item on the shortcut menu.
- Click the device's entry in the Source pane and then click the Eject iPod button or Eject Mobile Phone button in the lower-right corner of the iTunes window.
- Click the device's entry in the Source pane and then choose Controls | Eject *device's name* or press CTRL-E (Windows) or ⌘-E (Mac).

Click the Eject button for the iPod or iPhone.

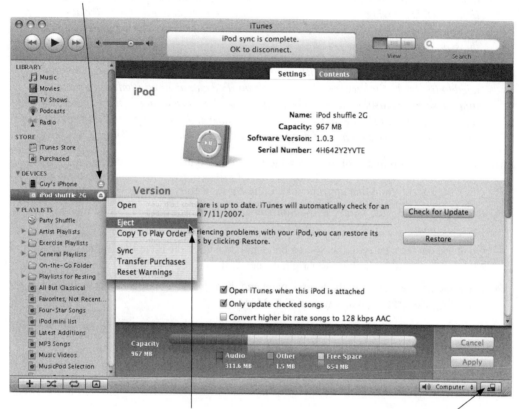

Right-click the iPod's or iPhone's entry, and then choose Eject.

Select the iPod or iPhone's entry in the Devices list, and then click the Eject iPod button or Eject Mobile Phone button.

FIGURE 2-19   The three easiest ways to eject the iPod or iPhone are to click its Eject button, right-click its Source pane entry and choose Eject, or click the Eject iPod button or Eject Mobile Phone button.

Chapter 3

Listen to Music on an iPod or iPhone

How to...

■ Connect your headphones or speakers to an iPod or iPhone

■ Use the controls on the iPod classic and iPod nano

■ Use the controls on the iPhone and iPod touch

■ Navigate through the iPod's screens

■ Customize the settings on an iPod

■ Play music on the iPod shuffle

■ Play music on the iPhone and iPod touch

This chapter shows you how to get started using an iPod or iPhone. You'll start by connecting your headphones or speakers, using the controls to play music, and navigating through the screens of the graphical user interface. After that, you'll learn how to customize the settings to make the iPod easier and faster to use and how to make the most of the iPod's features (other than playing music).

Much of this chapter applies to the iPod classic and the iPod nano, so this chapter treats them together as much as possible. Where the iPod nano behaves differently, this chapter tells you. The iPod shuffle is substantially different, so this chapter discusses it separately in its own section. The iPhone and iPod touch are also different, but similar to each other, so this chapter discusses them together in a section of their own.

Connect Your Headphones or Speakers

The easiest way to get sound out of an iPod or iPhone is to connect your headphones or speakers to the headphones port. The headphones port is on the top of the iPod classic, the second-generation iPod shuffle, and the iPhone; on the iPod nano and the iPod touch, the port appears on the bottom. It's easy enough to recognize: a 1/8-inch (3.5mm) round hole, into which you slide a miniplug of the corresponding size.

Connecting the miniplug and the port couldn't be easier, but a couple of things are worth mentioning:

■ The headphone port delivers up to 60 milliwatts (mW) altogether—30 mW per channel. To avoid distortion or damage, turn down the volume when connecting the player to a different pair of headphones, powered speakers, or an amplifier. Make the connection, set the volume to low on the speakers or amplifier, and then start playing the audio.

■ If you have an iPod Dock, you can play music from the iPod when it's docked. The same goes for the iPhone Dock that comes with the iPhone. Plug a cable with a stereo miniplug into the Line Out port on the Dock, and then connect the other end of the cable to your powered speakers or your stereo. Use the iPod's or iPhone's controls to navigate to the music, play it, pause it, and so on. Use the volume control on the speakers or the receiver to control the volume at which the songs play. The Line Out port delivers a standard volume and better audio quality than the headphone port.

Use Headphones with an iPod or iPhone

At this writing, each iPod comes with a pair of ear-bud headphones—the kind that fit in your ear rather than sit on your ear or over your ear. The iPhone includes a similar pair of headphones that incorporates a pause button and a microphone in the cord.

The headphones are designed to look good with the iPod—and in fact their distinctive white has helped muggers in many countries target victims with iPods rather than those with less desirable audio players. iPhone headphones seem destined to play a similar role.

Beyond that, these are good-quality headphones with a wide range of frequency response: from 20 Hz (hertz) to 20 KHz (kilohertz; 1,000 hertz), which is enough to cover most of the average human's hearing spectrum. Apple emphasizes that the headphones have drivers (technically, *transducers*) made of neodymium, a rare earth magnet that provides better frequency response and higher sound quality than alternative materials (such as cobalt, aluminum, or ceramics).

A wide range of frequency response and high sound quality are desirable, but what's more important to most people is that their headphones be comfortable and that they meet any other requirements, such as shutting out ambient sound or enhancing the wearer's charisma. See the sidebar "Choose Headphones to Suit You" for suggestions on evaluating and choosing headphones.

How to ...   Choose Headphones to Suit You

If you don't like the sound the iPod's headphones deliver, or if you just don't find them comfortable, use another pair of headphones instead. Any headphones with a standard miniplug will work; if your headphones have a quarter-inch jack, get a good-quality miniplug converter to make the connection to the iPod.

You can use another set of headphones with the iPhone, but you lose the benefit of the pause button and microphone built into the headphone cord. You also need to ensure that the jack on the headphones can fit into the iPhone's recessed socket. Many jacks, especially those that plug in at a right angle to the cord rather than straight in line with it, do not fit.

Headphones largely break down into three main types, although you can find plenty of exceptions:

- **Ear-bud headphones**   The most discreet type of headphones and the easiest to fit in a pocket. Most ear buds wedge in your ears like the iPod's ear buds do, but others sit on a headband and poke in sideways.

(Continued)

- **Supra-aural headphones** These headphones sit on your ears but don't fully cover them. Supra-aural headphones don't block out all ambient noise, which makes them good for situations in which you need to remain aware of the sounds happening around you. They also tend not to get as hot as circumaural headphones, because more air can get to your ears.

- **Circumaural headphones** These headphones sit over your ears, usually enclosing them fully. *Open* circumaural headphones allow external sounds to reach your ears, whereas *sealed* circumaural headphones block as much external sound as possible. Sealed headphones are good for noisy environments, but even better are noise-canceling circumaural headphones such as Bose's QuietComfort headphones (www.bose.com), which use electronics to reduce the amount of ambient noise that you hear.

Headphones can cost anywhere from a handful of dollars to many hundred dollars. Even ear buds can be impressively expensive: Shure's top-of-the-line set, the SE530 ear buds, cost $499 (www.shure.com), and Etymotic Research, Inc.'s ER6i Isolator Earphones go for $149 (www.etymotic.com). When choosing headphones, always try them on for comfort and listen to them for as long as possible, using a variety of your favorite music on the iPod or iPhone, to evaluate their sound as fully as you can.

Whichever type of headphones you choose to use, don't turn the volume up high enough to cause hearing damage. Instead, if you use an iPod or iPhone often with a high-end pair of headphones, get a headphone amplifier to improve the sound. A headphone amplifier plugs in between the sound source and your headphones to boost and condition the signal. You don't necessarily have to listen to music *louder* through a headphone amplifier—the amplifier can also improve the sound at a lower volume. Many headphone amplifiers are available from various manufacturers, but HeadRoom's Total AirHead and Total BitHead seem especially well regarded (www.headphone.com). You can also find plans on the Web for building your own headphone amplifier.

Use Speakers with an iPod or iPhone

Instead of using headphones, you can also connect an iPod or iPhone to a pair of powered speakers, a receiver or amplifier, or your car stereo. Chapter 5 discusses this topic in detail, but briefly, there are two main ways of making such a connection:

- **Direct connection** Use a standard cable with a 1/8-inch stereo headphone connector at the iPod end and the appropriate type of connector at the other end. For example, to connect an iPod to a conventional amplifier, you need two phono plugs on the other end of the cable.

- **Dock connection** If you have a dock for the iPod or iPhone, you can get higher-quality sound by connecting the receiver or amplifier to the dock's line-out port instead of the player's headphone port. The line-out port on the dock also gives a consistent level of signal, so you won't need to adjust the volume on the iPod or iPhone.

NOTE *Powered speakers are speakers that contain an amplifier, so you don't need to use an external amplifier. Many speaker sets designed for use with portable CD players, MP3 players, and computers are powered speakers. Usually, only one of the speakers contains an amplifier, making one speaker far heavier than the other. Sometimes the amplifier is hidden in the subwoofer, which lets you put the weight on the floor rather than on the furniture.*

The iPod and iPhone will work with any pair of speakers or stereo that can accept input, but you can also get various speakers designed specifically for these players. Chapter 4 discusses some of the options and suggests how to choose among them.

Get Familiar with the Controls on an iPod classic or iPod nano

To keep the various iPod models as streamlined as possible, Apple has reduced the number of controls to a minimum by making each control fulfill more than one purpose. You'll get the hang of the controls' basic functions easily, but you also need to know how to use the controls' secondary functions to get the most out of the iPod—so keep reading.

NOTE *This section discusses the controls on the iPod classic and iPod nano; most of the information also applies to various older iPod models that have Click Wheels, including the iPod with video and the fourth-generation iPod. For instructions on the iPod shuffle's controls, see the section "Play Music on the iPod shuffle," later in this chapter. For instructions on the controls on the iPhone and iPod touch, see the section "Play Music on the iPhone and iPod touch," toward the end of this chapter.*

Read the iPod's Display

The iPod has an LCD display that shows a handful of lines of text (exactly how many depends on the model of iPod) and multiple icons. Figure 3-1 shows the display with labels.

The title bar at the top of the display shows the title of the current screen—for example, "iPod" for the main menu (the top-level menu), "Now Playing" when the iPod's playing a song, "Cover Flow" when you're browsing using Cover Flow, or "Artists" when you're browsing by artist.

To turn on the display's backlight, hold down the Menu button for a moment. The backlight uses far more power than the LCD screen, so don't use the backlight unnecessarily when you're trying to extract the maximum amount of playing time from a single battery charge. You can configure how long the iPod keeps the backlight on after you press a button (see "Set the Backlight Timer," later in this chapter).

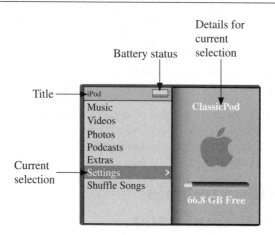

FIGURE 3-1   The iPod's LCD display contains around six lines of text and key icons.

Use the iPod's Controls

Below the iPod's display are the iPod's main controls, which you use for accessing songs and playing them back. The control buttons are integrated into the Click Wheel. Figure 3-2 shows an iPod classic.

Use the Buttons and the Click Wheel

Use the buttons and the Click Wheel as follows:

- Press any button to switch on the iPod.

- Press the Menu button to move up to the next level of menus. Hold down the Menu button for a second to turn the backlight on or off.

- Press the Previous/Rewind button or the Next/Fast-Forward button to navigate from one song to another and to rewind or fast-forward the playing song. Press one of these buttons once (and release it immediately) to issue the Previous command or the Next command. Hold down the button to issue the Rewind command or the Fast-Forward command. The iPod rewinds or fast-forwards slowly at first, but then speeds up if you keep holding down the button.

- Press the Play/Pause button to start playback or to pause it. Hold down the Play/Pause button for three seconds or so to switch off the iPod.

- Press the Select button to select the current menu item.

- Scroll your finger around the Click Wheel to move up and down menus, change the volume, or change the place in a song.

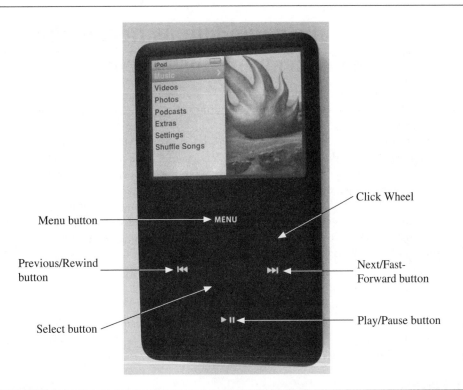

FIGURE 3-2   The control buttons on the iPod classic (shown here) and the iPod nano are integrated into the Click Wheel.

The Click Wheel adjusts the scrolling speed in response to your finger movements on the Click Wheel and the length of time you scroll for: When you're scrolling a long list, it speeds up the scrolling as you continue the scroll, and then slows down as you ease back on the scroll. This behavior makes scrolling even long lists (such as the Songs list, which lists every song on the iPod) swift and comfortable once you get used to it.

Browse and Access Your Music

The iPod's menu-driven interface makes browsing and accessing your music as easy as possible on the device's compact display.

Once you've accessed a list of songs—a playlist, an album, or a listing of all songs by an artist or composer—you can press the Play button to play the list from the start. Alternatively, you can scroll down to another song, and then press the Play button to start playing from that song.

How to ...   Add the Compilations Item to the Main Menu or Music Menu

If you listen to many compilation albums—*Ultimate Aerosmith Hits*, *Lost Stoner Rock of the Desert*, and so on—you may want to add the Compilations item to the Main Menu or Music menu.

To add the Compilations item, go to the Settings screen, select Main Menu or Music Menu (as appropriate), scroll to the Compilations item, and then press the Select button to apply a check mark to it. You can then browse a list of compilations easily from the Main menu or Music menu (depending on which you chose).

You can control what iTunes considers a compilation by selecting or clearing the Part Of A Compilation check box on the Info tab of the Song Information dialog box or choosing Yes or No in the Part Of A Compilation drop-down list in the Multiple Song Information dialog box. You'll meet both these dialog boxes in detail in Chapter 6.

NOTE   *You can customize the main menu on the iPod (see "Customize the Main Menu for Quick Access to Items," later in this chapter, for details). This chapter assumes you're using the default menu layout.*

Play a Playlist

To access your playlists, choose the Music item and press the Select button, then scroll to the Playlists item and press the Select button again. On the resulting screen, scroll down to the playlist you want to play, and then press the Select button.

Browse Your Music

To browse your music, select the Music item on the main menu. The iPod displays the Music menu, which contains entries for the various ways you can browse the songs and other audio items on the iPod.

Scroll to the browse category you want to use, and then press the Select button to access that category. Here's what you need to know about the browse categories:

- **Cover Flow**   Displays the songs as a sequence of CD covers, as shown here. You can move from one cover to the next by pressing the Previous button or the Next button. To flick through the covers faster, scroll to the left or to the right. When you've highlighted the cover you want, press the Play button to start it playing.

- **Playlists**   Displays an alphabetical list of the playlist folders and playlists you have created. To access a playlist within a folder, choose the folder, and then press the Select button to display its contents. Once you've chosen the playlist you want, press either the Select button or the Play button to start it playing.

- **Artists**   Displays an alphabetical list of all the songs on the iPod sorted by artist. The first entry, All Albums, displays an alphabetical list of all the albums on the iPod. Otherwise, scroll down to the artist and press the Select button to display a list of the albums by the artist. (If there's only one album, the iPod displays that album's songs immediately.) This menu also has a first entry called All Songs that displays an alphabetical list of all songs by the artist.

- **Albums**   Displays an alphabetical list of all the albums on the iPod. Scroll down to the album you want, and then press the Select button to display the songs it contains.

NOTE   *The data for the artist, album, song title, genre, composer, and so on comes from the tag information in the song file. An album shows up in the Artists category, the Albums category, the Genre category, or the Composers category even if only one file on the iPod has that album entered in the Album field on its tag. So the entry for an album doesn't necessarily mean that you have that entire album on the iPod—you may have only one song from that album.*

- **Songs**   Displays an alphabetical list of every song on the iPod. Scroll down to the song you want to play, and then press the Select button to start playing the song.

- **Genres**   Displays a list of the genres you've assigned to the music on the iPod. (The iPod builds the list of genres from the Genre field in the tags in AAC files, Apple Lossless Encoding files, and MP3 files.) Scroll to a genre, and then press the Select button to display the artists whose albums are tagged with that genre. You can then navigate to albums and songs by an artist.

- ■ **Composers**   Displays a list of the composers for the songs on the iPod. (The iPod builds the list of composers from the Composer field in the tags in the song files.) Scroll to a composer, and then press the Select button to display a list of the songs by that composer.

- ■ **Audiobooks**   Displays a list of the audiobooks on the iPod. (The iPod can play audiobooks in the Audible format, which you can buy either from the iTunes Store or from the Audible.com website.) Scroll down to the audiobook you want, and then press the Select button to start it playing.

- ■ **Search**   Displays a screen for searching by strings of text you dial in using the Click Wheel—for example, the key word in a song title. Searching initially seems clumsy, but once you get the hang of it, you may find it a handy way to find songs whose full names escape you.

Play Songs

Playing songs on the iPod is largely intuitive.

How to ... **Use the Composers Category Effectively to Find Music**

The Composers category is primarily useful for classical music, because these songs may be tagged with the name of the recording artist rather than that of the composer. For example, an album of The Fargo Philharmonic playing Beethoven's *Ninth Symphony* might list The Fargo Philharmonic as the artist and Beethoven as the composer. By using the Composers category, you can access the works by composer: Bach, Beethoven, Brahms, and so on.

However, there's no reason why you shouldn't use the Composers category to access nonclassical songs as well. For example, you could use the Composers category to quickly access all your Nick Drake cover versions as well as Drake's own recordings of his songs. The only disadvantage to doing so is that the tag information for many CDs in the CD Database (CDDB) doesn't include an entry in the Composer field, so you'll need to add this information if you want to use it. In this case, you may be better off using iTunes to create a playlist that contains the songs you want in the order you prefer.

There's also no reason why you should confine the contents of the Composer field to information about composers. By editing the tags manually, you can add to the Composer fields any information by which you want to be able to sort songs on the iPod or iPhone.

Start and Pause Play

To start playing a song, take either of the following actions:

- Navigate to the song, and then press the Play/Pause button or the Select button.
- Navigate to a playlist or an album, and then press the Play/Pause button or the Select button.

To pause play, press the Play/Pause button.

Change the Volume

To change the volume, scroll counterclockwise (to reduce the volume) or clockwise (to increase it) from the Now Playing screen. The volume bar at the bottom of the screen shows the volume setting as it changes (see Figure 3-3).

Change the Place in a Song

As well as fast-forwarding through a song by using the Next/Fast-Forward button, or rewinding through a song by using the Previous/Rewind button, you can *scrub* through a song to quickly change the location.

Scrubbing can be easier than fast-forwarding or rewinding because the iPod displays a readout of how far through the song the playing location currently is. Scrubbing is also more peaceful, because whereas Next/Fast-Forward and Previous/Rewind play blips of the parts of the song you're passing through (to help you locate the passage you want), scrubbing keeps the song playing until you indicate you've reached the part you're interested in.

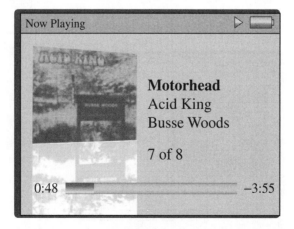

FIGURE 3-3   Scroll counterclockwise or clockwise to change the volume from the Now Playing screen.

To scrub through a song, follow these steps:

1. Display the Now Playing screen.
2. Press the Select button to display the scroll bar (see Figure 3-4).
3. Scroll counterclockwise to move backward through the song or clockwise to move forward through the song.
4. Press the Select button to cancel the display of the scroll bar, or wait a few seconds for the iPod to cancel its display automatically.

TIP *To display the lyrics for the currently playing song, press the Select button twice from the Now Playing screen. Scroll down to see more lyrics (if there are more). Press the Select button again to access the Ratings screen, again to reach the repeat-mode screen, and press it once more to return to the Now Playing screen.*

Use the Hold Switch

The Hold switch, located on the top of the iPod classic and the bottom of the iPod nano, locks the iPod controls in their current configuration. The Hold switch helps protect the controls against being bumped in active environments—for example, when you're exercising at the gym or barging your way onto a packed bus or subway train. When the Hold switch is pushed to the Hold side so that the orange underlay shows, the iPod is on hold.

The Hold switch is equally useful for keeping music playing without unintended interruptions and for keeping the iPod locked in the Off position, which prevents the battery from being drained by the iPod being switched on accidentally when you're carrying it.

If the iPod seems to stop responding to its other controls, check first that the Hold switch isn't on.

FIGURE 3-4 To "scrub" forward or backward through the current song, press the Select button, and then scroll clockwise (to go forward) or counterclockwise (to go backward).

Recharge the iPod's Battery to Keep the Songs Coming

The battery icon on the iPod's display shows you the status of the iPod's battery power.

The easiest way to recharge the iPod is to plug it into a high-power USB port on a computer. If the USB port provides enough power, you will see the battery indicator add a charging symbol. (If the port doesn't provide enough power, try another port.)

Alternatively, you can use an iPod power adapter, an optional accessory. See Chapter 4 for details. The power adapter is useful when you need to recharge the iPod away from any computer. You can also run the iPod from the adapter even while the battery is charging.

> **TIP** *Using the power adapter to charge an iPod is more reliable than using the USB cable, and the power adapter is useful for troubleshooting problems such as the iPod becoming nonresponsive. For this reason, a power adapter should be near the top of the list of accessories you buy for an iPod.*

How long the battery in an iPod takes to recharge depends on the iPod model, but most take between three and five hours. After about half of the charging time, the battery should be at about 80 percent of its charge capacity—enough for you to use the iPod for a while. (This is because the battery charges quickly at first, up to around the 80 percent level, and then charges more slowly the remainder of the way.)

When recharging from a computer, the iPod displays a charging symbol.

When recharging from an AC adapter, the iPod flashes a large battery icon and displays the word *Charging* at the top of the screen. When charging is complete, the iPod displays the battery icon without flashing it as well as the word *Charged* at the top of the screen.

Navigate the Extras Menu

The Extras menu provides access to the iPod's Clocks, Calendars, Contacts, Alarms, Games, Notes, Screen Lock, and Stopwatch features:

- To use the iPod's clock features, scroll to the Clocks item on the Extras menu, and then press the Select button. On the first Clock screen, which lists the clocks already configured, select the clock you want, or press the Select button to pop up a panel that allows you to add a new clock or either edit or delete an existing clock.

- To use the calendars, scroll to the Calendar item on the Extras menu, and then press the Select button. The iPod displays the list of calendars. Scroll to the calendar you want and press the Select button to display the calendar in month view. Scroll to access the day you're interested in, and then press the Select button to display the events listed for that day. The one-month display shows empty squares for days that have no events scheduled and dots for days that have one or more events. If the day contains more appointments than will fit on the iPod's display, scroll up and down. See Chapter 11 for a discussion of how to transfer your calendars to the iPod.

- To access a contact, scroll to the Contacts item on the Extras menu, and then press the Select button. On the Contacts screen, scroll to the contact, and then press the Select button. See Chapter 11 for details on how to put contacts onto the iPod.

- To play the games included with the iPod, scroll to the Games item on the Extras menu, and then press the Select button. From the Games menu, scroll to the game you want, and then press the Select button.

TIP   *You can buy further games for the iPod from the iTunes Store. Be warned that not all games work on all iPod models, so before you buy a game, verify that it supports your iPod model.*

- To access your text notes, scroll to the Notes item on the Extras menu, and then press the Select button. Chapter 11 discusses how to put notes on the iPod.

Choose Settings for the iPod

To choose settings for the iPod, scroll to the Settings item on the main menu, and then press the Select button. Work through those of the following sections that interest you.

Check the "About" Information for an iPod

To see an iPod's details, display the first About screen by choosing Settings | About. Press the Select button to move on to the second About screen, and then press again to display the third About screen. The About screens include the following information:

- The number of songs, videos, photos, podcasts, games, contacts, and other items the iPod contains

- The iPod's capacity and the amount of disk space available

- The iPod's name, serial number, and model

- The iPod Software version number of the iPod's software

- On some iPod models, whether the iPod is formatted for Windows or for the Mac

Apply Shuffle Settings to Randomize Songs or Albums

Instead of playing the songs in the current list in their usual order, you can tell the iPod to shuffle them into a random order by changing the Shuffle setting to Songs. Similarly, you can tell the iPod to shuffle the albums by a particular artist or composer into a random order by changing the Shuffle setting to Albums.

To change the Shuffle setting, scroll up to the Shuffle item on the Settings menu and press the Select button to choose the Shuffle setting you want. The settings are Off (the default), Songs, and Albums.

NOTE   *To shuffle songs on an iPod shuffle, move the slider on the bottom to the Shuffle position.*

Repeat One Song or All Songs

The Repeat item on the Settings menu lets you choose among:

- **Repeat the current song**   Choose the One setting.
- **Repeat all the songs in the current list**   Choose the All setting.
- **Don't repeat any songs**   Choose Off, the default setting.

Scroll to the Repeat item, and then press the Select button one or more times to change the setting.

Customize the Main Menu and Music Menu for Quick Access to Items

You can customize the iPod's main menu by controlling which items appear on it. By removing items you don't want, and adding items you do want, you can give yourself quicker access to the items you use most. For example, you might want to promote the Playlists item from the Music menu to the main menu, or you might want to put the Screen Lock item on the main menu so that you could lock the iPod's screen more easily.

To customize the main menu, follow these steps:

1. Choose Settings | Main Menu to display the Main Menu screen.
2. Scroll to the item you want to affect.
3. Press the Select button to toggle the item's setting between on (with a check mark next to it) and off (without a check mark).
4. Make further changes as necessary. Then press the Menu button twice to return to the main menu and see the effect of the changes you made.

To reset your main menu to its default settings, choose the Reset Main Menu item at the bottom of the Main Menu screen, and then choose Reset from the Menus screen.

> **TIP**
>
> *Another way of resetting your main menu is to reset all settings on the iPod by choosing the Reset Settings item at the bottom of the Settings screen. All settings includes the main menu.*

You can also customize the Music menu in a similar way by selecting the Music Menu item on the Settings screen, and then working on the Music Menu screen.

Set the Volume Limit

To prevent the iPod from playing back audio too loudly, follow these steps:

1. Scroll to the Volume Limit item, and then press the Select button.
2. On the Volume Limit screen, scroll to set the maximum audio volume, and then press the Select button to apply the change.

3. On the Enter Combination screen, dial each of the four digits to create the combination number for locking the volume limit, and then press the Select button to apply the locking.

TIP   *When setting the volume limit, connect the headphones that you or the listener will use. Set a song playing before you access the Volume Limit screen so that you can tell how loud the volume is.*

Set the Backlight Timer

To customize the length of time that the display backlight stays on after you press one of the iPod's controls, scroll to the Backlight option, and then press the Select button. Then you can choose from the following settings:

■ Choose the Off setting to keep the backlight off until you turn it on manually by holding down the Menu button for a second. You can then let the backlight go off automatically after the set delay or hold down the Menu button again for a couple of seconds to turn it off.

■ Specify the number of seconds for the backlight to stay on after you press a control.

■ Choose the Always On setting to keep the backlight on until you choose a new setting from this screen. (Even holding down the Menu button doesn't turn off the backlight when you choose Always On.) This setting is useful when you're using the iPod as a sound source in a place that's too dark to see the display without the backlight and when you need to change the music frequently. Be warned that Always On gets through battery power surprisingly quickly.

Set the Screen Brightness

You can change the screen brightness by choosing the Brightness item on the Settings menu, and then selecting the desired brightness on the resulting Brightness screen.

Change the Speed at Which Audiobooks Play

If you listen to audiobooks on an iPod, you may want to make them play faster or slower. To do so, choose the Audiobooks item on the Settings menu and choose Slower, Normal, or Faster from the Audiobooks screen.

Choose Equalizations to Make Your Music Sound Better

The iPod contains a graphical equalizer—a device that alters the sound of music by changing the level of different frequency bands. Here are two examples of how equalizations work:

■ A typical equalization for rock music boosts the lowest bass frequencies and most of the treble frequencies, while reducing some of the midrange frequencies. The normal effect of this arrangement is to punch up the drums, bass, and vocals, making the music sound more dynamic.

■ A typical equalization for classical music leaves the bass frequencies and midrange frequencies at their normal levels while reducing the treble frequencies, producing a mellow effect overall and helping avoid having the brass section blast the top off of your head.

NOTE   *The iPod shuffle doesn't include a graphical equalizer.*

The iPod typically includes the following equalizations: Acoustic, Bass Booster, Bass Reducer, Classical, Dance, Deep, Electronic, Flat, Hip Hop, Jazz, Latin, Loudness, Lounge, Piano, Pop, R & B, Rock, Small Speakers, Spoken Word, Treble Booster, Treble Reducer, and Vocal Booster. You might long for a Vocal Reducer setting for some artists or for karaoke, but the iPod doesn't provide one.

The names of most of these equalizations indicate their intended usage clearly, but Flat and Small Speakers deserve a word of explanation:

■ Flat is an equalization with all the sliders at their midpoints—an equalization that applies no filtering to any of the frequency bands. If you don't usually use an equalization, there's no point in applying Flat to a song, because the effect is the same as not using an equalization. But if you *do* use an equalization for most of your songs, you can apply Flat to individual songs to turn off the equalization while they play.

■ Small Speakers is for use with small loudspeakers. This equalization boosts the frequency bands that are typically lost by smaller loudspeakers. If you listen to the iPod through portable speakers, you may want to try this equalization for general listening. Its effect is to reduce the treble and enhance the bass.

TIP   *Don't take the names of the equalizations too literally, because those you find best will depend on your ears, your earphones or speakers, and the type of music you listen to. For example, if you find crunk sounds best played with the Classical equalization, don't scorn the Classical equalization because of its name. Or you may prefer to use different equalizations even for different songs that belong to the same genre—or even to the same CD.*

To apply an equalization, scroll to the EQ item on the Settings menu. The EQ item shows the current equalization—for example, EQ – Rock. To change the equalization, press the Select button. On the EQ screen, scroll to the equalization you want, and then press the Select button to apply it. Choose the Off "equalization" at the top of the list if you want to turn equalizations off.

Specifying an equalization from the Settings menu works well enough when you need to adjust the sound balance for the music you're playing during a listening session. But if you want to use different equalizations for the different songs in a playlist, you should use the iPod's other method of applying an equalization—by using iTunes to specify the equalization for the song, as described in "Specify an Equalization for an Individual Song" in Chapter 9. The iPod then applies this equalization when you play back the song on the iPod. The equalization also applies when you play the song in iTunes.

Use Sound Check to Standardize the Volume

Sound Check is a feature for normalizing the volume of different songs so you don't have to crank up the volume to hear a song encoded at a low volume and then suffer ear damage because the next song was recorded at a far higher volume. Scroll to the Sound Check item on the Settings menu, and then press the Select button to toggle Sound Check on or off.

For Sound Check to work on the iPod, you must also turn on the Sound Check feature in iTunes. Press CTRL-COMMA or choose Edit | Preferences to display the iTunes dialog box in Windows, or press ⌘-COMMA or choose iTunes | Preferences on the Mac to display the Preferences dialog box. Click the Playback tab to display its controls. Select the Sound Check check box, and then click the OK button to close the dialog box.

Turn the Clicker Off or Redirect the Clicks

By default, the iPod plays a clicking sound as you move the Click Wheel to give you feedback. You can turn off this clicking sound if you don't like it. Choose Settings | Clicker | Off. On the iPod nano, you can also choose to direct the clicking sound to the headphones, the iPod's tiny built-in (and hidden) speaker, or both, instead of turning them off: choose Settings | Clicker | Headphones, Settings | Clicker | Speaker, or Settings | Clicker | Both.

Set the Date and Time

To set the date and time on an iPod, choose Extras | Date & Time to display the Date & Time screen. From here, you can take the following actions:

- **Set the date**   Use the Date item to access a screen on which you can set the date.
- **Set the time**   Use the Time item to reach a screen on which you can set the time.
- **Set the time zone**   Use the Set Time Zone item to access the Time Zone screen, on which you can set the time zone (for example, U.S. Mountain). Scroll the Click Wheel to move the red dot to the city you want.
- **Turn daylight saving time on or off**   To turn daylight saving time off or on, scroll to the DST item on the Date & Time screen, and then press the Select button to toggle between Off and On.
- **Choose between 12-hour clocks and 24-hour clocks**   To choose the clock type, scroll to the Time item on the Date & Time screen, and then press the Select button to toggle between 12-Hour and 24-Hour.
- **Display the time in the iPod's title bar**   To make the iPod display the time in the title bar, set the Time In Title item on the Date & Time screen to On.

Choose How to Sort Your Contacts

To specify how the iPod should sort your contacts' names and display them onscreen, scroll to the Sort By item on the Settings screen, and then press the Select button to toggle between First (sorting the contacts by their first names) and Last (sorting them by their last names).

Make the Most of the iPod's Extra Features

The iPod classic and the iPod nano include a Sleep Timer for putting you to sleep, an Alarm Clock for waking you up, and alerts to help you avoid missing calendar appointments. You can even create playlists and rate songs on the iPod and have those playlists and ratings transferred back to iTunes when you synchronize the iPod.

NOTE   *The iPhone and the iPod touch have most of the extra features discussed here—plus many more. See Chapter 20 for coverage of these features.*

Use the Sleep Timer to Lull You to Sleep

The iPod's Sleep Timer is like the Sleep button on a clock radio or boom box: It lets you determine how long to continue playing music, presumably to lull you to sleep. You can set a value of 15, 30, 60, 90, or 120 minutes.

Choose Extras | Alarms, and then choose Sleep Timer. Scroll to the number of minutes, and then press the Select button. The Sleep Timer starts running. To turn off the Sleep Timer, access the Sleep screen again, and then select the Off setting.

Use the iPod's Alarm Clock to Wake You Up
or Remind You of an Appointment

The iPod's Alarm Clock feature lets you blast yourself awake—or give yourself a reminder—either with a beep or with one of your existing playlists. To use the Alarm Clock, follow these steps:

1. Create a custom playlist for waking up if you like (or create several—one for each day of the week, maybe). If you don't have your computer at hand, and the iPod doesn't contain a suitable playlist, create an On-the-Go playlist on the iPod.

2. Choose Extras | Alarms, and then choose Create Alarm to display the Alarm Clock screen.

3. Scroll to the Alarm item, and then press the Select button to toggle the alarm on or off, as appropriate.

4. Scroll to the Date item, and then press the Select button to access a screen on which you can set the date for the alarm.

5. Scroll to the Time item, and then press the Select button to access a screen on which you can set the time for the alarm.

6. If you want the alarm to repeat, scroll to the Repeat item, and then press the Select button to access a screen on which you can set up repeating. The default is Once (in other words, without repeating), but you can also choose Every Day, Weekdays, Weekends, Every Week, Every Month, or Every Year.

7. Scroll to the Sound item, and then press the Select button to display a screen on which you can choose between Tones and Playlists. If you just want a beep, select the Tones item, and then select the Beep item on the following screen. More likely, you'll want a playlist—in which case, select the Playlists item, and then choose the playlist on the resulting screen.

8. If you want to name the alarm, scroll to the Label item, and then press the Select button to access a screen on which you can choose from various predefined labels—for example, Wake Up, Work, Class, or Prescription.

9. If you're setting an alarm to wake you, connect the iPod to your speakers or stereo (unless you sleep with headphones on), and then go to sleep. Otherwise, use the iPod as normal.

When the appointed time arrives, the iPod wakes itself (if it's sleeping) and then unleashes the alarm.

Get Alerts for Your Calendar Appointments

The iPod can remind you of appointments in your calendar when their times arrive. Choose Extras | Calendars, scroll down to the Alarms item, and then press the Select button. Choose the Beep setting for Alarms to receive a beep and a message on the screen. Choose the None setting to receive only the message. Choose the Off setting to receive neither the beep nor the message.

Create a Playlist on the iPod

One of the features that iPod users pressed Apple for was the ability to create playlists on the fly on their iPods rather than having to create all playlists through iTunes ahead of time. Apple obliged, enabling you to create a new playlist called On-the-Go. You can even save this playlist under a different name, so you can keep it for later enjoyment and also create another On-the-Go playlist.

To create your On-the-Go playlist, follow these steps:

1. If you've previously created an On-the-Go playlist, decide whether to clear it or add to it. To clear it, choose Music | Playlists | On-the-Go | Clear Playlist | Clear.

2. Navigate to the song, album, artist, or playlist you want to add to the playlist.

3. Press the Select button and hold it down until the item's name starts flashing.

4. Repeat Steps 2 and 3 for each additional item that you want to add to the On-the-Go playlist.

To play your On-the-Go playlist, choose Playlists | On-the-Go. (Until you create an On-the-Go playlist, selecting this item displays an explanation of what the On-the-Go playlist does.)

To save your On-the-Go playlist under a different name, choose Playlists | On-the-Go | Save Playlist. The iPod saves the playlist under the name *New Playlist 1* (or *New Playlist 2*, or the next available number). After synchronizing the iPod with iTunes, click the playlist in the Source pane, wait a moment and click it again, type the new name, and then press ENTER (Windows) or RETURN (Mac).

Rate Songs on the iPod

To assign a rating to the song that's currently playing, follow these steps:

1. Display the Now Playing screen if it's not currently displayed. For example, from the main screen, scroll to the Now Playing item, and then press the Select button.

2. Press the Select button three times. (If the song has no CD cover art, you need only press twice.) The iPod displays five hollow dots under the song's name on the Now Playing screen.

3. Scroll to the right to display the appropriate number of stars in place of the five dots. Then press the Select button to apply the rating.

Use the iPod as a Stopwatch

The iPod classic and the iPod nano include stopwatch functionality. To use it, choose Extras | Stopwatch, and then press the Select button.

Lock the Screen on an iPod

You can even lock the screen to protect the iPod's contents. First, you need to set a combination:

1. Choose Extras | Screen Lock, and then use the resulting screen to set the four-digit code you want. Scroll each number to the appropriate digit, and then press the Select button to move to the next digit.

2. Press the Select button to apply the combination. The Confirm Combination screen appears.

3. Enter the combination again, and then press the Select button to apply it.

4. If you want to lock the iPod immediately, select the Lock button on the screen that appears, and then press the Select button. If you don't want to lock the iPod yet, select the Cancel button, and then press the Select button.

To lock the screen, choose Extras | Screen Lock, select the Lock button, and then press the Select button.

TIP   *If you forget your combination, all shouldn't be lost: Just connect the iPod to its home computer, and it unlocks. But if this doesn't work (don't ask why not), you'll need to restore the iPod's software to unlock it. See Chapter 18 for instructions on restoring the iPod's software.*

Play Music on the iPod shuffle

With no screen, the iPod shuffle needs only a limited set of controls for playing music (see Figure 3-5). These are largely intuitive but have a couple of hidden tricks:

- To start playing the songs on the iPod shuffle in the order of the playlist, move the mode switch on the bottom of the iPod shuffle to play mode, and then press the Play/Pause button.

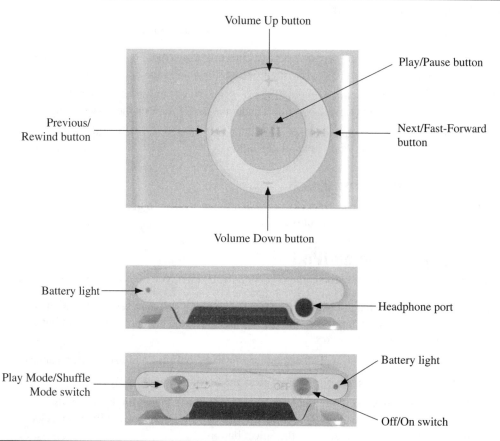

Volume Up button

Play/Pause button

Previous/
Rewind button

Next/Fast-Forward
button

Volume Down button

Battery light

Headphone port

Play Mode/Shuffle
Mode switch

Battery light

Off/On switch

FIGURE 3-5   The iPod shuffle's limited set of controls includes a couple of hidden tricks.

NOTE   *If the iPod shuffle blinks green and amber several times in succession when you press the Play/Pause button, it probably contains no songs. Move the switch to the Off position, wait for five seconds or more, move the switch back to the On position, and press the Play/Pause button again. If you see green and amber blinking again, connect the iPod shuffle to your computer and make sure that some songs are loaded on it.*

■   To start playing the songs in random order, move the mode switch to shuffle mode, and then press the Play/Pause button. When you hit a part of the playlist that you want to hear in sequence, move the mode switch to play mode to continue in sequence.

■   Press the Play/Pause button three times in immediate succession to move to the start of the playlist. To get to the end of the playlist, press the Play/Pause button three times, and then press the Previous/Rewind button once.

NOTE *When the iPod shuffle is in shuffle mode and you move to the beginning of the playlist, it shuffles the playlist again.*

■ Press the Next/Fast-Forward button to skip to the next song. Hold it down to fast-forward through the song.

NOTE *When the iPod shuffle is paused, you can press the Next/Fast-Forward button to start the next song playing, or press the Previous/Rewind button to start the previous song playing. The iPod shuffle doesn't remain paused when you press the Next/Fast-Forward button or the Previous/Rewind button, unlike other iPod models.*

■ Press the Previous/Rewind button to return to the start of the current song; press it again to go to the start of the previous song. Hold the button down to rewind through the current song.

■ Press the Volume Up button to increase the volume, or press the Volume Down button to decrease the volume.

■ To put the iPod shuffle on hold, hold down the Play/Pause button for several seconds. The top light gives three orange blinks to indicate that hold is applied. To remove hold, press the Play/Pause button for several seconds again until the status light blinks green.

■ To reset the iPod shuffle, turn it off, wait five seconds, and then turn it on again.

NOTE *If, when you press a button on the iPod shuffle, you see only the top light blink orange, it means that the iPod shuffle is on hold. Hold down the Play/Pause button for several seconds until the green light blinks three times to take it off hold.*

The iPod shuffle's lights give you feedback on the battery's status, as explained in the following list.

Battery Light Color	Battery Status
Green (when in dock)	30 percent or more charge
Amber (bottom light, when in dock)	10 to 30 percent charge
Red (bottom light, when in dock)	Critically low (less than 10 percent)—needs more charging
No light (bottom light, when in dock)	No charge
Blinking red (top light, while playing)	Critically low—recharge at once

Play Music on the iPhone or iPod touch

The touch screen on the iPhone and iPod touch makes playing music easy, although the techniques you use are necessarily different from those on the iPod classic and iPod nano.

Switch to iPod Mode

To play a song, first switch to iPod mode. Follow these steps:

1. Press the Home button to go to the Home screen unless you're already there (or you're already in iPod mode).

2. On the iPhone, touch the iPod button at the bottom of the Home screen. The iPhone switches to iPod mode and displays the last browse category you were using. On the iPod touch, touch the Music button.

Switch to the Browse Category You Want

In iPod mode, four browse buttons appear at the bottom of the screen: Playlists, Artists, Songs, and Videos or Albums, together with a More button. Touch the browse button by which you want to browse. For example, touch the Songs browse button to browse by song name, as shown on the left in Figure 3-6, or touch the Artists browse button to browse by artist name, as shown on the right in Figure 3-6.

The Playlists list contains the On-the-Go playlist that the iPhone or iPod touch creates for you, together with any other playlists you've created in iTunes.

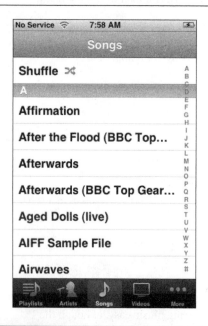 

FIGURE 3-6   Use the browse buttons at the bottom of the screen to switch among playlists, artists, songs, videos, and other items (touch the More button).

How to ...

Change the Browse Buttons at the Bottom of the iPod Screen

To change the browse buttons at the bottom of the iPod screen, follow these steps:

1. Touch the More button to display the More screen.

2. Touch the Edit button to display the Configure screen, shown here.

3. Drag the icon from the main part of the screen to the browse button whose current icon you want to replace. (You can't replace the More button.)

4. Change other browse buttons as needed, and then touch the Done button.

The icon you removed from the browse button appears on the More screen, so you can easily restore it if you want to.

NOTE   *The Songs list has a Shuffle item at the top that you can touch to play the songs in random order.*

To browse by albums, audiobooks, compilations, composers, genres, or podcasts, touch the More button. The iPhone or iPod touch displays the More screen (shown on the left in Figure 3-7). From here, you can touch one of the browse categories shown to browse by that category. For example, touch the Albums category to browse by album name, as shown on the right in Figure 3-7.

Find the Song or Other Item You Want to Play

To move down one of the lists, either drag your finger up the screen to pull the list upward, or touch one of the letters on the right to jump to that letter's section of the list. Once you find the song, playlist, album, artist, or other item you want to play, touch it. If the item is a song, video, or podcast, the iPhone or iPod touch starts playing it. If the item contains other items (such as songs), the iPhone or iPod touch displays a list of the contents. Touch the item you want to start playing.

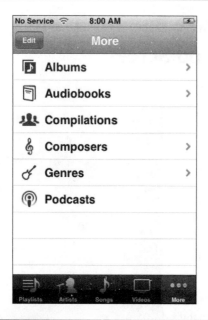 

FIGURE 3-7   The More screen lets you browse by any albums, audiobooks, compilations, composers, genres, or podcasts.

Play a Song or Other Item

When you start a song or other item playing, the iPhone or iPod touch displays any available art for it, together with play controls. Figure 3-8 shows an example of a song playing.

Touch the Back button to go back to the screen from which you started the song or other item playing.

Touch the Track List button to display a list of the items in the album or playlist (see Figure 3-9). You can then rate the item by touching the appropriate start or go to another item in the album or playlist by touching it.

Touch the cover art to display the additional play controls (see Figure 3-10). You can then:

■ **Play a different part of the song**   Drag the Playhead (the dot that shows the current playing position in the song) back or forward.

■ **Turn repeat on or off**   Touch the Repeat button once to repeat the album or playlist, a second time to repeat the playing item, and a third time to turn off repeating.

■ **Turn shuffle on or off**   Touch the Shuffle button to toggle shuffle on or off.

Back button

Artist, Song Name, and
Album Name readout

Track List button

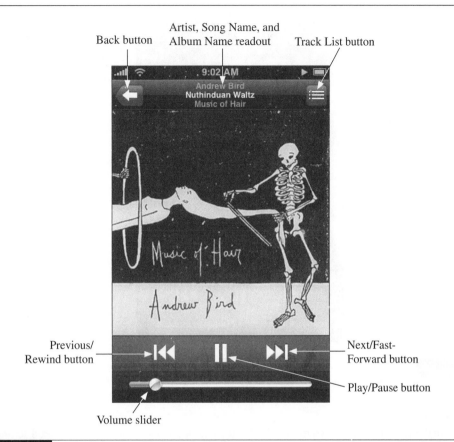

Previous/
Rewind button

Next/Fast-
Forward button

Play/Pause button

Volume slider

FIGURE 3-8   The iPhone or iPod touch displays the cover art for the item you're playing.

Use Cover Flow View

Once you've started a song or other audio item playing, you can turn the iPhone or iPod touch
to landscape orientation to switch to Cover Flow view (see Figure 3-11). You can then browse
through songs by touching the cover whose songs you want to view. Drag your finger left or
right to scroll through the covers more quickly.

Apply an Equalization to the Music

To apply an equalization on the iPhone or iPod touch, follow these steps:

1. Press the Home button to go to the Home screen unless you're already there.

2. Touch the Settings button to display the Settings screen.

FIGURE 3-9   The Track List screen lets you rate the playing item or go to another item on the album or playlist.

3. On the iPhone, scroll down to the iPod button, and then touch it to display the iPod settings screen. On the iPod touch, touch the Music button to display the Music settings screen.

4. Touch the EQ item to display the EQ screen (see Figure 3-12).

5. Touch the iPod button or Music button at the top to return to the iPod settings screen or Music settings screen, or simply press the Home button to go to the Home screen.

6. On the iPhone, touch the iPod button to switch to iPod mode. On the iPod touch, touch the Music button.

Create an On-the-Go Playlist

To create an On-the-Go playlist on an iPhone or iPod touch, follow these steps:

1. Touch the Playlists button.

2. At the top of the list, touch the On-the-Go item to display the Add Songs To The On-the-Go Playlist screen.

3. Touch the first song you want to add to the playlist.

Elapsed Time
readout

Playhead

Remaining Time readout

Shuffle button

Repeat button

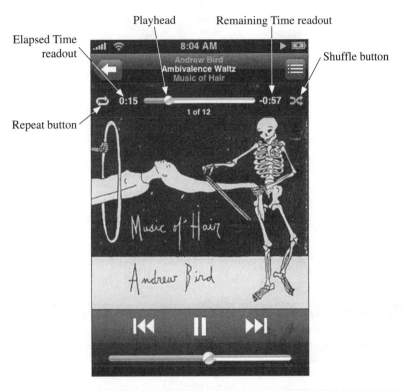

FIGURE 3-10   Display the additional play controls if you want to change the position of the
Playhead or turn repeating or shuffle on or off.

FIGURE 3-11   Cover Flow view lets you browse through songs or other items by their covers.

FIGURE 3-12 Use the EQ screen to apply an equalization to the iPhone or iPod touch. Usually, it's easier to apply the required equalization to each song, but you may need to adjust EQ on the iPhone or iPod touch sometimes.

TIP *While adding to the On-the-Go playlist, you can switch to another browse category. For example, touch the Artists button to view songs by artist.*

4. Touch additional songs in the order in which you want to add them.

5. When your playlist is complete, touch the Done button. The iPhone displays the On-the-Go playlist screen. From here, you can start the playlist playing (by touching a song or the Shuffle button) or touch the Edit button to edit it further.

NOTE *To delete the On-the-Go playlist, touch the Edit button on the On-the-Go screen, and then touch the Clear Playlist button.*

Control Your Music While You're Using Other Programs

When you're listening to music on the iPhone or iPod touch but you've moved to another program (for example, Safari), you can pop up a panel of play controls by pressing the Home button twice. These controls let you check the song information, pause and restart play, move forward and back, and change the volume.

When you've finished using the play controls, touch the Close button to hide the panel again.

Chapter 4

Extend the iPod's or iPhone's Capabilities with Hardware Accessories

How to...

- Approach buying accessories the right way
- Select alternative cases for an iPod or iPhone
- Learn about power adapters and car adapters for the iPod or iPhone
- Choose iPod stands, docks, and remote controls
- Choose a radio transmitter

Like many a consumer product that's been a runaway success, the iPod has spawned a huge market for accessories—from cases to stands, from microphones for input to speakers for output, from radio transmitters to remote controls. Apple makes some of the accessories, and third-party companies make far more. Some of these accessories are widely useful (although you may not need any of them yourself). Others are niche products, some of which are for very small niches.

Most of the accessories are for the regular iPod models, but there are plenty for the iPod nano as well. Fewer accessories are available for the iPod shuffle, partly because both of its generations are so different in form from the regular iPod and the iPod nano, but also because it has less functionality.

At this writing, the iPhone is new, so there are only a few accessories available for it—but there will likely be many more soon. The iPod touch is even newer, but accessories for it are already being released.

This chapter discusses the major categories of accessories (leaving you to choose the types you need) and highlights some of the less obvious and more innovative accessories that you might want to know about for special needs. This chapter focuses primarily on the iPod classic, iPod touch, iPod nano, iPod shuffle, and iPhone, but also mentions some accessories for earlier iPods where appropriate.

Approach Buying iPod or iPhone Accessories

Before you buy any iPod or iPhone accessories, run a quick reality check:

- *First, do you really need the accessory, or is it just cool or cute?* These are your dollars, so this is your decision.

- *Second, is there a less expensive alternative?* For some types of accessories, such as power adapters and cassette adapters, you don't need to restrict your horizons to iPod- or iPhone-specific accessories—you can choose generic accessories as well. Often, generic accessories are substantially less expensive than custom accessories, give you much more flexibility, or both.

- *Third, will this accessory work only with your current iPod or iPhone, or will it work with other devices you may buy in the future?* (You can be sure that Apple will release such compelling new iPod or iPhone models that you'll want to upgrade sooner or later.)

For example, if you get a radio transmitter designed for the third-generation iPod nano only, you'll need to upgrade the transmitter as well if you buy an iPod classic or an iPhone. In this case, buying a perhaps less stylish but more flexible accessory might make better financial sense.

Cases

The iPod and iPhone are built to be carried, so it's hardly surprising that a wide variety of cases has been developed for them—everything from bifold cases to armband cases to armored cases and waterproof cases. Early iPod models included sturdy cases, but Apple has dropped the cases along with the prices, so the first accessory you might need is a protective case for the iPod or iPhone.

> **TIP** *Many stores sell iPod cases and iPhone cases, but at this writing, the prime sources are the Apple Store (http://store.apple.com), Netalog's everythingiPod.com (www.everythingipod.com), and Gadget Locker (http://thinkdifferentstore.com).*

The Apple Store has user ratings for all third-party cases (but not for Apple cases), which can help you weed out superficially attractive losers.

Choosing a Case

Choosing a case is as fiercely personal as choosing comfortable underwear or choosing a car. Different aspects of cases are important to different people, and although one size may suit many, it doesn't fit all. As with underwear (or a car), you may prefer not to use a case at all—but the iPod's or iPhone's shiny surfaces will tend to get scratched, and you'll need to be careful not to drop the device onto any unforgiving surface.

But as with underwear (and, to a lesser extent, a car), it's vital to make sure the case you choose is the right size for the model of iPod or iPhone you have. You don't need me to tell you that the iPod shuffle and the iPod nano will rattle around in cases designed for an iPod classic, but the six generations and various capacities of the regular iPod have different sizes as well, and the iPhone and iPod touch are different sizes yet.

> **CAUTION** *The 160GB iPod classic is substantially thicker than the 80GB iPod classic, because its hard drive is not only higher in capacity but also physically larger.*

Beyond getting the size right, the remaining choices are yours. The following paragraphs summarize the key ways in which the cases differ. You get to decide which points are important for you:

- **How the case attaches to you (if at all)**   Many cases attach to your belt, whereas some hook on to a lanyard that goes around your neck or a strap that goes over your shoulder. Still others attach to an armband, which some people find better for performing vigorous activities. Some cases come with a variety of attachments—for example, a belt clip and an armband, or a mounting for sticking the iPod to a flat surface. Other cases are simply protective, designed to be carried in a pocket or a bag.

NOTE
Examples of armband cases include the Action Jacket from Digital Lifestyle Outfitters ($19.99 to $29.99; www.dlo.com). The Action Jacket is made of thick neoprene with holes that let you see the screen and access the front-panel controls. It attaches to either a belt clip or an armband.

- **The amount of protection the case provides** In general, the more protection a case provides, the larger and uglier it is, the more it weighs, and the more it costs. Balance your need for style against the iPod's or iPhone's need for protection when gravity gets the better of your grip.

- **Whether or not the case is waterproof** If you plan to take the iPod outdoors for exercise, you may want to get a case that's water-resistant or waterproof. Alternatively, carry a sturdy plastic bag in your pocket for weather emergencies. Either way, if the iPod has a Dock Connector port, it's a good idea to protect it.

- **Whether or not the case lets you access the iPod's controls** Access to the controls is pretty vital unless have a remote control for the iPod, in which case your need to access the iPod's controls once you've set the music playing will be much less. Generally speaking, the more waterproof the case, the less access it offers to the iPod's controls— although some case makers have been more successful than others at letting you reach the most important buttons.

- **Whether or not the case can hold the iPod's or iPhone's headphones and remote control** If you'll be toting the iPod in a bag or pocket, a case that can hold the ear-bud headphones and remote control as well as the player itself may be a boon. You may even want a case that can accommodate a USB cable and power adapter for traveling. But if you're more interested in a case that straps firmly to your body and holds the iPod securely, you probably won't want the case to devote extra space to store other objects.

TIP
If you're looking for an inexpensive case that'll take the iPod's complete entourage, consider the type of case designed for portable CD players and built into a padded belt.

- **Whether or not you need to take the iPod or iPhone out of the case to dock or recharge it** Some cases are designed to give you access to the Dock Connector port, so you can leave the iPhone in the case unless you need to admire it. With more protective cases, usually you need to remove the iPod or iPhone more often.

- **What the case is made of and how much it costs** Snug cases tend to be made of silicone or neoprene. Impressive cases tend to be made of leather. Leather and armor cost more than lesser materials.

- **Whether the case is single-purpose or multipurpose** Most cases are designed for carrying, either in your pocket or attached to your belt or clothing. Some cases convert to mount the iPod in your car or home.

TIP *When shopping for a case, look for special-value bundles that include other accessories you need—for example, a car cassette adapter or cables for connecting the iPod or iPhone to a stereo.*

Cases for the iPod classic

There are too many cases available for the iPod classic to round up here—and new cases are being released every month, if not every week. But here are some standout cases:

- If you have a rugged lifestyle and want the iPod to share it, consider the Matias Armor case from Matias Corporation ($19.95; http://matias.ca/armor/index5.php). The Matias Armor case cradles the iPod in a full metal jacket made of anodized aluminum padded with open-cell EVA foam. If you land on this case, you're more likely to damage yourself than the iPod.

- The ToughSkin from Speck Products ($24.95; www.speckproducts.com) is a series of ruggedized covers for various iPods, including the iPod classic. The ToughSkin (see Figure 4-1) is a polymer case with rubber bumpers, providing protection, a good grip, and easy access to the iPod's controls.

FIGURE 4-1   The ToughSkin provides a stylish way to protect the iPod from moderate harm.

■ The Sleevz for iPod 6G (classic) from RadTech ($20.95; www.radtech.us) is a thin protective case made of a soft-but-tough material through which you can press the buttons. The form-fitting Sleevz has a window for the iPod's screen and a die-cut knockout at the bottom for cable access to the Dock Connector. The Sleevz comes in several different colors.

■ The Otterbox from RadTech ($49.95; www.radtech.us) offers "waterproof impact protection" and a fully sealed audio jack interface that lets you use an iPod on the water— or even in the water. The Otterbox (see Figure 4-2) works with any headphones, but RadTech's H2O Audio Waterproof iPod Headphones ($39.95) seem an obvious match.

■ The Showcase from Contour Design ($34.95; www.contourdesign.com) is a protective case with a hard shell of impact-resistant plastic softened with shock-absorbing rubber. The Showcase opens like a book for when you want to access the iPod directly.

FIGURE 4-2   The Otterbox provides waterproof protection for the iPod.

- The Streamline ($29.99) and tempo ($24.99) from Griffin Technology (www .griffintechnology.com) are low-profile sport armbands that keep an iPod firmly anchored to your arm. These cases work for the third-, fourth-, fifth-, and sixth-generation iPods, the iPod touch, and the iPhone, and both the first- and second-generation iPod nano.

- Peter Kinne Design (www.peterkinne.com) makes wooden cases for iPods. Each case costs $39.00.

Cases for the iPod nano

The iPod nano's three generations have different styles and so typically need different cases.

Cases for the Third-Generation iPod nano

Here are some standout cases for the third-generation iPod nano:

- The iPod nano Armband from the Apple Store ($29.00; http://store.apple.com) is a lightweight armband that straps the iPod nano firmly to your wrist or arm.

- The Reflect from Griffin Technology ($24.99; www.griffintechnology.com) is a polycarbonate case whose front has a mirrored chrome finish that hides the iPod's screen until you turn the iPod on. If you wear mirror shades, you'll want one of these.

- The TechStyle Classic from Speck Products ($19.95; www.speckproducts.com) is a tight-fitting leather case that gives the iPod nano fair protection while still allowing you access to the Click Wheel.

Cases for the Second-Generation iPod nano

Standout cases for the second-generation iPod nano include the following:

- The iSkin for iPod nano 2nd Generation from the Apple Store ($29.95 for a three-pack; http://store.apple.com) is a flexible silicone case that fits the iPod nano snugly and protects it from dirt and damage. The iSkin for iPod nano 2nd Generation pack includes a belt clip.

- The iVault nano from Griffin Technologies ($24.99; www.griffintechnology.com) is a machined-aluminum case that provides robust protection for an iPod nano. The iVault (see Figure 4-3) works for the first-generation iPod nano as well.

- The disko nano from Griffin Technologies ($29.99; www.griffintechnology.com) is a polycarbonate case with a ring of colored LEDs around the Click Wheel. The LEDs light up in response to movement.

- The ToughSkin from Speck Products ($19.95; www.speckproducts.com) is a rubberized skin that provides good protection. If you're into extreme sports, you may want to go for the ToughSkin 2Tough ($24.95) instead.

FIGURE 4-3   The iVault provides heavy-duty protection for a first- or second-generation
iPod nano.

Cases for the First-Generation iPod nano

Cases for the first-generation iPod nano include the following:

- iPod nano Tubes from the Apple Store are slim silicone cases that the iPod
  nano can snuggle into. These cases cost $29 for a set of five different colors
  (http://store.apple.com).

- Incase nano Wallet ($19.95) and Incase Zip Folio for iPod nano ($24.95), both from the
  various retailers, provide sleek protection for the first-generation iPod nano.

- DecalGirl iPod nano Skin ($5.99; www.decalgirl.com) come in various flashy designs.
  Figure 4-4 shows some examples.

- invisibleSHIELD ($8.99; http://thinkdifferentstore.com) is a full-body wrap of
  protective film.

The Apple Store also offers iPod nano Armbands ($29) and the iPod nano Lanyard
Headphones ($39) that offer a means of carrying a first-generation iPod nano.

FIGURE 4-4   The DecalGirl iPod nano Skins come in a variety of striking designs.

Cases for the iPod shuffle

The two generations of the iPod shuffle are so different from each other that they require completely different cases.

Cases for the Second-Generation iPod shuffle

The second-generation iPod shuffle is small and tough in its aluminum shell, so you may prefer not to put it in a case. Besides, its built-in clip provides an effective means of securing the iPod shuffle to your clothing or belt.

But if you need a case, here are a couple you may want to consider:

- The Power Support Silicone Jacket for 2nd Generation iPod shuffle ($14.95; www.powersupportusa.com) is a tight-fitting silicone cover that protects most of the iPod.

- The TechStyle-Puck from Speck Products ($19.95; www.speckproducts.com) is a hard-shell case that can hold a second-generation iPod shuffle and its headphones. The Puck features a cable-management system to prevent the headphone cable from getting tangled.

Cases for the First-Generation iPod shuffle

Cases for the first-generation iPod shuffle include the following:

- The Apple iPod shuffle Sport Case from the Apple Store ($29.00; http://store .apple.com) is a waterproof case with an integrated lanyard. You can access the iPod shuffle's controls through the case.

- The Apple iPod shuffle Armband from the Apple Store ($29.00; http://store.apple.com) is an armband onto which the iPod shuffle clips. The iPod shuffle is still exposed to the elements; you take care of the consequences.

- The iPod shuffle cases from Cute Cases from ($24; www.cute-cases.com/ ipod_shuffle.html) let you disguise the iPod shuffle as a furry beast. Various hues and color combinations are available.

Cases for the iPhone

The iPhone presents a challenge for cases, because even if you use the headphones for listening to music, you'll presumably need to be able to whip the iPhone out at any moment to take or make a phone call—or to surf the Web, check your e-mail, watch a YouTube video, or use many of the other features. At the same time, the iPhone is an expensive gadget and is worth protecting.

Manufacturers have responded to the challenge in various ways, including the following:

- The Speck ToughSkin for iPhone ($29.95; www.speckproducts.com) provides protection for your iPhone while giving you extra grip and full access to the controls. The ToughSkin (see Figure 4-5) includes a holster with a belt clip.

- The Sidewinder from Marware ($24.95; http://store.apple.com) is a rubberized cradle with a retractable side arm on which you can wind the headset.

- The Incase Leather Fitted Sleeve for iPhone ($34.95; http://store.apple.com) is a leather case that fits snugly around the iPhone while providing access to its controls. At this writing, you have a choice of brown, black, or pink leather.

- The Incase Leather and Nylon Folio for iPhone ($39.95; http://store.apple.com) is a wallet-style case that covers the iPhone completely, so you have to remove the iPhone from the case for use. The Folio case clips to your belt or to a strap.

Cases for the iPod touch

At this writing, the iPod touch is new, but various cases are available already. Here are two models you may want to check out:

- The SeeThru from Speck Products ($29.95; www.speckproducts.com) is a translucent case made of hard plastic that keeps your iPod touch protected but fully visible.

FIGURE 4-5   The ToughSkin for iPhone allows access to the iPhone's controls.

■   The Courier from Griffin Technology (price to be announced; www.griffintechnology
.com) is a utility case built of compression-molded EVA. Inspired (so Griffin claims) by
bicycle messengers' need for hard-wearing gear, the Courier attaches via a dog-lead clip
and contains two pockets for carrying keys, ID, headphones, or even a mobile phone.

Stands and Docks

Cases can be great, but you won't always want to carry the iPod or iPhone. Sometimes, you'll
want to park it securely so you can use it without worrying about knocking it down, or so you
can contemplate its lustrous beauty.

If you have an iPhone, the dock that comes with it may be all you need. But while
early iPods came with docks, now the second-generation iPod shuffle is the only iPod that
includes a dock. However, plenty of iPod docks are available from Apple and from third-party
manufacturers.

TIP *The advantage of playing audio from an iPod Dock that includes a line-out port is that the port delivers a standard volume rather than a variable volume. The standard volume means that you're less likely to damage your receiver or speakers by putting too great a volume through them. It also means that you can't adjust the volume on the iPod, only on the receiver or speakers.*

If you want standard dock features, start by looking at the Apple Universal Dock ($49; http://store.apple.com). This dock works with any iPod that has the Dock Connector port and includes assorted Dock Adapters to make the iPods fit well. The Universal Dock includes a line-out port for producing high-quality audio (via the iPod's Dock Connector port) and an S-video out port for displaying photos, videos, or slideshows on a TV.

TIP *Another option for docking the iPod is to get a set of portable speakers designed to include an iPod stand. See "Portable Speakers for the iPod," later in this chapter, for examples.*

Stands and Docks for the iPod classic

If you decide that an Apple Universal Dock isn't what you need for an iPod classic, you should be able to find third-party alternatives that offer extra features. At this writing, docks designed specifically for the iPod classic are not yet available, but here are two examples of docks for the iPod with video that may be updated in the future for the iPod classic:

- ■ The FlipSkin from Speck Products ($24.95; www.speckproducts.com) is a protective case for the iPod that also acts as a stand when you flip the kickstand down. The FlipSkin fits the various models of iPod with video.
- ■ TuneCenter from Griffin Technology ($109.99; www.griffintechnology.com) is a dock that lets you play music through your home stereo and show photos and videos on a TV screen. TuneCenter displays the iPod's menus on the TV screen, allowing you to navigate the iPod via the remote control included in the package.

Stands and Docks for the iPod nano

The first-, second-, and third-generation iPod nanos need different types of docks.

TIP *If you already have another iPod Dock with a Dock Connector (for example, from a iPod with video or an iPhone), you will probably be able to use it for any iPod nano. If the iPod nano's iPod Dock Adapter doesn't fit the dock, try connecting the iPod nano using only the Dock Connector. Because the iPod nano is so light, the Dock Connector usually provides enough support even without an adapter.*

Stands and Docks for the Third-Generation iPod nano

At this writing, your best bet for a dock for the third-generation iPod nano is the Apple Universal Dock ($49.00; http://store.apple.com). However, other manufacturers will probably soon release docks for this model.

Stands and Docks for the Second-Generation iPod nano

Here are a couple of the docks available for the second-generation iPod nano:

- The Apple iPod nano Dock (2nd generation) ($29; http://store.apple.com) is a dock specifically tailored for the second-generation iPod nano. The iPod nano Dock provides only a Dock Connector port (for connecting the Dock to a USB cable) and a line-out port for high-quality audio playback.

- The PedN nano stand from THOUGHT OUT (from $14.99; http://thoughtout.biz) is a solid-steel stand that's available in either black or white.

Stands and Docks for the First-Generation iPod nano

Here are a couple of the docks available for the first-generation iPod nano:

- The Apple iPod nano Dock (1st generation) ($29; http://store.apple.com) is a dock made for the first-generation iPod nano. This deck is less expensive than the Apple iPod Universal Dock, but you won't be able to use it with any other iPod models you own. This Dock provides a Dock Connector port and a line-out port for high-quality audio playback.

- The mTUNE-N with iPod nano Dock from Macally ($49.99; www.macally.com) is a pair of cordless headphones that has a dock pocket for the iPod nano built in, so that the iPod nano sits just above your ear. If you can stand oversized circumaural headphones and can't stand headphone cords, this might be just what you need.

Stands and Docks for the iPod shuffle

The second-generation iPod shuffle comes with its own dock, so you probably will not need to get another. However, if you want a fractionally more compact arrangement for traveling, look at the Marware USB Travel Dock for 2nd Generation iPod shuffle ($19.95; http://store.apple.com). Instead of a cable, this dock has a built-in USB connector that goes straight into your computer's USB socket.

The first-generation iPod shuffle is designed to plug straight into a USB socket in much the same way, so you may not need a dock unless the USB socket is inaccessible or you like to keep your computer area neat. If so, consider the following options:

- The Apple iPod shuffle Dock ($29.00; http://store.apple.com) is Apple's own dock for the iPod shuffle—a straightforward base with a cap-like USB connection standing up. The iPod shuffle Dock simplifies the process of connecting the iPod shuffle to your computer, especially if your computer's USB ports are hard to reach, but it seems to be a poor value.

CAUTION   *Unlike most other Apple Docks, the iPod shuffle Dock doesn't have a line-out connector, so you can't play music directly from the iPod shuffle.*

- The DecoDock from Pressure Drop ($15; www.pressuredropinc.com) is an art-techno-styled dock that works only with the iPod shuffle. The DecoDock (see Figure 4-6) makes a pleasant alternative to scrabbling for a free USB port on your computer, but it costs far more than a USB extension cable, which can offer much of the same convenience.

FIGURE 4-6 The DecoDock is designed to recharge the iPod shuffle in style—and even includes an integrated holder for the iPod shuffle's cap.

Stands and Docks for the iPod touch

At this writing, the best dock for the iPod touch is the Apple Universal Dock ($49.00; http://store .apple.com). However, other manufacturers will probably soon release docks for this model.

NOTE *The iPod touch has a different body shape than the iPhone and doesn't fit into the iPhone's dock. However, the iPod touch does fit (albeit loosely) into various docks designed for older models of regular iPods—so if you have an old dock, or can scrounge one from someone who's just trashed their old iPod, try it with the iPod touch.*

Car and Bike Mounting Kits

The iPod on your body or desk gets you only so far. To get further, you'll probably want to use the iPod in your car or on your bike. To prevent it from shifting around as you shift gears, you'll probably want to secure it.

Car Mounts

If you want to secure the iPod in your car, you can choose between many types of holders and mounts, including the following:

■ The TuneDok Car Holder for iPod from Belkin ($29.99; www.belkin.com) lets you mount a regular iPod (such as the iPod classic) in your car's cup holder. The TuneDok includes large and small bases to fit securely in any cup holder.

- The iGrip ($8.99; http://thinkdifferentstore.com) from Handstands is an adhesive pad that you can use to secure the iPod to your car dashboard or another convenient location. Refreshingly low-tech, the iGrip will also stick to other objects, such as your mobile phone or the case for your shades.

- The iSqueez from Griffin Technology ($4.99; www.griffintechnology.com) is a low-tech foam cup that fits into most cup holders and will hold most iPod models or an iPhone securely.

All-in-One Adapters for the Car

Securing the iPod or iPhone in your car tends to be only half the problem. The other half is playing the sound from the iPod or iPhone through the car's stereo system. Chapter 5 discusses this problem in more detail, but one solution is to use an all-in-one gadget. Most of these combine three main components:

- A power adapter that connects to your car's 12-volt accessory outlet or cigarette-lighter socket.

- A means of piping the iPod's or iPhone's output to your stereo. This can use a direct cable connection, a cassette adapter, or a radio transmitter.

- A cradle or other device for holding the iPod or iPhone, either built onto the power adapter (using the power adapter as its support) or fitting into a cup holder or onto the dash.

Many different all-in-one gadgets are available, including the following:

- TransDock from Digital Lifestyle Outfitters (www.dlo.com) is a series of car gadgets for iPods. The TransDock Deluxe costs $129.99 and lets you not only broadcast music from the iPod to your car's radio but also show video from the iPod on your in-car video system. A remote control clips to the steering wheel, improving your chances of staying in lane as well as in tune. The nondeluxe model, the TransDock, offers the same audio and video features for $99.99 but not the remote control. Both models include an adapter to fit an iPod nano.

- The TuneBase and TuneCast series from Belkin (www.belkin.com) provide a variety of ways to play audio from an iPod through a car stereo. For example, the TuneBase FM for iPod ($79.99) mounts the iPod on a flexible steel neck from the accessory outlet and transmits audio wirelessly to the car stereo. The TuneCast Auto for iPod ($59.99) connects to the iPod via a Dock Connector, charges the iPod from the 12-volt accessory outlet or cigarette-lighter outlet, and transmits audio wirelessly to the car stereo.

- The Kensington Digital FM Transmitter/Auto Charger ($79.95; http://store.apple.com) charges the iPod from the accessory outlet and transmits audio wirelessly to the car stereo. You take care of securing the iPod. This accessory comes in a choice of white or black.

Bike Mounts

If you want to mount the iPod on your bike, your options are more limited. Here are a couple of examples:

- The iPod Mobility Pack ($19.95; http://store.apple.com) from Marware includes a bike holder, swivel clip, and car holder that work with Marware cases that use the Multidapt clip system. The Bike Holder Accessory lets you strap the iPod to your bike's handlebars so that you can manipulate the music when you have a hand free.

- The iBikeMount nano from Strata Systems LC ($29.99; www.ibikemount.com) attaches a first-generation iPod nano to your bike's handlebars or another tube.

Almost everyone who pronounces on the subject of road safety is adamant that you shouldn't listen to audio using earphones when riding a bike lest you fail to hear the vehicles thundering past with their own music blasting. But if you do listen to an iPod, keep your eyes on the road rather than on the iPod's screen. An iPod shuffle is great for biking, because there's no screen to distract you and you can easily attach the player to your clothing rather than to your bike.

Power Adapters and Battery Packs

Each iPod comes with a USB cable that allows you to recharge it from a computer. The iPhone also includes a power adapter that lets you recharge it from an electrical socket. You may want to get a power adapter for the iPod, or you may need to prolong your AC-free playing time by using a backup battery pack.

TunePower Rechargeable Battery Pack

The TunePower Rechargeable Battery Pack from Belkin ($79.99; www.belkin.com) is a rechargeable lithium-ion external battery that works with most iPods. The TunePower clips on to the back of the iPod, using any of several included sleeves to make a good fit, and connects via the Dock Connector. Belkin claims 8–10 hours of play time for the TunePower.

iLuv Battery Booster Series

The iLuv battery boosters (from around $59.95; www.thinkdifferentstore.com) are clip-on rechargeable lithium-ion batteries that boost your playing time significantly. For example, the iLuv iPod Video Battery Booster claims to deliver up to 55 hours of playback.

TuneJuice 2

The TuneJuice 2 from Griffin Technology ($29.99; www.griffintechnology.com) is an external backup battery that runs off four AAA batteries. The TuneJuice 2 can provide up to 14 hours of extra power to any iPod that has a Dock Connector port, but it doesn't recharge the iPod's battery.

Apple iPod Shuffle External Battery Pack

The Apple iPod shuffle External Battery Pack ($29.00; http://store.apple.com) takes two AAA batteries, delivers up to 20 hours of battery life to a first-generation iPod shuffle, and replaces the iPod shuffle's cap. The iPod shuffle connects to the External Battery Pack through its USB connector. The battery cap includes a lanyard so that you can still hang the iPod shuffle around your neck.

MicroPack

The MicroPack Portable Dock and Battery from XtremeMac ($79.95; http://store.apple.com) is a dock with a built-in lithium-ion rechargeable battery. The MicroPack can recharge any iPod that has a Dock Connector port and can provide up to 80 hours of audio playback.

JBox

The JBox from Macally ($49.99; www.macally.com) is an external lithium-ion battery that connects to any iPod or iPhone via a Dock Connector or a USB socket. The JBox gives up to eight hours extra battery life.

Basic AC Power Adapters

If you want to be able to recharge an iPod without connecting it to a USB port, you can buy an Apple USB Power Adapter ($29; http://store.apple.com). Alternatively, you can find a third-party USB power adapter for less.

Car Adapters

If you drive extensively (or live in a vehicle), you may find that even the iPod's impressive battery life isn't enough for your lifestyle. To recharge the iPod in your car, you need a power adapter that'll run from your car's 12-volt accessory outlet or cigarette-lighter socket. Technically, such an adapter is an *inverter*, a device that converts DC into AC, but we'll stick with the term *adapter* here.

You can choose between a generic car adapter and a custom car adapter for the iPod. Another option is an all-in-one device that combines a power adapter with a radio transmitter and (in some cases) a means of mounting the iPod, as discussed in "All-in-One Adapters for the Car," earlier in this chapter.

Generic Car Adapter

The simplest and most versatile option is to get a generic car adapter that plugs into your car's 12-volt accessory outlet or cigarette-lighter socket. Models vary, but the most effective types give you one or more conventional AC sockets. You plug an iPod or iPhone power adapter into one of these AC sockets, just as you would any other AC socket, and then plug the USB cable into the power adapter.

The advantage to these adapters is that you can run any electrical equipment off them that doesn't draw too heavy a load—a portable computer, your cell phone charger, a portable TV, or whatever. The disadvantage is that such adapters can be large and clumsy compared with custom adapters.

Cost usually depends on the wattage the adapter can handle; you can get 50-watt adapters from around $20 and 140-watt adapters for around $50, whereas 300-watt adapters cost more like $80. A 50-watt adapter will take care of an iPod and portable computer easily enough.

iPod-Specific Adapters

If the only thing you want to power from your car is the iPod, you can get a car adapter designed specially for the iPod. Many different models are available, including the following:

- The Belkin Auto Kit for iPod with Dock Connector ($39.99; www.belkin.com) is a charger for iPods with the Dock Connector. This kit also includes an adjustable amplifier and a 3.5mm audio-out jack for playing music from the iPod through the car stereo.

- The Griffin PowerJolt ($19.99; www.griffintechnology.com) is an adapter with a USB socket and a USB-to–Dock Connector cable. Figure 4-7 shows the PowerJolt.

- The XtremeMac InCharge Auto ($19.95; www.xtrememac.com) is an adapter into which you can plug any iPod that has a dock connector port.

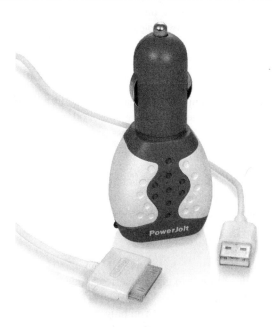

FIGURE 4-7 You can power the iPod from a car's cigarette-lighter socket or 12-volt accessory outlet with an adapter such as the PowerJolt.

World Travel Adapters

If you travel abroad with an iPod or iPhone, the lightest and easiest way to recharge it is from your laptop—provided that you have your computer with you, and you have access to an electric socket so that you don't deplete your computer's battery by charging the iPod or iPhone.

If you need to recharge the iPod or iPhone directly from the electric socket, get an adapter that lets you plug the iPod's or iPhone's power adapter into electric sockets in different countries. The adapter can handle multiple voltages, so you can plug it safely in even in countries that think 240 volts is just a refreshing tingle.

For such adapters, you have the choice between a set of cheap and ugly adapters and a set of stylish and sophisticated adapters. You can get the cheap and ugly adapters from any competent electrical-supply shop; they consist of an assortment of prong-converter receptacles into which you plug the power adapter U.S. prongs. The resulting piggyback arrangement is clumsy, and sometimes you have to jiggle the adapters to get a good connection. But these adapters are inexpensive (usually from $5 to $10) and functional, and they work for any electrical gear that can handle the different voltages.

The stylish and sophisticated adapters are designed by Apple and are (collectively) called the World Travel Adapter Kit. The kit costs $39.95 from the Apple Store (http://store.apple.com) or an authorized reseller. You slide the U.S. prongs off the iPod or iPhone power adapter and replace them with a set of prongs suited to the country you're in. The kit includes six prongs that'll juice up the iPod or iPhone in continental Europe, the United Kingdom, Australia, Hong Kong, South Korea, China, and Japan, as well as in the United States. These adapters also work with Apple laptops, but they won't help you plug in any of your other electrical equipment.

TIP   *If you're going somewhere sunny that lacks electricity, or you live somewhere sunny that suffers frequent power outages, consider a solar charger such as the Solio (www.solio.com/v2/).*

Remote Controls

If you connect an iPod to your stereo (as discussed in "Connect an iPod to Your Stereo" in Chapter 5), you'd probably appreciate being able to control the iPod from across the room. You can do so by using a wireless remote control.

Apart from price and looks, consider the following points when evaluating a remote control:

- Does it use infrared (IR) or radio frequency (RF)? RF typically gives better range and works around corners. On the other hand, if you have a universal remote control, you may be able to teach it the commands from an IR iPod control so that you can control the iPod remotely using the universal remote.

- Do you simply want to play back music, or do you need to be able to control other features, such as displaying photos or running videos?

HomeDock Music Remote

The HomeDock Music Remote from Digital Lifestyle Outfitters ($129.99; www.dlo.com) is a remote-control kit that works with all iPods that have a Dock Connector port. You place the iPod in the HomeDock, which you connect to your stereo, and then control the iPod using the Music Remote. The Music Remote includes a display that allows you to navigate the iPod's screens.

Aerolink

The Aerolink family of remote controls from Engineered Audio, LLC ($45 each; www.engineeredaudio.com) includes radio-frequency (RF) remotes designed for the iPods that have Dock Connector ports. The transmitter is a five-button key fob that offers control buttons but no screen.

Microphones and Camera Connectors

If you have one of the iPods that supports audio recording (such as an iPod classic, an iPod with video, or a second- or third-generation iPod nano), you may want to add a microphone so that you can use the iPod to take audio notes.

TuneTalk Stereo

The TuneTalk Stereo from Belkin ($69.95; http://store.apple.com) is a digital recorder that clips onto the base of an iPod classic, an iPod with video, or a second- or third-generation iPod nano and enables you to record CD-quality audio (16-bit, 44.1 KHz). The TuneTalk Stereo has a real-time gain control. You can also plug in an external microphone and record through that instead of through the TuneTalk Stereo's two built-in microphones.

MicroMemo

The MicroMemo from XtremeMac ($59.99; http://store.apple.com) is a digital recorder for recording CD-quality audio (16-bit, 44.1 KHz) onto an iPod with video. There is also a MicroMemo for iPod nano 2G that allows you to record in this quality on the second-generation iPod nano. You can record either through the attached microphone or through an external microphone that you plug in.

iTalk Pro

The iTalk Pro from Griffin Technologies ($49.95; www.griffintechnology.com) is a digital recorder that clips onto the base of an iPod with video and enables you to record CD-quality audio (16-bit, 44.1 KHz). You can also plug in an external microphone and record through that instead of through the iTalk Pro's two built-in microphones.

Did you know?

You Can Record on Third- and Fourth-Generation iPods—But Only at Lower Quality

The third- and fourth-generation regular iPods can record audio—but only at a lower quality suitable for voice, not at the CD quality that the iPod with video and the second-generation iPod nano can manage.

If you have a third- or fourth-generation regular iPod, you need a different type of microphone. Look for the following:

- The Belkin Voice Recorder for iPod (www.belkin.com) is a compact microphone that makes basic recordings easy.

- The Griffin iTalk is also a compact microphone, but it lets you connect an external microphone. This is an older model that you may be able to find on eBay or other trading sites.

- The Belkin iPod Mic Adapter for iPod (www.belkin.com) is a small adapter that lets you connect an external microphone.

If the manufacturers have discontinued these items, try searching on eBay or a similar site.

iPod Camera Connector

The iPod Camera Connector from Apple ($29.00; http://store.apple.com) is a device for transferring photos from a USB-equipped digital camera to the iPod. The iPod Camera Connector works with the iPod photo and iPod with video.

iPod Media Reader

The iPod Media Reader from Belkin (originally $69.99; www.belkin.com) is a compact unit that enables you to transfer pictures from media cards (including CompactFlash cards, Secure Digital cards, and Memory Stick cards) to the iPod. You may need to search the Internet for this product.

Digital Camera Link for iPod

The Digital Camera Link for iPod from Belkin (originally $49.99; www.belkin.com) is a device that enables you to transfer photos from a USB-equipped digital camera to a third-generation or later regular iPod. You connect the Digital Camera Link to the iPod via the Dock Connector and to the camera via the camera's USB cable, and then you press a button to transfer the photos. The Digital Camera Link runs off two AA batteries. You may need to search the Internet for this product.

Portable Speakers for the iPod and iPhone

You can use the iPod as the sound source for just about any stereo system, as you'll see in "Connect the iPod to Your Stereo" in the next chapter. But if you travel with an iPod, or simply prefer a compact lifestyle, you may want portable speakers that will treat the iPod as the center of their universe. You can find a variety of iPod-specific speakers to meet most constraints of budgets and portability.

Some of the speakers mentioned here work for the iPhone as well. However, the iPhone has the advantage of having its own built-in speakers for low-volume listening.

Choosing Portable Speakers for the iPod or iPhone

If you've decided that you need portable speakers specifically for an iPod or iPhone, you've already narrowed down your choices considerably. Bear the following in mind when choosing portable speakers:

- ■ *How much sound do the speakers make?* The best design in the world is useless if the speakers deliver sound too puny for your listening needs.

- ■ *Do the speakers recharge the device?* Some speakers recharge the iPod or iPhone as it plays. Others just wear down the battery.

- ■ *Do the speakers work with all iPods?* Some speakers are designed to work only with a particular iPod model. Others can recharge various iPods (for example, all models with the Dock Connector) and the iPhone but can accept input from other players via a line-in port.

- ■ *How are the speakers powered?* Some speakers are powered by replaceable batteries; others by rechargeable batteries; and others by AC power. A pairing of rechargeable batteries and AC power gives you the most flexibility.

- ■ *Do the speakers include a remote control?* If you're planning to use the speakers from across the room, look for speakers that include a remote control.

SoundDock

The SoundDock from Bose ($299.00; www.bose.com) is one of the larger and more powerful speaker systems designed for the iPod. The SoundDock works with all iPods that have a Dock Connector. The SoundDock runs on AC power and recharges the iPod as it plays.

Radial Micro Loudspeaker Dock

The JBL Radial Micro Loudspeaker Dock ($149.95; http://store.apple.com) is a round speaker unit that runs off AC power and delivers up to 10W per channel. The Radial Micro Loudspeaker Dock is designed for iPods with the Dock Connector port, but you can also use other sound sources through an auxiliary audio input cable.

Despite running on AC power, the Radial Micro Loudspeaker Dock weighs only 1.1 lb and is portable enough to be a fair travel solution.

inMotion Series

The inMotion series from Altec Lansing (various prices; http://store.apple.com) includes portable and ultraportable stereo systems designed for iPods with Dock Connector ports. The larger models are AC powered, while the smaller models can run from batteries.

Radio Transmitters

Portable speakers are a great way of getting a decent amount of audio out of an iPod or iPhone when you're at home or traveling with a moderate amount of kit. But where portable speakers aren't practical, or when you need to travel light, you can use a radio transmitter to play audio from an iPod or iPhone through a handy radio. This is useful in hotels, in cars, in friends' houses—and even in your own home.

Choosing a Radio Transmitter

Many models of radio transmitters are available. Apart from price and esthetics, consider the following when choosing between them:

- *Does the transmitter fit only one model, or will it work for any device?* You may find that the choice is between a transmitter designed to fit only your current model of iPod or iPhone or a less stylish transmitter that will work with any model—or indeed any sound source.

- *Is the transmitter powered by the iPod (or iPhone), or does it have its own power source?* Drawing power from the player's battery is a neater arrangement, because you don't have to worry about keeping the battery in the transmitter charged (or putting in new batteries) or connecting an external power supply. But drawing power from the player tends to limit the transmitter to working with certain models only.

- *Is the transmitter powerful enough for your needs?* Even among low-power transmitters that are legal for unlicensed use, power and range vary widely.

- *How many frequencies can the transmitter use?* Some transmitters are set to broadcast on a single frequency, which means you're out of luck if a more powerful local station happens to be using that frequency. Many transmitters offer several preset frequencies among which you can switch. Some transmitters provide a wide range of frequencies.

- *Does the transmitter have other tricks?* Some transmitters are designed for use in your car or another vehicle, whereas others are general purpose.

NOTE *Low-power radio transmitters are legal in the United States and the United Kingdom, but some other countries don't permit them. If you don't know whether your country permits radio transmitters, check before buying one.*

PodFreq

The PodFreq from Sonnet Technologies ($29.95 to $79.95; www.podfreq.com) is a family of relatively powerful radio transmitters built in the shape of an iPod case. The iPod slips inside the PodFreq (see Figure 4-8), and the PodFreq's aerial extends past the top of the iPod. The PodFreq offers a full range of digital tuning from 88.3 to 107.7 MHz, enabling you to avoid other stations even if the airwaves are jammed.

FIGURE 4-8   The PodFreq is one of the larger radio transmitters built for the iPod—and one of the most powerful.

Instead of taking the audio from the iPod's headphone port, the PodFreq takes it from the Dock Connector, which gives a line-out signal at a standard volume that should be cleaner than the audio from the headphone port. The bottom of the PodFreq includes FireWire and mini-USB 2.0 ports, enabling you to synchronize and recharge the iPod even when it's installed in the PodFreq. The PodFreq includes a car charger and car cradle.

iTrip

The iTrip family from Griffin Technology ($49.99 each; www.griffintechnology.com) consists of compact radio transmitters designed to work with most iPods. The iTrip models connect to the Dock Connector port, adding an extra section to the bottom of the iPod, and draw power from the iPod's battery rather than using batteries of their own. The iTrip (see Figure 4-9) lets you set it to broadcast on any frequency between 87.7 and 107.9 FM, so you should be able to get the signal through even in a busy urban area.

FIGURE 4-9   The iTrip family offers models for the regular iPod and the iPod nano.

Chapter 5

Use an iPod or iPhone as Your Home Stereo or Car Stereo

How to...

- Equip an iPod or iPhone with speakers
- Connect an iPod or iPhone to your stereo
- Play music throughout your house from an iPod or iPhone
- Play music through an AirPort Express network
- Connect an iPod or iPhone to your car stereo
- Use your computer to play songs directly from an iPod or iPhone

By the time you've loaded hundreds or thousands of songs onto your iPod or iPhone, you'll probably have decided that headphones only get you so far. To enjoy your music the rest of the time, chances are that you'll want to play it from the iPod or iPhone and through your home stereo or your car stereo. This chapter shows you the various ways of doing so, from using cables to using radio waves.

Equip an iPod or iPhone with Speakers

The simplest way to get a decent volume of sound from an iPod or iPhone is to connect it to a pair of powered speakers (speakers that include their own amplifier). You can buy speakers designed especially for the iPod or iPhone (see the section "Portable Speakers for the iPod and iPhone" in Chapter 4), but you can also use any iPod or iPhone with any powered speakers that accept input via a miniplug connector (the size of connector used for the iPod's or iPhone's headphones).

Speakers designed for the iPod or iPhone tend to be smaller and more stylish than general-purpose speakers, but also considerably more expensive.

TIP *To get the highest sound quality possible from an iPod or iPhone, use a dock rather than the headphone port. If you've got an iPhone, you already have a dock, so you're set. If you have an iPod, you'll need to buy an iPod dock if you don't have one already. Connect the dock's line-out port to the speakers or receiver, and you're in business any time you've docked the iPod or iPhone.*

Connect an iPod or iPhone to a Stereo

If you already have a stereo that produces good-quality sound, you can play songs from an iPod or iPhone through the stereo. There are three main ways of doing this:

- Connect the iPod or iPhone directly to the stereo with a cable, either via the device's headphone port or (better) via a dock.
- Use a radio transmitter to send the music from the iPod or iPhone to your radio, which plays it.

■ Use your computer to play the music from an iPod through an AirPort Express wireless access point that's connected to your stereo. At this writing, this approach doesn't work for an iPhone, because the iPhone does not allow manual management of music, which is required for playing back music from the iPod or iPhone via the computer.

Connect an iPod or iPhone to a Stereo with a Cable

The most direct way to connect an iPod or iPhone to a stereo system is with a cable. For a typical receiver, you'll need a cable that has a miniplug at one end and two RCA plugs at the other end. Figure 5-1 shows an example of an iPod connected to a stereo via the amplifier.

NOTE *Some receivers and boom boxes use a single stereo miniplug input rather than two RCA ports. To connect an iPod or iPhone to such devices, you'll need a stereo miniplug-to-miniplug cable. Make sure the cable is stereo, because mono miniplug-to-miniplug cables are common. A stereo cable has two bands around the miniplug (as on most headphones), whereas a mono cable has only one band.*

If you have a high-quality receiver and speakers, get a high-quality cable to connect the iPod or iPhone to them. After the amount you've presumably spent on the iPod or iPhone and stereo, it'd be a mistake to degrade the signal between them by sparing a few bucks on the cable.

TIP *You can find various home-audio connection kits that contain a variety of cables likely to cover your needs. These kits are usually a safe buy, but unless your needs are peculiar, you'll end up with one or more cables you don't need. So if you do know which cables you need, make sure a kit offers a cost savings before buying it instead of the individual cables.*

Connect the iPod or iPhone to your receiver as follows:

1. Connect the miniplug to the player's headphone port. If you have a dock, connect the miniplug to the dock's line-out port instead, because this gives better sound quality than the headphone port.

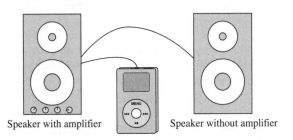

Speaker with amplifier   Speaker without amplifier

FIGURE 5-1 A miniplug-to-RCA-plugs cable is the most direct way of connecting an iPod or iPhone to your stereo system.

2. If you're using the headphone port, turn down the volume on the iPod or iPhone all the way.

3. Whichever port you're using, turn down the volume on the amplifier as well.

4. Connect the RCA plugs to the left and right ports of one of the inputs on your amplifier or boom box—for example, the AUX input or the Cassette input (if you're not using a cassette deck).

CAUTION   *Don't connect the iPod or iPhone to the Phono input on your amplifier. The Phono input is built with a higher sensitivity to make up for the weak output of a record player. Putting a full-strength signal into the Phono input will probably blow it.*

5. Start the music playing. If you're using the headphone port, turn up the volume a little.

6. Turn up the volume on the receiver so that you can hear the music.

7. Increase the volume on the two controls in tandem until you reach a satisfactory sound level.

NOTE   *Too low a level of output from the player may produce noise as your amplifier boosts the signal. Too high a level of output from the player may cause distortion.*

If you plug a player directly into your stereo, get a remote control for the player so that you don't need to march over to it each time you need to change the music. See "Remote Controls" in Chapter 4 for details of some of the remote controls available for the iPod and iPhone.

Use a Radio Transmitter Between an iPod or iPhone and a Stereo

If you don't want to connect the iPod or iPhone directly to your stereo system, you can use a radio transmitter to send the audio from the player to the radio on your stereo. See "Radio Transmitters" in Chapter 4 for examples of radio transmitters designed for the iPod and iPhone.

The sound you get from this arrangement typically will be lower in quality than the sound from a wired connection, but it should be at least as good as listening to a conventional radio station in stereo. If that's good enough for you, a radio transmitter can be a neat solution to playing music from the iPod or iPhone throughout your house.

TIP   *Using a radio transmitter has another advantage: You can play the music on several radios at the same time, giving yourself music throughout your dwelling without complex and expensive rewiring.*

Use an AirPort Express, a Computer, and an iPod

If you have an AirPort Express (a wireless access point that Apple makes), you can use it not only to network your home but also to play music from your computer or iPod through your stereo system. This method doesn't work for the iPhone.

To play music through an AirPort Express, follow these general steps:

1. Connect the AirPort Express to the receiver via a cable. The line-out port on the AirPort Express combines an analog port and an optical output, so you can connect the AirPort Express to the receiver in either of two ways:

   ■ Connect an optical cable to the AirPort Express's line-out socket and to an optical digital-audio input port on the receiver. If the receiver has an optical input, use this arrangement to get the best sound quality possible.

   ■ Connect an analog audio cable to the AirPort Express's line-out socket and to the RCA ports on your receiver.

2. If your network has a wired portion, connect the Ethernet port on the AirPort Express to the switch or hub using an Ethernet cable. If you have a DSL that you will share through the AirPort Express, connect the DSL via the Ethernet cable.

3. Plug the AirPort Express into an electric socket.

4. Install the software that accompanies the AirPort Express on your computer. Then use the AirPort Admin Utility for Windows or the AirPort Setup Assistant (on the Mac only) to configure the network.

5. Connect the iPod to your computer.

6. Launch iTunes if it isn't already running.

7. If the iPod is set for automatic updating of songs and playlists, click its entry in the Source pane to display the iPod's screens. On the Music tab, select the Manually Manage Songs And Playlists option button, click the Yes button in the confirmation dialog box, and then click the Apply button to apply the changes.

8. Click the Choose Speakers button (the large button at the bottom of the iTunes window) and choose the entry for the AirPort Express from the drop-down list. (This button appears only if iTunes has detected an AirPort Express within striking distance.)

9. Click the iPod's entry in the Source pane to display its contents. You can then play the songs on the iPod back via your computer to the speakers connected to the AirPort Express.

10. To switch back to playing through the computer's speakers, click the Choose Speakers button at the bottom of the iTunes window again. This time, choose the Computer entry from the drop-down list.

NOTE   *If you changed the iPod's updating preferences in Step 7, remember to change updating back to your preferred setting before you disconnect the iPod.*

Figure 5-2 shows a typical setup for playing music from an iPod through an AirPort Express.

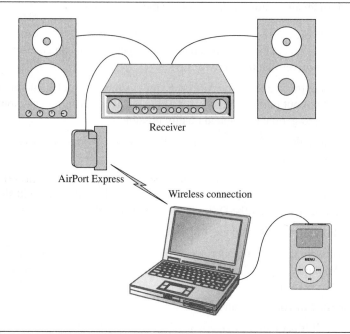

FIGURE 5-2   If you have an AirPort Express, you can play music on your computer or iPod through your stereo system across the wireless network.

Connect an iPod or iPhone to a Car Stereo

You can connect an iPod or iPhone to a car stereo in any of the following ways:

- Use a cassette adapter to connect the iPod or iPhone to the car's cassette player.
- Use a radio-frequency device to play the device's output through the car's radio.
- Wire the device directly to the car stereo and use it as an auxiliary input device.
- Get a car with a built-in iPod or iPhone connection or add an after-market iPod- or iPhone-integration device.

Each of these methods has its pros and cons. The following sections tell you what you need to know to choose the best option for your car stereo.

Use a Cassette Adapter

If the car stereo has a cassette player, your easiest option is to use a cassette adapter to play audio from the iPod or iPhone through the cassette deck. You can buy such adapters for between $10 and $20 from most electronics stores or from an iPod specialist.

The adapter is shaped like a cassette and uses a playback head to input analog audio via the head that normally reads the tape as it passes. A wire runs from the adapter to the iPod or iPhone.

A cassette adapter can be an easy and inexpensive solution, but it's far from perfect. The main problem is that the audio quality tends to be poor, because the means of transferring the audio to the cassette player's mechanism is less than optimal. But if your car is noisy, you may find that road noise obscures most of the defects in audio quality.

If the cassette player's playback head is dirty from playing cassettes, audio quality will be that much worse. To keep the audio quality as high as possible, clean the cassette player regularly using a cleaning cassette.

If you find it awkward to control the music from the iPod or iPhone rather than from the car stereo, look at the SmartDeck from Griffin Technology ($29.95 U.S.; www.griffintechnology .com). The SmartDeck connects to the iPod or iPhone via the dock connector and lets you control play by using the controls built into the cassette deck. You can't navigate the iPod's or iPhone's screens from the cassette deck, so what you do is choose the music using the iPod's or iPhone's controls, and then use the controls on the cassette deck to start play, stop it, move to the previous or next song, or eject the player (to pause playback on the player).

CAUTION   *If you use a cassette adapter in an extreme climate, try to make sure you don't bake it or freeze it by leaving it in the car.*

Use a Radio Transmitter

If the car stereo doesn't have a cassette deck, your easiest option for playing music from an iPod or iPhone may be to get a radio transmitter. This device plugs into the iPod or iPhone and broadcasts a signal on an FM frequency to which you then tune your radio to play the music. Better radio transmitters offer a choice of frequencies to allow you easy access to both the device and your favorite radio stations.

NOTE   *See the section "Radio Transmitters" in Chapter 4 for a discussion of how to choose among the many radio transmitters offered and examples of transmitters designed for the iPod and iPhone.*

Radio transmitters can deliver reasonable audio quality. If possible, try before you buy by asking for a demonstration in the store (take a portable radio with you, if necessary).

The main advantages of these devices are that they're relatively inexpensive (usually between $15 and $50) and they're easy to use. They also have the advantage that you can put the iPod or iPhone out of sight (for example, in the glove compartment—provided it's not too hot) without any telltale wires to help the light-fingered locate it.

On the downside, most of these devices need batteries (others can run off the 12-volt accessory outlet or cigarette-lighter socket), and less expensive units tend not to deliver the highest sound quality. The range of these devices is minimal, but at close quarters, other radios nearby may be able to pick up the signal—which could be embarrassing, entertaining, or irrelevant, depending on the circumstances. If you use the radio transmitter in an area where the airwaves are busy, you may need to keep switching the frequency to avoid having the transmitter swamped by the full-strength radio stations.

If you decide to get a radio transmitter, you'll need to choose between getting a model designed specifically for the iPod or iPhone and getting one that works with any audio source. Radio transmitters designed for the iPod or iPhone typically mount on the iPod or iPhone, making them a neater solution than general-purpose ones that dangle from the headphone socket. Radio transmitters designed for use with iPods or iPhones in cars often mount on the accessory outlet or dash and secure the device as well as transmitting its sound.

TIP *A radio-frequency adapter works with radios other than car radios, so you can use one to play music through your stereo system (or someone else's). You may also want to connect a radio-frequency adapter to a PC or Mac and use it to broadcast audio to a portable radio. This is a great way of getting streaming radio from the Internet to play on a conventional radio.*

Wire an iPod or iPhone Directly to a Car Stereo

If neither the cassette adapter nor the radio-frequency adapter provides a suitable solution, or if you simply want the best audio quality you can get, connect the iPod or iPhone directly to your car stereo. How easily you can do this depends on how the stereo is designed:

- If your car stereo is one of the few that has a miniplug input built in, get a miniplug-to-miniplug cable, and you'll be in business.

- If your stereo is built to take multiple inputs—for example, a CD player (or changer) and an auxiliary input—you may be able to simply run a wire from unused existing connectors. Plug the iPod into the other end, press the correct buttons, and you'll be ready to rock-and-roll down the freeway.

- If no unused connectors are available, you or your local friendly electronics technician may need to get busy with a soldering iron.

If you're buying a new car stereo, look for an auxiliary input that you can use with an iPod or iPhone.

Use a Built-in iPod or iPhone Connection

If the car has a special provision for an iPod or iPhone hookup, you need only get this feature or adapter installed, and you'll be away. At this writing, vehicles from companies and marques including Acura, Audio, BMW, Chrysler, Dodge, Form, GM, Honda, Infiniti, Jeep, Mercedes, Nissan, Scion, Suzuki, Volkswagen, and Volvo have iPod integration—and the list is continuing to grow. To see the latest list, go to www.apple.com/ipod/carintegration.html. Manufacturers are still working on iPhone integration, but it seems imminent.

If your car manufacturer hasn't yet provided its own means of integrating an iPod or iPhone, look for a third-party solution. Check out the list of after-market solutions on the www.apple .com/ipod/ipodyourcar/ webpage. Some adapters not only let you play back music from the device through the car's stereo and control it using the stereo system's controls, but also let you display the song information from the device on the stereo's display, making it easier to see what you're listening to.

Part II

Create and Manage Your Library

Chapter 6

Create Audio Files, Edit Them, and Tag Them

How to . . .

■ Choose where to store your library

■ Choose suitable audio-quality settings in iTunes

■ Convert audio files from other audio formats to AAC or MP3

■ Create AAC files or MP3 files from cassettes, vinyl, or other sources

■ Remove scratches, hiss, and hum from audio files

■ Trim or split song files

■ Rename song files efficiently

■ Save audio streams to disk

In Chapter 2, you learned how to start creating your library by copying music from your CDs and importing your existing music files. This is a great way to put songs on an iPod or iPhone quickly, but to get the most enjoyment out of your music, you'll probably want to customize iTunes' settings rather than use the defaults.

You may also want to do things with AAC files and MP3 files that iTunes doesn't support. For example, you may receive (or acquire) files in formats the iPod or iPhone can't handle, so you'll need to convert the files before you can use them on an iPod or iPhone. You may want to create song files from cassettes, LPs, or other media you own, and you may need to remove clicks, pops, and other extraneous noises from such recordings you make. You may want to trim intros or outros off audio files, split files into smaller files, or retag batches of files in ways iTunes can't handle. Last, you may want to record streaming audio to your hard disk.

Although iTunes now prefers AAC to MP3, most of the world is still using MP3. For this reason, at this writing there are many more—and more capable—MP3 applications than AAC applications. You'll find that the coverage in this chapter reflects this situation. But unless you've been creating AAC files with an application other than iTunes, you'll probably need to edit and tag MP3 files rather than AAC files, so the slight bias toward MP3 shouldn't be a problem.

NOTE   *Where many applications offer similar functionality, this book mentions freeware applications and applications that offer functional evaluation versions in preference to applications that insist you buy them outright without giving you a chance to try them.*

Choose Where to Store Your Library

Because your library can contain dozens—or even hundreds—of gigabytes of files, you must store it in a suitable location if you choose to keep all your files in it.

By default, iTunes stores your library in a folder named iTunes Music. This folder, the library folder, contains not only songs (in subfolders named after the artist) but also other items. For example, iTunes stores your movies in the Movies folder within the library folder, and your TV shows in the TV Shows folder.

NOTE *The alternative to keeping all your song files in your library is to instead store references to where the files are located in other folders. Doing so enables you to minimize the size of your library. But for maximum flexibility and to make sure you can access all the tracks in your library all the time, keeping all your song files in your library folder is best—if you can do so.*

To change the location of your library from now on, follow these steps:

1. Display the iTunes dialog box or the Preferences dialog box:

   ■ In Windows, choose Edit | Preferences or press CTRL-COMMA or CTRL-Y to display the iTunes dialog box.

   ■ On the Mac, choose iTunes | Preferences or press ⌘-COMMA or ⌘-Y to display the Preferences dialog box.

2. Click the Advanced tab to display its contents, and then click the General subtab. Figure 6-1 shows the Advanced tab of the iTunes dialog box in Windows.

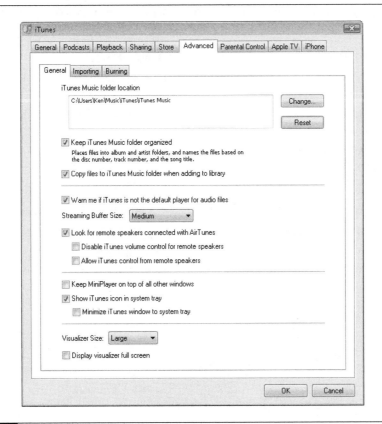

FIGURE 6-1   You may need to move your library folder from its default location to a folder that has more disk space available.

3. Click the Change button to display the Browse For Folder dialog box (Windows) or Change Music Folder Location dialog box (Mac).

4. Navigate to the folder that will contain your library, select the folder, and then click the Open button (Windows) or Choose button (Mac). iTunes returns you to the Advanced tab.

5. Click the OK button to close the iTunes dialog box or the Preferences dialog box. iTunes displays a message box as it updates your iTunes library, as shown here.

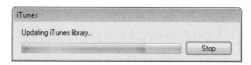

NOTE *To reset your library folder to its default location (the iTunes\iTunes Music folder in Windows or the iTunes/iTunes Music folder on the Mac), click the Reset button on the General subtab of the Advanced tab of the iTunes dialog box or the Preferences dialog box.*

When you change the location of your library like this, iTunes doesn't actually move the files that are already in your library. To move the files, make sure the new folder contains enough space, and then follow these steps:

1. Display the iTunes dialog box or the Preferences dialog box:
   - ■ In Windows, choose Edit | Preferences or press CTRL-COMMA or CTRL-Y to display the iTunes dialog box.
   - ■ On the Mac, choose iTunes | Preferences or press ⌘-COMMA or ⌘-Y to display the Preferences dialog box.

2. Click the Advanced tab to display its contents, and then click the General subtab (see Figure 6-1).

3. Select the Keep iTunes Music Folder Organized check box.

4. Select the Copy Files To iTunes Music Folder When Adding To Library check box.

5. Click the OK button to close the iTunes dialog box or the Preferences dialog box.

6. Choose Advanced | Consolidate Library. iTunes displays a message box telling you that consolidating your library will copy all the songs to the iTunes Music folder, as shown here.

7. Click the Consolidate button. iTunes copies the files, showing you its progress (as shown here) until it has finished.

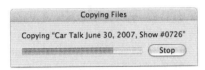

Configure iTunes for the Audio Quality You Want

Before you rip and encode your entire CD collection, check that the settings in iTunes are suitable for your needs. iTunes' default is to encode to AAC files at 128 Kbps in stereo: a fair choice for defaults, but you may well want to change them. It's worth investing a little time in choosing the right settings for ripping and encoding, because ripping CDs more than once quickly becomes a severe waste of time.

First, decide which music format and audio quality you want. Then choose the appropriate settings in iTunes.

Choose the Best Audio Format for Your Needs

iTunes can encode audio in five formats: AAC, MP3, Apple Lossless Encoding, WAV, and AIFF. AAC, MP3, and Apple Lossless Encoding are compressed audio formats, whereas WAV and AIFF are not compressed.

AAC

AAC is the abbreviation for Advanced Audio Coding, a *codec* (*co*der/*dec*oder) for compressing and playing back digital audio. AAC was put together by a group of heavy hitters in the audio and digital audio fields, including Fraunhofer IIS-A (the German company that developed MP3), Sony Corporation, Dolby Laboratories, AT&T, Nokia, and Lucent.

AAC is newer than MP3 (which is discussed in the next section), is generally agreed to deliver better sound than MP3, and is more tightly controlled than MP3. It is one of the key audio components of the MPEG-4 specification, which covers digital audio and video.

AAC files can be either protected with digital rights management (DRM) technology or unprotected.

The iTunes Store (discussed in Chapter 7) uses AAC for its songs, so if you buy songs from it, you won't have any choice about using AAC. If necessary, you can convert unprotected AAC songs to other formats. For example, you might convert an unprotected AAC song to MP3 so that you can use it with an MP3 player that can't handle AAC.

QuickTime includes an AAC codec. iTunes uses QuickTime's capabilities to encode audio and play back audio and video.

How to ... Understand CD-Quality Audio and Lossy and Lossless Compression

CD-quality audio samples audio 44,100 times per second (a sampling rate of 44.1 KHz) to provide coverage across most of the human hearing range. Each sample contains 16 bits (2 bytes) of data, which is enough information to convey the full range of frequencies. There are two tracks (for stereo), doubling the amount of data. CD-quality audio consumes around 9MB (megabytes) of storage space per minute of audio, which means that around 74 minutes of music fits on a standard 650MB CD and 80 minutes on a 700MB CD. The data on audio CDs is stored in *pulse code modulation (PCM),* a standard format for uncompressed audio.

To make more music fit on a device with a limited capacity (for example, an iPod or iPhone), you need to compress it so that it takes up less space. AAC and MP3 use *lossy compression,* compression that discards the parts of the audio data that your ears won't be able to hear or that your brain won't be able to pick out even though your ears hear it. Lossy audio codecs use *psychoacoustics,* the science of how the human brain processes sound, to select which data to keep and which to discard. As a basic example, when one part of the sound is masked by another part of the sound, the encoder discards the masked part, because you wouldn't hear it even if it were there.

How much data the encoder keeps depends on a setting called the *bitrate.* Almost all encoders let you choose a wide range of bitrates. In addition, most MP3 encoders can encode either at a constant bitrate (CBR) or a variable bitrate (VBR). The pros and cons of CBR and VBR are discussed in the sidebar "Choose Between CBR and VBR, and a Suitable Stereo Setting, for MP3," later in this chapter.

The advantage of lossy compression is that a well-designed codec can produce good-sounding audio at a fraction of the file size of uncompressed audio. For example, AAC and MP3 sound good to most people at a bitrate of 128 Kbps, which produces files around a tenth of the size of the uncompressed audio. The disadvantage of lossy compression is that the audio can never sound perfect, because some data has been discarded.

Better than lossy compression is *lossless compression,* which reduces the file size without discarding any of the audio data. Apple Lossless Encoding is lossless compression and produces extremely high-quality results.

The advantage of lossless compression is that it produces audio that is as high in quality as the uncompressed audio. The disadvantage is that lossless compression reduces the file size by much less than lossy compression, because it doesn't discard audio data.

NOTE *AAC can work with up to 48 full-frequency audio channels. This gives it a huge advantage over MP3, which can work with only two channels (in stereo) or a single channel (in mono). If you're used to listening to music in stereo, 48 channels seems an absurd number. But typically, only a small subset of those channels would be used at the same time. For example, conventional surround-sound rigs use 5.1 or 7.1 setups, using six channels or eight channels, respectively. Other channels can be used for different languages, so that an AAC player can play a different vocal track for differently configured players. Other tracks yet can be used for synchronizing and controlling the audio.*

Advantages of AAC   For music lovers, AAC offers higher music quality than MP3 at the same file sizes, or similar music quality at smaller file sizes. Apple claims that 128-Kbps AAC files sound as good as 160-Kbps MP3 files—so you can either save a fair amount of space and enjoy the same quality or enjoy even higher quality at the same bitrate. Around 24 Kbps, AAC streams provide quite listenable sound, whereas MP3 streams sound quite rough. (*Streaming* is the method of transmission used by Internet radio, in which you can listen to a file as your computer downloads it.)

Small file sizes are especially welcome for streaming audio over slow connections, such as modem connections. AAC streamed around 56 Kbps sounds pretty good (though not perfect), whereas MP3 sounds a bit flawed.

The main advantage of AAC for the music industry is that the format supports DRM. This means that AAC files can be created in a protected format with custom limitations built in. For example, most of the song files you can buy from the iTunes Store are protected by DRM so that, even if you distribute them to other people, those people can't play them.

NOTE *To tell whether an AAC file is protected, click it in iTunes, choose File | Get Info, and then check the Kind readout on the Summary tab of the Song Information dialog box. If the file is protected, the Kind readout reads "Protected AAC Audio File." If not, Kind reads "AAC Audio File." Alternatively, check the file extension: The .m4p extension indicates a protected file, whereas the .m4a extension indicates an unprotected file.*

Disadvantages of AAC   AAC's disadvantages are largely acceptable to most users of iTunes and the iPod or iPhone:

- AAC files are not widely available except by using iTunes and the iTunes Store. Even though Apple has made AAC the default format for iTunes and the iTunes Store, most other sources of digital audio files use other formats—typically either WMA or MP3.

- Encoding AAC files takes more processor cycles than encoding MP3 files. But as processors continue to increase in speed and power by the month if not by the week, this becomes less and less of a problem. Even relatively antiquated Macs (such as my PowerBook G3/333) and PCs (for example, a Celeron 600) have plenty of power to encode and decode AAC—they just do so more slowly than faster computers.

■ For consumers, the largest potential disadvantage of AAC is the extent to which DRM can limit their use of the files. At the time of writing, Apple has delivered a relatively flexible implementation of DRM in the protected files sold by the iTunes Store. However, if Apple and the record companies tighten the licensing terms of the files in the future, consumers may have cause for concern. In this sense, AAC could act as a Trojan horse to wean customers off MP3 and onto AAC, and then gradually lock them in to a format that the music industry can control. It's encouraging that the iTunes Store now also provides some unprotected song files.

MP3

Like AAC, MP3 is a file format for compressed audio. MP3 became popular in the late 1990s and largely sparked the digital music revolution by making it possible to carry a large amount of high-quality audio with you on a small device and enjoy it at the cost of nothing but the device, battery power, and time.

Among Mac users, MP3 has been overshadowed recently by AAC since Apple incorporated the AAC codec in iTunes, QuickTime, and the iPod. But MP3 remains the dominant format for compressed audio on computers running Windows (where its major competition comes from WMA, Microsoft's proprietary Windows Media Audio format) and computers running Linux.

MP3's name comes from the Motion Picture Experts Group (MPEG; www.chiariglione.org/ mpeg/—*not* www.mpeg.org), which oversaw the development of the MP3 format. MP3 is both the extension used by the files and the name commonly used for them. More correctly, MP3 is the file format for MPEG-1 Layer 3—but most people who listen to MP3 files neither know that nor care to know such details.

MP3 can deliver high-quality music in files that take up as little as a tenth as much space as uncompressed CD-quality files. For speech, which typically requires less fidelity than music, you can create even smaller files that still sound good, enabling you to pack that much more audio in the same amount of disk space.

Apple Lossless Encoding

Apple Lossless Encoding is an encoder that gives results that are mathematically lossless—there is no degradation of audio quality in the compressed files. The amount that Apple Lossless Encoding compresses audio depends on how complex the audio is. Some songs compress to around 40 percent of the uncompressed file size, whereas others compress to only 60–70 percent of the uncompressed file size.

Apple Lossless Encoding is a great way to keep full-quality audio on your computer—at least, if it has a large hard disk (or several large hard disks). Apple Lossless Encoding gives great audio quality on the iPod and iPhone as well, of course, but it's not such a great solution for most people. This is for three reasons:

■ The large amount of space that Apple Lossless Encoding files consume means that you can't fit nearly as many songs on an iPod or iPhone as you can using AAC or MP3.

- The Apple Lossless Encoding files are too large for the memory chip in hard drive–based iPods to buffer effectively. As a result, the iPod has to read the hard drive more frequently, which reduces battery life. (This isn't a concern for the iPod nano, iPod touch, or iPhone, which use flash memory rather than a hard drive.)

- Most non-Apple hardware and software players can't play Apple Lossless Encoding files. If you want to be able to play your song files on various devices, either now or in the future, a format other than Apple Lossless Encoding may be a better bet.

NOTE   *The iPod shuffle doesn't play Apple Lossless Encoding files at all, even though it plays WAV files and AIFF files. But what you can do is select the Convert Higher Bit Rate Files To 128 Kbps AAC check box on the Settings tab for the iPod shuffle. You can then add Apple Lossless Encoding files to the iPod shuffle, with iTunes converting the files to AAC files on-the-fly. (iTunes converts other file formats that use a bitrate higher than 128 Kbps as well.)*

WAV and AIFF

WAV files and AIFF files are basically the same thing—uncompressed PCM audio, which is also referred to as "raw" audio. WAV files are PCM files with a WAV header, whereas AIFF files are PCM files with an AIFF header. The *header* is a section of identification information contained at the start of the file.

NOTE   *AIFF tends to be more widely used on the Mac than in Windows, which favors WAV. However, iTunes can create and play both AIFF files and WAV files on both Windows and Mac OS X.*

If you want the ultimate in audio quality, you can create AIFF files or WAV files from your CDs and store them on your computer and iPod or iPhone. However, there are three reasons why you shouldn't do this:

- Each full-length CD will take up between 500MB and 800MB of disk space, compared to the 50MB to 80MB it would take up compressed at 128 Kbps. Apple Lossless Encoding gives a better balance of full audio quality with somewhat reduced file size.

- The iPod won't be able to buffer the audio effectively, will need to access the hard drive more frequently, and will deliver poor battery life. This is a consideration only for iPods that have hard drives, not for the iPod nano, iPod touch, or iPhone, which all use memory chips rather than a hard drive.

- Neither AIFF files nor WAV files have containers for storing tag information, such as the names of the artist, the CD, and the song. iTunes does its best to help by maintaining the tag information for AIFF files or WAV files in its database, but if you move the files (for example, if you copy them to a different computer), the tag information doesn't go with them. By contrast, Apple Lossless Encoding files have containers for their tag information.

That all sounds pretty negative—yet if you need the highest quality for music, WAV or AIFF is the way to go. Another advantage is that WAV files are widely playable—all versions of Windows, Mac OS X, and most other operating systems have WAV players. The AIFF format is not as widely used on Windows (although iTunes for Windows can play AIFF), being primarily a Mac format.

How to Choose the Best Format for iTunes, the iPod, and the iPhone

Choosing the best audio format for iTunes, the iPod, and the iPhone can be tough. You'll probably be torn between having the highest-quality audio possible when playing audio on your computer and packing the largest possible number of good-sounding songs on the player—and making sure it has enough battery life for you to listen to plenty of those songs each day.

For the highest possible audio quality on your computer, use Apple Lossless Encoding. (WAV and AIFF are also possible, but they use more space, have no tag containers, and offer no advantage over Apple Lossless Encoding.) For the largest possible number of songs on an iPod or iPhone, use AAC.

Unless you can keep two copies of each song in your library (or at least two copies of each song that you want to be able to play both on your computer and on the iPod or iPhone), you'll probably be best off going with AAC at a high enough bitrate that you don't notice the difference in quality between the AAC files and Apple Lossless Encoding files.

NOTE   *AAC delivers high-quality audio, small file size, and enough flexibility for most purposes. But if you want to use the files you rip from a CD on a portable player that doesn't support AAC, or you need to play them using a software player that doesn't support AAC, choose MP3 instead. Similarly, if you want to share your music files with other people in any way other than sharing your library via iTunes, MP3 is the way to go—but remember that you need the copyright holder's explicit authorization to copy and distribute music.*

Check or Change Your Importing Settings

To check or change the importing settings, follow these steps:

1. Display the iTunes dialog box or the Preferences dialog box:
   - In Windows, choose Edit | Preferences or press CTRL-COMMA or CTRL-Y to display the iTunes dialog box.
   - On the Mac, choose iTunes | Preferences or press ⌘-COMMA or ⌘-Y to display the Preferences dialog box.

2. Click the Advanced tab, and then click the Importing subtab to display its contents. Figure 6-2 shows the Importing subtab on iTunes for the Mac. The Importing tab on iTunes for Windows has the same controls.

3. In the On CD Insert drop-down list, choose the action you want iTunes to perform when you insert a CD: Show CD, Begin Playing, Ask To Import CD, Import CD, or Import CD

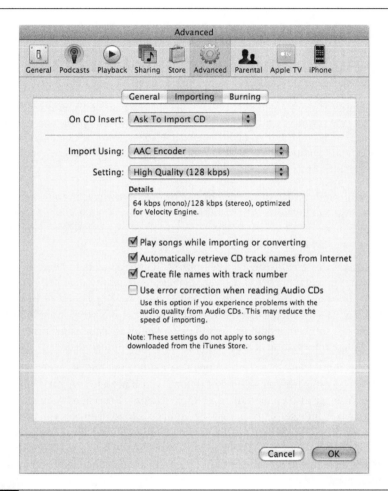

FIGURE 6-2   Configure your audio quality settings on the Importing subtab of the Advanced
tab of the iTunes dialog box or the Preferences dialog box.

And Eject. These settings are easy to understand, but bear in mind that Show CD, Import
CD, and Import CD And Eject all involve looking up the song names on the Internet
(unless you've already played the CD and thus caused iTunes to look up the names
before), so iTunes will need to use your Internet connection.

4. In the Import Using drop-down list, specify the file format you want to use by choosing
the appropriate encoder:

  ■ The default setting is AAC Encoder, which creates compressed files in AAC format.
    AAC files combine high audio quality with compact size, making AAC a good
    format for both iTunes and the iPod or iPhone.

Did you know?

Digital Audio Formats iTunes, the iPod, and the iPhone Can't Play

For most of the music you store on your computer and enjoy via iTunes or an iPod or iPhone, you'll want to use AAC, MP3, or whichever combination of the two you find most convenient. Both iTunes and the iPod and iPhone can also use WAV files and AIFF files.

For you as a digital audio enthusiast, other formats that may be of interest include the following:

- WMA is an audio format developed by Microsoft. It's the preferred format of Windows Media Player, the Microsoft audio and video player included with all desktop versions of Windows. WMA supports DRM, but its DRM is incompatible with iTunes and the iPod and iPhone.

- mp3PRO was designed to be a successor to MP3 but appears to have stalled shortly after takeoff. mp3PRO delivers higher audio quality than MP3 at the same bitrates. For example, mp3PRO files encoded at the 64-Kbps bitrate are similar in quality to MP3 files encoded at the 128-Kbps bitrate. Like MP3, mp3PRO requires hardware and software manufacturers to pay royalties to Thomson Corporation. You can find some information at mp3PROzone (www.mp3prozone.com).

- Ogg Vorbis is an open-source format that's patent free but not yet widely used. To play Ogg Vorbis files on an iPod or iPhone, you'll need to convert them to AAC or MP3. (You can also convert them to Apple Lossless Encoding, WAV, or AIFF, but doing so makes little sense, because Ogg Vorbis is a lossy format.) You can convert Ogg Vorbis files to WAV by using the freeware program Audacity (discussed later in this chapter) and then use iTunes to convert the WAV files to AAC or MP3, or convert them directly to AAC or MP3 by using Total Audio Converter (www .coolutils.com).

- FLAC, Free Lossless Audio Codec, is an open-source audio codec that creates lossless compressed files comparable in quality to Apple Lossless Encoding. To play FLAC files on an iPod or iPhone, you'll need to convert them to AAC or MP3. The best tool is Total Audio Converter (www.coolutils.com).

- The other setting you're likely to want to try is MP3 Encoder, which creates compressed files in the MP3 format. MP3 files have marginally lower audio quality than AAC files for the same file size, but you can use them with a wider variety of software applications and hardware players than AAC files.

- Apple Lossless Encoding files have full audio quality but a relatively large file size. They're good for iTunes but typically too large for the iPod or iPhone.

- AIFF files and WAV files are uncompressed audio files, so they have full audio quality (and are widely playable, as noted earlier) but take up a huge amount of space. You'll seldom need to use either of these formats.

5. In the Setting drop-down list, choose the setting you want to use:

   - For the AAC Encoder, the Setting drop-down list offers the settings High Quality (128 Kbps), Higher Quality (256 Kbps), Spoken Podcast, and Custom. When you select Custom, iTunes displays the AAC Encoder dialog box so you can specify custom settings. See the next section, "Choose Custom AAC Encoding Settings," for a discussion of these options.

   - For the MP3 Encoder, the Setting drop-down list offers the settings Good Quality (128 Kbps), High Quality (160 Kbps), Higher Quality (192 Kbps), and Custom. When you select Custom, iTunes displays the MP3 Encoder dialog box so you can specify custom settings. See "Choose Custom MP3 Encoding Settings," later in this chapter, for a discussion of these options.

   - The Apple Lossless Encoder has no configurable settings. (The Setting drop-down list offers only the Automatic setting.)

   - For the AIFF Encoder and the WAV Encoder, the Setting drop-down list offers the settings Automatic and Custom. When you select Custom, iTunes displays the AIFF Encoder dialog box or the WAV Encoder dialog box (as appropriate) so you can specify custom settings. See "Choose Custom AIFF and WAV Encoding Settings," later in this chapter, for a discussion of these options.

6. If you want iTunes to play each CD as you import it, leave the Play Songs While Importing Or Converting check box selected (it's selected by default). Listening to the CD may slow down the rate of ripping and encoding, so usually it's best not to use this option.

7. If you want iTunes to include track numbers in song names (creating names such as *01 Cortez the Killer* instead of *Cortez the Killer*), leave the Create File Names With Track Number check box selected (it's selected by default).

Including the track numbers in the filenames isn't necessary for iTunes itself to keep the tracks in order, because iTunes can use the track-number information in a track's tag. (Some utilities for downloading songs from an iPod or iPhone can sort songs by tag information, too.) But you may want to include the numbers so that you can sort the songs easily into album order in the Finder.

Including the track number is useful for keeping tracks in order when you create MP3 CDs. This is a consideration only when you're encoding the songs as MP3 files, because you can't create MP3 CDs using audio file formats other than MP3.

How to ... Choose an Appropriate Compression Rate, Bitrate, and Stereo Settings

To get suitable audio quality, you must use an appropriate compression rate for the audio files you encode with iTunes.

iTunes' default settings are to encode AAC files in stereo at the 128-Kbps bitrate using automatic sample-rate detection. iTunes calls those settings High Quality, and they deliver great results for most purposes. If they don't suit you, you can opt for the Higher Quality setting, choose the Podcast setting to create files suitable for podcasting (in other words, with lower quality and a smaller file size), or specify custom AAC settings for the files you create. With AAC you can change the bitrate, the sample rate, and the channels.

iTunes' MP3 Encoder gives you more flexibility. The default settings for MP3 are to encode MP3 files in stereo at the 160-Kbps bitrate, using CBR and automatic sample-rate detection. iTunes calls those settings High Quality, and they deliver results almost as good as the High Quality settings with the AAC Encoder, although they produce significantly larger files because the bitrate is higher.

For encoding MP3 files, iTunes also offers preset settings for Good Quality (128 Kbps) and Higher Quality (192 Kbps). Beyond these choices, you can choose the Custom setting and specify exactly the settings you want: bitrates from 16 Kbps to 320 Kbps, CBR or VBR, sample rate, channels, the stereo mode, whether to use Smart Encoding Adjustments, and whether to filter frequencies lower than 10 Hz.

If possible, invest a few days in choosing a compression rate for your library. Choosing an unsuitable compression rate can cost you disk space (if you record at too high a bitrate), audio quality (too low a bitrate), and the time it takes to rip your entire collection again at a more suitable bitrate.

Choose a representative selection of the types of music you plan to listen to using your computer and iPod or iPhone. Encode several copies of each test track at different bitrates, and then listen to them over several days to see which provides the best balance of file size and audio quality. Make sure some of the songs test the different aspects of music that are important to you. For example, if your musical tastes lean to female vocalists, listen to plenty of those types of songs. If you prefer bass-heavy, bludgeoning rock, listen to that. If you go for classical music as well, add that to the mix. You may find that you need to use different compression rates for different types of music to achieve satisfactory results and keep the file size down.

Choose Custom AAC Encoding Settings

To choose custom AAC encoding settings, follow these steps:

1. On the Importing subtab of the Advanced tab of the iTunes dialog box or the Preferences dialog box, choose AAC Encoder in the Import Using drop-down list.

2. In the Setting drop-down list, choose the Custom item to display the AAC Encoder dialog box:

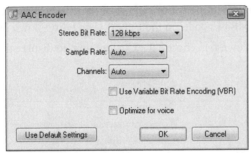

3. In the Stereo Bit Rate drop-down list, choose the bitrate. You can use from 16 Kbps to 320 Kbps. The default is 128 Kbps.

    The 128 Kbps setting provides high-quality audio suitable for general music listening. You may want to experiment with higher bitrates to see if you can detect a difference. If not, stick with 128 Kbps so as to get the largest possible amount of quality music on the iPod or iPhone.

    If you listen to spoken-word audio, experiment with the bitrates below 64 Kbps to see which bitrate delivers suitable quality for the material you listen to, and select the Optimize For Voice check box.

4. In the Sample Rate drop-down list, specify the sample rate by choosing Auto, 44.100 KHz, or 48.000 KHz. 44.100 KHz is the sample rate used by CD audio; unless you have a data source that uses a 48.000-KHz sampling rate, there's no point in choosing this option. For most purposes, you'll get best results by using the Auto setting (the default setting), which makes iTunes use a sampling rate that matches the input quality. For example, for CD-quality audio, iTunes uses the 44.100-KHz sampling rate.

5. In the Channels drop-down list, select Auto, Stereo, or Mono, as appropriate. In most cases, Auto (the default setting) is the best bet, because it makes iTunes choose stereo or mono as appropriate to the sound source. However, you may occasionally need to produce mono files from stereo sources.

6. If you want to use VBR encoding rather than CBR encoding, select the Use Variable Bit Rate Encoding (VBR) check box.

7. If you want to optimize the encoding for voice instead of music, select the Optimize For Voice check box.

8. Click the OK button to close the AAC Encoder dialog box.

Choose Custom MP3 Encoding Settings

To choose custom MP3 encoding settings, follow these steps:

1. On the Importing subtab of the Advanced tab of the iTunes dialog box or the Preferences dialog box, choose MP3 Encoder in the Import Using drop-down list.

2. In the Setting drop-down list, choose the Custom item to display the MP3 Encoder dialog box:

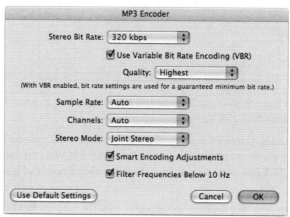

3. In the Stereo Bit Rate drop-down list, select the bitrate you want to use.

The choices range from 16 Kbps to 320 Kbps. 16 Kbps produces shoddy-sounding audio even for the spoken word, but it may be useful when you need to get long passages of low-quality audio into a small file. At the other extreme, 320 Kbps produces audio high enough in quality that most people can't distinguish it from CD-quality audio.

iTunes uses the bitrate you select as the exact bitrate for CBR encoding and as the minimum bitrate for VBR encoding.

See the section "Understand CD-Quality Audio and Lossy and Lossless Compression" earlier in this chapter for a discussion of CD-quality audio. "Choose an Appropriate Compression Rate, Bitrate, and Stereo Settings," also earlier in this chapter, offers advice on choosing a compression rate that matches your needs.

4. Select the Use Variable Bit Rate Encoding (VBR) check box if you want to create VBR-encoded files instead of CBR-encoded files.

See the sidebar "Choose Between CBR and VBR, and a Suitable Stereo Setting, for MP3" later in this chapter, for a discussion of CBR and VBR.

If you select this check box, choose a suitable setting in the Quality drop-down list. The choices are Lowest, Low, Medium Low, Medium, Medium High, High, and Highest. iTunes uses the bitrates specified in the Stereo Bit Rate drop-down list as the guaranteed minimum bitrates. The Quality setting controls the amount of processing iTunes applies to making the file sound as close to the original as possible. More processing requires more processor cycles, which will make your computer work harder. If your computer is already working at full throttle, encoding will take longer— but again, it will get done in the end, and each song needs encoding only once.

5. In the Sample Rate drop-down list, set a sample rate manually only if you're convinced you need to do so.

   You may want to use a lower sample rate if you're encoding spoken-word audio rather than music and don't need such high fidelity.

   Choices range from 8 KHz to 48 KHz (higher than CD-quality audio, which uses 44.1 KHz).

   The default setting is Auto, which uses the same sample rate as does the music you're encoding. Using the same sample rate usually delivers optimal results.

6. In the Channels drop-down list, select Auto, Mono, or Stereo. The default setting is Auto, which uses mono for encoding mono sources and stereo for stereo sources.

7. In the Stereo Mode drop-down list, choose Normal Stereo or Joint Stereo. See the sidebar "Choose Between CBR and VBR, and a Suitable Stereo Setting, for MP3," later in this chapter, for a discussion of the difference between normal stereo and joint stereo. If you select Mono in the Channels drop-down list, the Stereo Mode drop-down list becomes unavailable because its options don't apply to mono.

8. Select or clear the Smart Encoding Adjustments check box and the Filter Frequencies Below 10 Hz check box, as appropriate. These check boxes are selected by default. In most cases, you'll do best to leave them selected.

   Smart Encoding Adjustments allows iTunes to tweak your custom settings to improve them if you've chosen an inappropriate combination.

   Frequencies below 10 Hz are infrasound and are of interest only to animals such as elephants, so filtering them out makes sense for humans.

NOTE *To restore iTunes to using its default settings for encoding MP3 files, click the Use Default Settings button in the MP3 Encoder dialog box.*

9. Click the OK button to close the MP3 Encoder dialog box.
10. Click the OK button to close the iTunes dialog box or the Preferences dialog box.

How to ...   Choose Between CBR and VBR, and a Suitable Stereo Setting, for MP3

After choosing the bitrate at which to encode your MP3 files, you must choose between constant bitrate (CBR) and variable bitrate (VBR). You must also choose whether to use joint stereo or normal stereo.

CBR simply records each part of the file at the specified bitrate. CBR files can sound great, particularly at higher bitrates, but generally VBR delivers better quality than CBR. This is because VBR can allocate space more intelligently as the audio needs it. For example, a complex passage of a song will require more data to represent it accurately than will a simple passage, which in turn will require more data than the two seconds of silence before the massed guitars come crashing back in.

The disadvantage to VBR, and the reason why most MP3 encoders are set to use CBR by default, is that many older decoders and hardware devices can't play it. If you're using iTunes and an iPod or iPhone, you don't need to worry about this. But if you're using an older decoder or hardware device, check that it can manage VBR.

So VBR is probably a better bet. A harder choice is between the two different types of stereo that iTunes offers: joint stereo and normal stereo. (iTunes also offers mono—a single channel that gives no separation among the sounds. The only reason to use mono is if your sound source is mono; for example, a live recording that used a single mono microphone.)

Stereo delivers two channels: a left channel and a right channel. These two channels provide positional audio, enabling recording and mixing engineers to separate the audio so that different sounds appear to be coming from different places. For example, the engineer can make one guitar sound as though it's positioned on the left and another guitar sound as though it's positioned on the right. Or the engineer might fade a sound from left to right so it seems to go across the listener.

Normal stereo (sometimes called *plain stereo*) uses two tracks: one for the left stereo channel and another for the right stereo channel. As its name suggests, normal stereo is the normal form of stereo. For example, if you buy a CD that's recorded in stereo and play it back through your boom box, you're using normal stereo.

Joint stereo (sometimes called *mid/side stereo*) divides the channel data differently to make better use of a small amount of space. The encoder averages out the two original channels (assuming the sound source is normal stereo) to a mid channel. It then encodes this channel, devoting to it the bulk of the available space assigned by the bitrate. One channel contains the data that's the same on both channels. The second channel contains the data that's different on one of the channels. By reducing the channel data to the common data (which takes the bulk of the available space) and the data that's different on one of the channels (which takes much less space), joint stereo can deliver higher audio quality at the same bitrate as normal stereo.

Use joint stereo to produce better-sounding audio when encoding at lower bitrates, and use normal stereo for all your recordings at your preferred bitrate. Where the threshold for lower-bitrate recording falls depends on you. Many people recommend using normal stereo for encoding at bitrates of 160 Kbps and above, and using joint stereo for lower bitrates (128 Kbps and below). Others recommend not using normal stereo below 192 Kbps. Experiment to establish what works for you.

The results you get with joint stereo depend on the quality of the MP3 encoder you use. Some of the less-capable MP3 encoders produce joint-stereo tracks that sound more like mono tracks than like normal-stereo tracks. Better encoders produce joint-stereo tracks that sound very close to normal-stereo tracks. iTunes produces pretty good joint-stereo tracks.

Using the same MP3 encoder, normal stereo delivers better sound quality than joint stereo—at high bitrates. At lower bitrates, joint stereo delivers better sound quality than normal stereo, because joint stereo can retain more data about the basic sound (in the mid channel) than normal stereo can retain about the sound in its two separate channels. However, joint stereo provides less separation between the left and right channels than normal stereo provides. (The lack of separation is what produces the mono-like effect.)

Choose Custom AIFF and WAV Encoding Settings

The AIFF Encoder dialog box (shown on the left in Figure 6-3) and the WAV Encoder dialog box (shown on the right in Figure 6-3) offer similar settings. AIFFs and WAVs are essentially the same apart from the file header, which distinguishes the file formats from each other.

In either of these dialog boxes, you can choose the following settings:

- **Sample Rate**   Choose Auto (the default setting) to encode at the same sample rate as the original you're ripping. Otherwise, choose a value from the range available (8 KHz to 48 KHz).

FIGURE 6-3   If you choose to encode to AIFF or WAV files, you can set encoding options in the AIFF Encoder dialog box (left) or the WAV Encoder dialog box (right).

- ■ **Sample Size**   Select Auto to have iTunes automatically match the sample size to that of the source. Otherwise, select 8 Bit or 16 Bit, as appropriate. PCM audio uses 16 bits, so if you're encoding files from CDs, iTunes automatically uses a 16-bit sample size.
- ■ **Channels**   Select Auto (the default setting) to encode mono files from mono sources and stereo files from stereo sources. Otherwise, select Mono or Stereo, as appropriate.

Deal with CDs That Your Computer Can't Rip

This book's discussion of importing audio from CDs so far has assumed that you're dealing with regular audio CDs: CDs that comply with the Red Book format, the basic format for putting audio data on a CD without any anticopying protection or DRM. Some unprotected CDs use the CD Extra format (a subset of Red Book) to put nonaudio data on the CD as well.

NOTE   *Philips and Sony defined the Red Book format in 1980. (The standard was published in a red binder—hence the name. Subsequent standards include Orange Book and Yellow Book, named for similar reasons.) Red Book ensures the disc will work with all drives that bear the Compact Disc logo and entitles the disc to bear the Compact Disc Digital Audio logo.*

You can import audio from any Red Book or CD Extra CD without a problem using iTunes (or another application) on Windows, Mac OS X, or Linux. But because many music enthusiasts have shared the songs they've ripped from CDs with other people over the Internet, the music industry has taken to including protection on some of the CDs they release.

Understand Copy-Protection Techniques on Audio Discs

Since the MP3 format, the original Napster program for sharing music, and faster Internet connections made exchanging music via the Internet easy around the turn of the millennium, the music industry has tried applying various copy-protection technologies to audio discs to prevent them from being copied to digital files.

Some of these technologies have been partly successful, and you will still find them in use on audio discs today. For example, CDS-300 from Macrovision Corporation (www.macrovision.com) is a combined hardware and software solution that dynamically encodes the CD's audio to DRM-protected WMA files so that PC users can use the files with Windows Media Player and portable devices that support Windows Media DRM.

Others have proved disastrous and have been withdrawn—but you may still run into them. For example, Sony BMG used a copy-protection system named Extended Copy Protection (XCP) on some audio discs in 2005 that installed what computer hackers call a *rootkit* on Windows computers that tried to play the discs. The rootkit severely compromised the computers' security, and caused a storm of protest. Sony BMG eventually withdrew the XCP-protected discs and offered to exchange those that had been bought.

Some copy-protection solutions add deliberate errors to the data on the disc to make it harder for optical drives to read while allowing audio-only CD players (which have more effective error-correction mechanisms) to read the discs successfully. Other copy-protection solutions

Did you know?

Who Benefits from Copy-Protected Audio Discs?

The companies that make copy protection for audio discs present the copy protection as being good for all parties concerned: the record companies, the artists, and the customers. Most customers—and even some artists—disagree.

For record companies, copy-protected audio discs are mostly positive, because the discs help to reduce the amount of piracy the companies suffer. However, copy-protected audio discs have drawn many complaints from customers unable to play the discs on their computers or specialized optical-disc players (for example, DVD players)—and some means of protection have drawn severely adverse publicity, not to mention lawsuits. Artists also benefit from reduced piracy of their music but suffer from negative feedback from fans who can't play the discs as they expect to.

Customers benefit little or not at all from copy-protected audio discs:

■ Protected discs can cause computers to hang (freeze) or crash.

■ Those discs that do not play on computers severely restrict the customers' ability to enjoy the music, preventing them from putting the songs on their computers or portable devices.

■ Those discs that permit playback only of lower-quality audio files included in a separate session on the disc, or that create DRM-restricted WMA files on-the-fly, also limit the customers' choice, and are useless for anyone wanting to play the music with iTunes or put it on an iPod or iPhone.

■ Those discs that include deliberate errors on the discs to make them harder or impossible for CD drives to play make the error-correction mechanisms on the players work harder to compensate. Using the error-correction mechanism on the player like this makes the disc less resistant to real damage (for example, scratches), because the player will be unable to correct many damage-related errors on top of the deliberate copy-protection errors. The discs may also degrade more quickly than unprotected CDs. Copy-protection solutions may cause CD players to fail sooner than they would otherwise have done, because they make the players work harder than unprotected CDs do, much as driving at full-speed over rough roads will wear out your car's suspension far more quickly than driving at the same speed on freeways will.

include compressed audio in a separate session on the disc, usually with a player that is intended to spring into action when the disc is loaded on a computer.

Most of the copy-protection solutions are aimed at Windows users and work only with Windows Media Player. These solutions don't work for iTunes on either Windows or the Mac, nor for Windows Media Player on the Mac. Other copy-protection solutions, such as MediaMax, work on the Mac as well.

Recognize Copy-Protected Discs

Copy-protected discs won't play on all CD drives. This means that they don't conform to the Red Book CD standard, so they are technically and legally *not* CDs. You should be able to recognize them as follows:

- The discs shouldn't bear the Compact Disc Digital Audio logo (because they're not CDs), but some do. And in any case, many Red Book CDs don't bear this logo, usually for reasons of label design or laziness. So the presence or lack of the CDDA logo isn't a good way to distinguish a copy-protected disc.

- The disc may carry a disclaimer, warning, or notice such as "Will *not* play on PC or Mac," "This CD [*sic*] cannot be played on a PC/Mac," "Copy Control," or "Copy Protected."

- The disc may attempt to install on your computer software that you must use to access the music on the disc.

- The disc won't play on your computer, or it will play but won't rip.

Know What May Happen When You Try to Use a Copy-Protected Disc on a Computer

When you try to use a copy-protected disc on a computer, any of the following may happen:

- The disc may play back without problems. You may even be able to rip it by using a conventional audio program (such as iTunes) or a specialized, heavy-duty ripper (such as Exact Audio Copy). If you can rip the disc, the copy protection has failed (or your drive has defeated it).

NOTE   *Exact Audio Copy is a free application that you can download from www.exactaudiocopy.de. Exact Audio Copy is postcard-ware—if you like it, you send a postcard to register.*

- The disc may not play at all.

- The disc may cause your computer's operating system to hang.

- You may be unable to eject the disc on some PCs and many Macs. (If this happens to you, see the sidebar "Eject Stuck Audio Discs.")

Learn about Ways to Get Around Copy Protection

Customers annoyed by copy-protected audio discs quickly found ways to circumvent the copy protection. In many cases, the most effective solution is to experiment with different drives. Some drives can play audio discs protected with some technologies; others can't.

How to ...   **Eject Stuck Audio Discs**

If you insert a non-CD audio disc into your CD drive and your PC or Mac can't handle it, you may be unable to eject the disc. The PC or Mac may hang. If your computer is a Mac, and you restart it with the disc in the CD drive, your Mac may start up to a gray screen.

On PCs and some Macs, you can use the manual eject hole on the CD drive to eject the disc. Straighten one end of a sturdy paper clip and push it into the hole to eject the disc.

If your Mac doesn't have a manual eject hole, don't go prodding the wrong hole. Instead, follow as many of these steps as necessary to fix the problem:

1. Restart your Mac. If it's too hung to restart by conventional means, press the Reset button (if it has one) or press ⌘-CTRL-POWER. At the system startup sound, hold down the mouse button until your Mac finishes booting. This action may eject the disc.

2. Restart your Mac again. As before, if the Mac is too hung to restart by conventional means, press the Reset button or press ⌘-CTRL-POWER. At the system startup sound, hold down ⌘-OPTION-O-F to boot to the Open Firmware mode. You'll see a prompt screen that contains something like the text shown here (the exact text varies depending on the model of Mac).

```
Apple PowerBook3, 5 4.5.3f2 BootROM built on 10/25/02 at 10:31:30
Copyright 1994-2002 Apple Computer, Inc.
All Rights Reserved

Welcome to Open Firmware, the system time and date is:  10:27:06 02/03/2003

To continue booting, type "mac-boot" and press return.
To shut down, type "shut-down" and press return.

ok
0> _
```

3. Type **eject cd** and press RETURN. If all is well, the CD drive will open. If not, you may see the message "read of block0 failed. can't OPEN the EJECT device." Either way, type **mac-boot** and press RETURN to reboot your Mac.

If Open Firmware mode won't fix the problem, you'll need to take your Mac to a service shop.

CAUTION   *Title I of the Digital Millennium Copyright Act (DMCA), which was passed in 1998, states that it's illegal to circumvent "effective technological measures" protecting a copyrighted work. There are various ifs and buts (for example, you can circumvent such measures to make another program interoperate with a copyrighted work), but essentially Title I says if someone has protected a copyrighted work with a technological measure that could be argued to be "effective" (whatever that means), it's illegal to crack that measure. There are heavy penalties if you do so deliberately and for "commercial advantage" or private gain—fines of up to $500,000 and five years' imprisonment for a first offense, and double those for a second offense.*

If you don't have multiple CD or DVD drives to experiment with, you might be interested to hear of two crude solutions that have proved successful with some copy-protected audio discs:

- Stick a strip of tape on the disc to mask the outermost track. This track contains extra information intended to confuse computer CD drives. By masking the track, people have managed to obviate the confusion.

- Use a marker to color the outermost track on the disc dark so the laser of the drive won't read it.

TIP   *Many DVD drives are better at playing copy-protected discs than many plain CD-ROM drives. This is because the DVD drives are designed to work with multiple types of discs—DVDs, CDs, recordable CDs (CD-Rs), rewritable CDs (CD-RWs), and (for DVD recorders) various types of recordable DVDs, depending on the capabilities of the drive. These extra capabilities include greater tolerance for faults on the discs.*

Both of these techniques require a steady hand—and both constitute willful circumvention of the copy protection, possibly exposing those performing them to retribution under the DMCA.

Some versions of the MediaMax copy-protection mechanism can be disabled by holding down SHIFT while loading the CD on a Windows PC for the first time. Holding down SHIFT prevents the CD from automatically loading a driver used to protect the music.

Holding down SHIFT might be interpreted as an active attempt to bypass the copy-protection mechanism. But you can also turn off the AutoPlay feature for an optical drive permanently on either Windows Vista or Windows XP, as described next.

Turn Off AutoPlay on Windows Vista

To turn off AutoPlay for an optical drive on Windows Vista, follow these steps:

1. Choose Start | Control Panel to open a Control Panel window.

2. If the window shows a list of categories rather than many icons, click the Classic View link in the upper-left corner to switch to Classic view.

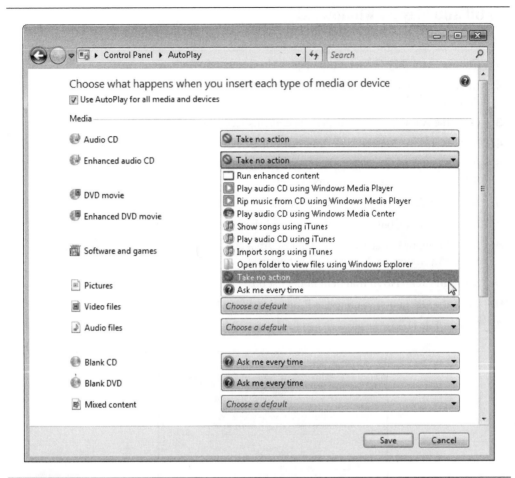

FIGURE 6-4   Turning off AutoPlay for audio CDs and enhanced audio CDs can help you avoid installing CD copy-protection software unintentionally on your PC.

3. Double-click the AutoPlay icon to open the AutoPlay window (see Figure 6-4).

4. In the Audio CD drop-down list, choose Take No Action.

5. In the Enhanced Audio CD drop-down list, choose Take No Action.

6. Click the Save button.

7. Click the Close button (the × button) to close the AutoPlay window.

Turn Off AutoPlay on Windows XP

To turn off AutoPlay for an optical drive on Windows XP, follow these steps:

1. Choose Start | My Computer to open a My Computer window.

2. Right-click the optical drive and choose Properties from the shortcut menu to display the Properties dialog box.

3. Click the AutoPlay tab to display its contents (see Figure 6-5).

4. In the Select A Content Type drop-down list, select the Music CD item.

5. If the Prompt Me Each Time To Choose An Action option button is selected, select the Select An Action To Perform option button.

6. Select the Take No Action item in the list box.

7. In the Select A Content Type drop-down list, select the Mixed Content item.

8. If the Prompt Me Each Time To Choose An Action option button is selected, select the Select An Action To Perform option button.

9. Select the Take No Action item in the list box.

10. Click the OK button to close the Properties dialog box.

11. Choose File | Close or press ALT-F4 to close the My Computer window.

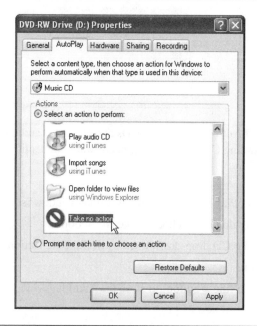

FIGURE 6-5   Turning off AutoPlay on your optical drive can help you avoid installing CD copy-protection software unintentionally on your PC.

Convert Other File Types to Formats an iPod or iPhone Can Play

Most iPods and the iPhone can play AAC files, MP3 files (including Audible files), Apple Lossless Encoding files, AIFF files, and WAV files. The iPod shuffle can play all these file types except Apple Lossless Encoding. These common formats should take care of all your regular listening in iTunes and on the iPod or iPhone.

But if you receive files from other people, or download audio from the Internet (as described in Chapter 7), you'll encounter many other digital audio formats. This section describes a couple of utilities for converting files from one format to another—preferably to a format the iPod or iPhone can use, or to a format from which you can encode a format that the iPod or iPhone can manage.

What Happens When You Convert a File from One Compressed Format to Another

Don't convert a song from one compressed format to another compressed format unless you absolutely must, because such a conversion gives you the worst of both worlds.

For example, say you have a WMA file. The audio is already compressed with lossy compression, so some parts of the audio have been lost. When you convert this file to an MP3 file, the conversion utility expands the compressed WMA audio to uncompressed audio—essentially, to a PCM file (such as WAV or AIFF)—and then recompresses it to the MP3 format, again using lossy compression.

The uncompressed audio contains a faithful rendering of all the defects in the WMA file. So the MP3 file contains as faithful a rendering of this defective audio as the MP3 encoder can provide at that compression rate, plus any defects the MP3 encoding introduces. But you'll be able to play the file on the iPod or iPhone—which may be your main concern.

So if you still have the CD from which you imported the song, import the song again using the other compressed format rather than converting the song from one compressed format to another. Doing so will give you significantly higher quality. But if you don't have the CD—for example, because you bought the song in the compressed format—converting to the other format will produce usable results.

Convert a Song from AAC to MP3 (or Vice Versa)

Sometimes, you may need to convert a song from the format in which you imported it, or (more likely) in which you bought it, to a different format. For example, you may need to convert a song in AAC format to MP3 so that you can use it on an MP3 player that can't play AAC files.

NOTE *If the AAC file is a protected song you bought from the iTunes Store, you cannot convert it directly. Instead, you must burn it to a CD, and then rip that CD to the format you need.*

To convert a song from one compressed format to another, follow these steps:

1. In iTunes, display the Advanced menu and see which format is listed in the Convert Selection To command (for example, Convert Selection To AAC or Convert Selection To MP3). If this is the format you want, you're all set, but you might want to double-check the settings used for the format.

NOTE *You can also right-click a file (or CTRL-click on the Mac) and look at the Convert Selection To item on the shortcut menu.*

2. Display the iTunes dialog box or the Preferences dialog box:
   - In Windows, choose Edit | Preferences or press CTRL-COMMA or CTRL-Y to display the iTunes dialog box.
   - On the Mac, choose iTunes | Preferences or press ⌘-COMMA or ⌘-Y to display the Preferences dialog box.

3. Click the Advanced tab, and then click the Importing subtab to display its contents.

4. In the Import Using drop-down list, select the encoder you want to use. For example, choose MP3 Encoder if you want to convert an existing file to an MP3 file; choose AAC Encoder if you want to create an AAC file; or choose Apple Lossless Encoder if you want to create an Apple Lossless Encoding file.

NOTE *Unless the song file is currently in WAV or AIFF format, it's usually not worth converting it to Apple Lossless Encoding, because the source file is not high enough quality to benefit from Apple Lossless Encoding's advantages over AAC or MP3.*

5. If necessary, use the Setting drop-down list to specify the details of the format. (See "Check or Change Your Importing Settings" earlier in this chapter for details.)

6. Click the OK button to close the dialog box.

7. In your library, select the song or songs you want to convert.

8. Choose Advanced | Convert Selection To *Format*. (The Convert Selection To item on the Advanced menu changes to reflect the encoder you chose in Step 4.) iTunes converts the file or files, saves it or them in the folder that contains the original file or files, and adds it or them to your library.

NOTE *Because iTunes automatically applies tag information to converted files, you may find it hard to tell in iTunes which file is in AAC format and which is in MP3 format. The easiest way to find out is to issue a Get Info command for the song (for example, right-click or CTRL-click the song and choose Get Info from the shortcut menu) and check the Kind readout on the Summary tab of the Song Information dialog box.*

After converting the song or songs to the other format, remember to restore your normal import setting on the Importing subtab of the Advanced tab in the iTunes dialog box or the Preferences dialog box before you import any more songs from CD.

Convert WMA Files to MP3 or AAC

If you buy music from any of the online music stores that focus on Windows rather than on the Mac, chances are that the songs will be in WMA format. WMA is the stores' preferred format for selling online music because it offers DRM features for protecting the music against being stolen.

In iTunes for Windows, you can convert a WMA file to your current importing format (as set on the Importing subtab of the Advanced tab in the iTunes dialog box) by dragging the file to your library or by using either the File | Add File To Library or the File | Add Folder To Library command. iTunes for the Mac doesn't have this capability—but if you have access to a PC running Windows, you can then copy or transfer the converted files to the Mac.

If you buy WMA files protected with DRM, you'll be limited in what you can do with them. In most cases, you'll be restricted to playing the songs with Windows Media Player (which is one of the underpinnings of the WMA DRM scheme), which won't let you convert the songs directly to another format. But most online music stores allow you to burn the songs you buy to CD. In this case, you can convert the WMA files to MP3 files or AAC files by burning them to CD and then use iTunes to rip and encode the CD as usual.

Create Audio Files from Cassettes or Vinyl Records

If you have audio on analog media such as cassette tapes, vinyl records, or other waning technologies, you may want to transfer that audio to your computer so you can listen to it using iTunes or an iPod or iPhone. Dust off your gramophone, cassette deck, or other audio source, and then work your way through the following sections.

CAUTION *You may need permission to create audio files that contain copyrighted content. If you hold the copyright to the audio, you can copy it as much as you want. If not, you need specific permission to copy it, unless it falls under a specific copyright exemption. For example, the Audio Home Recording Act (AHRA) personal use provision lets you copy a copyrighted work (for example, an LP) onto a different medium so you can listen to it—but only provided that you use a "digital audio recording device," a term that doesn't cover computers.*

Connect the Audio Source to Your Computer

Start by connecting the audio source to your computer with a cable that has the right kinds of connectors for the audio source and your sound card. For example, to connect a typical cassette player to a typical sound card, you'll need a cable with two RCA plugs at the cassette player's end (or at the receiver's end) and a male-end stereo miniplug at the other end to plug into your sound card. If the audio source has only a headphone socket or line-out socket for output, you'll need a miniplug at the source end too.

NOTE   *Because record players produce a low volume of sound, you'll almost always need to put a record player's output through the Phono input of an amplifier before you can record it on your computer.*

If your sound card has a Line In port and a Mic port, use the Line In port. If your sound card has only a Mic port, turn the source volume down to a minimum for the initial connection, because Mic ports tend to be sensitive.

TIP   *If you have a Mac that doesn't have an audio input, consider a solution such as the Griffin iMic (www.griffintechnology.com), which lets you record via USB.*

Record on Windows

To record audio on Windows, you can use the minimalist sound-recording application, Sound Recorder, or add (and usually pay for) a more powerful application. This section discusses how to use Sound Recorder.

Sound Recorder doesn't automatically sync the recording with the playback, so unless you manage some cute cueing, you'll end up with empty audio at the beginning and end of the file. You can remove this empty audio later using iTunes; see the section "Trim Audio Files to Get Rid of Intros and Outros You Don't Like," later in this chapter, for details.

TIP   *One of the best cross-platform solutions for recording and editing audio files is Audacity (freeware; http://audacity.sourceforge.net). Audacity runs on Windows, Mac OS X, and Linux, using very nearly the same interface on each platform. The section "Record Audio with Audacity," later in this chapter, shows you how to use Audacity on the Mac (which doesn't come with an equivalent of Sound Recorder). However, the steps for using Audacity on Windows are almost identical.*

The next two subsections show you how to specify the audio source on Windows Vista and then record using Sound Recorder. The two subsections after those show you how to specify the audio source and record using Sound Recorder on Windows XP.

TIP   *If you have a lot of records and tapes that you want to copy to digital audio files, consider buying an audio-cleanup application that includes recording capabilities instead of an application whose strengths lie mainly in recording. For example, applications such as Magix's Audio Cleaning Lab focus mainly on audio cleanup (removing crackle, pops, hiss, and other defects) but include more-than-adequate recording capabilities.*

Specify the Audio Source for Recording in Windows Vista

To set Windows Vista to accept input from the source so you can record from it, follow these steps:

1. Start your audio source playing so that you'll be able to check the volume level.

2. Right-click the Volume icon in the notification area, and then choose Recording Devices from the shortcut menu to display the Recording tab of the Sound dialog box (see Figure 6-6).

3. If the device you want to use is marked as Currently Unavailable (as in the figure), click the device, and then click the Set Default button. Windows makes the device available and moves the green circle with the white checkmark from the other device to this device.

FIGURE 6-6   Before recording in Windows Vista, you may need to change the recording device on the Recording tab of the Sound dialog box.

4. Verify that the signal level is suitable—for example, somewhere between the halfway point and the top of the scale for much of the input, as shown here.

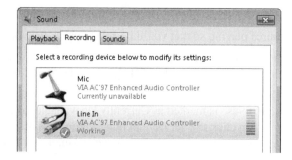

5. To change the recording level for the device, click the device in the list box, and then click the Properties button. In the Properties dialog box for the device, click the Levels tab to display its contents (see Figure 6-7). You can then drag the input slider to the level needed. Click the OK button when you've finished.

FIGURE 6-7   Use the Properties dialog box if you need to change the input level for a device.

You can also change the left–right balance by clicking the Balance button and then dragging the L and R sliders in the Balance dialog box.

Record with Sound Recorder in Windows Vista

To record with Sound Recorder in Windows Vista, follow these steps:

1. Choose Start | All Programs | Accessories | Sound Recorder to open Sound Recorder (shown here).

2. Get the audio source ready to play.

3. Click the Start Recording button when you're ready to start recording.

4. Click the Stop Recording button when you're ready to stop recording, and then stop the audio source. Sound Recorder automatically displays the Save As dialog box.

5. Type the filename, change the folder if necessary, and then click the Save button. Sound Recorder saves the file, closes it, and then automatically starts a new file in case you want to record something else.

Specify the Audio Source for Recording in Windows XP

To set Windows XP to accept input from the source so you can record from it, follow these steps:

1. If the notification area includes a Volume icon, double-click this icon to display the Volume Control window. Otherwise, choose Start | Control Panel to display the Control Panel, click the Switch To Classic View link if it appears in the upper-left corner, double-click the Sounds And Audio Devices icon, and then open the Volume Control window from there. For example, click the Advanced button in the Device Volume group box on the Volume tab of the Sounds And Audio Devices Properties dialog box.

NOTE   *Depending on your audio hardware and its drivers, the Volume Control window may have a different name (for example, Play Control).*

2. Choose Options | Properties to display the Properties dialog box. Then select the Recording option button to display the list of devices for recording (as opposed to the devices for playback). The left screen in Figure 6-8 shows this list.

3. Select the check box for the input device you want to use—for example, select the Line-In check box or the Microphone check box, depending on which you're using.

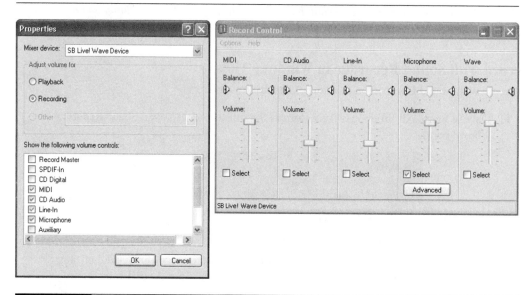

FIGURE 6-8   Click the Recording option button in the Properties dialog box (left) to display the Record Control window (right) instead of Volume Control.

4. Click the OK button to close the Properties dialog box. Windows displays the Record Control window, an example of which is shown on the right in Figure 6-8. (Like the Volume Control window, this window may have a different name—for example, Recording Control.)

5. Select the Select check box for the source you want to use.

6. Leave the Record Control window open for the time being so you can adjust the input volume on the device if necessary.

Record with Sound Recorder in Windows XP

To open Sound Recorder, choose Start | All Programs | Accessories | Entertainment | Sound Recorder.

Sound Recorder works fine except that it can't record files longer than 60 seconds, which makes it next to useless for recording music. (This limitation doesn't apply to the version of Sound Recorder in Windows Vista.) But you can sidestep around this limitation by creating a blank file longer than the longest item you want to record and then recording over this blank file. This takes a little effort but is worth the trouble.

There are two parts to making Sound Recorder record files longer than 60 seconds. The first part, which is compulsory, is to create a blank dummy file long enough to contain whatever you want to record. The second part, which is optional, is to make Sound Recorder open this file automatically when you start it so that you don't have to open it manually.

Create the Dummy File   To create the blank dummy file, follow these steps:

1. Choose Start | All Programs | Accessories | Entertainment | Sound Recorder to launch Sound Recorder:

2. Mute your sound source.

3. Click the Record button (the button with the red dot) to start recording a blank file. Sound Recorder makes the file 60 seconds long, its default maximum.

4. Let the recording run until it stops automatically at 60 seconds.

5. Choose File | Save to display the Save As dialog box.

6. Save the file under a descriptive name such as Dummy.wav.

7. Choose Edit | Insert File to display the Insert File dialog box.

8. Select the file you saved and click the Open button to insert it in the open version of the file. This adds another 60 seconds to the file's length, doubling it.

9. Repeat the procedure of inserting the saved file in the open file until the open file reaches the length you need. It's best to have the dummy file substantially longer than the longest song you expect to record, so that you don't run out of recording time.

TIP *To increase the file's size more quickly, save the open file after inserting another one or two minutes in it. You can then insert the saved file, adding two or three minutes to the open file at a time.*

10. When the file reaches the length you need, choose File | Save to save it.

11. Press ALT-F4 or choose File | Exit to close Sound Recorder.

Make Sound Recorder Open the Dummy File Automatically   To make Sound Recorder open the dummy file automatically, follow these steps:

1. Right-click the Sound Recorder entry on your Start menu and choose Properties from the shortcut menu to display its Properties dialog box (see Figure 6-9).

2. In the Target text box, enter the path and filename to the file you recorded, inside double quotation marks, after the path and filename of the executable, so that it looks something like this:

```
%SystemRoot%\System32\sndrec32.exe "C:\Documents and Settings\
Your Name\My Documents\Dummy.wav"
```

3. Click the OK button to close the Properties dialog box.

FIGURE 6-9   Use the Properties dialog box to configure Sound Recorder to open your dummy file automatically.

Now, when you start Sound Recorder, it automatically opens the dummy file. You can then record audio up to the length of the dummy file.

Record a Sound File   To record a file with Sound Recorder, follow these steps:

1. Choose Start | All Programs | Accessories | Entertainment | Sound Recorder to launch Sound Recorder and make it open the dummy file.

NOTE   *If you didn't change the Sound Recorder shortcut, open your dummy file manually.*

2. Get the audio source ready to play.
3. Click the Record button to start recording.
4. Start the audio playing.
5. To stop recording, click the Stop button.

6. Choose File | Save As to display the Save As dialog box:

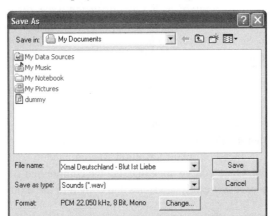

7. Specify the location and name for the file. (Don't overwrite your dummy file.)

8. Make sure the Format field, at the bottom of the Save As dialog box, is displaying the format in which you want to save the file. This field gives brief details of the format—for example, "PCM 22 050 KHz, 8 Bit, Mono" or "Windows Media Audio V2, 160 Kbps, 48 KHz, Stereo." To set a different format, click the Change button and work in the Sound Selection dialog box:

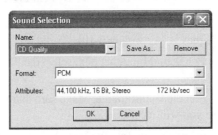

■ To select a predefined set of attributes, select CD Quality, Radio Quality, or Telephone Quality in the Name drop-down list. If you're recording music you want to turn into an AAC file or MP3 file, choose the CD Quality item. You can define your own named formats by choosing appropriate settings in the Format drop-down list and Attributes drop-down list and then clicking the Save As button. You can then reuse these formats more quickly the next time you need the same settings.

■ Otherwise, choose the format in the Format drop-down list and then select the appropriate attributes in the Attributes drop-down list. For example, you might choose PCM in the Format drop-down list and the 48 000 KHz, 16 Bit, Stereo setting in the Attributes drop-down list to record pulse code modulation audio at the highest quality that Sound Recorder supports.

9. Click the OK button to close the Sound Selection dialog box.

10. Click the Save button in the Save As dialog box to save the file.

TIP
The Format drop-down list in Sound Recorder includes an MPEG Layer-3 item, which creates MP3 files. Unfortunately, owing to a licensing issue, the encoder included with Windows XP can encode only up to 56 Kbps at 24 KHz, which makes it useless for high-quality audio. So you'll get much better results from creating WAV files with Sound Recorder and then using iTunes to encode them to MP3 files or AAC files.

Import the Sound File into iTunes and Convert It

After saving the sound file in an audio format that iTunes can handle (either the WMA format from Windows Vista or the WAV format from Windows XP), import the sound file into iTunes. If the file is WMA, iTunes automatically converts it to your current import format. If the file is WAV, you need to use the Advanced | Convert Selection To command to convert the sound file to your preferred import format. Once you've done that, tag the compressed file with the appropriate information so that you can access it easily in iTunes and copy it to the iPod or iPhone.

Record Audio on the Mac

To record audio on the Mac, specify the audio source, and then download and install Audacity.

Specify the Audio Source for Recording on the Mac

To specify the source on the Mac, follow these steps:

1. Choose Apple | System Preferences to display the System Preferences window.
2. Click the Sound item to display the Sound preferences.
3. Click the Input tab to display it (see Figure 6-10).
4. In the Choose A Device For Sound Input list box, select the device to use (for example, Line In).
5. Start some audio playing on the sound source. Make sure that it's representative of the loudest part of the audio you will record.
6. Watch the Input Level readout as you drag the Input Volume slider to a suitable level.

Install Audacity and Add an MP3 Encoder

Go to SourceForge (http://audacity.sourceforge.net) and download Audacity by following the link for the latest stable version and your operating system. At this writing, you download the file itself from one of various software-distribution sites.

Expand the downloaded file, and then drag the resulting Audacity folder to your Applications folder. Keep your browser open for the moment, and go back to the Audacity page. You'll need to download another file in a minute.

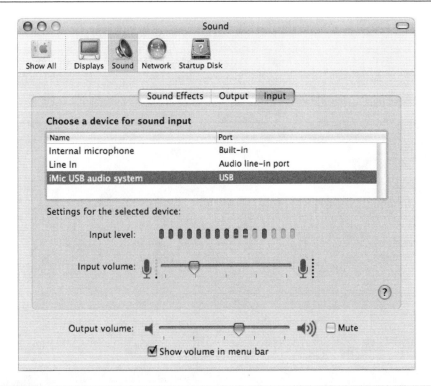

FIGURE 6-10   Configure your sound source on the Input tab of the Sound window.

Set Up Audacity

The first time you run Audacity, choose the language you want to use—for example, English. You then see Audacity (see Figure 6-11).

After you install Audacity, you'll need to add an MP3 encoder if you want to be able to create MP3 files with Audacity. (Instead of adding the MP3 encoder, you can create WAV files with Audacity and then use iTunes to create MP3 files or AAC files.)

Follow these steps to add an MP3 encoder to Audacity:

1. Download the latest stable version of the LAME encoder from the LAME Project home page (http://lame.sourceforge.net) or another site.

2. From the download package, extract the LameLib file and put it in a folder of your choosing, such as your ~/Library/Audio folder.

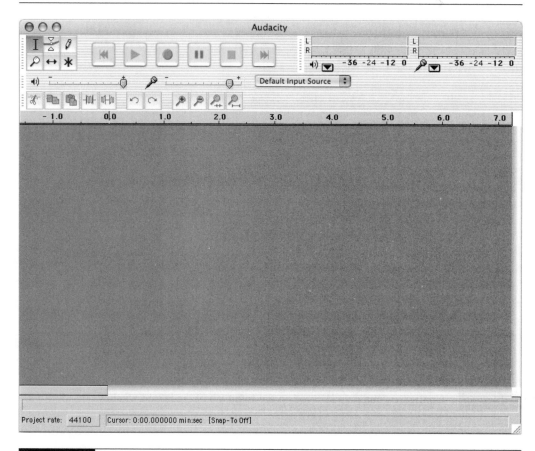

FIGURE 6-11 Audacity is a great freeware application for recording audio and fixing problems with it.

3. Display the Audacity Preferences dialog box by pressing ⌘-COMMA or choosing Audacity | Preferences.

4. Click the File Formats tab to display its contents (see Figure 6-12).

5. Check the MP3 Export Setup area. If the MP3 Library Version readout says "MP3 exporting plugin not found," you need to add an MP3 encoder.

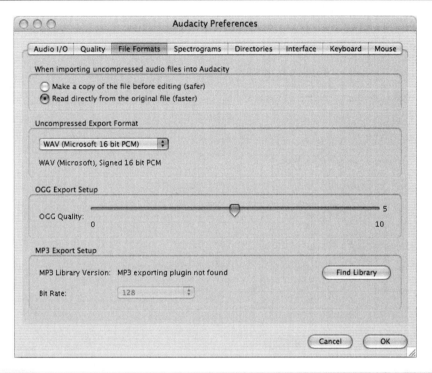

FIGURE 6-12   Use the File Formats tab of the Audacity Preferences dialog box to add an MP3 encoder to Audacity.

6. Click the Find Library button. Audacity displays the Export MP3 dialog box, which explains that you need to supply the LAME MP3 encoder and asks if you want to provide it:

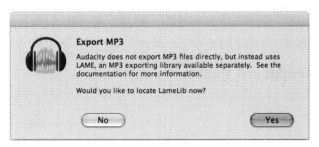

7. Click the Yes button and use the resulting dialog box to find LameLib in the folder to which you extracted it in Step 2.

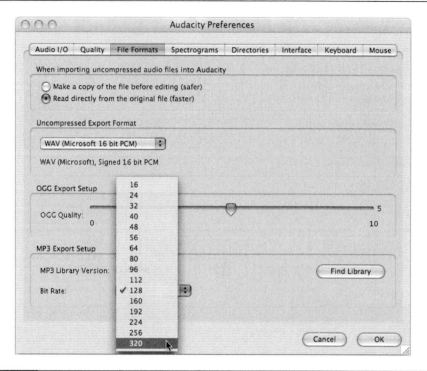

FIGURE 6-13 Once you've added the LAME encoder, you can choose the bitrate to use for exporting MP3 files.

8. Click the Open button. Audacity adds the LAME version to the MP3 Library Version readout.

9. In the Bit Rate drop-down list (see Figure 6-13), select the bitrate at which you want to export MP3 files. For example, choose 128 Kbps if you want acceptable-quality audio at small file sizes (so that you can cram more songs onto a low-capacity iPod or an iPhone) or choose 320 Kbps for maximum quality at the expense of file size.

Configure Input/Output and Quality Settings

With the Audacity Preferences dialog box still open, configure the audio input/output settings and the quality settings:

1. Click the Audio I/O tab to display its contents (see Figure 6-14).

2. Select your playback device, recording device, and the number of channels—for example, 2 (Stereo). You can also choose whether to play existing tracks while recording a new

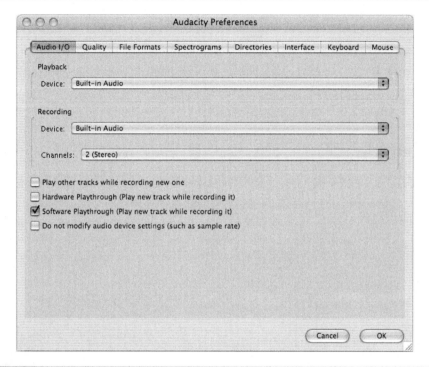

FIGURE 6-14 Choose your playback and recording devices, and the number of channels, on the Audio I/O tab of the Audacity Preferences dialog box.

track (which you won't need to do if you're recording a single audio track, such as a song) and whether to play the new track that's being recorded (this can help you stop the recording at the appropriate point).

3. Click the Quality tab to display its contents (see Figure 6-15).

4. In the Default Sample Rate drop-down list, select the sample rate you want to use. If you don't know the rate you want, use 44100 Hz. Leave the other settings on the Quality tab at their defaults unless you know you need to change them.

5. Click the OK button to close the Audacity Preferences dialog box.

Record Audio with Audacity

To record audio with Audacity, follow these steps:

1. Start Audacity if it's not already running.

2. If necessary, choose a different sound source in the Default Input Source drop-down list on the right side of the window.

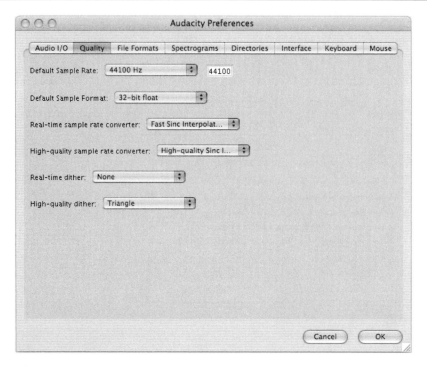

FIGURE 6-15 Choose the default sample rate on the Quality tab of the Audacity Preferences dialog box.

3. Cue your audio source.

4. Click the Record button (the button with the red circle) to start the recording (see Figure 6-16).

NOTE

If necessary, change the recording volume by dragging the Input Volume slider (the slider with the microphone at its left end). When you've got it right, stop the recording, create a new file, and then restart the recording.

5. Click the Record button again to stop recording.

6. Choose File | Save Project to open the Save Project As dialog box, specify a filename and folder, and then click the Save button.

7. When you are ready to export the audio file, choose File | Export As MP3 or File | Export As WAV.

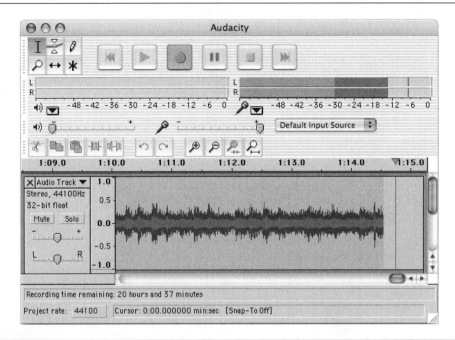

FIGURE 6-16   Adjust the input volume if the signal is too low or too high.

How to ... Remove Scratches and Hiss from Audio Files

If you record tracks from vinyl records, audio cassettes, or other analog sources, you may well get some clicks or pops, hiss, or background hum in the file. Scratches on a record can cause clicks and pops, audio cassettes tend to hiss (even with noise-reduction such as Dolby), and record players or other machinery can add hum.

All these noises—very much part of the analog audio experience, and actually appreciated as such by some enthusiasts—tend to annoy people accustomed to digital audio. The good news is that you can remove many such noises by using the right software.

Unless you already have an audio editor that has noise-removal features, your best choice is probably the freeware program Audacity. This chapter has shown you how to install and use Audacity on the Mac, but the program also works on Windows.

(Continued)

To remove noise from a recording using Audacity, follow these steps:

1. In Audacity, open the project containing the song.

2. Select a part of the recording with just noise—for example, the opening few seconds of silence (except for the stylus clicking and popping along).

3. Choose Effect | Noise Removal to open the Noise Removal dialog box:

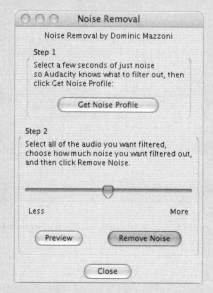

4. Click the Get Noise Profile button. The Noise Removal system analyzes your sample and applies the corresponding noise profile.

5. Select the part of the recording that you want to affect:

   ■ To affect the entire recording, choose Edit | Select | All. This is usually the easiest approach.

   ■ To affect only part of the recording, drag through it. For example, you might want to affect only the end of the recording if this is where all the scratches occur.

6. Choose Effect | Noise Removal to open the Noise Removal dialog box again. This time, drag the slider in the Step 2 box along the Less–More axis to specify how much noise you want to remove. Click the Preview button to get a preview of the effect this will have, and adjust the slider as needed. When you're satisfied with the effect, click the Remove Noise button to remove the noise.

7. Choose File | Save to save your project.

Trim Audio Files to Get Rid of Intros and Outros You Don't Like

If you don't like the intro of a particular song, you can tell iTunes to suppress it by setting the Start Time option on the Options tab of the Song Information dialog box to the point where you want the song to start playing. Similarly, you can suppress an outro by using the Stop Time option, also on the Options tab.

You can also use these options to trim an audio file. Follow these steps:

1. In iTunes, right-click (or CTRL-click on the Mac) the song you want to shorten, and then choose Get Info from the shortcut menu to display the Song Information dialog box. (This dialog box's title bar shows the song name, not the words "Song Information.")

TIP   *If you've recorded songs that have empty audio at the beginning or end (or both), use this technique to remove the empty audio.*

2. Click the Options tab to display its contents.

3. Set the Start Time, Stop Time, or both, as needed.

4. Click the OK button to close the Song Information dialog box.

5. Right-click (or CTRL-click on the Mac) the song, and then choose Convert Selection To *Format,* where *Format* is the import format set on the Importing subtab of the Advanced tab in the iTunes dialog box or the Preferences dialog box.

6. iTunes creates a shorter version of the song. It's a good idea to rename the song immediately to avoid confusing it with the source file.

TIP   *You can even use this trick to split a song file into two or more different files. For example, to create two files, work out where the division needs to fall. Create the first file by setting the Stop Time to this time, and then performing the conversion. Return to the source file, set the Start Time to the dividing time, and then perform the conversion again.*

Tag Your Compressed Files with the Correct Information for Sorting

The best thing about compressed audio formats such as AAC, MP3, and Apple Lossless Encoding—apart from their being compressed and still giving high-quality audio—is that each file format can store a full set of tag information about the song the file contains. The tag information lets you sort, organize, and search for songs on iTunes. The iPod and iPhone need correct artist, album, and track name information in tags to be able to organize your AAC files and MP3 files correctly. If a song lacks this minimum of information, iTunes doesn't transfer it to the device.

TIP *You can force iTunes to load untagged songs on an iPod or iPhone by assigning them to a playlist and loading the playlist. But in most cases it's best to tag all the songs in your library—or at least tag as many as is practicable.*

Your main tool for tagging song files should be iTunes, because it provides solid if basic features for tagging one or more files at once manually. But if your library contains many untagged or mistagged files, you may need a heavier-duty application. This section shows you how to tag most effectively in iTunes and then presents two more powerful applications—Tag&Rename for Windows, and MP3 Rage for the Mac.

Tag Songs Effectively with iTunes

The easiest way to add tag information to an AAC file or MP3 file is by downloading the information from CDDB (the CD Database) when you rip the CD. But sometimes you'll need to enter (or change) tag information manually to make iTunes sort the files correctly—for example, when the CDDB data is wrong or not available, or for existing song files created with software other than iTunes, such as song files you've created yourself.

How to ...   Tag Song Files after Encoding when Offline

Even if you rip CDs when your computer has no Internet connection, you can usually apply the CD information to the song files once you've reestablished an Internet connection. To do so, select the album or the songs in your library and then choose Advanced | Get CD Track Names. If the CD's details are in CDDB, iTunes should then be able to download the information.

If you imported the songs by using software other than iTunes, or if you imported the songs using iTunes on another computer and then copied them to this computer, iTunes objects with the "iTunes cannot get CD track names" dialog box shown here. In this case, you'll need to either reimport the songs on this computer or tag the songs manually.

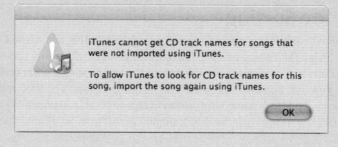

iTunes cannot get CD track names for songs that were not imported using iTunes.

To allow iTunes to look for CD track names for this song, import the song again using iTunes.

OK

NOTE *Often, MP3 files distributed illegally on the Internet lack tag information or include incorrect tags. That said, officially tagged files aren't always as accurate as they might be—so if you want your files to be as easy to find and manipulate as possible, it's worth spending some time checking the tags and improving them as necessary.*

If you need to change the tag information for a whole CD's worth of songs, proceed as follows:

1. In iTunes, select all the song files you want to affect.

2. Right-click (or CTRL-click on the Mac) the selection and choose Get Info from the shortcut menu to display the Multiple Item Information dialog box. Alternatively, choose File | Get Info or press CTRL-I (Windows) or ⌘-M (Mac). Figure 6-17 shows the Windows version of the Multiple Item Information dialog box.

FIGURE 6-17   Use the Multiple Item Information dialog box to enter common tag information for all the songs on a CD or album at once.

NOTE

By default, when you issue a Get Info command with multiple songs selected, iTunes displays a dialog box to check that you want to edit the information for multiple songs. Click the Yes button to proceed; click the Cancel button to cancel. If you frequently want to edit tag information for multiple songs, select the Do Not Ask Me Again check box in the confirmation dialog box to turn off confirmations in the future.

3. Enter as much common information as you can: the artist, year, album, total number of tracks, disc number, composer, comments, and so on. If you have the artwork for the CD available, drag it to the Artwork pane.

4. Click the OK button to apply the information to the songs.

5. Click the first song to clear the current selection. Right-click (or CTRL-click on the Mac) the song and choose Get Info from the shortcut menu to display the Item Information dialog box for the song. Click the Info tab to display it if iTunes doesn't display it automatically. Figure 6-18 shows the Windows version of the Item Information dialog box for the song "Instant Gravitation." The song's title appears in the title bar of the dialog box.

FIGURE 6-18   Use the Item Information dialog box (whose title bar shows the song's name) to add song-specific information.

6. Add any song-specific information here: the song name, the track number, and so on.

7. If you need to change the song's relative volume, equalizer preset, rating, start time, or stop time, work on the Options tab.

8. If you want to add lyrics to the song (either by typing them in or by pasting them from a lyrics site), work on the Lyrics tab.

9. Click the Previous button or the Next button to display the information for the previous song or next song.

10. Click the OK button to close the Item Information dialog box when you've finished adding song information.

How to ... Submit CD Information to CDDB Using iTunes

If a CD you want to rip turns out not to have an entry in CDDB (as indicated by the dialog box shown here), you can submit an entry yourself. Users submitting entries like this have added many of the entries in CDDB for older or less widely known CDs. Mainstream entries are submitted by the record companies themselves: They submit a listing to CDDB (and other online CD-information services, such as WindowsMedia.com) as a matter of course when they release a new CD.

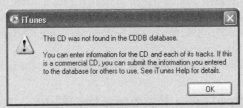

At this writing, CDDB contains entries for an enormous number of CDs—so unless you have an unusual CD, chances are any CD you want to rip already has an entry in CDDB. You may find that your CD is listed under a slightly different title or artist name than you're expecting—for example, the artist might be listed as "Sixpack, Joe" rather than "Joe Sixpack." Check carefully for any close matches before submitting an entry so you don't waste your time. You may also find CDDB contains two or more entries for the same CD.

When submitting an entry to CDDB, type the CD title, artist name, and song titles carefully using standard capitalization, and double-check all the information before you submit it. Otherwise, if your entry is accepted and entered in CDDB, anyone who looks up that CD will get the misspellings or wrong information you entered.

(Continued)

Here's how to submit an entry to CDDB:

1. Enter the tag information for the CD.

2. Choose Advanced | Submit CD Track Names to display the CD Info dialog box and then check the information in the Artist, Composer, Album, Disc Number, Genre, and Year fields. Select the Compilation CD check box if the CD is a compilation rather than a work by an individual artist.

3. Establish an Internet connection if you need to do so manually.

4. Click the OK button. iTunes connects to CDDB and submits the information.

Change Tags with Tag&Rename on Windows

Tag&Rename, from Softpointer, Inc., is a powerful tag-editing application for various types of files, including AAC and MP3. You can download a free 30-day evaluation version from www. softpointer.com/tr.htm and from various other sites on the Internet.

Tag&Rename can derive tag information by breaking down a file's name into its constituents. For example, if you set Tag&Rename on the file Aimee Mann - Lost in Space - 06 - Pavlov's Bell.mp3, Tag&Rename can derive the artist name (Aimee Mann), the album name (*Lost in Space)*, the track number (06), and the song name ("Pavlov's Bell") from the file and then apply that information to the tag fields.

Tag&Rename can also derive tag information from the folder structure that contains an MP3 file that needs tagging. For example, if you have the file 06 - Pavlov's Bell.mp3 stored in the folder Aimee Mann\Lost in Space, Tag&Rename will be able to tag the file with the artist name, album name, track name, and track number.

Figure 6-19 shows Tag&Rename in action, working on the tags of some MP3 files.

Change Tags with Media Rage on the Mac

Media Rage, from Chaotic Software (www.chaoticsoftware.com), is an impressive bundle of utilities for tagging, organizing, and improving your MP3 files. The tagging features in Media Rage include deriving tag information from filenames and folder paths and changing the tags on multiple files at once.

You can download a fully functional evaluation version of Media Rage from the Chaotic Software website. The registered version of Media Rage costs $29.95.

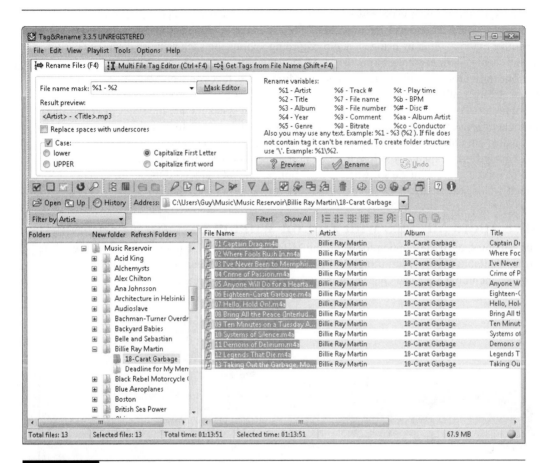

FIGURE 6-19   Tag&Rename can edit multiple tags at once.

Save Audio Streams to Disk So You Can Listen to Them Later

If you enjoy listening to Internet radio, you may want to record it so that you can play it back later. iTunes doesn't let you save streaming audio to disk because recording streaming audio without specific permission typically violates copyright. So you need to use either a hardware solution or a third-party application to record streams.

To solve the problem via hardware, use a standard audio cable to pipe the output from your computer's sound card to its Line In socket. You can then record the audio stream as you would any other external input by using an audio-recording application such as those discussed earlier in this chapter—for example, Sound Recorder or Audacity.

The only problem with using a standard audio cable is that you won't be able to hear the audio stream you're recording via external speakers. To solve this problem, get a stereo Y-connector. Connect one of the outputs to your external speakers and the other to your Line In socket. Converting the audio from digital to analog and then back to digital like this degrades its quality, but unless you're listening to the highest-bitrate Internet radio stations around, you'll most likely find the quality you lose to be a fair trade-off for the convenience you gain.

To solve the problem via software, get an application that can record the audio stream directly. This section discusses some possibilities for Windows and Mac OS X.

Save Audio Streams with Zinf on Windows

For Windows, the easiest option for recording MP3 streams is Zinf, a freeware open-source music player available from www.zinf.org. Zinf (shown on the left in Figure 6-20) can handle various formats, including MP3 and Ogg Vorbis files, and it can record streams to files.

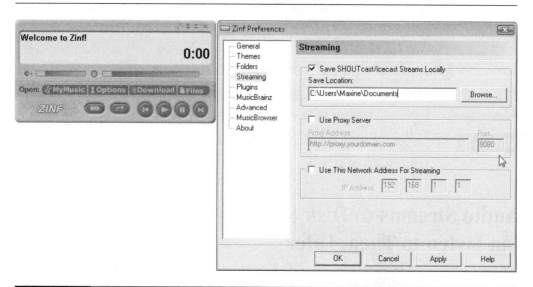

FIGURE 6-20 Zinf is an open-source freeware music player that can record audio streams to files so that you can listen to them later.

To record MP3 streams with Zinf, follow these steps:

1. Click the Options button to display the Zinf Preferences dialog box (shown on the right in Figure 6-20).

2. Click the Streaming category to display it.

3. Select the Save SHOUTcast/icecast Streams Locally check box.

4. Use the Browse button and the resulting Browse For Folder dialog box to specify the folder in which to save the streamed files. Make sure the drive on which the folder is located contains several gigabytes of free space.

5. Click the OK button to close the Zinf Preferences dialog box.

6. Tune into the audio stream. Zinf records the stream automatically under an autonamed file.

You may find that Windows Firewall tries to block Zinf, as shown here. Click the Unblock button to allow Zinf to connect to the Internet.

Save Audio Streams with Total Recorder on Windows

If you want to record stream types that Zinf can't record, try Total Recorder, from High Criteria, Inc. (www.highcriteria.com):

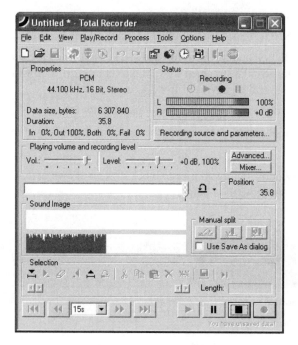

Total Recorder comes in a Standard Edition, a Professional Edition, and a Developer Edition but you probably won't want this unless you're developing software. Both Standard and Professional can save MP3 streams. High Criteria provides trial versions of Total Recorder, but they're so thoroughly crippled you'll need to open your wallet to actually get anything done.

Save Streams with RadioLover on the Mac

RadioLover, which you can download from VersionTracker.com (www.versiontracker.com), is shareware that can tap into and record iTunes' Internet radio streams.

Save Streams with Audio Hijack on the Mac

Audio Hijack, from Rogue Amoeba Software (www.rogueamoeba.com/audiohijack/), is a full-featured application for recording the audio output of applications and manipulating that output. Audio Hijack (see Figure 6-21) includes timers that you can set ahead of time to record the shows you're interested in. It can also apply equalization to applications that don't have equalizers themselves. For example, you can use Audio Hijack to equalize the output of Apple's DVD player. You can also buy Audio Hijack Pro, which has extra features.

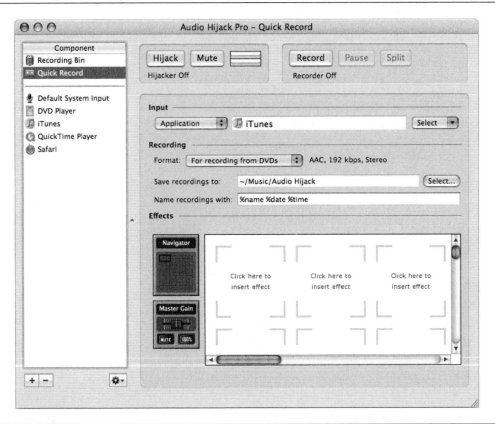

FIGURE 6-21   Audio Hijack can record the audio output of various applications and apply effects to that output.

Chapter 7

Buy and Download Songs, Videos, and More Online

How to...

- Understand what the iTunes Store is
- Understand digital rights management (DRM)
- Set up an account with the iTunes Store
- Configure iTunes Store settings
- Access the iTunes Store
- Buy songs and videos from the iTunes Store
- Listen to songs and watch videos you've purchased
- Authorize and deauthorize computers for the iTunes Store
- Buy and download music from other online music stores
- Download music from other online sources

Instead of creating song files by ripping your own CDs, tapes, and records, you can buy songs online. You can also buy videos, audio books, and other content.

If iTunes has its way, your first stop for buying content will be the iTunes Store, Apple's online service for songs, videos, and more. This chapter discusses what the iTunes Store is, how it works, and how to use it. Because the iTunes Store works in almost exactly the same way on Mac OS X and Windows, this chapter discusses both operating systems together and, for balance, shows some screens from each.

This chapter also discusses digital rights management (DRM), because you'll benefit from understanding the essentials of DRM before buying content online. The end of the chapter discusses other online sources of songs, from online music stores other than the iTunes Store to free sources.

Understand Digital Rights Management (DRM)

Currently, the movie and music industry bodies are engaged in a vigorous struggle with consumers over how music and video are sold (or stolen) and distributed:

- The record companies have applied copy-protection mechanisms to some audio discs (see "Understand Current Copy-Protection Techniques on the Discs You Buy" in Chapter 6) to prevent their customers from making unauthorized pure-digital copies of music.

- Most video content is sold with copy-protection applied. For example, regular DVDs use the Content Scramble System (CSS) to protect their content. High-definition DVDs use the Advanced Access Content System (AACS) for protection.

- Some consumers are trying to protect their freedom to enjoy the music and video they buy in the variety of ways that law and case law have established to be either definitely legal or sort-of legal. For example, legal precedents that permit the use of VCRs, personal video recorders (PVRs), and home audio taping suggest that it's probably legal to create compressed audio files from a CD, record, or cassette, as long as they're for your personal use.

- Other people are deliberately infringing the media companies' copyrights by copying, distributing, and stealing music and video via peer-to-peer (P2P) networks, recordable CDs and DVDs, and other means.

- Also participating in this struggle is the movie industry, which suffers similar piracy problems. VCRs and PVRs provide plenty of precedent for making copies of copyrighted works for personal use and sharing them with other people (for example, on videotape or DVD), but widespread distribution of digital video files on P2P networks is another matter entirely.

Behind this struggle lies digital rights management (DRM), technologies for defining which actions a user may take with a particular work and restricting the user to those actions, preferably without preventing them from using or enjoying the work in the ways they expect to.

Understand That DRM Is Neither "Good" nor "Bad"

DRM is often portrayed by consumer activists as being the quintessence of the Recording Industry Association of America's and Motion Picture Association of America's dreams and of consumers' nightmares. The publisher of a work can use DRM to impose a wide variety of restrictions on the ways in which a consumer can use the work.

For example, some digital books are delivered in an encrypted format that requires a special certificate to decrypt, which effectively means that the consumer can read them only on one authorized computer. DRM also prevents the consumer from printing any of the book or copying any of it directly from the reader application. As you'd imagine, these restrictions are unpopular with most consumers, and such books have largely failed in the marketplace: Consumers prefer traditional physical books that they can read wherever they want to, lend to a friend, photocopy, rip pages out of, drop in the bath, and so on.

But how good or bad DRM is in practice depends on the implementation. DRM can also be a compromise—for example, when Apple launched the iTunes Store, the only way it could persuade the record companies to make the songs available was by agreeing to apply DRM to the songs to limit what buyers could do with them. The compromise worked adequately for both the record companies and the consumers. In May 2007, however, Apple convinced EMI to make songs available without DRM and at a higher quality. This move was welcomed by most consumers, although few welcomed the higher prices that initially accompanied the higher-quality files.

Music is almost ideal for digital distribution, and the record companies are sitting on colossal archives of songs that are out of print but still well within copyright. It's not economically viable for the record companies to sell pressed CDs of these songs, because demand for any given CD is likely to be relatively low. But demand is there, as has been demonstrated by the millions of illegal copies of such songs that have been downloaded from P2P services. If the record companies can make these songs available online with acceptable DRM, they'll almost certainly find buyers.

NOTE   *Some enterprising smaller operators* have *managed to make an economic proposition out of selling pressed CDs or recorded CDs of out-of-print music to which they've acquired the rights. By cutting out middlemen and selling directly via websites and mail order, and in some cases by charging a premium price for a hard-to-get product, such operators have proved that making such music available isn't impossible.*

Historically, video has not been a good candidate for digital distribution, because the files have been too big to transfer easily across the Internet. But now that faster broadband connections are becoming increasingly widespread, and YouTube is used for everything from promoting music to promoting presidential candidates, distributing even full-quality video files is workable.

Know a Store's DRM Terms Before You Buy Any Protected Songs

Before you buy any song (or video) that is protected by DRM, make sure you understand what the DRM involves, what restrictions it places on you, and what changes the implementer of the DRM is allowed to make. In most cases, when you "buy" a song that is protected by DRM, you buy not the song but a license to play the song in limited circumstances—for example, on a single computer or several computers, or for a limited length of time. You may or may not be permitted to burn the song to disc for storage or so that you can play it in conventional audio players (rather than on computers). In most cases, you are not permitted to give or sell the song to anyone else, nor can you return the song to the store for a refund or exchange.

The store that sells you the license to the song usually retains the right to change the limitations on how you can use the song. For example, the store can change the number of computers on which you can play the song, prevent you from burning it to disc, or even prevent you from playing it anymore. Any restrictions added may not take place immediately if your computer isn't connected to the Internet, but most online music stores require periodic authentication checks to make sure the music is still licensed for playing.

In general, "buying" DRM-protected songs online compares poorly to buying a physical CD, even though you have the option of buying individual songs rather than having to buy the entire contents of the CD. While you don't own the music on the CD, you own the CD itself, and can dispose of it as you want. For example, you can create digital copies of its contents (assuming that the CD is not copy-protected), lend the CD to a friend, or sell the CD to an individual or a store.

The sections in this chapter about the iTunes Store and other online music stores explain the current DRM the stores impose on the songs they sell. You should check the terms and conditions of each store for changes to the DRM before buying from that store.

Similar restrictions and considerations apply to video files you buy from the iTunes Store. In most cases, if the same content is available on a conventional medium (such as a DVD or a video cassette), buying it on that medium gives you more flexibility than buying a digital file.

Buy Songs and Videos from the iTunes Store

So far, the iTunes Store is one of the largest and most successful attempts to sell music online. (The latter part of this chapter discusses other online music services, including Wal-Mart, the second-generation Napster, and eMusic.) The iTunes Store is far from perfect, and its selection is still very limited compared to what many users would like to be able to buy, but it's an extremely promising start. At this writing, the iTunes Store is available to iTunes users on Windows and the Mac.

Here's the deal with the iTunes Store:

- Most songs cost $0.99 each for a DRM-protected version. If there's a DRM-free version, it may cost the same, but it may cost more. The cost of albums varies, but many cost $9.99 or so for the DRM-protected versions—around what you'd pay for a discounted CD in many stores. Some CDs are available only as "partial CDs," which typically means that you can't buy the songs you're most likely to want. Extra-long songs (for example, those 13-minute jam sessions used to max out a CD) are sometimes available for purchase only with an entire CD.

- Most video items cost $1.99 or more, but you can also buy them in bulk and save. For example, you might buy a whole season of *Desperate Housewives*.

- You can listen to a 30-second preview of any song to make sure it's what you want. After you buy a song, you download it to your music library.

- You can burn songs to CD an unlimited number of times, although you can burn any given playlist only seven times without changing it or re-creating it under another name. (The number of burns was originally ten but was reduced in early 2005.)

- The songs you buy are encoded in the AAC format (discussed in the section "AAC" in Chapter 6). Most songs are protected with DRM (discussed in the following section). The videos you buy are in the MPEG-4 video format and are also protected with DRM.

- You can play the songs you buy on any number of iPods or iPhones that you synchronize with your PC or Mac. You may also be able to play the songs on other music players that can use the AAC format (for example, some mobile phones can play AAC files).

- You can play the songs and videos you buy on up to three computers at once. These computers are said to be "authorized." You can change which computers are authorized for the songs bought on a particular iTunes Store account.

- You can download each item you buy only once (assuming the download is successful). After that, the item is your responsibility. If you lose the item, you have to buy it again. This means that you must back up the items you buy or risk losing them.

Understand What the iTunes Store DRM Means

At this writing, the iTunes Store uses FairPlay, a DRM implementation designed to be acceptable both to customers and to the record companies that provide the songs. As of summer 2007, the iTunes Store offers more than five million songs and has sold more than two billion songs altogether.

For customers, the attraction is being able to find songs easily, acquire them almost instantly for reasonable prices, and use them in enough of the ways they're used to (play the songs on their computer, play them on their iPod or iPhone, or burn them to disc). For the record companies, the appeal is a largely untapped market that can provide a revenue stream at minimal cost (no physical media are involved) and with an acceptably small potential for abuse. (For example, most people who buy songs won't burn them to CD, rip the CD to MP3, and then distribute the MP3 files.) To the surprise of many analysts, Steve Jobs claimed in late 2003 that Apple makes hardly any money from the iTunes Store, which seems to mean that most of the revenue (apart from the overheads of administering the service, running the servers, and providing bandwidth) goes to the record companies.

Being able to download music like this is great: You can get the songs you want, when you want them, and at a price that's more reasonable than buying a whole CD. But it's important to be aware of the following points, even if they don't bother you in the least:

- Even though the AAC format provides relatively high audio quality, the songs sold by the iTunes Store are significantly lower quality than CD-quality audio. At this writing, the DRM-protected songs are 128 Kbps AAC. The DRM-free songs are 256 Kbps AAC, which Apple claims gives "audio quality indistinguishable from the original recording." Audiophiles disagree.

- When you buy a CD, you own it. You can't necessarily do what you want with the music—not legally, anyway. But you can play it as often as you want on whichever player, lend it to a friend, and so on.

- When you buy a DRM-protected song from the iTunes Store, you don't own it. Instead, you have a very limited license. A DRM-free song gives you more freedom, but you must back it up. If your computer's hard disk crashes so that you lose your music library, you can't download the songs again from the iTunes Store without paying for them again.

- The record labels that provide the music reserve the right to change the terms under which they provide the music in the future. Apple has implemented several changes already, reducing the number of computers with which iTunes can share music and the number of CD burns allowed for any given playlist. Like these changes, future changes seem likely to be more restrictive than more liberal.

In October 2005, the iTunes Store added a modest selection of video files, and sold one million of them in the first 19 days. As with songs, the convenience of buying via download is wonderful, but some of the same concerns apply: The MPEG format provides good enough quality, but nothing compared to a DVD; you buy not a tangible object but a license to use the file; you need to back up your purchases to physical media to avoid loss; and the terms of service may change.

NOTE   *The success of the iTunes Store has greatly increased consumers' acceptance of DRM. The iTunes Store has been successful because it enables people to find and buy music with minimal fuss, and the DRM on iTunes, the iTunes Store, and the iPod or iPhone is implemented in a slick and effective package. Several other online music stores have taken their lead from the iTunes Store, even though they use different—and mostly Windows-only—types of DRM. Let's hope that other major online stores follow Apple's lead in offering more music without DRM. (As you'll see later in this chapter, a couple of major stores now offer DRM-free songs.)*

Set Up an Account with the iTunes Store

To use the iTunes Store, you need a PC or a Mac running iTunes as well as a .Mac account, an Apple ID, or an AOL screen name. (An Apple ID is essentially an account with the iTunes Store and takes the form of an e-mail address. The .Mac service is Apple's online service. If you have a .Mac account, you have an Apple ID, but you don't have to get a .Mac account to get an Apple ID.) To use the video features, you need iTunes 6.0 or later.

To get started with the iTunes Store, click the iTunes Store item in the Source pane in iTunes. (Alternatively, double-click the iTunes Store item to display a separate iTunes Store window.) iTunes accesses the iTunes Store and displays its home page, of which Figure 7-1 shows an example on the Mac.

To sign in or to create an account, click the Sign In button. iTunes displays the Sign In To Download Music From The iTunes Store dialog box (see Figure 7-2).

FIGURE 7-1   The iTunes Store home page

FIGURE 7-2   From the Sign In dialog box, you can sign in to an existing account or create a new account.

If you have a .Mac account or an Apple ID, type it in the Apple ID text box, type your password in the Password text box, and click the Sign In button. Likewise, if you have an AOL screen name, select the AOL option button, enter your screen name and password, and click the Sign In button.

NOTE   *Remember that your Apple ID is the full e-mail address, including the domain—not just the first part of the address. For example, if your Apple ID is a .Mac address, enter **yourname@mac.com** rather than just **yourname**.*

The first time you sign in to the iTunes Store, iTunes displays a dialog box pointing out that your Apple ID or AOL screen name hasn't been used with the iTunes Store and suggesting that you review your account information:

Click the Review button to review your account information. (This is a compulsory step. Clicking the Cancel button doesn't skip the review process, as you might hope—instead, it cancels the creation of your account.)

To create a new account, click the Create New Account button and then click the Continue button on the Welcome To The iTunes Store page. The subsequent screens then walk you through the process of creating an account. You have to provide your credit card details and billing address. Beyond this, you get a little homily on what you may and may not legally do with the items you download, and you must agree to the terms of service of the iTunes Store.

Understand the Terms of Service

Almost no one ever reads the details of software licenses, which is why the software companies have been able to establish as normal the sales model in which you buy not software itself but a limited license to use it, and you have no recourse if it corrupts your data or reduces your computer to a puddle of silicon and steel. But you'd do well to read the terms and conditions of the iTunes Store before you buy music from it, because you should understand what you're getting into.

TIP   *The iTunes window doesn't give you the greatest view of the terms of service. To get a better view, click the Printable Version link at the very bottom of the scroll box or direct your browser to www.apple.com/legal/itunes/us/service.html.*

The following are the key points of the terms of service:

- You can play songs and videos that you download on five Apple-authorized devices—computers, iPods, or iPhones—at any time. You can authorize and deauthorize computers, so you can (for example) transfer your songs and videos from your old computer to a new computer you buy.

- You can use, export, copy, and burn songs for "personal, noncommercial use." Burning and exporting are an "accommodation" to you and don't "constitute a grant or waiver (or other limitation or implication) of any rights of the copyright owners." If you think that your being allowed to burn what would otherwise be illegal copies must limit the copyright owners' rights, I'd say you're right logically but wrong legally.

- You're not allowed to burn videos. Period.

- After you buy and download songs and videos, they're your responsibility. If you lose them or destroy them, Apple won't replace them. (You have to buy new copies of the songs and videos if you want to get them back.)

- You agree not to violate the Usage Rules imposed by the agreement.

- You agree that Apple may disclose your registration data and account information to "law enforcement authorities, government officials, and/or a third party, as Apple believes is reasonably necessary or appropriate to enforce and/or verify compliance with any part of this Agreement." The implication is that if a copyright holder claims that you're infringing their copyright, Apple may disclose your details without your knowledge, let alone your agreement. This seems to mean that, say, Sony Music or the RIAA can get the details of your e-mail address, physical address, credit card, and listening habits by claiming a suspicion of copyright violation.

- Apple and its licensors can remove or prevent you from accessing "products, content, or other materials."

- Apple reserves the right to modify the Agreement at any time. If you continue using the iTunes Store, you're deemed to have accepted whatever additional terms Apple imposes.

- Apple can terminate your account for your failing to "comply with any of the provisions" in the Agreement—or for your being suspected of such failure. Terminating your account prevents you from buying any more songs and videos immediately, but you might be able to set up another account. More seriously, termination might prevent you from playing songs and videos you've already bought—for example, if you need to authorize a computer to play them.

Configure iTunes Store Settings

By default, iTunes displays a Store category in the Source pane with an iTunes Store item and (once you've bought a song or video from the iTunes Store) a Purchased item below it. iTunes also uses 1-Click buying and downloading. You may want to remove the iTunes Store category or use the shopping basket. To change your preferences, follow these steps:

1. Display the iTunes dialog box or the Preferences dialog box:

    - In Windows, choose Edit | Preferences or press CTRL-COMMA or CTRL-Y to display the iTunes dialog box.

    - On the Mac, choose iTunes | Preferences or press ⌘-COMMA or ⌘-Y to display the Preferences dialog box.

2. Click the Parental Control tab (Windows) or Parental button (Mac) to display the Parental Controls. Figure 7-3 shows the Parental Controls on the Mac.

3. Select the Disable iTunes Store check box if you want to remove the Store category from the Source pane. If you want to prevent anyone else from reenabling the iTunes Store, click the lock icon and then go through User Account Control for the iTunes Parental Controls Operation (on Windows Vista) or authenticate yourself (on the Mac).

4. If you didn't disable the iTunes Store, click the Store tab (Windows) or Store button (Mac) to display the Store tab. Figure 7-4 shows the Store tab on the Mac. The Store tab in Windows has the same controls.

5. Select the Buy And Download Using 1-Click option button or the Buy Using A Shopping Cart option button, as appropriate. 1-Click is great for impulse shopping and instant gratification, whereas the shopping cart enables you to round up a collection of songs, weigh their merits against each other, and decide which ones you feel you must have. (In other words, using the shopping cart is the more sensible approach—so Apple has made 1-Click the default setting.)

TIP

If you have a slow connection, use the Buy Using A Shopping Cart option to queue up a stack of tracks to download overnight when the download won't compete with your other online activities for your meager bandwidth.

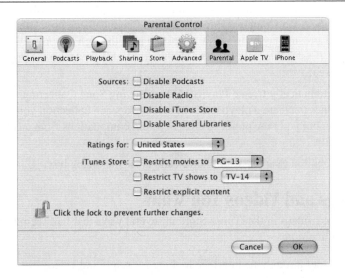

FIGURE 7-3 The Parental Control tab of the iTunes dialog box or Preferences dialog box lets you disable the iTunes Store if you don't want to use it.

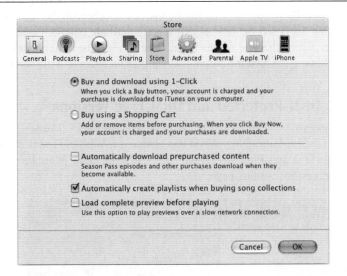

FIGURE 7-4 Configure the settings on the Store tab of the iTunes dialog box or the Preferences dialog box before you buy any songs unexpectedly.

6. If you're using a slow Internet connection (for example, dial-up or ISDN) to download songs, select the Load Complete Preview Before Playing check box. Otherwise, the download stream may be too slow to sustain play through the preview without interruptions. (Faster Internet connections should be able to stream the previews without breaking a sweat.)

7. Select the Automatically Create Playlists When Buying Song Collections check box if you want iTunes to create a playlist automatically for each collection you buy. Normally, this is helpful, but you may prefer to create custom compilations from a collection's songs manually.

8. Click the OK button to apply your choices and close the dialog box.

Find the Songs and Videos You Want

You can find songs and videos in the iTunes Store in several ways that will seem familiar if you've used other online stores:

-   You can meander through the interface looking for songs and videos by clicking links from the home page.

-   You can browse by genre, subgenre, artist, and album. Click the Browse button, click the Browse link in the Quick Links area on the home page, choose View | Show Browser, or press CTRL-B (Windows) or ⌘-B (Mac) to display the Browse interface (see Figure 7-5).

-   You can search for specific music or videos either by using the Search iTunes Store box or by clicking the Power Search link (in the Quick Links box on the right of the home page) and using the Power Search page to specify multiple criteria. Figure 7-6 shows the Power Search page with some results found. You can sort the search results by a column heading by clicking it. Click the column heading again to reverse the sort order.

Choose Between DRM-Protected and DRM-Free Versions

For some songs and videos, you can choose between the DRM-protected version and the DRM-free version, which is called iTunes Plus. When this choice is available, iTunes displays a note saying "Also available in iTunes Plus," as shown here. Click the Learn More link, and then click the iTunes Plus button on the resulting page.

FIGURE 7-5 Use the Browse feature to browse through the iTunes Store's offerings.

iTunes prompts you to set your iTunes Plus Preference, as shown here. (You will also see this dialog box if you try to access an iTunes Plus song without clicking a Learn More link.) Click the iTunes Plus button if you want to buy the DRM-free songs whenever they are available. If you have not already signed in, iTunes then prompts you to sign in.

NOTE *The first time you change your iTunes Plus setting, you must agree to revised Terms and Conditions.*

FIGURE 7-6 Use the Power Search feature to search for songs by song title, artist, album, genre, and composer.

Preview Songs and Videos

One of the most attractive features of the iTunes Store is that it lets you preview a song or video before you buy it. This feature helps you ensure both that you've found the right song or video and that you like it.

For some songs, the previews are of the first 30 seconds. For most songs, the previews feature one of the most distinctive parts of the song (for example, the chorus or a catchy line). For videos, the previews are 20 seconds of the most identifiable highlights.

A typical download of a 30-second audio clip involves around 600KB of data; 20 seconds of video takes considerably more. If you have a slow Internet connection, downloading the previews will take a while. It's best to select the Load Complete Preview Before Playing check box on the Store tab of the iTunes dialog box or the Preferences dialog box.

Double-click a song's or video's listing to start the preview playing (or downloading, if you choose to load complete previews before playing).

How to ... **Turn iTunes Plus Off Again**

If you decide that iTunes Plus doesn't suit you, follow these steps to turn it off:

1. Click the Account link in the Quick Links box on the right side of the home page. iTunes prompts you for your password.

2. Enter the password. iTunes then displays the Apple Account Information page.

3. At the top of the page, the iTunes Plus readout shows Enabled or Disabled. To change your preference, click the Manage iTunes Plus button. iTunes displays the iTunes Plus screen, as shown here.

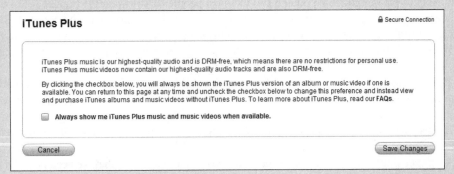

4. Clear the Always Show Me iTunes Plus Music And Music Videos When Available check box.

5. Click the Save Changes button. iTunes returns you to the Apple Account Information page.

6. Click the Home button to return to the iTunes Store home page.

Understand A******s, "Explicit," and "Clean"

The iTunes Store censors supposedly offensive words to help minimize offense:

■   Songs or videos deemed to have potentially offensive lyrics are marked EXPLICIT in the Song Name column. Where a sanitized version is available, it's marked CLEAN in the Name column. Some of the supposedly explicit items contain words no more offensive than "love." Some supposedly explicit songs are instrumentals.

- Strangely, other songs and videos that contain words that are offensive to most people aren't flagged as being explicit. So if you worry about what you and yours hear, don't trust the iTunes Store ratings too far.

- Any word deemed offensive is censored with asterisks (**), at least in theory. (In practice, some words sneak through.) When searching, use the real word rather than censoring it yourself.

Request Songs or Other Items You Can't Find

Five million songs sounds like an impressive number, but it's a mere cupful in the bucket of all the songs that have ever been recorded (and that music enthusiasts would like to buy). As a result, the iTunes Store's selection of music pleases some users more than others. Not surprisingly, Apple and the record companies seem to be concentrating first on the songs that are most likely to please (and to be bought by) the most people. If you want the biggest hits—either the latest ones or longtime favorites—chances are that the iTunes Store has you covered. But if your tastes run to the esoteric, you may not find the songs you're looking for in the iTunes Store.

If you can't find a song or other item you're looking for in the iTunes Store, you can submit a request for it. If a search produces no results, the iTunes Store offers you a Request link that you can click to display the Request Music form for requesting music by song name, artist name, album, composer, or genre. Despite the form's name, you can also use it to request other items, such as videos or audiobooks.

Beyond the immediate thank-you-for-your-input screen that the iTunes Store displays, requesting songs feels unrewarding at present. Apple doesn't respond directly to requests, so unless you keep checking for the items you've requested, you won't know that they've been posted. Nor will you learn if the items will ever be made available. Besides, given the complexities involved in licensing songs, it seems highly unlikely that Apple will make special efforts to license any particular song unless a truly phenomenal number of people request it. Instead, Apple seems likely to continue doing what makes much more sense—licensing as many songs as possible that are as certain as possible to appeal to plenty of people.

Navigate the iTunes Store

To navigate from page to page in the iTunes Store, click the buttons in the toolbar. Alternatively, use these keyboard shortcuts:

- In Windows, press CTRL-[to return to the previous page and CTRL-] to go to the next page.

- On the Mac, press ⌘-[to return to the previous page and ⌘-] to go to the next page.

Buy a Song or Video from the iTunes Store

To buy a song from the iTunes Store, simply click the Buy Song button. To buy a video, click the Buy Video button.

If you're not currently signed in, iTunes displays the Sign In To Download Music From The iTunes Store dialog box, as shown here.

Type your ID and password. Select the Remember Password For Purchasing check box if you want iTunes to remember your password so that you don't need to enter it in future. Then click the Buy button. iTunes then displays a confirmation message box like this:

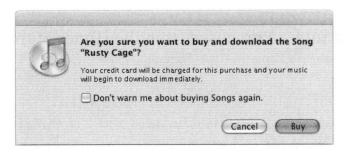

Click the Buy button to make the purchase. Select the Don't Warn Me About Buying Songs Again check box if appropriate. Some people prefer to have this double-check in place to slow down the pace at which they assault their credit cards. For others, even having to confirm the purchase is an annoyance.

iTunes then downloads the song or video to your library and adds an entry for it to your Purchased playlist.

Listen to Songs or Watch Videos You've Purchased

When you download a song or video from the iTunes Store, iTunes adds it to the playlist named Purchased in the Source pane. When you display the Purchased playlist, iTunes automatically displays a message box to explain what the playlist is. Select the Do Not Show This Message Again check box before dismissing this message box, because otherwise it will soon endanger your sanity.

The Purchased playlist is there to provide a quick-and-easy way to get to all the items you buy. Otherwise, if you purchase items on impulse without keeping a list, the songs might vanish into your huge media library.

To delete the entry for an item in the Purchased playlist, right-click it, choose Clear from the shortcut menu, and click the Yes button in the confirmation message box. However, unlike for regular song and video files, iTunes doesn't offer you the opportunity to delete the file itself—the file remains in your library on the basis that, having paid for it, you don't actually want to delete it.

You can drag items that you haven't purchased to the Purchased playlist as well.

Restart a Failed Download

If a download fails, you may see an error message that invites you to try again later. If this happens, iTunes terminates the download but doesn't roll back the purchase.

To restart a failed download, choose Store | Check For Purchases. Type your password in the Enter Account Name And Password dialog box, and then click the Check button. iTunes attempts to restart the failed download.

Review What You've Purchased from the iTunes Store

To see what you've purchased from the iTunes Store, follow these steps:

1. Click the Account button (the button that displays your account name) and then enter your password to display the Apple Account Information window.

2. Click the Purchase History button to display details of the items you've purchased.

3. Click the arrow to the left of an order date to display details of the purchases on that date.

4. Click the Done button when you've finished examining your purchases. iTunes returns you to your Apple Account Information page.

Authorize and Deauthorize Computers for the iTunes Store

As mentioned earlier in this chapter, when you buy an item from the iTunes Store, you're allowed to play it on up to five different computers or devices at a time. iTunes implements this limitation through a form of license that Apple calls *authorization*. iTunes tracks which computers are authorized to play items you've purchased and stops you from playing the items when you're out of authorizations.

If you want to play items you've purchased on another computer, you need to *deauthorize* one of the authorized computers so as to free up an authorization for use on the extra computer. You may also need to specifically deauthorize a computer to prevent it from playing the items you've bought. For example, if you sell or give away your Mac, you'd probably want to deauthorize it. You might also need to deauthorize a computer if you're planning to rebuild it.

NOTE   *Your computer must be connected to the Internet to authorize and deauthorize computers.*

Authorize a Computer to Use the iTunes Store

To authorize a computer, simply try to play an item purchased from the iTunes Store. For example, access a shared computer's Purchased playlist and double-click one of the songs. iTunes displays the Authorize Computer dialog box:

Enter your Apple ID and password and then click the Authorize button. iTunes accesses the iTunes Store and (all being well) authorizes the computer. iTunes starts playing the item and displays the Machine Authorization Was Successful dialog box, as shown here. Click the OK button.

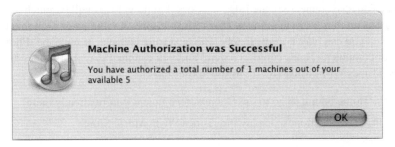

Deauthorize a Computer from Using the iTunes Store

To deauthorize a computer so that it can no longer play the items you've purchased from the iTunes Store, follow these steps:

1. Choose Store | Deauthorize Computer to display the Deauthorize Computer dialog box, shown here.

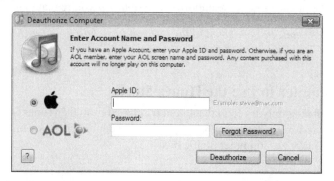

2. Type your Apple ID and password, and then click the Deauthorize button. iTunes deauthorizes the computer and displays a message box to tell you it has done so, as shown here.

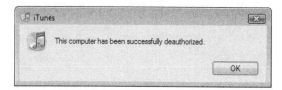

Buy Music from the iTunes Wi-Fi Music Store

If you have an iPhone or an iPod touch, you can buy songs and albums over the air from the iTunes Wi-Fi Music Store. With either device, you can connect to the iTunes Wi-Fi Music Store via a wireless network—for example, your home wireless network or a wireless hotspot. With the iPhone, you can also connect via the Edge network, but downloads will be much slower.

When you buy an item from the iTunes Wi-Fi Music Store, the iPhone or iPod touch downloads it, and you can play it immediately. The next time you synchronize the iPhone or iPod touch with your computer, iTunes copies the item, and you can then play it in iTunes as well.

To use the iTunes Wi-Fi Music Store, follow these steps:

1. Press the Home button to go to the Home screen unless you're already there.

2. Touch the iTunes button to display the iTunes Wi-Fi Music Store.

How to ... # Deauthorize a Computer You Can't Currently Access

The procedure you've just seen for deauthorizing a computer is easy—but you must be able to access the computer. If you've already parted with the computer, or if the computer has stopped working, this gives you a problem. The solution is to deauthorize *all* your computers at once, and then reauthorize those you want to be able to use.

To deauthorize all your computers, follow these steps:

1. Click the Account button (the button that displays your account name) and then enter your password to display the Apple Account Information window.

2. Click the Deauthorize All button. iTunes displays a confirmation dialog box, as shown here.

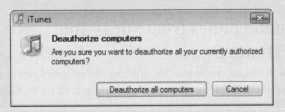

3. Click the Deauthorize All Computers button. iTunes deauthorizes all the computers, and then displays a message box to let you know it has done so.

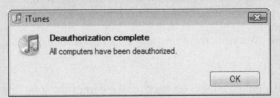

4. Click the OK button, and then click the Home button to return to the iTunes Store home screen.

3. Touch the buttons onscreen to navigate to the song or item you want. For example:

   ■ Touch the Featured button to view the songs that the iTunes Wi-Fi Music Store is featuring.

   ■ Touch the Top Tens button to display a list of Top Tens in different categories—for example, Pop, Alternative, or Rock. Touch the Top Ten item you want to view.

- To search, touch the Search button, touch the Search box to bring up the onscreen keyboard, and then type your search term. The iTunes Wi-Fi Music Store searches as you type, so you usually needn't touch the Search button to start the search.

- Touch one of the buttons at the top of the screen, such as New Releases, What's Hot, or Genres, to display a list of songs.

4. When you've found a song or item you're interested in, touch a song to start playing its preview. If what starts playing is unbearable, touch the Stop button at the left of the item's listing to end the torment.

5. To buy a song or other item, touch its price. The price changes to a Buy Now button.

6. Touch the Buy Now button. The iTunes Wi-Fi Music Store adds the song to your Downloads list and prompts you for your password.

7. Type the password, and then touch the OK button. iTunes starts downloading the song.

8. To see the progress of your downloads, touch the Downloads button.

Create iPhone Ringtones from Songs You Buy from the iTunes Store

If you have an iPhone, you can create custom ringtones from songs you purchase from the iTunes Store that have the ringtone mark (a bell symbol) next to them. Each ringtone costs an additional $0.99.

To create a ringtone, follow these steps:

1. In iTunes, right-click the song, and these choose Create Ringtone from the context menu. iTunes displays the Ringtone controls (see Figure 7-7).

NOTE   *At this writing, you can create ring tones only from songs you buy from the U.S. iTunes Store.*

2. Drag the blue highlighted section to cover the part of the song that you want to turn into the ringtone.

3. Click the Preview button to hear what you've selected. The ringtone loops, so you can take your time. If necessary, reposition the blue highlighted section. Also if necessary, click the Stop button to stop the music.

4. You can lengthen or shorten the selection by positioning the mouse pointer over the starting or ending line so that it turns into a two-headed arrow, and then clicking and dragging.

5. If you want the ringtone to start with a bang rather than fading in, clear the Fade In check box at the beginning of the blue highlighted section. Similarly, if you don't want the ringtone to fade out, clear the Fade Out check box at the end of the blue highlighted section.

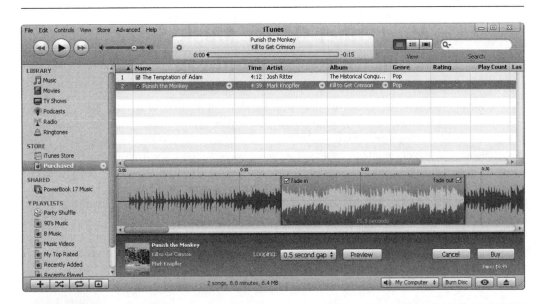

FIGURE 7-7   Use the Ringtone controls to create a custom ringtone from a song you've
purchased from the iTunes Store.

6. In the Looping drop-down list, choose the length of gap you want between each loop of
   the ringtone (assuming you don't answer the call). You can choose a gap of 0.5 seconds,
   1 second, 2 seconds, 3 seconds, 4 seconds, or 5 seconds.

7. When you've arranged the ringtone to your liking, click the Buy button.

Buy Music from Other Online Music Stores

If you use an iPod or iPhone, the iTunes Store is the best of the large online music stores,
because it sells songs in a format that the device can play, whereas most other online music
stores use incompatible formats (such as WMA). But you may want to use other online music
stores for a couple of reasons:

- Some sell songs that the iTunes Store doesn't have.
- Some offer subscription pricing that lets you download and listen to as much music as
  you want for a monthly fee.
- Some sell music in formats that the iPod or iPhone can play—and even without DRM
  restrictions on what you can do with the songs.

This section discusses some of the main online music stores at this writing, starting with the
one that is most likely to be of interest to iPod or iPhone owners—eMusic.

Did you know?

Most Other Online Music Stores Work Only with Windows

Most of the online music services work only with Windows at the time of writing. To complicate things still more for anyone using an iPod or iPhone, most of the online music services use WMA files protected with DRM for their songs. Some services are also tied to specific hardware players, some to their own software players, and some to Windows Media Player.

To use protected WMA files with an iPod or iPhone, you must burn them to CD, and then rip and encode the CD to AAC files or MP3 files. You could also use Apple Lossless Encoding, but because the WMA files are lower quality than Apple Lossless Encoding, doing so makes little sense.

Most of the online music services permit you to burn songs to CD, but creating further copies of the songs could be interpreted to be against the terms and conditions of some services.

eMusic

eMusic (www.emusic.com) offers more than two million songs for download—and the songs are in the unprotected MP3 format, so you can use them freely in iTunes, on an iPod or iPhone, or on almost any other music player.

eMusic offers various pricing plans, including yearly subscriptions. Each plan has a free 14-day trial, but you must provide valid credit card details. You download the songs using eMusic's software.

Amie Street

Amie Street (http://amiestreet.com) is a website that offers DRM-free songs with two twists. First, members who are artists can sell their songs via Amie Street—no record deal needed. Second, a song's price varies depending on its popularity: It starts off being free, and the price increases (up to a maximum of 98 cents) as it becomes more popular.

Amazon.com

Amazon.com (www.amazon.com) launched a public beta of a digital music download store in September 2007. The songs are in the MP3 format, and most are encoded at the 256 Kbps bitrate. Most songs cost 99 cents apiece.

At this writing, you can download an individual song directly to your computer (and then add it to iTunes manually), but you need to use Amazon's custom download program to download a full album. This program automatically adds the songs you've bought to your iTunes library.

Napster 2.0

Napster 2.0 (www.napster.com) offers more than three million songs at this writing. Napster 2.0 has nothing to do with the pioneering file-sharing application Napster except the name and logo. Napster uses the WMA format protected with DRM and works only on the PC—there is no Mac client at this writing.

A standard Napster subscription allows you to download as much music as you want to your PC, where you can play it as often as you like using the Napster player. You can use up to three PCs for the same Napster account, but the terms and conditions specify that the account is for one person only, so you're not allowed to share it with your friends. If you discontinue your subscription, you lose access to all songs you've downloaded except for those you've bought.

If you want to burn a song to CD, you must pay; you must also pay if you want to transfer the song to a music player that supports WMA DRM.

Even if you pay, you can't transfer songs to an iPod or iPhone. You can put songs on the iPod or iPhone in only two ways:

- Buy the songs, burn them to CD, and then rip the CD to a format that the iPod or iPhone can play (for example, use iTunes to rip the CD to AAC files).

- Use an audio-grabbing utility (such as Total Recorder, discussed in Chapter 6) that captures the audio stream from the PC's sound card, or route the output from your sound card to an input that you can capture with a conventional audio application (such as Sound Recorder). These maneuvers are against the Napster terms and conditions and are illegal in most circumstances.

The Napster To Go service enables you to transfer as many songs as you want to a portable player that supports Windows Media Player 10 DRM. (The Napster website lists supported players.)

Napster's restrictions may appear to be onerous, but Napster can be a great way to listen to a wide variety of music for a fixed fee. Being able to "try before you buy" takes the gamble out of buying CDs (or individual songs) that you're not sure you'll like.

NOTE   *Napster has been marketing its services aggressively to colleges and universities, which pay reduced fees for providing Napster access to all their students. Mac users are out of luck.*

RealPlayer Music Store and Real Rhapsody

The RealPlayer Music Store (www.real.com/musicstore/) provides 192 Kbps AAC files, which give very high audio quality. To access the RealPlayer Music Store, you must use RealPlayer 10, which is free and runs on Windows and Mac OS X. You can burn songs to CD and download them to some players, including iPods and iPhones.

Real Rhapsody is a service that provides unlimited streaming access to more than two million songs. You can buy songs and put them on a variety of devices, but not on the iPod or iPhone. Like Napster, Rhapsody provides a good way to listen to a wide variety of music for a fixed fee.

Walmart.com

Wal-Mart's website (www.walmart.com) includes a Music Downloads section that offers songs and albums. Songs from Walmart.com come as protected WMA files and work only with Windows Media Player and hardware players that Windows Media Player supports. You can use either Windows Media Player or Internet Explorer to buy and download music.

With an easy-to-use interface, 500,000 songs available, and low prices, Walmart.com is an attractive option for anyone using Windows Media Player. For iTunes and iPod or iPhone users, Walmart.com has little appeal. You can put songs on the iPod or iPhone in only two ways:

- Buy the songs, burn them to CD, and then rip the CD to a format that the iPod or iPhone can play (for example, use iTunes to rip the CD to AAC files).

- Use an audio-grabbing utility (such as Total Recorder, discussed in Chapter 6) that captures the audio stream from the PC's sound card, or route the output from your sound card to an input that you can capture with a conventional audio application (such as Sound Recorder). These maneuvers are against the Walmart.com terms and conditions and are illegal in most circumstances.

Yahoo! Music Jukebox

Yahoo! Music (http://music.yahoo.com) offers more than two million songs that you can access via the Yahoo! Music Unlimited subscription service. You can buy a yearly subscription or pay each month. Either way, you must pay extra for any songs you burn to CD.

Yahoo! Music Unlimited lets you transfer the music to a supported portable device without extra charge, so it offers great value for anyone with one of these devices, which include various model of Dell DJ, RCA Lycra, iRiver players, and the Creative Labs Zen Portable Media Player and the Samsung YH-999 Portable Media Center. Unfortunately, Yahoo! Music Unlimited doesn't support the iPod or iPhone directly from its subscription, although you can use the Yahoo! Music Engine to transfer songs that you have bought from the service to an iPod or iPhone.

Wippit

Wippit (www.wippit.com) uses a P2P network to provide a variety of tracks for download in a mixture of unprotected MP3 and protected WMA formats. Wippit lets you buy individual songs but favors a subscription model for access to its music: for a yearly fee, you get all-you-can-eat access to Wippit's catalog.

Wippit's unprotected MP3 files work in iTunes and on the iPod, whereas the protected WMA files need to be either burned and reripped or captured, like the protected WMA files discussed earlier in this chapter.

Russian MP3 Download Sites

You can also find high-quality MP3 files—without DRM—for download on sites hosted in Russia and other former Eastern Bloc countries. These sites typically offer a wide selection of music at very low prices.

At this writing, the legal position of these sites is not clear. While these sites insist they are operating legally, most Western legal experts disagree. Music industry bodies, such as the RIAA, are actively trying to close these sites down.

Find Free Songs Online

Beyond the iTunes Store and the other online music stores discussed so far in this chapter, you'll find many sources of free music online. Some of this free music is legal, but much of it is illegal.

Find Free Songs on the Online Music Stores

Most of the major online music stores provide some free songs, usually to promote either up-and-coming artists or major releases from established artists. For example, the iTunes Store provides a single for free download each week. The stores typically make you create an account before you can download such free songs as they're offering.

Find Free Songs for Legal Download

Sadly, many of the sites that provided free songs in the early days of the Internet have closed down. However, the Internet still contains some sources of songs that are distributed for free by the artists who created them. Usually, the best way to discover these sites is to visit an artist's own website or an independent site such as GarageBand.com (www.garageband.com).

> **TIP** *If you're always looking for new music recommendations, try The Filter (www.thefilter .com). The website has a tool that lets you choose your three favorite artists and generate a playlist of music you might like. If you like the results, you can download a program that lets you create playlists on your computer and transfer them to an iPod or iPhone. Sites such as Pandora (www.pandora.com) and Musicovery (www.musicovery .com) also provide interesting recommendations.*

Find Free Songs for Illegal Download

Beyond the legal offerings of the online music stores and the free (and legal) sites, you can find pretty much any song for illegal download on the Internet. Finding a song that you can't find anywhere else can be wonderful, and getting the song for free is even more so. But before you download music illegally, you should be aware of possible repercussions to your computer, your wallet, and even your future.

Threats to Your Computer

Downloading files illegally may pose several threats to your computer:

- Many companies that produce P2P software include other applications with their products. Some of these applications are shareware and can be tolerably useful; others are adware that are useless and an irritant; still others are spyware that report users' sharing and downloading habits.

TIP *To detect and remove spyware from your computer, use an application such as the free Ad-aware from LavaSoft (www.lavasoft.de) or Spybot Search & Destroy (www.safer-networking.org/; make sure you use the hyphen in the name, as there is also a www.safernetworking.org site).*

■ Many of the files shared on P2P networks contain only the songs they claim to contain. Others are fake files provided by companies working for the RIAA and the record companies to "poison" the P2P networks and discourage people from downloading files by wasting their time.

■ Other files *are* songs but also harbor a virus, worm, or Trojan horse. Even apparently harmless files can have a sting in the tail. For example, the tags in music files can contain URLs to which your player's browser component automatically connects. The site can then run a script on your computer, doing anything from opening some irritating advertisement windows, to harvesting any sensitive information it can locate, to deleting vital files or destroying the firmware on your computer.

TIP *Whether you're downloading songs illegally or not, use virus-checking software to scan all incoming files to your computer, no matter whom they come from—friends, family, coworkers, or the Internet.*

Threats to Your Wallet, Your ID, and Your Future

Even if your computer remains in rude health, downloading files illegally poses several threats. Unless you use a service (such as Anonymizer, www.anonymizer.com) that masks your computer's IP address, any action that you take on the Internet can be tracked back to your computer.

Sharing digital files of other people's copyrighted content without permission is illegal. So is receiving such illegal files. The No Electronic Theft Act (NET Act) of 1997 and the Digital Millennium Copyright Act (DMCA) of 1998 provide savage penalties for people caught distributing copyrighted materials illegally. Under the DMCA, you can face fines of up to $500,000 and five years' imprisonment for a first offense, and double those for a second offense.

P2P networks also expose users to social-engineering attacks through the chat features that most P2P tools include. However friendly other users are, and however attractive the files they provide, it can be a severe mistake to divulge personal information. A favored gambit of malefactors is to provide a quantity of "good" (malware-free) files followed by one or more files that include a Trojan horse or keystroke logger to capture sensitive information from your computer.

Find P2P Software

At this writing, there are various P2P networks, some of which interoperate with each other. However, for legal reasons, P2P networks frequently change their nature or close.

To find up-to-date information on P2P software, consult a resource such as Wikipedia (http://en.wikipedia.org/wiki/Main_Page; see the "peer-to-peer file sharing" entry) or a search engine.

Chapter 8

Burn CDs and DVDs from iTunes

How to...

- Understand why you should burn your iTunes Store purchases to CD or DVD
- Understand the basics of burning CDs and DVDs
- Configure iTunes for burning CDs and DVDs
- Burn CDs and DVDs
- Print CD covers and playlist listings
- Troubleshoot the problems you run into when burning CDs

iTunes makes it as easy as possible to burn playlists to CD, enabling you to create either regular audio CDs that will work in any CD player or MP3 CDs that will work only in MP3-capable CD players. You can also burn a playlist to a data CD or data DVD for backup or portability—for example, to back up your library. Such data DVDs work in computer DVD drives but not in commercial DVD players. However, because each DVD can store around 150 CDs' worth of audio compressed at 128 Kbps, they're great for backup.

Burning with iTunes works in the same way in Windows and on the Mac, so this chapter discusses both operating systems together, showing some screens from each. The chapter starts by quickly running through the basics of burning. You'll then learn how to choose suitable settings for burning, how to burn CDs and DVDs, and how to print covers and playlist listings for the discs. You'll also learn how to minimize avoidable problems and how to troubleshoot common problems you may run into.

Why Burn Song Files to CD or DVD?

Typically, you'll want to burn song files to CD or DVD for one of three reasons:

- You want to create an audio CD that will play either on a regular CD player or on a computer. An *audio CD* is a CD that contains uncompressed audio: up to 74 minutes for a 650MB CD, 80 minutes for a 700MB CD, and 90 minutes for an 800MB CD.

NOTE   *You can play audio CDs on CD players (for example, a boom box or a hi-fi component) as well as on CD drives. Audio CDs created on recordable CDs are compatible with all CD players and with most (but not all) DVD players.*

- You want to create an MP3 CD that will play on a computer or on a CD player that can handle MP3 CDs. MP3 CDs can store far more music than audio CDs. For example, if you encode your MP3 files at 128 Kbps, you can fit about 12 hours of music on a CD. The disadvantages are that most CD players can't play MP3 CDs, and you can't burn protected AAC files to an MP3 CD—at least, not without burning them to an audio CD, ripping the CD to MP3 files, and then burning those files to the CD.

NOTE *An MP3 CD can contain only MP3 files—not AAC, Apple Lossless Encoding, WAV, or AIFF files. If you've encoded your entire CD collection to AAC files, you won't be able to burn them to MP3 CDs without reencoding them. Because iTunes doesn't distinguish visibly among music file types in your library and in playlists, it's easy to trip up on this limitation: You happily queue a hundred or so files for burning to an MP3 CD, but iTunes burns only 20 or so files to the CD, because the rest are in AAC or other non-MP3 formats.*

- You want to back up part of your library to CD or DVD to protect it against loss. For example, you'll probably want to back up your Purchased playlist to CD or DVD, because if you lose those items, you'll need to buy them again. A backup disc is called a *data CD* or *data DVD*. Data discs won't play on most audio CD players, regular DVD players, or even most MP3-capable CD players; essentially, data discs are for computers only, but the occasional sophisticated CD player or DVD player may also be able to handle them.

NOTE *The iTunes Store terms of service specifically forbid you to burn videos purchased from the Store to disc—but iTunes does not prevent you from doing so. Given that you cannot download videos again if your computer loses them (for example, because it has a hard disk problem), making backups seems only prudent.*

Understand the Basics of Burning CDs and DVDs

At this writing, most new PCs and all new Macs sold include CD burners. Many also include DVD burners or drives that burn both DVDs and CDs.

To burn CDs with iTunes, your computer must have a CD burner or DVD burner. If your computer has a CD burner, it can be either a CD recorder (CD-R) drive or a CD rewriter (CD-RW) drive. Similarly, a DVD burner can be either a DVD recorder (DVD-R) or DVD rewriter (DVD-RW).

NOTE *A CD-R burner can burn only CD-recordable discs—discs that can be burned only one time. A CD-RW burner can burn both CD-recordable discs and CD-rewritable discs; the latter can be burned, erased, and burned again multiple times. Similarly, DVD-R discs can be burned only once, but DVD-RW discs can be rewritten multiple times.*

If your computer doesn't have a burner, you can add a compatible internal CD-R or CD-RW drive (to most desktop PCs, a PowerMac, or a Mac Pro) or a compatible external USB or FireWire CD-R or CD-RW drive (to any desktop or laptop PC or Mac).

TIP *Before buying a burner for a Mac, consult the Apple Support website (www.apple.com/ support/) for the latest list of compatible drives.*

To burn DVDs (either DVD-R discs or DVD-RW discs), your PC must have a DVD burner that's compatible with iTunes. Your Mac must have either an internal SuperDrive or another compatible DVD burner, and it must be running Mac OS X 10.2.4 or later.

NOTE *You can burn a playlist to a DVD-R disc or a DVD-RW disc, but not to a DVD-Audio disc.*

Burn CDs and DVDs

iTunes makes the process of burning CDs and DVDs straightforward. You can burn only a playlist to CD or DVD; you can't burn any other subdivision of your library, such as an album or an artist's entire works, unless you add it to a custom playlist. That means you need to arrange your music files into suitable playlists before attempting to burn them to CD or DVD.

Typically, you'll want to start by choosing burning options, as described first in this section. Then you'll be ready to burn a disc, as described second.

Choose Burning Options

iTunes keeps its options for burning discs on the Burning subtab of the Advanced tab in the iTunes dialog box or the Preferences dialog box.

Display the Burning Subtab

To choose burning options for iTunes, display the iTunes dialog box or the Preferences dialog box:

- In Windows, choose Edit | Preferences or press CTRL-COMMA or CTRL-Y to display the iTunes dialog box.

- On the Mac, choose iTunes | Preferences or press ⌘-COMMA or ⌘-Y to display the Preferences dialog box.

Click the Advanced tab, and then click the Burning subtab to display its contents. Figure 8-1 shows the Burning subtab for iTunes on the Mac. The Burning subtab for iTunes on Windows has the same controls.

Once you've displayed the Burning subtab, look at the CD Burner label or list. If your computer has two or more CD or DVD burners, this item appears as a list, so you need to make sure iTunes has chosen the right burner; if not, change it. If you have only one burner, this item appears as a label that you can't change, but you should verify that iTunes has recognized the burner. If you see the label No Supported Disc Burners Found, iTunes has either not recognized your burner or your burner is not compatible with iTunes.

Choose the Burning Speed You Want

Next, set the burning speed you want in the Preferred Speed drop-down list. You'll probably want to start with the Maximum Possible speed, which burns discs at the fastest speed that iTunes and the drive can manage.

If you don't get good results from the maximum possible speed, reduce the speed by choosing one of the other settings in the list. (See the section "Balance Quality, Speed, and Cost," later in this chapter, for further advice.) Test the setting and reduce the speed further if necessary.

NOTE   *The speeds shown in the Preferred Speed drop-down list are CD-rotation speeds, not DVD-rotation speeds, which are substantially slower.*

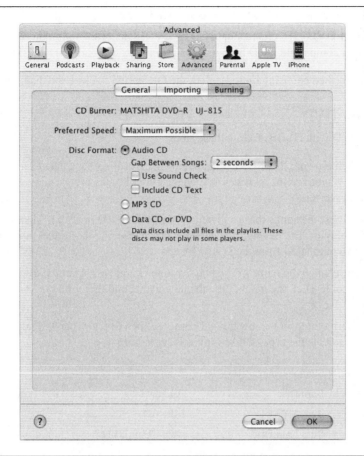

FIGURE 8-1 On the Burning subtab of the iTunes dialog box or the Preferences dialog box, configure options for burning CDs and DVDs.

Choose the Disc Format

The most important choice on the Burning subtab is which type of disc you want to create:

- **Audio CD**   Select this option button to create an audio CD. (This option button may be selected already.) Use the Gap Between Songs drop-down list to specify whether to include a gap between the tracks on the CD (you can choose from one second to five seconds; the default is two seconds) or not (choose None). Select the Use Sound Check check box to make iTunes use Sound Check to normalize the volume on the tracks. Using Sound Check should produce CDs with much more consistent volume across their tracks than CDs created without Sound Check.

- ■ **MP3 CD**   To create an MP3 CD, select the MP3 CD option button.
- ■ **Data CD Or DVD**   To create a data CD or DVD, select this option button. (If you don't have a compatible DVD burner, this option button is named Data CD.)

When you've finished choosing options, click the OK button to close the dialog box.

Burn a CD or DVD

To burn a CD or DVD with iTunes, follow these steps:

1. Decide which type of CD or DVD—an audio CD, an MP3 CD, a data CD, or a data DVD—you want to create. If necessary, change your iTunes preferences as discussed in the previous section.

2. Add to a playlist the songs that you want to have on the CD or DVD. Alternatively, open an existing playlist. For example, select your Purchased playlist so that you can burn the items you've purchased from the iTunes Store.

3. If necessary, change the name of the playlist to the name you want the disc to have. To do so, double-click the name, type the new name, and then press ENTER (Windows) or RETURN (Mac).

4. Click the Burn button in the lower-right corner of the iTunes window. The button's name changes to indicate the type of disc iTunes is set to burn:

Button Name	Disc Type
Burn Disc	Audio CD
Burn MP3 CD	MP3 CD
Burn Data Disc	Data CD or DVD

5. When iTunes prompts you to insert a blank disc, do so. (If you take too long inserting the disc, iTunes decides you don't really want to burn a disc and stops flashing the message at you.)

6. If the playlist you've chosen is too long to fit on the type of disc you've inserted in the format set in the Preferences dialog box or the iTunes dialog box, iTunes warns you and asks what you want to do:

   - ■ If your Burning preferences are set to create an audio CD, and the playlist you've chosen is too long, iTunes lets you choose whether to split the playlist across multiple CDs, as shown here. Click the Audio CDs button to split the playlist across as many CDs as necessary. Click the Cancel button if you want to fix the problem yourself.

How to ... Start Burning a Disc When You Haven't Selected a Playlist

If you insert a blank recordable disc in your burner before clicking the Burn button in iTunes, Mac OS X may display a dialog box inviting you to choose what to do with the disc, as shown here.

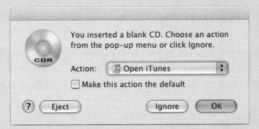

Choose the Open iTunes item in the Action drop-down list. Select the Make This Action The Default check box if you always want to launch iTunes when you insert a blank disc. Then click the OK button to close the dialog box. iTunes displays a dialog box explaining the basics of burning, as shown here.

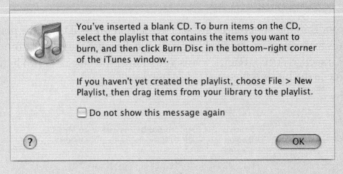

Select the Do Not Show This Message Again check box, and then click the OK button.

For example, you might slim down the playlist so that it will fit on a single CD, or you might change your burning preferences to burn a different type of CD.

- If your Burning preferences are set to create an MP3 CD, and the playlist you've chosen is too long, iTunes warns you that some of the tracks won't fit, and lets you choose whether to proceed, as shown here. Click the MP3 CD button if you want to go ahead.

- If your Burning preferences are set to create an MP3 CD, and the playlist contains songs that cannot be included (for example, because they're in a format other than MP3, such as AAC), iTunes warns you of the problem, as shown here. Click the arrow in the lower-left corner to see the details.

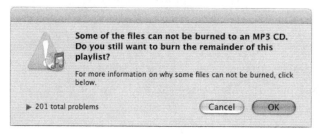

- If your Burning preferences are set to create a data disc, and the playlist you've chosen is too long, iTunes lets you choose whether to split the playlist across multiple discs, as shown here. Click the Data Discs button to have iTunes split the playlist automatically, or click the Cancel button if you want to change the playlist or the type of disc you're burning.

TIP *When you cancel a burn like this, you'll need to eject the unburned disc manually. If your drive has an Eject button, press it to eject the disc. If not, in Windows, choose Start | My Computer to display a My Computer window. Right-click the drive letter that represents the burner and then choose Eject from the shortcut menu to eject the disc. On the Mac, quit iTunes to force Mac OS X to eject the disc.*

■ If the playlist contains a video file, and you've set iTunes to create an audio CD or an MP3 CD, iTunes warns you that there is a problem. Click the Cancel button in the message box, open the iTunes dialog box or the Preferences dialog box, click the Advanced tab, click the Burning subtab, select the Data CD Or DVD button (if you have a DVD burner) or the Data CD option button (if you don't), click the OK button, and then restart the burn.

7. Click the Burn button to start burning the disc.

8. When iTunes has finished burning the disc, or the last disc, it plays a notification sound. Eject the disc by right-clicking its entry in the Source pane and choosing Eject Disc from the shortcut menu. Then label the disc carefully, test it to make sure it's playable, and store it safely.

9. If you're burning multiple CDs, iTunes ejects each completed CD in turn and prompts you to insert a blank disc. Insert the disc and then click the Burn button when iTunes prompts you to do so.

Print CD Covers and Playlist Listings

Follow these steps to print a CD jewel case insert, a song listing, or an album listing:

1. Select the playlist for which you want to produce the item. (If you've just burned a playlist to disc, the playlist should still be selected.)

2. Choose File | Print to display the Print dialog box. Figure 8-2 shows the Mac version of the Print dialog box.

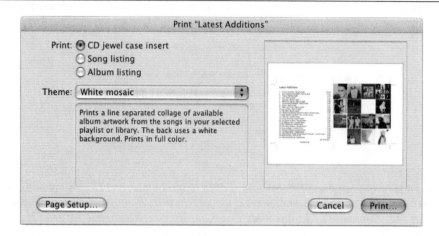

FIGURE 8-2   iTunes makes it easy to print out a CD jewel case insert, a song listing, or an album listing for a disc you've burned.

3. In the Print area, select the CD Jewel Case Insert option button, the Song Listing option button, or the Album Listing option button, as appropriate.

4. For a CD jewel case insert or a song listing, choose the theme you want in the Theme drop-down list. For example, choose Single Cover for a CD jewel case insert to create a single cover from one of the songs in the playlist, or choose Mosaic to create a cover that uses all the available art for the songs in the playlist.

5. Click the Print button to print the item you've chosen.

Troubleshoot Burning CDs and DVDs

Despite impressive progress in CD and DVD burning, many things can still go wrong, wasting your time, effort, and media. This section discusses how to avoid causing your burner problems and how to solve problems when they nonetheless occur.

Avoid Causing Your Burner Problems

First, avoid avoidable problems with burning CDs and DVDs. To do so, balance quality, speed, and cost sensibly; devote as many processor cycles as possible to the burning; make sure your computer has plenty of memory; and prevent your computer from going to sleep during a burn.

Balance Quality, Speed, and Cost

To get good results, you must select a sensible balance for the classic choice of quality, speed, and cost, in which you are allowed to choose any two of the three but not all three. For burning, this means considering the following:

- *Buy only high-quality recordable media.* Low-quality media isn't worth using: There's no upside to losing your data—at least, unless the Department of Justice is on your case. Expect to pay a market price for high-quality recordable media. If anyone offers you recordable media at bargain-basement prices, be duly suspicious. (Remember: once badly burnt, forever shy.)

- *In burning, speed is worthless without accuracy.* If your options are to record a CD at $60 \times$ with errors or $1 \times$ without errors, choose the $1 \times$ speed. Otherwise, your data will be useless.

- *If you're buying a burner, get a good one.* The latest, fastest, and most hyped drive probably costs much more than a more modest model—but delivers only a small speed increase. Look at the specs carefully. You may be able to save money by buying a slightly older drive that gives almost the same level of performance.

- *If you're buying a DVD burner for a Mac, your best bet is to buy an internal SuperDrive so that you can use it fully with the iLife applications.* If you must buy an external drive, double-check beforehand that it'll work with the relevant iLife applications.

> NOTE   *Different brands of recordable discs use different colors of dye: some green, some blue, some a faint shade of yellowy-brown. In theory, the color doesn't matter, although you'll hear some people claim that some colors are inferior to others—but in practice, it sometimes can make the difference between a burner being able to burn a disc or not, or between a player being able to play a disc back or not. So if you find your burner or player seems to prefer one color of recordable media to another, you're not necessarily imagining things. Stick with the brand and color that give best results. One other thing: Discs that are made in Japan seem generally to perform better than discs made elsewhere, even when the manufacturer is the same.*

Give the Burner as Many Processor Cycles as Possible

Windows Vista, Windows XP, and Mac OS X are multitasking operating systems in which you can have multiple applications working actively at the same time. But because burning CDs or DVDs is a processor-intensive activity, it's a good idea not to multitask actively while burning unless you've established that your PC or Mac can comfortably handle the demands of burning and of whatever other work you're doing.

To get the very best burning performance:

- Quit any applications you're no longer using.
- Reduce other tasks to a minimum. For example, don't run a video-processing task at the same time as you're burning a disc.
- Leave the burner as the foreground application (in other words, don't move the focus to another application window).
- Take your hands off the keyboard and mouse until the burn is complete.

Because the mouse can do so much in a graphical user interface, mouse-enabled operating systems squander many processor cycles on tracking exactly what the mouse is doing at any given moment if it's moving.

Get More Memory if You Don't Have Enough

Modern applications are memory hungry, modern operating systems doubly so. And burning CDs or DVDs is a demanding task.

Windows and Mac OS X run much better given plenty more RAM than the bare minimum they technically require. The following list shows the minimum RAM for Windows and Mac OS X versions, together with recommended RAM for better performance.

Operating System	Minimum RAM	Recommended RAM
Windows Vista	512MB	1GB or more
Windows XP	128MB	512MB or more
Mac OS X Tiger	256MB	1GB or more
Mac OS X Leopard	512MB	1GB or more

Prevent Your PC from Using Screen Savers or Powering Down During a Burn

Processor-intensive screen savers (in other words, most of the visually interesting screen savers) can cause problems with burns by diverting processor cycles from the burn at a critical moment. To avoid this, configure a long wait on your screen saver. Similarly, configure Windows so that it doesn't try to power down the computer during a burn.

In Windows Vista, follow these steps:

1. Right-click the Desktop and choose Personalize from the shortcut menu to display the Personalization window.

2. Click the Screen Saver link to display the Screen Saver Settings dialog box.

3. Either choose the None item in the Screen Saver drop-down list or increase the Wait setting to longer than the longest burn will take (for example, 90 minutes).

4. In the Power Management group box, click the Change Power Settings link to display the Power Options window, shown here.

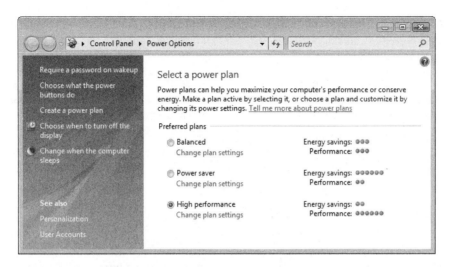

5. For best performance, select the High Performance option button.

NOTE   *Some computers include a manufacturer-recommended power plan that attempts to give a reasonable balance of performance and power saving. On most computers, the High Performance power plan is a better choice if you're burning many discs, even though it will cost you more power.*

6. Click the Change Plan Settings link under the High Performance option button to display the Edit Plan Settings window, shown here.

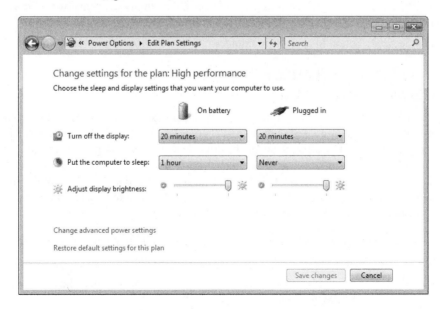

NOTE   *For a laptop computer, you can choose different settings in the On Battery column and the Plugged In column. Normally, it's best to have your computer plugged in while burning a disc, so you should adjust the Plugged In settings for burning.*

7. Choose a suitably long time in the Put The Computer To Sleep drop-down list. If you want to be able to view the progress of the burn without moving the mouse or pressing a key, set the same length of time in the Turn Off The Display drop-down list.

8. Click the Save Changes button to save the changes.

9. Click the Close button (the × button) to close the Power Options window.

In Windows XP, follow these steps:

1. Right-click the Desktop, and then choose Properties from the shortcut menu to display the Display Properties dialog box.

2. On the Screen Saver tab (shown on the left in Figure 8-3), increase the time shown in the Wait text box so it's far longer than even the slowest burn your burner will ever perform. (Better yet, choose None in the Screen Saver drop-down list to turn off your screen saver altogether.) Click the Apply button to apply your choices.

3. Click the Screen Saver tab's Power button to open the Power Options Properties dialog box, in which you can make adjustments to prevent your computer from going to sleep during a burn.

4. On the Power Schemes tab (shown on the right in Figure 8-3), specify suitably lengthy times (or choose the Never item) in the Turn Off Monitor, Turn Off Hard Disks, System Standby, and System Hibernates drop-down lists to prevent these events from occurring during a burn.

5. Click the Apply button to apply your choices.

Prevent Your Mac from Starting a Screen Saver or Going to Sleep During a Burn

Configure the sleep timing settings in the Energy Saver pane of System Preferences to ensure that neither your Mac nor its display goes to sleep during a burn. Even with modern burners, your Mac's going to sleep during a burn may cause errors on the disc. Having the display go to sleep during a burn shouldn't affect the burn in many cases, but in other cases it may—particularly if you press the wrong keys or buttons when reawakening the display. Unless you care to experiment with having your display go to sleep and checking the resulting discs, you may prefer to be safe than sorry.

To change your Mac's sleep timing settings, follow these steps:

1. Choose Apple | System Preferences to display the System Preferences window.

2. Click the Energy Saver item in the Hardware category to display the Energy Saver pane.

3. If the Energy Saver pane is in its small format, which hides the details, click the Show Details button to display the full pane (see Figure 8-4).

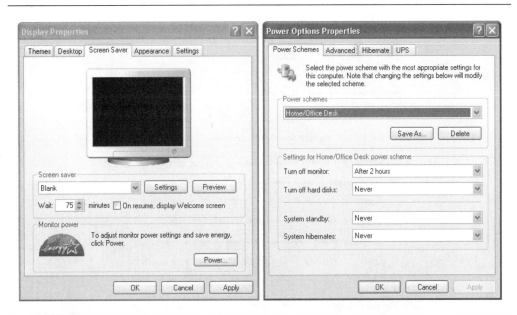

FIGURE 8-3   Configure your screen saver (left) and power schemes (right) to prevent interruptions to the burn.

4. For a desktop Mac, or for a 'Book running on the power adapter (rather than the battery), the easiest option is to choose the Automatic item in the Optimize Energy Settings drop-down list. This item puts the Mac to sleep after one hour of inactivity, which should be plenty long enough for burning any recordable CD—even at 2 × speed. For burning a full DVD with a slow burner, however, you may need to allow a longer period of inactivity. Alternatively, you may prefer the Highest Performance item, which prevents the Mac from ever going to sleep without your putting it to sleep manually.

5. For a 'Book running on battery power, you may find that the Automatic item in the Optimize Energy Settings drop-down list works okay for burning if your 'Book has a fast burner; the Automatic item puts the display to sleep after 9 minutes and the computer to sleep after 25 minutes. On older 'Books, or with a slow burner, you may find these sleep settings too aggressive for comfort. In this case, you can choose the Highest Performance item if you don't care about exhausting your batteries quickly. Or you can choose the Custom item and then choose custom settings as follows:

   ■ Drag the Put The Computer To Sleep When It Is Inactive For slider to a setting that will allow plenty of time for the burn to complete.

   ■ To configure a sleep setting for the display that is different from the setting for the computer, select the Put The Display To Sleep When The Computer Is Inactive For check box and drag the slider to a setting that will allow the burn to complete. For obvious reasons, you can't set a longer sleep delay for the display than for the computer.

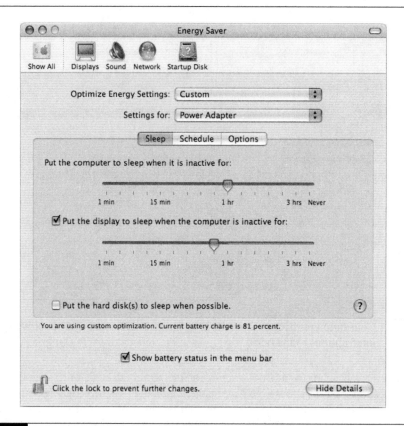

FIGURE 8-4   Configure the sleep timing settings in the Energy Saver pane of System
Preferences to prevent your Mac from going to sleep during a burn.

■ Select the Put The Hard Disk(s) To Sleep When Possible check box if you want Mac
OS X to shut down the hard disk whenever possible. Because the hard disk is used
extensively (though not quite continuously) during a burn, Mac OS X shouldn't try
to shut down the hard disk while the burn is happening.

TIP   *To prevent further changes to the Energy Saver configuration, click the lock icon at the
lower-left corner of the Energy Saver pane. This will prevent anyone from shortening
the sleep settings and throwing a monkey wrench into your burns. To unlock he Energy
Saver pane, click the lock icon again, and enter your account name and password in the
resulting Authenticate dialog box.*

6. Press ⌘-Q or choose System Preferences | Quit System Preferences to quit System
Preferences.

Troubleshoot Specific Problems

This section discusses how to troubleshoot problems in burning CDs and DVDs with iTunes. The section starts with the basics and then moves on to more challenging problems.

iTunes Doesn't List Your Burner on the Burning Sheet

If iTunes doesn't list your burner on the Burning subtab on the Advanced tab in the Preferences dialog box (on the Mac) or on the Burning subtab of the Advanced tab in the iTunes dialog box (in Windows), the problem is most likely that iTunes doesn't support your burner.

> **TIP** *If you need to get a new drive for a Mac, check the list of FireWire, USB, and internal CD burners at www.apple.com/macosx/upgrade/storage.html first.*

Check the CD Burner readout on the Burning subtab tab on the Advanced tab in the iTunes dialog box or the Preferences dialog box:

- In Windows, press CTRL-COMMA or CTRL-Y or choose Edit | Preferences to display the iTunes dialog box.

- On the Mac, press ⌘-COMMA or ⌘-Y or choose iTunes | Preferences to display the Preferences dialog box.

Click the Advanced tab to display its contents, and then click the Burning subtab. If the CD Burner readout lists your CD or DVD burner by name or by model number, the drive works with iTunes.

Burning Is Very Slow (Windows)

If you find that burning is much slower than your drive's stated speed and the speed claimed for the recordable disc, you may need to change your drive from programmed input/output (PIO) to direct memory access (DMA).

To change from PIO to DMA, follow these steps:

1. Press WINDOWS KEY–R to display the Run dialog box. Type **devmgmt.msc**, and then press ENTER to display the Device Manager window. In Windows Vista, you must go through User Account Control for the Microsoft Management Console feature (unless you've switched off User Account Control).

2. Double-click the IDE ATA/ATAPI Controllers category to expand its contents (see Figure 8-5).

3. Right-click the IDE bus to which the optical drive is connected, and then choose Properties from the shortcut menu to display the Properties dialog box.

> **NOTE** *If you're not sure which IDE bus is the right one, double-click the second one listed. When you display the Advanced Settings tab in Step 4, look at the Device Type readout in the Devices group box. If you've got the right bus, you'll see a readout such as ATAPI Cdrom. If the readout says ATA Disk, click the Cancel button, and then double-click the first bus listed.*

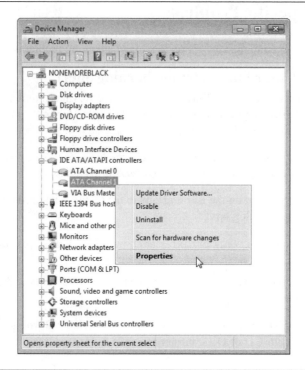

FIGURE 8-5   Use Device Manager to change the method your burner drive uses for transferring data.

4. Click the Advanced Settings tab to display its contents (see Figure 8-6).
5. In the Device Properties group box, select the Enable DMA check box.
6. Click the OK button to close the Properties dialog box.
7. Click the Close button (the × button) to close the Device Manager window.

External Burner Stops Responding

If you're using an external burner and you find that the drive stops responding after a burn fails, reset the drive by powering it down and then powering it back up—in lay terms, switching the drive off and then on again. If that doesn't work, you may need to restart your computer to regain control of the drive.

Solve Problems with an External USB CD Burner

If you're having problems with an external CD burner connected via USB, try the following actions to reduce the problems:

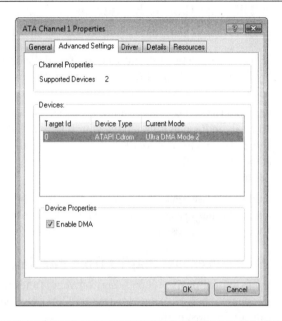

FIGURE 8-6   If burning is slow, make sure the burner is set to use DMA rather than PIO.

- Disconnect all nonessential USB devices (in other words, don't disconnect a USB keyboard or mouse).
- If the CD burner is connected through a USB hub, try removing the hub and plugging the burner directly into the computer's USB port.
- Reduce the burn speed to 2 × and see if that works. If so, increase the burn speed and test again.

Unable to Eject an Optical Disc (Mac)

Sometimes Mac OS X doesn't eject a CD or DVD the first time you issue a command to eject it. For example, if you drag the CD's icon to the Trash, Mac OS X sometimes fails to eject it. In iTunes, click the Eject button to eject the CD. You may need to click the button more than once. Allow a few seconds after each click to allow iTunes to respond.

External CD-RW Drive Stutters or Skips During Playback

Some external CD-RW drives don't play back CDs correctly, and you may hear stutters or apparent skips. To check whether the CD or the drive is the problem, try playing the CD in a CD player or in an internal CD drive (if you have one). If you don't have another CD player or CD drive, try playing another CD in the external CD-RW drive and see if that works.

"None of the Items in This List Can Be Burned to CD" Error Message

iTunes displays the error message "None of these items in this list can be burned to CD" in three cases:

- You try to burn a CD containing a playlist, but you've cleared the check boxes for all the songs on the playlist. To solve the problem, select the check boxes for the songs you want to burn to the CD.

- You try to burn a CD, but iTunes discovers that it can't locate any of the songs on the playlist. This is most likely to happen if you move your library to a different folder. You may need to change the iTunes Music Folder Location setting on the General subtab of the Advanced tab in the iTunes dialog box or the Preferences dialog box to show iTunes where your song files are.

- You try to burn a playlist that contains only protected AAC files that you've purchased from the iTunes Store, but iTunes is set to burn an MP3 CD rather than an audio CD or data CD. To solve the problem, choose a different CD type in the Preferences dialog box.

A Long Gap Between Songs Prevents Playlist from Burning

Choosing a Gap Between Songs setting of five seconds may prevent iTunes from burning a playlist successfully. If this happens, choose a shorter setting for Gap Between Songs. Two or three seconds should be adequate for most purposes.

"Songs in the Playlist Are Not Authorized" Error Message

The error message "One or more of the songs in this playlist are not authorized for use on this machine" means that you're trying to burn one or more songs that this computer isn't authorized to play. Click the OK button to close the message box.

The easiest way to fix this problem is to play each song on the playlist and go through the process of authorizing each song for which iTunes prompts you for authorization. (See Chapter 7 for details on authorization.) After doing this, start the burning process again.

"There Was a Problem with the Target Device" Error Message

The error message "There was a problem with the target device. Error code—7932" means that iTunes can't successfully write to the CD media you're using at the speed you're trying to use. Take one of the following actions to solve the problem:

- Reduce the burn speed to a lower setting on the Burning subtab of the Advanced tab of the iTunes dialog box or the Preferences dialog box.

- Use a different type of recordable CD—preferably a better-quality kind.

- If you're using CD-RW discs (rather than CD-R discs), don't use discs rated faster than 4 ×, because iTunes may not be able to write to them successfully.

"You Have Inserted a Blank DVD" Error Message

The error message "You have inserted a blank DVD but originally selected a CD format. Are you sure you wish to create a data DVD instead?" occurs when your Burning preferences specify an

How to ... Get the Highest Possible Audio Quality on the CDs You Burn

AAC and MP3 deliver high-quality compressed audio, especially when you use a high bitrate and other appropriate settings. But both AAC and MP3 use lossy compression, losing some of the data required to deliver a perfect audio signal.

If you need to burn CDs with the highest possible audio quality, make sure that your source files are either Apple Lossless Encoding or uncompressed, high-quality audio. If you rip song files from CD, rip them to Apple Lossless Encoding files, AIFF files, or WAV files rather than to AAC or MP3. If you record audio from your own sources, record it to Apple Lossless Encoding, AIFF, or WAV instead of recording it to a compressed format.

Arrange the uncompressed audio files into a playlist and then burn the playlist to CD.

If the CD turns out satisfactorily (as it should), you'll probably want to delete the Apple Lossless Encoding files or uncompressed source files from your hard disk to reclaim the space they take up.

audio CD but you insert a blank DVD instead. When you see this error message, you'll usually want to click the Cancel button, eject the DVD, and insert a blank CD-R or CD-RW disc instead. If you decide that you do want to burn a data DVD containing the discs instead of an audio CD, click the Data DVD button.

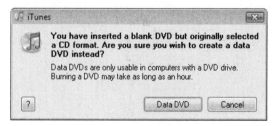

Remember that a data DVD has a huge capacity (typically more than 4.5GB) and that iTunes will store the songs on the DVD in their current format (for example, as AAC files or MP3 files) rather than writing them out to uncompressed audio files, so the DVD will probably end up with most of its capacity unused.

On the Mac, if you click the Cancel button, you may need to quit iTunes (press ⌘-Q) to force Mac OS X to eject the DVD.

iTunes Persistently Rejects a Blank Recordable Disc

If iTunes puzzles over a blank disc for a while and then ejects it without comment, chances are that the disc is either upside down or is not usable. Try the disc the other way up (this sounds dumb, but some brands of blank disc look almost identical on each side) and see if iTunes accepts it. If not, try another disc.

Chapter 9

Make the Most of iTunes

How to...

- Play music with iTunes
- Make iTunes run automatically when you log on
- Improve the sound that iTunes produces
- Change the iTunes interface to meet your preferences
- Enjoy visualizations as you listen to music

In Chapter 2, you learned how to rip CDs and create playlists; in Chapter 7, you learned the ins and outs of creating high-quality audio files from both CDs and other sources, such as your records and tapes. This chapter shows you how to enjoy that music using iTunes and how to change the sound you get and the interface you see. But first, you may want to make iTunes run automatically when you log onto your PC or Mac.

Play Music with iTunes

By following the techniques described in Chapter 2 and Chapter 7, you've probably created a fair-sized library. Now it's time to enjoy your library, using as many of iTunes' features as you need.

Play Back Music with iTunes

To play back music with iTunes, follow these general steps:

1. Navigate to the album, playlist, or song you want to play, select it, and then click the Play button.

2. Drag the diamond on the progress bar in the display to scroll forward or backward through the current track.

3. Use the Shuffle button to shuffle the order of the tracks in the current album or playlist. (To change whether iTunes shuffles by song or by album, select the Song option button or the Album option button on the Advanced tab of the Preferences dialog box.)

   TIP   *To reshuffle the current playlist on the Mac, OPTION-click the Shuffle button.*

4. Click the Repeat button one or more times to repeat a playlist, album, or song:

   - **Repeat the current playlist or album**   Click the Repeat button once, so that iTunes turns the arrows on the button to blue.

   - **Repeat the current song**   Click the Repeat button again, so that iTunes adds a blue circle bearing the number 1 to the blue arrows.

   - **Turn off repeat**   Click the Repeat button a third time.

How to ...   Run iTunes Frequently—or Always on Startup

Running iTunes from the iTunes icon on your desktop, from the Windows Start menu, or from the Dock works well enough for frequent use, but if you intend to run iTunes frequently, or always, you can do better.

In Windows, you can pin iTunes to the fixed part of the Start menu so that it always appears. To do so, navigate to the iTunes icon on the Start menu in Windows Vista or Windows XP, right-click it, and then choose Pin To Start Menu from the shortcut menu. If you keep the Quick Launch toolbar displayed, consider dragging an iTunes icon to the Quick Launch toolbar so that it's present there too.

To run iTunes even more quickly, configure a CTRL-ALT keyboard shortcut for it so that you can start iTunes by pressing the keyboard shortcut either from the Desktop or from within an application. Here's how to create the shortcut:

1. Right-click the iTunes icon on your Desktop or on your Start menu, and then choose Properties from the shortcut menu to display the iTunes Properties dialog box.

2. On the Shortcut tab, click in the Shortcut Key text box and then press the letter you want to use in the CTRL-ALT shortcut. For example, press I to create the shortcut CTRL-ALT-I.

3. Click the OK button to close the Properties dialog box.

But if you use iTunes whenever you're using your computer, the best solution is to make iTunes start automatically whenever you log on. To do so, follow these steps in Windows:

1. Right-click the iTunes icon on your Desktop or on your Start menu, and then choose Copy from the shortcut menu to copy the shortcut to the Clipboard.

2. On the Start menu's All Programs submenu, right-click the Startup folder and choose Open to open a Windows Explorer window showing the folder's contents.

3. Right-click in the Startup folder and choose Paste from the shortcut menu to paste a copy of the iTunes shortcut into the folder.

4. Click the Close button (the X button), press ALT-F4, or choose Organize | Close (on Windows Vista) or File | Close (on Windows XP) to close the Windows Explorer window.

To make iTunes start automatically on the Mac when you log in, simply right-click the iTunes icon on the Dock and select the Open At Login item from the shortcut menu.

5. If you've scrolled the Song list so that the current song isn't visible, click the arrow button on the right side of the readout at the top of the iTunes window to scroll back to the current song. Alternatively, press CTRL-L (Windows) or ⌘-L (Mac) to quickly scroll back to the current song. You can also simply wait until the next song starts, at which point iTunes automatically scrolls back to it.

6. To open a Windows Explorer window (in Windows) or a Finder window (on the Mac) to the folder that contains the selected song file, press CTRL-R (Windows) or ⌘-R (Mac).

7. To toggle the display of the artwork, click the Show Or Hide Song Artwork button, press CTRL-G (Windows) or ⌘-G (Mac), or choose Edit | Show Artwork or Edit | Hide Artwork.

8. On the Mac, you can also control iTunes by right-clicking or CTRL-clicking its Dock icon and making the appropriate choice from the shortcut menu. In Windows, if you've chosen to display an iTunes icon in the notification area, you can control iTunes from the icon, as shown here.

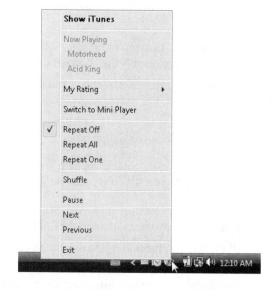

You can change the information shown in the display window by clicking the items in it. Click the Play icon at the left of the display window to toggle between the track information and the equalization graph. Click the time readout to move between Remaining Time and Total Time.

TIP

How to ...   Create a Gapless Album or Join Tracks Together Without Gaps

iTunes' default settings are to create a separate file (AAC, MP3, Apple Lossless Encoding, AIFF, or WAV, depending on your preferences) from each song on CDs you rip.

For most CDs, this works well. But sometimes you'll want to rip a CD so that it plays back without any gaps between songs. For example, most live CDs have applause or banter rather than silence between songs, so having a break in the playback tends to be distracting. To play back a CD without any gaps, you have two choices:

- ■ *Create a gapless album.* You can tell iTunes that an album shouldn't have a gap between songs. Creating a gapless album is a good idea when you will normally play the CD's songs in sequence rather than shuffle them.

- ■ *Join two or more songs—or even the full CD—into a single file so that you can treat those songs (or CD) as a single unit.* The advantage of this approach is that you can prevent Party Shuffle and other Smart Playlists from playing individual songs from the CD (or from your selection of songs) out of context. The disadvantage is that the joined-together songs tend to be long and hard to navigate through, especially on the iPod or iPhone.

You can create a gapless album either before or after you rip the CD:

- ■ **Before you rip the CD**   Right-click (or CTRL-click on the Mac) the CD's entry in the Source pane and choose Get Info. In the CD Info dialog box, select the Gapless Album check box and then click the OK button.

(Continued)

■ **After you rip the CD** Browse to the album, select it, and then choose File |
Get Info. If iTunes asks whether you're sure you want to edit information for
multiple tracks, click the Yes button. In the Multiple Song Information dialog box,
choose Yes in the Gapless Album drop-down list, and then click the OK button.
(Alternatively, right-click a song, choose Get Info, and then click the Options tab.
Select the Part Of A Gapless Album check box, and then click the OK button.)

To rip two or more tracks from a CD into a single file, select the tracks and then choose
Advanced | Join CD Tracks. iTunes brackets the tracks, as shown here. These tracks then rip
to a single file.

If you made a mistake with the tracks you joined, select one or more of the joined tracks
and then choose Advanced | Unjoin CD Tracks to separate the tracks again.

Listen to Audiobooks on Your iPod or iPhone

Even if your iPod or iPhone is laden nearly to the gunwales with songs, you may be able to cram
on a good amount of spoken-word audio, such as audiobooks and podcasts. This is because
spoken-word audio can sound great at much lower bitrates than music.

The iTunes Store provides a wide variety of content, including audiobooks, magazines,
plays, and poems. You can also get audiobooks from other sources, such as from the Audible
.com website (www.audible.com), which offers subscription plans for audio downloads.
(Audible.com provides many of the audiobooks on the iTunes Store.)

> TIP
>
> *When playing many audiobooks, you can press CTRL-SHIFT–RIGHT ARROW (Windows) or
> ⌘-SHIFT–RIGHT ARROW (Mac) to go to the next chapter. Press CTRL-SHIFT–LEFT ARROW
> (Windows) or ⌘-SHIFT–LEFT ARROW (Mac) to go to the previous chapter.*

Improve the Sound of Music

To make music sound as good as possible, you should apply suitable equalizations using iTunes' graphical equalizer. You can also crossfade one song into another, add automatic sound enhancement, and skip the beginning or end of a song.

Use the Graphical Equalizer to Make the Music Sound Great

iTunes includes a graphical equalizer that you can use to change the sound of the music (or other audio) you're playing. You can apply an equalization directly to the playlist you're currently playing, much as you would apply an equalization manually to a physical amplifier or receiver.

You can also apply a specific equalization to each song (or other item) in your iTunes library. Once you've done this, iTunes always uses that equalization when playing that song or item, no matter which equalization is currently applied to iTunes itself.

After playing an item that has an equalization specified, iTunes switches back to the equalization applied to iTunes itself for the next item that doesn't have an equalization specified.

Apply an Equalization to What's Currently Playing

To apply an equalization to what you're currently playing, follow these steps:

1. Display the Equalizer window (see Figure 9-1):

   ■ **Windows**   Choose View | Show Equalizer.

   ■ **Mac**   Choose Window | Equalizer or press ⌘-OPTION-2.

2. Select the equalization from the drop-down list. If you're playing an item, you'll hear the effect of the new equalization in a second or two.

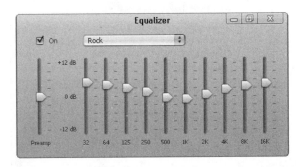

FIGURE 9-1   iTunes's Equalizer window offers preset equalizations, but you can also create custom equalizations.

Specify an Equalization for an Individual Item

To specify the equalization iTunes should use for a particular song or other item, follow these steps:

1. Select the item in your library or in a playlist.

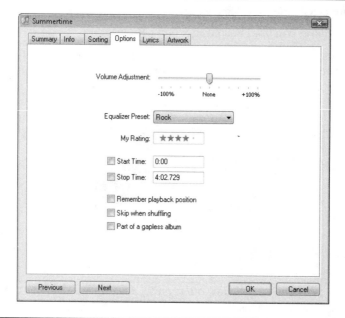

TIP   *It doesn't matter whether you apply the equalization to the item in the library or in a playlist, because applying the equalization even in a playlist affects the item in the library as a whole. So if you can access an item more easily through a playlist than through your library, start from the playlist.*

2. Press CTRL-I (Windows) or ⌘-I (Mac), or choose Get Info from the File menu or the shortcut menu, to display the Item Information dialog box. Alternatively, right-click (or CTRL-click on the Mac) the item and choose Get Info from the shortcut menu. This dialog box's title bar shows the item's name rather than the words "Item Information."

3. Click the Options tab to display its contents. Figure 9-2 shows the Options tab for iTunes for Windows. The Options tab for iTunes for the Mac has the same controls.

4. Select the equalization you want in the Equalizer Preset drop-down list.

FIGURE 9-2   You can specify the equalization for a particular song or other item on the Options tab of the Item Information dialog box.

Use the iPod's Diagnostic Tests to Pinpoint Problems

If you've read Chapter 18, you know that there's plenty that can go wrong with iPods. Some things you can fix by using the iPod's controls in special ways (see Chapter 18). Others you can fix using iTunes—for example, restoring the iPod's software. But others yet are more puzzling—and you have to turn to specialist techniques to find out what's wrong.

This Special Project shows you how to use the diagnostic tests built into the iPod classic and the third-generation iPod nano to troubleshoot problems. This Special Project does not cover other models of iPod or the iPhone.

Use the Diagnostic Tests on the iPod classic

This section shows you how to use the diagnostic tests on the iPod classic.

Access the Diagnostic Tests on the iPod classic

To access the various diagnostic tests on the iPod classic, you must enter diagnostic mode. Follow these steps:

1. Toggle the Hold switch on and off. (This step isn't always essential, but it's recommended.)

2. Hold down the Select button and the Menu button for about six seconds, until the Apple logo appears.

3. Hold down the Previous and Select buttons for a few seconds until the iPod displays the SRV Diag Boot screen, which looks like this drawing:

```
          SRV Diag Boot
         SRV Sep 11 2007
    ---------------------------

Menu    : Manual Test
Previous: Auto Test
```

4. Press the Menu button to access the main iPod Diagnostics screen, which looks like the following drawing:

```
    iPod Diagnostics d002
     SRV v.0056 Sep 11 2007
    ---------------------------
  NTF
 >Memory
  IO
  Power
  Accessories Test
  SysCfg
  Reset
```

CAUTION

Sometimes Apple changes the diagnostic tests in iPod firmware updates, so the iPod may show you different diagnostics from those listed here.

Navigate Through the Diagnostic Tests on the iPod classic

To navigate through and run the diagnostic tests on the iPod classic, use the following buttons:

- Press the Next and Previous buttons to navigate through the list of tests. You can also scroll up and down using the Click wheel.

- Press the Select button to run the highlighted test.

- Press the Menu button to return from the results of a test to the Diagnostics screen. You may also need to press the Menu button to move from one stage of a test to the next stage.

- To leave the Diagnostics screen, either run the Reset test or reset the iPod again by holding down the Menu button and the Play/Pause button for a few seconds.

The diagnostic tests on the iPod classic are arranged into a hierarchy of categories and subcategories, as shown here:

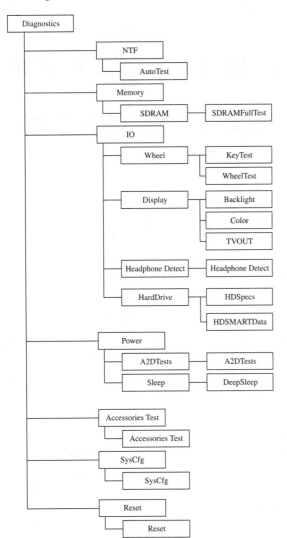

Understand the Diagnostic Tests for the iPod classic

Table 1 briefly explains all the diagnostic tests for the iPod classic, dividing them by menu and submenu so that you can easily access them.

Use Specific Diagnostic Tests on the iPod classic

This section shows you how to run some of the most useful diagnostic tests on the iPod classic. Before you follow the instructions for running these tests, put the iPod into diagnostic mode, as described in "Access the Diagnostic Tests on the iPod classic," earlier in this Special Project.

Check the USB Connection on an iPod classic

To check a USB connection on an iPod classic, choose Accessories Test | Accessories Test. You'll need to plug in a FireWire power source first and then a USB power source.

Check the RAM on an iPod classic

To check the RAM on a iPod classic, choose SDRAM | SDRAMFullTest. Again, you must plug in power to run this test.

Check the Buttons on an iPod classic

If one of the buttons on the iPod seems to stop working, you'll probably be able to tell without diagnostics. But before you call for backup, you may want to check that the iPod agrees with you that there's a problem.

To do so, choose IO | Wheel | KeyTest, and then press the iPod's buttons when prompted.

> **NOTE**
>
> If the iPod classic doesn't register you pressing one of the listed buttons in the KeyTest, it continues to wait until you reset it by holding down the Select button and the Menu button for a few seconds. (If one or both of these buttons aren't working, you're in trouble here. You may need professional help.)

SUBMENU	TEST	DESCRIPTION
NTF MENU		
AutoTest	[AutoTest]	Runs a battery of tests: SDRAMQuickTest, KeyTest, WheelTest, HeadphoneDetect, Accessory Test, Backlight, and Color. You can move to a particular item in the menu to start running that test and those that follow it.
MEMORY MENU		
SDRAM	SDRAMFullTest	You must plug in power to run the test. The test checks the SDRAM on the iPod.
IO MENU		
Wheel	KeyTest	Prompts you to press each button on the Scroll wheel, and displays KEY PASS if each press registers successfully.
Wheel	WheelTest	Returns the TouchWheelID data, and then prompts you to scroll around the wheel. Displays "Pass!" if the wheel is working okay.
Display	Backlight	Lets you check that different degrees of backlighting are working.
Display	Color	Displays a sequence of colors, gradients, and patterns to check that the display is working correctly. Press the Select button to move through the sequence.
Display	TVOUT	Lets you press the Previous button or Next button to toggle between NTSC and PAL TV standards.
Headphone Detect	Headphone Detect	Runs the HoldSwitch Detect test and then the HeadPhone Detect test. HoldSwitch Detect lets you test whether the Hold switch is working. You must toggle the Hold switch on and then off before pressing the Menu button to continue. HeadPhone Detect displays a readout of whether a device is connected to the headphone socket. You must connect and then disconnect the headphones (or a similar connector) before pressing the Menu button to continue.
HardDrive	HDSpecs	Displays information about the hard disk, including its serial number and firmware revision.
HardDrive	HDSMARTData	Displays information on the Self-Monitoring, Analysis, and Reporting Technology (S.M.A.R.T.) in the drive. The information includes the drive's current, maximum, and minimum temperatures.

Table 1. Diagnostic Tests for the iPod classic

POWER MENU		
A2DTests	Various Tests	These tests display information on the iPod's ID; the analog-to-digital converter; the battery, battery system, and battery temperature; and USB information.
Sleep	DeepSleep	Puts the iPod into deep sleep, like switching it off. Press the Select button to restart the iPod.
ACCESSORIES TEST MENU		
Accessories Test	[Accessories Test]	Displays the LCD ID and prompts you to plug in a FireWire power source and then a USB power source.
SYSCFG MENU		
SysCfg		Displays information on the iPod's serial number, manufacturer number, and hardware version.
RESET MENU		
Reset		Resets the iPod. Use this command to quit diagnostic mode.

Table 1. Diagnostic Tests for the iPod classic (*continued*)

Check the Click Wheel on an iPod classic

To test the Click wheel on the iPod classic, choose IO | Wheel | WheelTest. The iPod verifies the wheel's ID, and then prompts you to press the Menu button. After you press the button, the iPod prompts you to spin the wheel. If the wheel registers correctly, the iPod displays "Pass!" and then prompts you to press the Menu button to continue.

Check That Sleep Mode Is Working on the iPod classic

To check that Sleep mode is working on the iPod, choose Power | Sleep | DeepSleep. If the test works, you'll need to reset the iPod to get it working again. If the iPod doesn't go to sleep, the test has failed.

Check How the iPod classic Is Receiving Power

To check whether the iPod classic is receiving power across a USB cable or FireWire cable connected to an

iPod Power Adapter, choose Accessories Test from the iPod Diagnostics screen. On the Accesorize Test (*sic*) screen, connect the FireWire adapter when prompted.

If the iPod detects power, it changes the FW_DETECT=0 readout to FW_DETECT=1 and prompts you to plug in the USB. After you plug in a USB cable connected to an iPod Power Adapter, the USB_DETECT=0 readout changes to USB_DETECT=1, the screen displays PASS, and the test ends.

CAUTION

If you don't have a FireWire cable connected to a FireWire iPod Power Adapter and a USB cable connected to a USB iPod Power Adapter, you won't be able to complete the Accessories test. To escape from the test, hold down the Select button and the Menu button for several seconds to reset the iPod.

Check How Hot the iPod classic Is Running

To check the temperature of an iPod classic, choose IO | HardDrive | HDSMARTData. Run the HDSpecs test on the HardDrive menu, and then check the Temp: Current readout. The Min and Max readouts give the drive's minimum and maximum operating temperatures.

Exit Diagnostic Mode on the iPod classic

To exit diagnostic mode, choose Reset from the Diagnostics screen. The iPod classic resets itself, and then restarts.

Use the Diagnostic Tests on the iPod nano

This section shows you how to use the diagnostics on the third-generation iPod nano.

Access the Diagnostic Tests on the iPod nano

To access the various diagnostic tools on the iPod nano, you must enter diagnostic mode. Follow these steps:

1. Toggle the Hold switch on and off.

2. Hold down the Select button and the Menu button for about six seconds, until the Apple logo appears.

3. Hold down the Previous and Select buttons for a few seconds until the iPod displays the Diagnostics screen, which looks like the following drawing:

```
iPod Diagnostics BuildID: d002
SVC Sep 10 2007 V. 0072
--------------------------------
>Power
 Sleep
 Audio
 Video
 LCD
 IO
 Memory
 TouchWheel
 About
```

CAUTION

Sometimes Apple changes the diagnostic tests in iPod firmware updates, so the iPod may show you different diagnostics from those listed here.

Navigate Through the Diagnostic Tests on the iPod nano

To navigate through and run the diagnostic tests on the iPod nano, use the following buttons:

- Press the Next and Previous buttons to navigate through the list of tests.

- Press the Select button to run the highlighted test.

- Press the Menu button to return from the results of a test to the Diagnostics screen. You may also need to press the Menu button to move from one stage of a test to the next stage.

- To leave the Diagnostics screen, either run the Reset test or reset the iPod again by holding down the Menu button and the Play/Pause button for a few seconds.

The diagnostic tests on the iPod nano are arranged into a hierarchy of categories, as shown here:

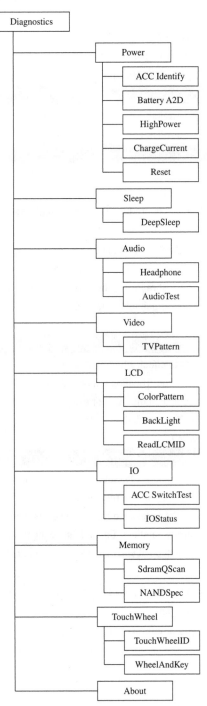

The following sections discuss the diagnostic tests you'll most likely want to perform.

Understand the Diagnostic Tests for the iPod nano

Table 2 briefly explains all the diagnostic tests for the iPod nano.

Use Specific Diagnostic Tests on the iPod nano

This section shows you how to run some of the most useful diagnostic tests on the third-generation iPod nano. Before you follow the instructions for running these tests, put the iPod into diagnostic mode, as described in "Access the Diagnostic Tests on the iPod nano," earlier in this Special Project.

Get an Executive Summary of the iPod nano's Status

Normally, the best place to start diagnosing the iPod nano is by running the IOStatus test. You'll see a screen like this:

```
IO Status Test
HP_DETECT:1
LCD_ID1:0
LCD_ID0:0
USB_DETECT:0
FW_DETECT:0
ACC_DETECT:0
HOLD_SWITCH:1
```

Among other things, these readouts let you quickly tell three important items:

- **Whether headphones are connected** HP_DETECT:0 means the iPod nano doesn't detect a jack in the headphone socket. HP_DETECT:1 means that it does detect a jack.

TEST	DESCRIPTION
POWER MENU	
ACC Identify	Displays the ACC battery level.
BatteryA2D	Displays the battery voltage level.
HighPower	Displays an ongoing evaluation of the battery voltage and the current level.
ChargeCurrent	Displays the battery charge level in milliamps and the battery voltage in volts.
Reset	Resets the iPod, exiting diagnostic mode and resuming normal behavior.
SLEEP MENU	
DeepSleep	Puts the iPod into a deep sleep. When you awaken it by holding down the Select button, the iPod will be running normally—it will not be in diagnostic mode.
AUDIO MENU	
Headphone	Displays HP_DETECT:0 if the iPod nano does not detect a compatible jack in the headphone socket and displays HP_DETECT:1 if it does. Change the headphone state by unplugging or plugging in a headphone jack to produce a prompt that allows you to press the Menu button to continue.
AudioTest	Displays a screen on which you can press the Play/Pause button to play a tone, press the Previous/Rewind button to check the line-in recording capability, or press the Next/Fast Forward button to play the file just recorded (by pressing the Previous/Rewind button). Be warned that the Play tone is painfully loud if you're wearing standard headphones.
VIDEO MENU	
TVPattern	Outputs a series of patterns that allows you to check whether a connected TV is receiving the signal correctly from the iPod. The iPod's screen displays a text description of what you should be seeing on the TV—for example, DisplayScaleFullRGB or DisplayFullWhite. Press the Select button to move through the series of patterns until you reach DisplayEND.
LCD MENU	
ColorPattern	Displays a series of colors and patterns to let you verify that the screen is working. Press the Select button to display each color or pattern. You can press the Previous/Rewind button to turn the backlight off, and then press the Next/Fast Forward button to turn it back on, but this capability seems pretty pointless. Continue pressing the Select button until you reach the last screen, at which point you can press the Menu button to exit the test.
BackLight	Displays a screen on which you can press the Play/Pause button to turn the backlight off and press the Select button to turn it back on.
ReadLCMID	Displays information about the LCD screen's ID information.

Table 2. Diagnostic Tests for the Third-Generation iPod nano

IO MENU

ACC SwitchTest	Displays a diagnostics screen on which you can press the Select button to change the ACC Switch Mode setting between On and Off.
IOStatus	Displays a summary of input and output status for the headphone socket, LCD screen, USB and FireWire connection on the Dock Connector socket, ACC Detect feature, and the Hold switch.

MEMORY MENU

SdramQScan	Performs a quick scan of the SDRAM memory chip.
NANDSpec	Displays a readout such as "NandLBA = 1982464," giving the address of the logical block address of the NAND flash memory, and a NAND SIZE readout that indicates the available amount of flash memory.

TOUCHWHEEL MENU

TouchWheelID	Displays register information about the Scroll wheel.
WheelAndKey	Lets you check that the iPod's Click wheel is working by spinning it with your finger, and check the iPod's buttons by pressing them. This test doesn't check the Hold switch. Keep pressing and scrolling until the iPod displays the "MENU to continue" message.

ABOUT

[About]	Displays information about the iPod, including its serial number, model number, and hardware version.

Table 2. Diagnostic Tests for the Third-Generation iPod nano (*continued*)

- **Whether a USB connection is working**   USB_DETECT:0 means the iPod nano doesn't detect a connection. USB_DETECT:1 means that it does detect a connection.

- **Whether a FireWire connection is working**   FW_DETECT:0 means the iPod nano doesn't detect a connection. FW_DETECT:1 means that it does detect a connection. The iPod nano uses FireWire for power only, not for synchronizing.

Check Whether Headphones Are Connected

To check whether the iPod nano detects headphones (or something else that uses a headphone jack, such as speakers) plugged into the headphone socket, choose Audio | Headphone.

If you see HP_DETECT:0, the iPod thinks nothing is connected to the headphone socket. HP_DETECT:1 means that the iPod detects a headphone jack.

Unlike the readout on the IOStatus test, the Headphone test keeps monitoring the status of the headphone port. When you plug in or unplug a headphone jack, the status changes.

Determine the iPod's Serial Number, Model Number, and Hardware Version

Run the About test (that is, press the Next button to reach the About item on the Diagnostics menu, and then press the Select button).

The SrNm readout shows the serial number. Usually, it's easier to look at the tiny characters engraved on the back of the iPod, but you may enjoy doing things the hard way on occasion. The model number (Mod#) and hardware version (HwVr) may be more useful when you're troubleshooting problems.

Check Whether the iPod nano's SDRAM Is Okay

To check whether the iPod nano's SDRAM memory chip is functional, choose Memory | SdramQScan.

Check the Audio Subsystem on an iPod nano

To check the audio subsystem on an iPod nano, run the AudioTest:

1. Plug a pair of headphones into the headphone port. Put the headphones somewhere you can hear their output but not directly in or on your ears (because the output may be uncomfortably loud).

2. Plug a microphone or other audio input into the Dock Connector port. (You'll need an accessory specifically designed for the iPod nano.)

3. From the Diagnostics screen, choose Audio | AudioTest. The iPod displays the Test Audio screen.

4. Press the Play button and listen for the tone.

5. Press the Previous/Rewind button to record some audio via your input.

6. Press the Next/Fast Forward button to listen to the audio you just recorded.

7. Press the Menu button to quit the test.

Check the Click Wheel and Buttons on an iPod nano

If you think that one or more of the buttons on the iPod nano has stopped working, or if the Click wheel doesn't seem to be responding correctly, run the WheelAndKey test to check. Follow these steps:

1. From the Diagnostics screen, choose TouchWheel | WheelAndKey. The iPod displays the WheelAndKey Test screen, which lists the button names.

2. Press each of the buttons in turn. Each button name fades to blue as the iPod recognizes the press.

3. Scroll the wheel until each of the hexadecimal digits has been replaced with an asterisk.

4. Press the Menu button again to quit the test.

Exit Diagnostic Mode on the iPod nano

To exit diagnostic mode, choose Power | Reset. The iPod nano resets itself, and then restarts.

5. Choose other options as necessary, and then click the OK button to close the Item Information dialog box. Alternatively, click the Previous button or the Next button to display the information for the previous item or next item in the Item Information dialog box.

NOTE   *If the equalization you apply to an item is one of the equalizations built into the iPod or iPhone, the iPod or iPhone also automatically uses the equalization for playing back the item. But if the equalization is a custom one your iPod or iPhone doesn't have, the player can't use it. The iPod and iPhone don't pick up custom equalizations you create in iTunes. Equalizations don't apply to the iPod shuffle, because this player doesn't use equalizations.*

Create a Custom Equalization That Sounds Good to You

The preset equalizations in iTunes span a wide range of musical types—but even if there's one named after the type of music you're currently listening to, you may not like the effects it produces. When this happens, try all the other equalizations, however unsuitable their names may make them seem, to see if any of them just happens to sound great with this type of music. (For example, some people swear the Classical equalization is perfect for many Grateful Dead tracks.) If none of them suits you, create a custom equalization that delivers the goods.

To create a new custom equalization, follow these steps:

1. Open the Equalizer window.

2. Drag the frequency sliders to the appropriate positions for the sound you want the equalization to deliver. When you change the first slider in the current preset, the drop-down list displays Manual.

3. If you need to change the overall volume of the song or item, drag the Preamp slider to a different level. For example, you might want to boost the preamp level on all the songs to which you apply a certain equalization.

4. Choose Make Preset from the drop-down list. iTunes displays the Make Preset dialog box:

5. Type the name for the equalization, and then click the OK button.

You can then apply your equalization from the drop-down list in the Item Information dialog box as you would any other preset equalization.

Delete and Rename Preset Equalizations

If you don't like a preset equalization, you can delete it. If you find an equalization's name unsuitable, you can rename it.

To delete or rename an equalization, start by following these steps:

1. Select the Edit List item from the drop-down list in the Equalizer window. iTunes displays the Edit Presets dialog box:

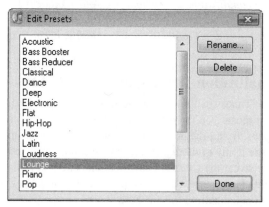

2. Select the preset equalization you want to affect.

To rename the equalization, follow these steps:

1. Click the Rename button to display the Rename dialog box, as shown here.

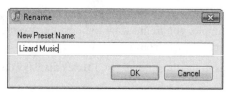

2. Type the new name in the New Preset Name text box.

3. Click the OK button. iTunes displays a dialog box like this, asking whether you want to change all songs currently set to use this equalization under its current name to use the equalization under the new name you've just specified.

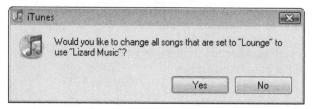

4. Click the Yes button or the No button as appropriate.

5. Click the Done button if you want to close the Edit Presets dialog box. If you want to work with other presets, leave it open.

To delete a preset equalization, follow these steps:

1. Click the Delete button.

2. iTunes displays a dialog box like the one shown here, asking you to confirm the deletion. Click the Delete button or the Cancel button, as appropriate.

3. To stop iTunes from confirming the deletion of preset equalizations, select the Do Not Warn Me Again check box before clicking the Delete button or the Cancel button. If you delete the preset, iTunes prompts you to choose whether to remove the equalization from all songs that are set to use it, as shown here. Click the Yes button or the No button as appropriate.

4. Click the Done button to close the Edit Presets dialog box.

Choose Crossfading, Sound Enhancer, and Sound Check Settings

The Playback tab of the iTunes dialog box (Windows) or the Preferences dialog box (Mac) offers options for crossfading playback, changing the Sound Enhancer, and controlling whether iTunes uses its Sound Check feature to normalize the volume of songs. Figure 9-3 shows the Playback tab of iTunes for the Mac. The Playback tab for iTunes for Windows has the same controls.

■ **Crossfade Playback** Makes iTunes fade in the start of the next song as the current song is about to end. This option lets you eliminate gaps between songs the way most DJs do. Drag the slider to increase or decrease the length of time that's crossfaded. This check box is selected by default. Turn off crossfading if you don't like it.

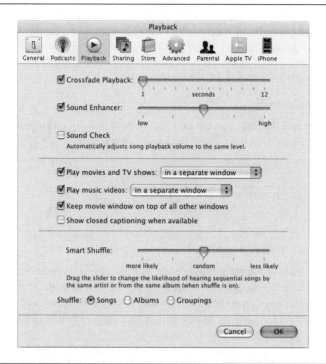

FIGURE 9-3
Choose crossfading, Sound Enhancer, and Sound Check options on the Audio tab of the Preferences dialog box.

CAUTION   *Turning on crossfading prevents iTunes from using gapless playback for any song that does not have the gapless playback option explicitly turned on.*

- **Sound Enhancer**   Applies iTunes' sound enhancement to the audio you're playing. The Sound Enhancer check box is selected by default, so you've probably been listening to it all along. Experiment with different settings on the Low–High scale by dragging the slider to see which setting sounds best to you—or turn off sound enhancement if you don't like it. Sound enhancement can make treble sounds appear brighter and can add to the effect of stereo separation, but the results don't suit everybody. You may prefer to adjust the sound manually by using the graphical equalizer.

- **Sound Check**   Controls whether iTunes uses its Sound Check feature to normalize the volume of different songs so that you don't experience widely varying audio levels in different songs. Many people find Sound Check useful. If you don't like Sound Check, or if you find that the extra processing power it requires makes your computer struggle to play music back satisfactorily, turn it off.

Skip the Boring Intro or Outro on a Song

If you disagree with the producer of a song about when the song should begin or end, use the Start Time and Stop Time controls on the Options tab of the Item Information dialog box (shown in Figure 9-2, earlier in this chapter) to specify how much of the track to lop off. This trimming works both in iTunes and on the iPod or iPhone.

To trim the intro, enter in the Start Time text box the point at which you want the song to start. For example, enter **1:15** to skip the first minute and a quarter of a song. When you start typing in the Start Time text box, iTunes selects the Start Time check box for you, so you don't need to select it manually.

Similarly, you can change the value in the Stop Time text box to stop the song playing before its end. By default, the Stop Time text box contains a time showing when the song ends, down to thousandths of a second—for example, 4:56.769. When you reduce this time, iTunes selects the Stop Time check box automatically.

> TIP   *When skipping an intro or outro isn't enough, you can edit a song file down to only that part you want. See Chapter 6 for details.*

Tweak the iTunes Interface

You can change the iTunes interface in several ways, which include resizing the window, turning off the display of the arrows linked to the iTunes Store, and changing the columns of data displayed.

> TIP   *For an extreme makeover of iTunes—and other applications—on the Mac, try ShapeShifter (www.unsanity.com/haxies/shapeshifter), which allows you to either apply existing themes that other people have created or design custom themes of your own.*

This section also shows you how to control iTunes by using keyboard shortcuts, how to use iTunes' visualizations, and how to control iTunes with the iTunes widget on Mac OS X.

Resize the iTunes Window to the Size You Need

iTunes offers various window sizes to suit the amount of space you're prepared to dedicate to it:

- In Windows, iTunes has four sizes: normal, maximized, small, and minute. The small and minute sizes are considered mini mode.

- On the Mac, iTunes has three sizes: normal, small, and minute. The small and minute sizes are considered mini mode. You can also use the iTunes widget to control iTunes from the Dashboard instead of using the main iTunes window.

By default, iTunes opens in a normal window that you can resize by dragging any of its borders or corners (on Windows) or by dragging the sizing handle in the lower-right corner (on the Mac).

In Windows, you can click the Maximize button to maximize the window so that it occupies all the space on your screen (apart from the taskbar, if you have it displayed), and you can click the Restore Down button to restore the maximized window to its previous size. You can also toggle the iTunes window between its maximized and normal states by double-clicking the title bar.

Once you've set the music playing, you'll often want to reduce the iTunes window to its essentials so that you can get on with your work (or play). To do so, in Windows, press CTRL-M or choose Advanced | Switch To Mini Player to display iTunes in mini mode.

On the Mac, there's no way of maximizing the iTunes window. You can click the Zoom button (the green button on the title bar) or press ⌘-CTRL-Z to toggle between normal mode and mini mode (shown here). You can minimize the iTunes window by double-clicking the title bar, by clicking the Minimize button, or by pressing ⌘-M.

From here, you can drag the sizing handle in the lower-right corner to shrink iTunes down even further to its minute size. This can be handy when you're pushed for space, but it isn't very informative:

Here's how to restore iTunes to its normal size from mini mode:

- In Windows, press CTRL-M or click the Restore button.
- On the Mac, click the Zoom button, choose Window | Zoom, or press ⌘-CTRL-Z.

Remove the iTunes Store Link Arrows

Unless you're desperate to buy music or other items from the iTunes Store at a moment's notice, you'll probably find the arrows that iTunes displays in the Name, Artist, Album, and Composer columns an irritant rather than a boon. You can click an arrow to search the iTunes Store for related items.

To remove the arrows, follow these steps:

1. Display the iTunes dialog box or the Preferences dialog box:

    - In Windows, choose Edit | Preferences or press CTRL-COMMA or CTRL-Y to display the iTunes dialog box.
    - On the Mac, choose iTunes | Preferences or press ⌘-COMMA or ⌘-Y to display the Preferences dialog box.

2. Click the General tab if it's not already displayed.

3. Clear the Show Links To The iTunes Store check box.

4. Click the OK button to close the dialog box.

Change the Columns Displayed to Show the Information You Need

By default, iTunes displays the following columns: Name, Time, Artist, Album, Genre, My Rating, Play Count, and Last Played. You can change the columns displayed for the current item (for example, your music library or a playlist) by using either of two techniques.

To change the display of multiple columns in the same operation, press CTRL-J (Windows) or ⌘-J (Mac), or choose Edit | View Options, to display the View Options dialog box. Figure 9-4 shows the View Options dialog box for Windows; the View Options dialog box for the Mac has the same controls. The icon and label in the upper-left corner of the dialog box indicate which item's view you're customizing—for example, Music for your music library, or Party Shuffle for the Party Shuffle playlist. Select the check boxes for the columns you want to display, and then click the OK button to close the dialog box and apply your choices.

To change the display of a single column in the current item, right-click (or CTRL-click on the Mac) the heading of one of the columns currently displayed. iTunes displays a menu of the available columns, showing a check mark next to those currently displayed. Select an unchecked column to display it. Select a checked column to remove it from the display.

NOTE   *The Play Count item stores the number of times you've played each item in iTunes. iTunes uses this information to determine your favorite items—for example, to decide which songs Smart Playlist should add to a playlist. You can also use this information yourself if you so choose. For example, you can create a Never Played playlist (with the criterion Play Count Is 0) to pick out all the items you've never played.*

FIGURE 9-4   Use the View Options dialog box to specify which columns iTunes displays for the current item.

To change the order in which your selected columns appear, drag a column heading to the left or right. For example, if you want the Album column to appear before the Artist column, drag the Album column heading to the left until iTunes moves the column.

From the shortcut menu, you can also select the Auto Size Column command to automatically resize the column whose heading you clicked so that the column's width best fits its contents. Select the Auto Size All Columns command to automatically resize all columns like this.

TIP   *You can change the column width by dragging a column heading to the left or right.*

Control iTunes via Keyboard Shortcuts

Controlling iTunes via the mouse is easy enough, but you can also control most of iTunes' features by using the keyboard. This can be useful both when your mouse is temporarily out of reach and when you've reduced the iTunes window to its small size or minute size, and thus hidden some of the controls.

Table 9-1 lists the keyboard shortcuts you can use to control iTunes. Most of these shortcuts work in any of iTunes' four display modes in Windows (normal, maximized, small, and mini) and iTunes' three display modes on the Mac (maximized, small, and mini), but the table notes the shortcuts that work only in some modes.

Accompany Your Music with Visualizations

Like many music programs, iTunes can produce stunning visualizations to accompany your music. You can display visualizations at any of three sizes within the iTunes window (which can provide visual distraction while you work or play) or display them full-screen to make your computer the life of the party.

Here's how to use visualizations:

■ To start visualizations, press CTRL-T or choose View | Show Visualizer (Windows) or press ⌘-T or choose Visualizer | Turn On Visualizer (Mac).

■ To stop visualizations, press CTRL-T or choose View | Hide Visualizer (Windows) or press ⌘-T or choose Visualizer | Turn Off Visualizer (Mac).

■ To launch full-screen visualizations, press CTRL-F (Windows) or ⌘-F (Mac) or choose View | Full Screen.

■ To stop full-screen visualizations, click your mouse button anywhere or press ESC or CTRL-T (Windows) or ⌘-T (Mac)

Configure Visualizations to Get the Best Results

iTunes even lets you configure visualizations to make them look as good as possible on your computer. To configure visualizations, follow these steps:

1. If iTunes is displayed at its small or minute size, click the Restore button (Windows) or the green button on the window frame (Mac) to return iTunes to a normal window.

Action	Windows Keystroke	Mac Keystroke
Controlling Playback		
Play or pause the selected song.	SPACEBAR	SPACEBAR
Skip to the next song.	RIGHT ARROW CTRL–RIGHT ARROW	RIGHT ARROW ⌘–RIGHT ARROW
Skip to the previous song.	LEFT ARROW CTRL–LEFT ARROW	LEFT ARROW ⌘–LEFT ARROW
Rewind the song.	CTRL-ALT–LEFT ARROW	⌘-OPTION–LEFT ARROW
Fast forward the song.	CTRL-ALT–RIGHT ARROW	⌘-OPTION–RIGHT ARROW
Skip to the next album in the list.	ALT–RIGHT ARROW	OPTION–RIGHT ARROW
Skip to the previous album in the list.	ALT–LEFT ARROW	OPTION–LEFT ARROW
Controlling the Volume		
Increase the volume.	CTRL–UP ARROW	⌘–UP ARROW
Decrease the volume.	CTRL–DOWN ARROW	⌘–DOWN ARROW
Toggle muting.	CTRL-ALT–UP ARROW CTRL-ALT–DOWN ARROW	⌘-OPTION–UP ARROW ⌘-OPTION–DOWN ARROW
Controlling the iTunes Windows		
Toggle the display of the iTunes main window.	n/a	⌘-1
Toggle the display of the Equalizer window.	n/a	⌘-2
Windows: Toggle between the mini player and full player. Mac: Minimize iTunes.	CTRL-M	⌘-M
Move the focus to the Find box	CTRL-ALT-F	⌘-ALT-F
Display the Open Stream dialog box.	CTRL-U	⌘-U
Controlling the Mini Player		
Increase the volume.	UP ARROW	UP ARROW
Decrease the volume.	DOWN ARROW	DOWN ARROW
Turn the iTunes volume to maximum.	SHIFT–UP ARROW	SHIFT–UP ARROW
Turn the iTunes volume down to minimum.	SHIFT–DOWN ARROW	SHIFT–DOWN ARROW
Controlling the Visualizer		
Toggle the Visualizer on and off.	CTRL-T	⌘-T
Toggle full-screen mode on the Visualizer.	CTRL-F	⌘-F

TABLE 9-1   Keyboard Shortcuts for iTunes

2. Start a song playing.

3. Start visualizations as described in the preceding section. For example, press CTRL-T (Windows) or ⌘-T (Mac).

4. Choose View | Visualizer | Options to display the Visualizer Options dialog box. Figure 9-5 shows the Visualizer Options dialog box for Windows on the left and the Visualizer Options dialog box for the Mac on the right.

5. Select and clear the check boxes to specify the options you want:

■ **Display Frame Rate**   Controls whether iTunes displays the frame rate (the number of frames being generated each second) superimposed on the upper-left corner of the visualization. This check box is cleared by default. The frame rate is useless information that adds nothing to the visualization, but it can be useful as a point of reference. For example, you may want to compare the visualization frame rates generated by different computers, or you might want to try the Faster But Rougher Display option (discussed in a moment) to see how much difference it produces. Bear in mind that the frame rate will vary depending on the size of the iTunes window, the complexity of the visualization, and what other tasks your computer is working on at the time.

■ **Cap Frame Rate At 30 fps**   Controls whether iTunes stops the frame from exceeding 30 frames per second (fps). This check box is selected by default. iTunes is configured to cap the frame rate to reduce the demands on the visualization on your computer's graphics card and processor. The cap is at 30 fps because most people find that 30 fps provides smooth and wonderful visualizations—so there's no point in trying to crank out extra frames.

■ **Always Display Song Info**   Controls whether iTunes displays the song information overlaid on the visualization all the time or just at the beginning of a song and when you change the Visualizer size while playing a song. This check box is cleared by default.

FIGURE 9-5   Use the Visualizer dialog box to configure visualizations for Windows (on the left) and the Mac (on the right).

- **Use DirectX**   (Windows only.) Controls whether iTunes uses DirectX, a graphics-rendering system, to create the visualizations. This check box is selected by default if your computer supports DirectX (as most recent computers do). If this check box is selected, leave it selected for best results.

- **Use OpenGL**   (Mac only.) Controls whether iTunes uses OpenGL, a graphics-rendering system, to create the visualizations. This check box is selected by default. Leave it selected for best results.

- **Faster But Rougher Display**   Lets you tell iTunes to lower the quality of the visualizations to increase the frame rate. This check box is cleared by default. You may want to try selecting this check box on a less-powerful computer if you find the visualizations are too slow.

> **TIP**   *You can also trigger most of these options from the keyboard while a visualization is playing, without displaying the Visualizer Options dialog box. Press F to toggle the frame rate display, T to toggle frame rate capping, I to toggle the display of song information, and D to restore the default settings.*

6. Click the OK button to close the Visualizer Options dialog box.

Control iTunes with the iTunes Widget on Mac OS X

If you're using Mac OS X, you can use the built-in iTunes widget to control iTunes from the Dashboard. To set the Dashboard to display the iTunes widget, follow these steps:

1. Click the Dashboard button on the Dock to display the Dashboard.

2. Click the + button superimposed on the left end of the Dock to display the bar showing the available widgets.

3. Click the iTunes widget, as shown here, to display it.

4. Click the × button superimposed on the left end of the Dock to close the widget bar.

You can then control iTunes by displaying the Dashboard and using the iTunes widget. Figure 9-6 shows the controls on the widget.

Previous/Rewind   Volume ring   Next/Fast Forward

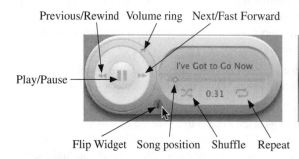

Play/Pause

Flip Widget   Song position   Shuffle   Repeat

FIGURE 9-6   The iTunes widget lets you control your music from the Dashboard. Flip the widget (right) to select another playlist.

> **TIP**
>
> *Apart from clicking the Dashboard button on the Dock, you can display the Dashboard by pressing the hot key assigned to it on the Dashboard & Exposé tab of System Preferences (choose Apple | System Preferences and then click the Dashboard & Exposé icon). On this tab, you can also set an active screen corner for the Dashboard so that Mac OS X displays the Dashboard when you move the mouse pointer into that corner of the screen.*

To open a playlist, click the Flip Widget button (the button showing the lowercase *i*). The iTunes widget rotates to show its other side. Select the playlist in the drop-down list and then click the Done button to flip the widget back to its regular position.

> **TIP**
>
> *If you use Yahoo! Widgets (free; http://widgets.yahoo.com), you can use similar widgets to run iTunes in both earlier versions of Mac OS X and Windows.*

Chapter 10

Manage Your Library with iTunes

How to...

- Browse quickly through your library
- Search for songs and other items
- Create regular playlists and Smart Playlists
- Move your library from one folder to another
- Remove duplicate items from your library
- Use multiple libraries on the same computer
- Share your library with other iTunes users and access their shared library
- Build a media server for your household
- Enjoy podcasts

This chapter shows you how to use iTunes to manage your library. You'll learn how to browse quickly by using the Browser panes, how to search for songs, how to create playlists and Smart Playlists, and how to mix up your music with the Party Shuffle feature. After that, you'll meet iTunes' features for applying ratings and artwork to songs, for consolidating your library so that it contains all your song files (or moving it to a different folder), and for removing any duplicate files that are wasting space.

Finally, you'll see how to export playlists so that you can share them with other people and import the playlists they share with you, and how to export your library to an XML file to store details of your playlists and ratings. You'll also learn how to build a media server for your household and how to enjoy podcasts.

Browse Quickly by Using the Browser Panes

iTunes provides the Browser panes (see Figure 10-1) to browse items quickly by artist, album, or (if you choose) genre. You can toggle the display of the Browser panes in any of these ways:

- Click the Browse button in the lower-right corner of the iTunes window.
- Press CTRL-B (Windows) or ⌘-B (Mac).
- Choose View | Show Browser or View | Hide Browser.

Once the Browser panes are displayed, click an item in the Artist column to display the albums by that artist in the Album column. Then click an item in the Albums column to display that album in the lower pane.

TIP   *When you have the Genre pane displayed but you don't want to restrict the view by genre, select the All item at the top of the Genre pane so that you see all genres at once.*

FIGURE 10-1   iTunes' Browser panes let you browse by artist, album, and genre.

To control whether iTunes displays the Genre pane in the Browser, follow these steps:

1. Display the iTunes dialog box or the Preferences dialog box:

   ■ In Windows, choose Edit | Preferences or press CTRL-COMMA or CTRL-Y to display the iTunes dialog box.

   ■ On the Mac, choose iTunes | Preferences or press ⌘-COMMA or ⌘-Y to display the Preferences dialog box.

2. Click the General tab if it isn't already displayed.

3. Select or clear the Show Genre When Browsing check box, as appropriate.

4. Click the OK button to close the dialog box.

The line of text at the bottom of the full iTunes window shows you how many songs are in the current selection and how long they last. This readout has two formats: 5738 songs, 17.4 days, 22.98 GB, and 5738 songs, 17:10:06:58 total time, 22.98 GB. To toggle between the two formats, click the songs-and-time display.

Use Views to Skim Through Your Library

Browsing can be an effective way of finding the songs or other items you want, but you may make better progress—or have more fun browsing—if you change the view iTunes is using.

iTunes provides three views: List view, Album view, and Cover Flow view. You can switch among views by clicking the View buttons to the left of the Search box (as shown in the next illustration); by using the View | List View, View | Album View, and View | Cover Flow View commands; or by pressing these keyboard shortcuts:

Windows	Mac	Switches to This View
CTRL-ALT-3	⌘-OPTION-3	List view
CTRL-ALT-4	⌘-OPTION-4	Album view
CTRL-ALT-5	⌘-OPTION-5	Cover Flow view

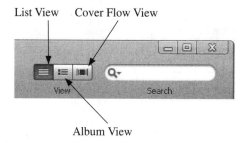

Sort Your Songs in List View

List view is the view in which iTunes normally starts. List view shows a simple list of the songs in the selected item—for example, your library or a playlist. Figure 10-2 shows List view.

To move to the first item in the current sort column that matches a certain letter or sequence of letters, click in the list, and then type the letter or sequence. For example, with the list sorted by the Album column, you might type **Tang** to jump to the first item by Tangerine Dream.

To sort the songs in List view or in Album view (discussed next), click the heading of the column by which you want to sort. Click once for an ascending sort (alphabetical order and

FIGURE 10-2   In List view, you can sort the songs quickly by any column heading.

smaller numbers before larger numbers). Click again for a descending sort (reverse alphabetical order, larger numbers before smaller numbers). The column heading shows an upward-pointing arrow for an ascending sort and a downward-pointing arrow for a descending sort.

The exception is the Album column, which works a little differently:

■ Click the column heading (but not the sort arrow) to cycle through the views: Album, Album By Artist, and Album By Year.

■ Click the sort arrow to reverse the direction of the sort.

See Your Songs Divided into Albums

In Album view, iTunes displays the songs divided by album (or single, EP, maxi-EP, CD, or what you will). Album view lets you scroll down the list of albums, pick the one you want by its cover, and then start playing the song you want (or add that song to a playlist). Figure 10-3 shows album view.

FIGURE 10-3   Album view divides the songs into albums and displays all available cover art.

To switch to Album view, click the Album View button to the left of the Search box. In Album view, you can sort by clicking the column headings as described in the previous section.

Flick Through Your CDs in Cover Flow View

If you've ever had a record collection, you'll remember the joy of browsing through the records by cover, finding the record you wanted by color and picture. (If you haven't done this—finding a record by reading the tiny print on its spine was far less fun.)

Cover Flow view is the iTunes equivalent of that experience—and it's pretty good. In Cover Flow view (see Figure 10-4), iTunes displays a carousel of covers. You can click a cover to move to it or scroll the scroll bar to move in larger jumps.

Full Screen

FIGURE 10-4   In Cover Flow view, you can click the Full Screen button to view your album covers full screen.

Search for Particular Songs or Other Items

Sometimes you may need to search for particular songs. You can also turn up interesting collections of unrelated songs by searching on a word that appears somewhere in the artist name, song name, or album name.

To search all categories of information, type the search text in the Search box and press ENTER (Windows) or RETURN (Mac). To constrain the search to artists, albums, composers, or songs, click the drop-down button and make the appropriate choice from the menu:

Then type the search text and press ENTER (Windows) or RETURN (Mac). To clear the Search box after searching, click the × button:

Use Playlists, Smart Playlists, and Party Shuffle

Typically, a CD presents its songs in the order the artist or the producer thought best, but often you'll want to rearrange the songs into a different order—or mix the songs from different CDs and files in a way that suits only you. To do so, you create playlists in iTunes, and iTunes automatically shares them with the iPod or iPhone so that you can use them there as well.

You'll probably want to start by creating playlists that contain songs. But playlists can also contain other items, such as TV shows, movies, or podcasts.

You can create playlists manually or use iTunes' Smart Playlist feature to create playlists automatically based on criteria you specify.

Create a Playlist Manually

To create a standard playlist, follow these steps:

1. Click the + button in the Source pane, choose File | New Playlist, or press CTRL-N in Windows or ⌘-N on the Mac. iTunes adds a new playlist to the Source pane, names it *untitled playlist* (or the next available name, such as *untitled playlist 2)*, and displays an edit box around it.

2. Type the name for the playlist, and then press ENTER (Windows) or RETURN (Mac), or click elsewhere, to apply the name.

3. Select the Music item in the Source pane to display your songs. If you want to work by artist and album, press CTRL-B (Windows) or ⌘-B (Mac), or choose Edit | Show Browser, to display the Browser pane.

4. Select the songs you want to add to the playlist and then drag them to the playlist's name. You can drag one song at a time, multiple songs, a whole artist, or a whole CD—whatever you find easiest. You can also drag an existing playlist to the new playlist.

5. Click the playlist's name in the Source pane to display the playlist.

6. Drag the songs into the order in which you want them to play.

NOTE *For you to be able to drag the songs around in the playlist, the playlist must be sorted by the track-number column. If any other column heading is selected, you won't be able to rearrange the order of the songs in the playlist.*

You can also create a playlist by selecting the songs or other items you want to include and then pressing CTRL-N (Windows) or ⌘-SHIFT-N (Mac) or choosing File | New Playlist From Selection. iTunes organizes the songs into a new playlist provisionally named *untitled playlist* and displays an edit box around the title so that you can change it immediately. Type the new name, and then press ENTER (Windows) or RETURN (Mac), or click elsewhere, to apply the name.

To delete a playlist, select it in the Source pane and press DELETE (Windows) or BACKSPACE (Mac). Alternatively, right-click the playlist (or CTRL-click it on the Mac) and choose Delete from the shortcut menu. iTunes displays a confirmation dialog box:

Click the Delete button to delete the playlist. If you want to turn off the confirmation for playlists you delete from now on, select the Do Not Ask Me Again check box before clicking the Delete button.

iTunes also offers more complex ways of deleting playlists and their contents:

- If you choose not to turn off confirmation of deleting playlists, you can override confirmation by pressing CTRL-DELETE (Windows) or ⌘-DELETE (Mac) when deleting a playlist.

- On the Mac, to delete a playlist *and the songs it contains* from your library, select the playlist and press OPTION-BACKSPACE. iTunes displays a confirmation dialog box for the deletion, as shown here. Click the Delete button. As before, you can select the Do Not Ask Me Again check box to suppress this confirmation dialog box in the future, but because you're removing song files from your library, it's best not to do so.

- On the Mac, to delete a playlist and the songs it contains from your library *and* to temporarily suppress the confirmation dialog box while doing so, select the playlist and press ⌘-OPTION-DELETE. iTunes prompts you to decide whether to move the selected songs to the Trash or keep them in the iTunes Music folder, as shown here. Click the Keep Files button or the Move To Trash button as appropriate. If you click the Move

To Trash button, iTunes deletes only those songs that are in your iTunes Music folder, not those that are in other folders.

Automatically Create Smart Playlists Based on Your Ratings and Preferences

Smart Playlist is a great feature that lets you instruct iTunes how to build a list of songs automatically for you.

You can tell Smart Playlist to build playlists by artist, composer, or genre; to select up to a specific number of songs at random, by artist, by most played, by last played, or by song name; and to automatically update a playlist as you add tracks to or remove tracks from your library. For example, if you tell Smart Playlist to make you a playlist of songs by Ashlee Simpson, Smart Playlist can update the list with new Ashlee tracks after you import them into your library.

By using Smart Playlist's advanced features, you can even specify multiple rules. For example, you might choose to include songs tagged with the genre Gothic Rock but exclude certain artists by name that you didn't want to hear.

NOTE *Smart Playlist maintains playlists such as the My Top Rated playlist, the Recently Played playlist, and the Top 25 Most Played playlist, which iTunes creates by default.*

Here's how to create a Smart Playlist:

1. Press CTRL-ALT-N (Windows) or ⌘-OPTION-N (Mac), or choose File | New Smart Playlist, to display the Smart Playlist dialog box (see Figure 10-5). On the Mac, you can also OPTION-click the Add button.

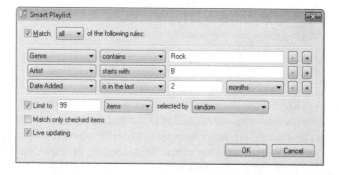

FIGURE 10-5   Smart Playlists are playlists that iTunes automatically populates with songs that match the criteria you specify.

2. Make sure the Match The Following Rules check box is selected so that you can specify criteria. (The other option is to create a random Smart Playlist, which can sometimes be entertaining.) If you create multiple rules, this check box offers the choices Match All Of The Following Rules and Match Any Of The Following Rules. Choose the appropriate one.

3. Use the controls in the first line to specify the first rule:

   ■ The first drop-down list offers an extensive range of choices: Album, Album Artist, Artist, BPM, Bit Rate, Category, Comment, Compilation, Composer, Date Added, Date Modified, Genre, Grouping, Kind, Last Played, Last Skipped, My Rating, Name, Play Count, Playlist, Podcast, Sample Rate, Season, Show, Size, Skip Count, Sort Album, Sort Album Artist, Sort Artist, Sort Composer, Sort Name, Sort Show, Time, Track Number, Video Kind, and Year.

   ■ The second drop-down list offers options suitable to the item you chose in the first drop-down list—for example, Contains, Does Not Contain, Is, Is Not, Starts With, or Ends With for a text field, or Is, Is Not, Is Greater Than, Is Less Than, or Is In The Range for the bitrate.

4. To create multiple rules, click the + button at the end of the line. iTunes adds another line of rule controls, which you can then set as described in Step 3. To remove a rule, click the – button at the end of the line.

5. To limit the playlist to a maximum number of tracks, time, or disk space, select the Limit To check box and then specify the limit and how iTunes should select the songs. For example, you could specify Limit To 30 Songs Selected By Least Often Played or Limit To 8 Hours Selected By Random.

6. To make iTunes omit songs whose check boxes you've cleared, select the Match Only Checked Items check box.

How to ... Use the Playlist Item Effectively When Creating Smart Playlists

The Playlist item in the first drop-down list in the Smart Playlist dialog box lets you specify a relationship between the Smart Playlist you're creating and an existing playlist (Smart or regular).

For example, you might specify in a Smart Playlist the criterion "Playlist Is Not Recently Played" to prevent any songs that appear in your Recently Played playlist from appearing in the Smart Playlist. Similarly, you could create a Smart Playlist called, say, "Rock Types" that uses several rules to define all the types of music you consider "rock": Genre Contains Rock, Genre Is Alternative, Genre Contains Gothic, and so on.

You could then use the criterion Playlist Is Rock Types in a Smart Playlist to create a subset of your rock music—for example, 90s rock or rock by artists not named Bryan or Brian.

7. Select the Live Updating check box if you want iTunes to update the playlist periodically according to your listening patterns. If you prefer not to update the playlist, clear this check box.

8. Click the OK button to close the Smart Playlist dialog box. iTunes creates the playlist, assigns a name to it (for example, *untitled playlist*), and displays an edit box around the name so you can change it.

9. Type the new name for the playlist and then press ENTER (Windows) or RETURN (Mac).

TIP   *A Smart Playlist limited by size can be a good way of selecting songs for an iPod or iPhone whose capacity is substantially less than the size of your library. For example, you might create a Smart Playlist with the parameter Limit To 950 MB for loading on an iPod shuffle or with the parameter Limit To 3 GB for an iPhone.*

Mix Up Your Music with Party Shuffle

If you like having someone else choose music for you, you may well love iTunes' Party Shuffle feature. Party Shuffle (see Figure 10-6) automatically selects music for you based on four parameters that you specify.

FIGURE 10-6   Party Shuffle is like a giant Smart Playlist.

To use Party Shuffle, follow these steps:

1. Click the Party Shuffle item in the Source pane.

NOTE *If the Source pane doesn't include Party Shuffle, press CTRL-COMMA (Windows) to display the iTunes dialog box or ⌘-COMMA (Mac) to display the Preferences dialog box. On the General tab, select the Party Shuffle check box in the Show area, and then click the OK button to close the dialog box.*

2. Choose options at the bottom of the pane:
   - Select the source for the Party Shuffle: your library or a playlist.
   - Select the Play Higher Rated Songs More Often check box if you want iTunes to weight the selection toward songs that you've given a higher rating.
   - Choose how many recently played songs and how many upcoming songs to display. The display of recently played songs can be useful for finding out the song details of songs you didn't recognize when Party Shuffle chose them.

3. Click the Play button to start the songs playing.

4. If you don't like the selection, click the Refresh button to display a new selection of songs.

TIP *If you find that Party Shuffle dredges up many songs you don't like, you can use it as a means of finding songs for playlists. From the songs that Party Shuffle picks, select those you want to hear, and drag them to a playlist. Click the Refresh button to find more songs, add those you want to hear to the playlist, and repeat the process until you've got a long enough playlist. Then start that playlist playing.*

Apply Ratings to Items

iTunes' My Rating feature lets you assign a rating of no stars to five stars to each item in your library. You can then sort the songs by rating or tell Smart Playlist to add only songs of a certain ranking or better to a playlist. (See "Automatically Create Smart Playlists Based on Your Ratings and Preferences," earlier in this chapter, for a discussion of Smart Playlist.)

You can apply a rating in three ways:

- Select the song in iTunes, and then click in the My Rating column to select the number of stars.
- Right-click a song or several selected songs (or CTRL-click on the Mac), choose My Rating from the shortcut menu, and then select the appropriate number of stars from the submenu. This technique is useful when you've selected several songs and want to apply the same rating to them.

■ Use the My Rating box on the Options tab of the Song Information dialog box (press CTRL-I in Windows or ⌘-1 on the Mac, or choose Get Info from the File menu or the shortcut menu) to specify the number of stars.

You can also rate a song on any iPod that has a screen (other than first- and second-generation iPods) or on an iPhone or iPod touch. On Click-Wheel iPods, press the Select button twice from the Now Playing screen while the song is playing, scroll left or right to select the appropriate number of stars, and then press the Select button again. On the iPhone or iPod touch, drag your finger across the row of stars to select the rating you want. iTunes picks up the rating the next time you synchronize the iPod or iPhone.

Add Artwork to Items

iTunes lets you add artwork to songs and other items, and then display the artwork while the item is playing or is selected.

Most songs or other items you buy from the iTunes Store include artwork—for example, the cover of the single, EP, album, or CD that includes the song, or the cover of a video. And once you've created an account with the iTunes Store, you can have iTunes automatically add art to songs in your library that do not already have art.

Better yet, when you add songs to your library, or when you convert songs in your library to another format, iTunes adds art to the songs from online sources wherever possible.

Set iTunes to Automatically Add Art from the iTunes Store to Songs

To set iTunes to download art from the iTunes Store for songs that do not have art, follow these steps:

1. Click the iTunes Store item in the Source pane to access the iTunes Store.

2. If iTunes doesn't automatically sign you in, click the Sign In button, type your name and password in the Sign In dialog box, and then click the Sign In button.

3. Choose Advanced | Get Album Artwork. iTunes displays a confirmation dialog box, as shown here.

4. Select the Do Not Ask Me Again check box if you want to suppress this confirmation dialog box when you give the command in the future.

5. Click the Get Album Artwork button.

Set iTunes to Automatically Download Missing Album Artwork

To set iTunes to download missing album artwork automatically, follow these steps:

1. Create an account for the iTunes Store, and then sign in to it.

2. Display the iTunes dialog box or the Preferences dialog box:

   ■ In Windows, choose Edit | Preferences or press CTRL-COMMA or CTRL-Y to display the iTunes dialog box.

   ■ On the Mac, choose iTunes | Preferences or press ⌘-COMMA or ⌘-Y to display the Preferences dialog box.

3. Click the General tab if it's not already displayed.

4. Select the Automatically Download Missing Album Artwork check box. iTunes displays a confirmation message box, as shown here.

5. Select the Do Not Warn Me Again check box if you want to suppress this confirmation when you turn automatic downloading on in the future.

6. Click the Enable Automatic Downloading button to close the confirmation message box.

7. Click the OK button to close the iTunes dialog box or Preferences dialog box.

Add Artwork to Songs Manually

If iTunes can't find art for a song automatically, or if you want to add another piece of art to a song that already has art, you can add the art manually. You can use either the artwork pane in the iTunes window or the Artwork box in the Song Information dialog box or the Multiple Song Information dialog box. The artwork pane is usually easiest.

You can apply any image you want to a song, provided that it is in a format that QuickTime supports. (QuickTime's supported formats include JPG, GIF, TIFF, PNG, BMP, and PhotoShop.) For example, you might download album art or other pictures from an artist's website and then apply those to the song files you ripped from the artist's CDs. Or you might prefer to add images of your own to favorite songs or to songs you've composed yourself.

TIP   *Amazon.com (www.amazon.com) has cover images for millions of CDs and records. For most music items, you can click the small picture on the item's main page to display a larger version of the image. Another source is Allmusic (www.allmusic.com), a service that requires registration.*

Add Artwork to Songs by Using the Artwork Pane

To add an image by using the artwork pane, follow these steps:

1. Open iTunes, and then select the song or songs you want to affect.

2. If the artwork pane isn't displayed (below the Source pane), display it in one of these ways:

   - Click the Show Or Hide Artwork button.
   - Press CTRL-G (Windows) or ⌘-G (Mac).
   - Choose View I Show Artwork.

3. If the title bar of the artwork pane says Now Playing, click the title bar to change it to Selected Song.

4. Open a Windows Explorer window or a Finder window to the folder that contains the image you want to use for the artwork, or open a browser window to a URL that contains the image. For example, open an Internet Explorer window to Amazon.com, and then navigate to the image you want.

5. Arrange iTunes and the Windows Explorer window, Finder window, or browser window so that you can see them both.

6. Drag the image to the artwork pane and drop it there.

7. Add further images to the song or songs if you want while you have them selected.

> **NOTE** *Most CD cover images are relatively small in dimensions and are compressed, so their file size is fairly small. Adding an image to a song increases its file size a little, but not by a large amount. If you add a large image to a song, iTunes uses a compressed version of the image rather than the full image.*

Add Artwork to Songs by Using the Song Information Dialog Box or the Multiple Song Information Dialog Box

Follow these steps to add artwork by using the Song Information dialog box (for a single song) or the Multiple Song Information dialog box:

1. Select the songs, right-click (or CTRL-click on the Mac), and choose Get Info from the shortcut menu to display the dialog box. (You can also choose File I Get Info or press CTRL-I in Windows or ⌘-I on the Mac to display the dialog box.)

2. If you've opened the Song Information dialog box, click the Artwork tab to display it. (The Multiple Song Information dialog box does not have tabs.)

3. Open a Windows Explorer window or a Finder window to the folder that contains the picture you want to use for the artwork, or open a browser window to a URL that contains the picture.

4. Drag the image to the Artwork box in the Multiple Song Information dialog box or the open area on the Artwork tab of the Song Information dialog box.

5. If you're using the Song Information dialog box, add further images as needed. To change the order of the images, drag them about in the open area (see Figure 10-7). You may need to reduce the zoom by dragging the slider to get the pictures small enough to rearrange.

When you've added two or more pictures to the same song, the artwork pane displays a Previous button and a Next button for browsing from picture to picture.

You can display the current picture at full size by clicking it in the artwork pane. Click the Close button (the × button) to close the artwork window.

NOTE   *Adding artwork to your songs can be not only esthetic but also practical. For a way of selecting music by cover art, see "Improve the iTunes Interface with Clutter (Mac)" in Chapter 16.*

To remove the artwork from a song, right-click (or CTRL-click on the Mac) the song and choose Get Info from the shortcut menu. Click the Artwork tab of the Song Information dialog box, click the picture, and then click the Remove button.

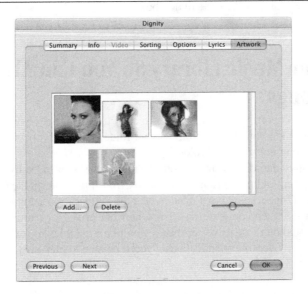

FIGURE 10-7   The Song Information dialog box lets you add multiple images to a song and rearrange them into the order you want.

How to ... Copy a Picture from a Song to Other Songs

You can also paste a picture into the Artwork box or the Artwork tab. For example, if your library already contains one song that has a picture you want to apply to other songs, you can copy the picture from that song, and then paste it into the other songs. Follow these steps:

1. Display the artwork pane if it isn't already displayed. If the artwork pane is showing Now Playing, click its title bar to make it show Selected Item.

2. Click the song that contains the picture you want to use.

3. Right-click (or CTRL-click on the Mac) the picture in the artwork pane, and then choose Copy from the shortcut menu.

4. Select the songs to which you want to apply the picture.

5. Right-click (or CTRL-click on the Mac) in the selection, and then choose Get Info from the shortcut menu to display the Multiple Song Information dialog box.

6. Right-click in the Artwork box, and then choose Paste from the shortcut menu.

7. Click the OK button to close the dialog box.

Consolidate Your Music Library So You Can Always Access All Its Songs

As you saw earlier in this book, you can set iTunes to copy to your iTunes Music folder the file for each song that you add to your library from another folder. Alternatively, you can have iTunes add a reference to the song in its original folder.

Whether iTunes copies the song or simply adds the reference is controlled by the Copy Files To iTunes Music Folder When Adding To Library check box. You'll find this on the General subtab of the Advanced tab in the iTunes dialog box (Windows) or the Preferences dialog box (Mac).

If you add references, when your external drives, network drives, or removable media aren't available, the songs stored on those drives or media won't be available. For example, when you grab your laptop and head over to a friend's house, you'll be able to play only the songs on the laptop's own drive.

TIP   *Use the Consolidate command when you want to move your library to another folder.*

To make sure you can play the music you want wherever you want, you can *consolidate* your library, making iTunes copy all the files currently outside your library folder to the library folder.

Understand the implications before you consolidate your library:

1. Consolidation can take a long time, depending on the number of files to be copied and the speed of the network connection you're using. Don't consolidate your library just as the airport shuttle is about to arrive.

2. The drive that holds your library must have enough space free to hold all your files. If lack of space was the reason you didn't copy the files to your music library in the first place, you probably don't want to consolidate your library.

3. Files on removable media such as CDs, DVDs, or USB sticks won't be copied unless the medium is in the drive at the time.

To consolidate your library, follow these steps:

1. Choose Advanced | Consolidate Library. iTunes displays the following dialog box:

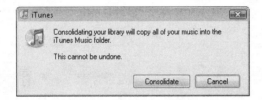

2. Click the Consolidate button. iTunes displays the Copying Files dialog box as it copies the files to your library.

TIP   *If consolidation goes wrong, see "Letting iTunes Copy All Song Files to Your Library Runs You Out of Hard-Disk Space" in Chapter 18 for help.*

Remove Duplicate Items from Your Library

Even if your library isn't huge, it's easy to get duplicate songs or videos in it, especially if you add folders of existing files as well as rip and encode your CDs and other audio sources. Duplicates waste disk space, particularly on an iPod or iPhone, so iTunes offers a command to help you identify them so that you can remove them.

To remove duplicate items, follow these steps:

1. In the Source pane, click the appropriate item in the Library category. For example, to look for duplicate songs, click the Music item. If you want to confine the duplicate-checking to a playlist, click that playlist in the Source pane.

2. Choose View | Show Duplicates. iTunes displays a list of duplicate items. Figure 10-8 shows an example on Windows.

FIGURE 10-8   Use the View | Show Duplicates command to display a list of duplicate songs and videos in a playlist or in your library.

NOTE
iTunes identifies duplicates by artist and name, not by album, length, or other often-useful details. Before deleting any duplicates, check that they're actually duplicates, not just different versions or mixes of the same item.

3. Decide which copy of each item you want to keep. To find out where an item is stored, right-click it (or CTRL-click it on the Mac) and choose Show In Windows Explorer (Windows) or Show In Finder (Mac) from the shortcut menu. You'll see a Windows Explorer window or a Finder window that shows the contents of the folder that includes the file.

TIP
If your library contains various file formats, you may find it helpful to display the file type in iTunes so that you can see which item is which format. For example, when you have duplicate song files, you might want to delete the MP3 files rather than the AAC files. Right-click (or CTRL-click on the Mac) the heading of the column after which you want the Kind column to appear, and then select the Kind item from the shortcut menu.

4. To delete an item, select it and press DELETE (Windows) or BACKSPACE (Mac). Click the Remove button in the confirmation dialog box; select the Do Not Ask Me Again check box first if you want to turn off the confirmation.

5. If the file is stored in your library folder, iTunes prompts you to move it to the Recycle Bin (Windows) or to the Trash (Mac). Click the Keep Files button if you want to keep the files or the Move To Recycle Bin button or Move To Trash button if you want to get rid of them.

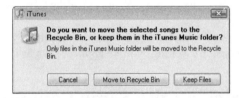

To display all items again, click the Show Songs button at the bottom of the iTunes window or choose View | Show All Songs.

Export and Import Playlists

If you create a great playlist, chances are that you'll want to share it with others. You can do so by exporting the playlist so that someone else can import it—provided that they have the items in their music library. Follow these steps:

1. Select the playlist in the Source pane.

2. Choose File | Export to display the Save As dialog box (Windows) or the Save: iTunes dialog box (Mac).

3. Specify the filename for the list, and then choose the folder in which to store it.

4. Choose the format for the file. Windows lets you choose between Text Files and XML Files. Mac OS X lets you choose among Plain Text, Unicode Text, and XML. Text Files or Plain Text is usually the best choice.

5. Click the Save button to save the playlist.

You can then share the playlist with someone else—for example, by sending it via e-mail.

When you receive a playlist, you can import it by choosing File | Import, selecting the file in the Import dialog box (change the Files Of Type setting in Windows if necessary), and then clicking the Open button. iTunes checks the playlist against your library and creates a playlist that contains as many of the items as you have available. If one or more items are unavailable, iTunes warns you, as shown here.

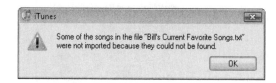

Export Your Library

You can export the details of your entire library and all your playlists as a backup in case your computer suffers data loss or damage. To export the library, choose File | Export Library, specify the name and folder in the Save As dialog box (Windows) or the Save: iTunes dialog box (Mac), and then click the Save button.

As well as your playlists, your exported library contains details of your play count, ratings, equalizations, and other item-specific settings you've applied, such as start times and stop times.

Use Multiple Libraries on the Same Computer

Normally, you put all your songs, videos, and other items into a single iTunes library. This has several advantages, including simplicity and having all of your media items instantly accessible from iTunes.

However, in some cases you may want to create different libraries for different categories of items. For example, you can have a family library containing songs that are safe for the kids, and an adult library that contains explicit material. Or you can have a library that contains only the songs on your laptop, plus a library that contains all those songs and those that appear on your removable drives or network drives.

You already have the standard library that iTunes has created for you, so your first step is to create a new library.

Create a New Library

To create a new library, follow these steps:

1. If iTunes is running, close it. For example, press ALT-F4 (Windows) or ⌘-Q (Mac).

2. Start iTunes using the special command for changing libraries:

   ■ **Windows**   SHIFT-click the iTunes icon. For example, click the Start button, click All Programs, click the iTunes folder, and then SHIFT-click the iTunes icon.

   ■ **Mac**   OPTION-click the iTunes icon—for example, in the Dock.

3. iTunes displays the Choose iTunes Library dialog box. The next illustration shows the Mac version of this dialog box.

4. Click the Create Library button. iTunes displays the New iTunes Library dialog box. The next illustration shows the Mac version of this dialog box.

5. Type the name for the new library folder, choose the folder in which to store it, and then click the Save button. iTunes closes the New iTunes Library dialog box, creates the new library, and then opens itself, showing the contents of the new library.

6. Add songs and other items to the library using the techniques you learned in Chapter 9.

Switch to Another Library

To switch from one library to another, follow these steps:

1. If iTunes is running, close it. For example, press ALT-F4 (Windows) or ⌘-Q (Mac).

2. Start iTunes using the special command for changing libraries:

   ■ **Windows** SHIFT-click the iTunes icon. For example, click the Start button, click All Programs, click the iTunes folder, and then SHIFT-click the iTunes icon.

   ■ **Mac** OPTION-click the iTunes icon—for example, in the Dock.

3. iTunes displays the Choose iTunes Library dialog box. The next illustration shows the Windows version of this dialog box.

4. Click the Choose Library button. iTunes displays the Open iTunes Library dialog box. The next illustration shows the Windows version of this dialog box.

5. Open the folder in which you stored the library, select the iTunes Library.itl file, and then click the Open button.

6. iTunes opens, showing the contents of the library you selected.

Share Items and Access Shared Items

Listening to your own music collection is great, but it's often even better to be able to share your music with your friends or family—and to enjoy as much of their music as you can stand. iTunes provides features for sharing your music with other iTunes users on your network and for playing the music they're sharing. You may also want to share music with other users of your computer—which, interestingly, requires a little more effort. Similarly, you may want to share other file types that iTunes supports.

Share Your Library with Other Local iTunes Users

You can share either your entire library or selected playlists with other users on your network. You can share most items, including MP3 files, AAC files, Apple Lossless Encoding files, AIFF files, WAV files, and links to radio stations. You can't share Audible files or QuickTime sound files.

NOTE *Technically, iTunes' sharing is limited to computers on the same TCP/IP subnet as your computer is on. (A subnet is a logical division of a network.) If your computer connects to a medium-sized network, and you're unable to find a computer that you know is connected to the same network somewhere, it may be on a different subnet.*

At this writing, you can share your library with up to five other computers per day, and your computer can be one of up to five computers accessing the shared library on another computer on any given day. (The sharing privileges used to be more generous: five concurrent computers at any time. See the sidebar "Apple May Change the Details of Library Sharing" for details.)

Did you know?

Apple May Change the Details of Library Sharing

If you read through the license agreements for iTunes and the iTunes Store, you'll notice that Apple reserves the right to change the details of what you can and can't do with iTunes and the files you buy. This isn't unusual, but it's worth taking a moment to consider.

At this writing, Apple has made several changes. Some changes are no big deal. For example, Apple has reduced the number of times you can burn an individual playlist to CD from ten times to seven times. (You can create another playlist with the same songs and burn that seven times too, and then create another.)

More of a big deal are the changes Apple has made to sharing songs and other files on the network. The first versions of iTunes 4 could share songs not only on the computer's local network but also across the Internet. Apple quickly reduced this to the local network only, which seemed fair enough. iTunes could share music with five other computers at a time—enough to reach a good number of people, especially in a dorm situation with many people sharing music and listening to shared music.

But in iTunes 4.7.1, Apple reduced the sharing from five computers at a time to five computers *per day* total. This still works fine for most homes, but on bigger networks, it's very restrictive. Once a computer has shared library items with its five computers for the day, you'll see one of the messages shown here if you try to connect.

All the changes so far have been restrictive and have benefited the media providers (such as the record companies) rather than iTunes users. Further changes seem likely, so if iTunes doesn't behave as described here, check the latest license agreement on the Apple website.

The shared library remains on the computer that's sharing it, and when a participating computer goes to play a song or other item, that item is streamed across the network. This means that the item isn't copied from the computer that's sharing it to the computer that's playing it in a way that leaves a usable file on the playing computer.

When a computer goes offline or is shut down, library items it has been sharing stop being available to other users. Participating computers can play the shared items but can't do anything else with them; for example, they can't burn shared songs to CD or DVD, download them to an iPod or iPhone, or copy them to their own libraries.

To share some or all of your library, follow these steps:

1. Display the iTunes dialog box or the Preferences dialog box:

    ■ In Windows, choose Edit | Preferences or press CTRL-COMMA or CTRL-Y to display the iTunes dialog box.

    ■ On the Mac, choose iTunes | Preferences or press ⌘-COMMA or ⌘-Y to display the Preferences dialog box.

2. Click the Sharing tab to display it. Figure 10-9 shows the Sharing tab of the iTunes dialog box with settings chosen.

3. Select the Share My Library On My Local Network check box. (This check box is cleared by default.) By default, iTunes then selects the Share Entire Library option button. If you want to share only some playlists, select the Share Selected Playlists option button, and then select the check boxes in the list box for the playlists you want to share.

4. By default, your shared library items are available to any other user on the network. To restrict access to people with whom you share a password, select the Require Password check box, and then enter a strong (unguessable) password in the text box.

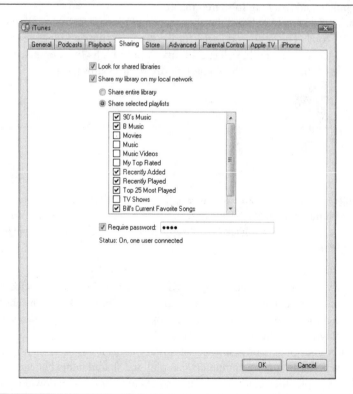

FIGURE 10-9   On the Sharing tab of the iTunes dialog box or the Preferences dialog box, choose whether to look for shared libraries and whether to share part or all of your library.

TIP *If there are many computers on your network, use a sharing password to help avoid running up against the five-users-per-day limit. If your network has only a few computers, you may not need a password to avoid reaching this limit.*

5. Click the General tab to display its contents. In the Shared Name text box near the bottom of the dialog box, set the name that other users trying to access your library will see. The default name is *username*'s Library, where *username* is your username—for example, Anna Connor's Library. You might choose to enter a more descriptive name, especially if your computer is part of a well-populated network (for example, in a dorm).

6. Click the OK button to apply your choices and close the dialog box.

NOTE *When you set iTunes to share your library, iTunes displays a message reminding you that "Sharing music is for personal use only"—in other words, remember not to violate copyright law. Select the Do Not Show This Message Again check box if you want to prevent this message from appearing again.*

Disconnect Other Users from Your Shared Library

To disconnect other users from your shared library, follow these steps:

1. Display the iTunes dialog box or the Preferences dialog box:

- In Windows, choose Edit | Preferences or press CTRL-COMMA or CTRL-Y to display the iTunes dialog box.

- On the Mac, choose iTunes | Preferences or press ⌘-COMMA or ⌘-Y to display the Preferences dialog box.

2. Click the Sharing tab to display it.

3. Clear the Share My Library On My Local Network check box.

4. Click the OK button. If any other user is connected to your shared library, iTunes displays this message box to warn you:

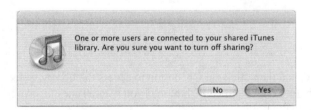

5. Click the Yes button or the No button, as appropriate. If you click the Yes button, anyone playing an item from the library will be cut off abruptly without notice.

Access and Play Another Local iTunes User's Shared Library

To access another person's shared library, you must first set your computer to look for shared libraries. You may already have done so when you turned on sharing on your own computer.

Set Your Computer to Look for Shared Libraries

First, set your computer to look for shared libraries. Follow these steps:

1. Display the iTunes dialog box or the Preferences dialog box:

   - In Windows, choose Edit | Preferences or press CTRL-COMMA or CTRL-Y to display the iTunes dialog box.

   - On the Mac, choose iTunes | Preferences or press ⌘-COMMA or ⌘-Y to display the Preferences dialog box.

2. Click the Sharing tab to display its contents.

3. Select the Look For Shared Libraries check box.

4. Click the OK button to close the dialog box.

Access Shared Libraries on Your Local Network

Once you've selected the Look For Shared Libraries check box on the Sharing tab of the iTunes dialog box or the Preferences dialog box, iTunes automatically detects shared libraries when you launch the program while your computer is connected to a network. If iTunes finds shared libraries or playlists, it displays them in the Source pane. Figure 10-10 shows an example of browsing the music shared by another computer.

If a shared library has a password, iTunes displays the Shared Library Password dialog box:

Type the password, and then click the OK button to access the library. Select the Remember Password check box before clicking the OK button if you want iTunes to save the password to speed up future access to the library.

TIP   *Double-click the entry for a shared library in the Source pane to open a separate window that shows its contents.*

FIGURE 10-10 Computers sharing libraries appear in the iTunes Source pane, allowing you to quickly browse the songs and other items that are being shared.

Disconnect a Shared Library

To disconnect a shared library you've connected to, take one of these actions:

- Click the Eject icon next to the library in the Source pane.
- Click the library in the Source pane, and then press CTRL-E (Windows) or ⌘-E (Mac).
- Click the library in the Source pane, and then click the Eject icon in the lower-right corner of the iTunes window.
- Click the library in the Source pane, and then choose Controls | Disconnect *Library* from the shortcut menu (where *Library* is the name of the shared library).
- Right-click the library in the Source pane (or CTRL-click on the Mac), and then choose Disconnect from the shortcut menu.

Share Your Music More Effectively with Other Local Users

As you saw in the previous section, iTunes makes it easy for you to share either your music library or specific playlists with other iTunes users on your local area network (LAN). You can share with up to five different computers per day, and of course your computer must be attached to the network and powered on for them to be able to access your music.

You may also want to share your music with other users of your computer. The security features built into Windows Vista, Windows XP, and Mac OS X mean that you have to do a little work to share it.

This section focuses on music files, but you can use the same approach for other media files—for example, video files.

Share Your Library with Other Users of Your PC

Windows automatically prevents other users from accessing your personal files, assigning each user a user account and keeping them out of other users' accounts. The result of this is that your iTunes library, which is stored by default in your Music\iTunes\iTunes Music folder on Windows Vista or the My Music\iTunes\iTunes Music folder on Windows XP, is securely protected from other users of your computer. That's great if you want to keep your music to yourself, but not so great if you want to share it with your friends, family, or coworkers.

NOTE   *Windows Media Player, the audio and video player that Microsoft includes with Windows at this writing, gets around this restriction by making the music and video files that any user adds to their music library available to all users. This is great if you want to share all your files but less appealing if you want to keep some of them private.*

The easiest way to give other users access to your library is to move it to the Public Music folder (on Windows Vista) or the Shared Music folder (on Windows XP). This is a folder created automatically when Windows is installed, and which Windows automatically shares with other users of your computer but not with other computers on the network.

Here's where to find this folder:

- **Windows Vista**   The Public Music folder is located in the Public folder.
- **Windows XP**   The Shared Music folder is located in the \Documents and Settings\All Users\Documents\My Music folder.

Alternatively, you can put the library in another shared folder. This example uses the Public Music folder on Windows Vista and the Shared Music folder in Windows XP. If you're using another folder, substitute it where appropriate.

Moving your library to the Public Music folder or the Shared Music folder involves two steps: moving the files, and then telling iTunes where you've moved them to.

To move your library files to the Public Music folder or the Shared Music folder, follow these steps:

1. Close iTunes if it's running. (For example, press ALT-F4 or choose File | Exit.)
2. Open your library folder:
   - **Windows Vista**   Choose Start | Music to open a Windows Explorer window showing your Music folder.
   - **Windows XP**   Choose Start | My Music to open a Windows Explorer window showing your My Music folder.

3. Double-click the iTunes folder to open it. You'll see an iTunes Music Library.xml file, an iTunes 4 Music Library.itl file, and an iTunes Music folder. The first two files must stay in your library folder. If you remove them, iTunes won't be able to find your library, and it will create these files again from scratch.

4. Right-click the iTunes Music folder, and then choose Cut from the shortcut menu to cut it to the Clipboard.

5. Open the Public Music folder or the Shared Music folder:

■ **Windows Vista**   In the Music folder, double-click the shortcut to the Sample Music folder. The Sample Music folder is in the Public Music folder. In the Address bar, click the Public Music item to display the folder's contents.

■ **Windows XP**   In the Other Places task pane, click the Shared Music link to display the Shared Music folder. (If the Shared Music folder doesn't appear in the Other Places task pane, click the My Computer link, click the Shared Documents link, and then double-click the Shared Music folder.)

6. Right-click an open space in the Public Music folder or the Shared Music folder, and then choose Paste from the shortcut menu to paste the iTunes Music folder into the folder.

7. Close the Windows Explorer window. (For example, press ALT-F4 or choose File | Close.)

Next, you need to tell iTunes where the song files and other media files are. Follow these steps:

1. Start iTunes. (For example, double-click the iTunes icon on your desktop.)

2. Press CTRL-COMMA or choose Edit | Preferences to display the iTunes dialog box.

3. Click the Advanced tab to display its contents.

4. Click the Change button to display the Browse For Folder dialog box.

5. Navigate to the Public Music folder or the Shared Music folder, and then click the OK button to close the Browse For Folder dialog box.

6. Click the OK button to close the iTunes dialog box.

After you've done this, iTunes knows where the files are, and you can play them back as usual. When you rip further song files from CD or import files, iTunes stores them in the Public Music folder or Shared Music folder.

You're all set. The other users of your PC can do either of two things:

■ Move their library to the Public Music folder or Shared Music folder, using the techniques described here, so that all files are stored centrally. Instead of moving the library folder itself, move the folders it contains. Users can then add songs they import to the shared library, and all users can access them.

■ Keep their library separate, but add the contents of the shared library folder to it. Here's how:

   1. Choose File | Add Folder To Library to display the Browse For Folder dialog box.

   2. Navigate to the Public Music folder or Shared Music folder.

   3. Select the iTunes Music folder.

   4. Click the Open button. iTunes adds all the latest songs to your library.

Whichever approach the other users of your PC choose, the songs that they add to the shared library don't appear automatically in your library. To add all the latest tracks, use the Add To Library dialog box, as described in the previous list.

Share Your Library with Other Users of Your Mac

Mac OS X's security system prevents other users from accessing your Home folder or its contents—which by default includes your library. So if you want to share your library with other users of your Mac, you need to change permissions to allow others to access your Home folder (or parts of it) or move your library to a folder they can access.

The easiest way to give other users access to your songs and other items is to put your library in the Users/Shared folder and put an alias to it in its default location. To do so, follow these steps:

   1. Use the Finder to move the iTunes Music folder from your ~/Music/iTunes folder to the /Users/Shared folder.

   2. Press ⌘-COMMA (or ⌘-Y) or choose iTunes | Preferences to display the Preferences dialog box.

   3. Click the Advanced button to display the Advanced tab.

   4. Click the General subtab if this tab isn't already displayed.

   5. Click the Change button, and then use the resulting Change Music Folder Location dialog box to navigate to and select the /Users/Shared/iTunes Music folder.

   6. Click the Choose button to close the Change Music Folder Location dialog box and enter the new path in the iTunes Music Folder Location text box on the General subtab of the Advanced tab.

   7. Make sure the Keep iTunes Music Folder Organized check box is selected.

   8. Click the OK button to close the Preferences dialog box.

If you want other users to be able to put song files in the shared library (for example, if they import songs from CD), you need to give them Write permission for it. To do so, follow these steps:

1. Open a Finder window to the /Users/Shared folder.

2. CTRL-click or right-click the iTunes Music folder, and then choose Get Info from the shortcut menu to display the iTunes Music Info window:

3. In the Ownership & Permissions area, click the Details arrow to expand its display, if necessary.

4. In the Others drop-down list, select the Read & Write item instead of the Read Only item.

5. Click the Apply To Enclosed Items button. Mac OS X displays this dialog box:

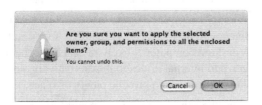

6. Click the OK button.

7. Click the Close button (the × button) to close the Info window for the library folder.

After you move your library to the /Users/Shared folder, the other users of your Mac can do one of two things:

■ Move their library to the /Users/Shared folder, using the technique described here, so that all files are stored centrally. Users can then add songs they import to the shared library, and all users can access them.

■ Keep their library separate, but add the contents of the shared library folder to it. Here's how:

　　1. Press ⌘-o or choose File | Add To Library to display the Add To Library dialog box.

　　2. Navigate to the /Users/Shared/iTunes Music folder.

　　3. Click the Choose button. iTunes adds all the latest songs to your library.

Whichever approach the other users of your Mac choose, the songs that they add to the shared library don't appear automatically in your library. To add all the latest tracks, use the Add To Library dialog box, as described in the previous list.

Build a Media Server for Your Household

If you find that trying to play songs stored in libraries that keep disappearing off the network is too tedious, another option is to build a media server for your household. You can either build a server from scratch on a new computer or change the role of one of your existing computers—even a pensioned-off computer that's too old to run Mac OS X or Windows Vista or XP at a decent speed.

Whether you buy (or build) a new computer or repurpose an existing computer will color your choices for your server. Here are notes on the key components for the server:

- **Operating system**   The server can run Windows or Mac OS X if you have a copy that you can spare; if not, you might consider using a less expensive (or even free) operating system, such as one of the many distributions of Linux.

- **Processor**   The server can run on a modest processor—even an antiquated one by today's standards, such as a 500-MHz or faster processor for a Windows or Linux server or a slower G3 processor for a Mac server.

- **RAM**   The server needs only enough RAM to run the operating system unless you'll need to run applications on it. For example, 256MB of RAM is adequate for a server running Windows XP or Mac OS X Tiger. Windows Vista and Mac OXS X Leopard require 512MB or (preferably) 1GB.

- **Disk space**   The server must have enough disk space to store all the songs and other files you want to have available. A desktop computer is likely to be a better bet than a notebook computer, because you can add internal drives to it. Alternatively, you might use one or more external USB or FireWire drives to provide plenty of space.

- **Network connection**   The server must be connected to your network, either via network cable or via wireless. A wireless connection is adequate for serving a few computers, but in most cases, a wired connection (Fast Ethernet or Gigabit Ethernet) is a much better choice.

- **Monitor**   If the server will simply be running somewhere convenient (rather than being used for other computing tasks, such as running applications), all you need is an old monitor capable of displaying the bootup and login screens for the operating system. After that, you can turn the monitor off until you need to restart or configure the server.

- **Keyboard and mouse**   Like the monitor, the keyboard and mouse can be basic devices, because you'll need to use them only for booting and configuring the server.

- **CD-ROM drive**   Your server needs a CD-ROM drive only if you'll use it for ripping. If you'll rip on the clients, the server can get by without one.

- **Sound card**   Your server needs a sound card only if you'll use it for playing music or other media files.

- **Reliability**   Modest your server may be, but it must be reliable—otherwise the music won't be available when you want to play it. Make sure also that the server has plenty of cooling, and configure its power settings so that it doesn't go to sleep. See the end of Chapter 8 for instructions on how to make sure a PC or Mac doesn't go to sleep at the wrong time.

- **Location**   If you choose to leave your server running all the time, locate it somewhere safe from being switched off accidentally. Because the running server will probably make some noise, you may be tempted to hide it away in a closet. If you do, make sure there's enough ventilation so that it doesn't overheat.

To set up the server, follow these general steps. The specifics will depend on which operating system you're using for the server.

1. Create a folder that will contain the songs.

2. Share that folder on the network so that all the users you want to be able to play music are allowed to access it.

3. On each of the client computers, move the library into the shared folder.

Enjoy Podcasts

A *podcast* is a downloadable show that you can play in iTunes or transfer to an iPod or iPhone. Some podcasts are downloadable versions of professional broadcast radio shows, while others are put together by enthusiasts.

Apple makes selected podcasts available through the iTunes Store, which makes an easy way to get started listening to podcasts or watching video podcasts. You can also find many more podcasts on the Internet.

Configure Podcast Preferences

Before you start working with podcasts, you should configure podcast preferences. These preferences cover how iTunes handles podcasts and which podcasts are synchronized with the iPod or iPhone. To control how iTunes handles podcasts, follow these steps:

1. Display the iTunes dialog box or the Preferences dialog box:

   ■ In Windows, choose Edit | Preferences or press CTRL-COMMA or CTRL-Y to display the iTunes dialog box.

   ■ On the Mac, choose iTunes | Preferences or press ⌘-COMMA or ⌘-Y to display the Preferences dialog box.

2. Click the Podcasts tab. Figure 10-11 shows the Podcasts tab for iTunes on the Mac. The Windows version has the same controls.

FIGURE 10-11   Choose podcast settings on the Podcasts tab in iTunes.

3. In the Check for New Episodes drop-down list, choose the appropriate frequency: Every Hour, Every Day, Every Week, or Manually.

4. In the When New Episodes Are Available drop-down list, choose what to do: Download All, Download The Most Recent One, or Do Nothing.

5. In the Keep drop-down list, choose which episodes of the podcasts to keep: All Episodes, All Unplayed Episodes, Most Recent Episodes, or the last 2, 3, 4, 5, or 10 episodes.

6. Click the OK button to close the dialog box.

Once you've set up iTunes to handle podcasts, tell the iPod or iPhone which podcasts you want to synchronize. Follow these steps:

1. Connect the iPod or iPhone to your computer if it's not already connected.

2. Click the iPod's or iPhone's entry in the Source pane to display its contents.

3. Click the Podcasts tab to display that tab's contents (see Figure 10-12).

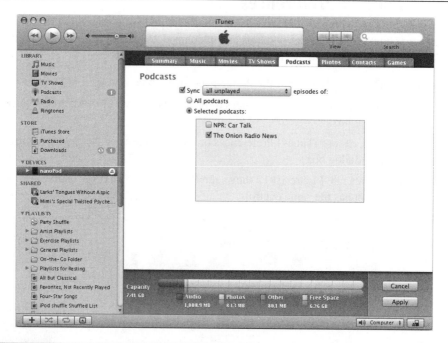

FIGURE 10-12   Use the Podcasts tab to tell iTunes which podcasts you want to put on the iPod or iPhone.

4. To synchronize podcasts automatically, select the Sync check box, and then choose which episodes in the drop-down list: All; 1, 3, 5, or 10 Most Recent; All Unplayed; 1, 3, 5, or 10 Most Recent Unplayed; All New; or 1, 3, 5, or 10 Most Recent New.

5. Choose which podcasts to synchronize by selecting either the All Podcasts option button or the Selected Podcasts option button (and then selecting the check box for each podcast that you want to have updated).

6. Click the Apply button to apply the changes. iTunes synchronizes the podcasts with the iPod or iPhone.

Explore Podcasts on the iTunes Store

To explore podcasts on the iTunes Store, click the iTunes Store item in the Source pane, and then click the Podcasts link in the iTunes Store box on the home page. iTunes displays the Podcasts page (see Figure 10-13).

From here, you can follow the links to the various podcasts. When you find a podcast that interests you, you can either click the Get Episode button to download a particular episode or click the Subscribe button to subscribe to the podcast. When you click the Subscribe button,

FIGURE 10-13   You can find a wide variety of podcasts on the Podcasts page of the iTunes Store.

iTunes displays a confirmation dialog box, as shown here. Select the Do Not Ask About Subscribing Again check box if you want to suppress confirmation in the future, and then click the Subscribe button to proceed with the subscription.

Add Podcasts from the Internet

If the range of podcasts available on the iTunes Store doesn't sate your appetite, you can find many other podcasts on the Internet. To add a podcast whose URL you know, choose Advanced | Subscribe To Podcast to display the Subscribe To Podcast dialog box (shown here), type or paste the URL of the podcast, and then click the OK button.

Listen to Podcasts

To listen to the podcasts that you've subscribed to, click the Podcasts item in the Source pane, and then double-click the podcast that you want to hear. You can then control the podcast by using the iTunes play controls as usual. From here, you can unsubscribe from a podcast by selecting it and clicking the Unsubscribe button. When you do so, iTunes adds a Subscribe button to the podcast, so that you can easily subscribe to it again if you choose.

To play a podcast on the iPod, choose the Podcasts item on the Music menu; on the iPhone, go to the iPod, touch the More button, and then touch the Podcasts item. Select the podcast you want to play, and then use the device's play controls as usual.

TIP

If you want to create your own podcasts, you can find plenty of suitable software online—but you may already have all you need on your Mac. GarageBand, the music-composition tool that comes as part of the iLife suite, is quite capable of creating podcasts. Use the File | Export To iTunes command to export the resulting file to iTunes, select it in iTunes, and then use the Advanced | Convert Selection To command to convert it to the format in which you want to distribute it (for example, AAC using the Podcast quality).

Part III

Put Text and Photos on the iPod

Chapter 11

Put Your Contacts and Calendars on the iPod

How to...

- Put your Outlook contacts and calendars on the iPod automatically
- Put your Windows Address Book contacts on the iPod automatically
- Put your Address Book contacts on the iPod automatically from the Mac
- View your contacts on the iPod
- View your calendars on the iPod
- Put your contacts and calendars on the iPod manually from Windows
- Put your contacts and calendars on the iPod manually from the Mac

Together with your songs, photos, and videos, the iPod lets you carry around your contacts and calendars so that you can view them whenever you need.

The easiest way to put your contacts and calendars on the iPod is to synchronize them automatically. On Windows, you can synchronize calendars from Outlook and synchronize contacts from either Outlook or Windows Contacts (on Windows Vista) or Windows Address Book (on Windows XP). On the Mac, you can synchronize contacts from Address Book and synchronize calendars from iCal. You can even synchronize contacts' photos, though you may find the small versions of the photos on the iPod less helpful than those on your desktop.

If you use other calendar or contact programs, you can put your calendars and contacts on the iPod manually.

You can also put your contacts and calendars on the iPhone and iPod touch. These devices display contacts and calendars differently from the other iPods; both let you create contacts, and the iPhone lets you create calendar appointments as well. Chapter 19 shows you how to work with contacts on the iPhone and iPod touch, and Chapter 20 explains how to work with calendars on the iPhone and iPod touch.

NOTE   *You can't display contacts or calendars on an iPod shuffle because it doesn't have a screen.*

Put Your Outlook Contacts and Calendars on the iPod Automatically

If you use Outlook, you can easily put your contacts and calendars on the iPod. Follow these steps:

1. Connect the iPod to your PC. Windows launches iTunes (if it wasn't running) or activates iTunes (if it was running).
2. In iTunes, click the iPod's entry in the Devices list in the Source pane.

FIGURE 11-1   iTunes makes it easy to put your Outlook contacts and calendars onto the iPod.

3. Click the Contacts tab to display its contents. Figure 11-1 shows the Contacts tab with settings chosen for Outlook.

4. Select the Sync Contacts From check box, and then select Microsoft Outlook in the drop-down list.

5. If you want to sync all your contacts, select the All Contacts option button. If you prefer to sync only some groups, click the Selected Groups option button, and then, in the list box, select the check box for each group you want to have on the iPod.

6. Select the Include Contacts' Photos check box if you want to include photos with the contact records.

7. If you want to put your Outlook calendars on the iPod, select the Sync Calendars From Microsoft Outlook check box.

8. Select the All Calendars option button if you want to sync all your calendars. To sync only some, click the Selected Calendars option button, and then, in the list box, select the check box for each calendar you want to have on the iPod.

9. Click the Apply button to apply the changes to the iPod. iTunes synchronizes the contacts, calendars, or both with the iPod.

Put Your Windows Address Book Contacts on the iPod Automatically

If you keep your contacts in the Windows Contacts folder (on Windows Vista) or the Windows Address Book (on Windows XP), you can put your contacts on the iPod automatically. Follow these steps:

1. Connect the iPod to your PC. Windows launches iTunes (if it wasn't running) or activates iTunes (if it was running).

2. In iTunes, click the iPod's entry in the Devices list in the Source pane.

3. Click the Contacts tab to display its contents.

4. Select the Sync Contacts From check box. For Windows Vista, then select Windows Contacts in the drop-down list. For Windows XP, select Windows Address Book in the drop-down list.

5. Select the Include Contacts' Photos check box if you want to include photos with the contact records.

6. Click the Apply button to apply the changes. iTunes synchronizes the contacts with the iPod.

Put Your Mac Contacts and iCal Calendars on the iPod Automatically

On the Mac, if you keep your contacts in Address Book, you can put them on the iPod automatically. Likewise, if you keep your calendars in iCal, you can synchronize these calendars with the iPod automatically.

To synchronize Address Book contacts and iCal calendars, follow these steps:

1. Connect the iPod to your Mac. Mac OS X launches iTunes (if it wasn't running) or activates iTunes (if it was running).

2. In iTunes, click the iPod's entry in the Devices list in the Source pane.

3. Click the Contacts tab to display its contents (shown in Figure 11-2 with settings chosen).

4. Select the Sync Address Book Contacts check box.

5. If you want to sync all your contacts, select the All Contacts option button. If you prefer to sync only some groups, click the Selected Groups option button, and then, in the list box, select the check box for each group you want to have on the iPod.

6. Select the Include Contacts' Photos check box if you want to include photos with the contact records.

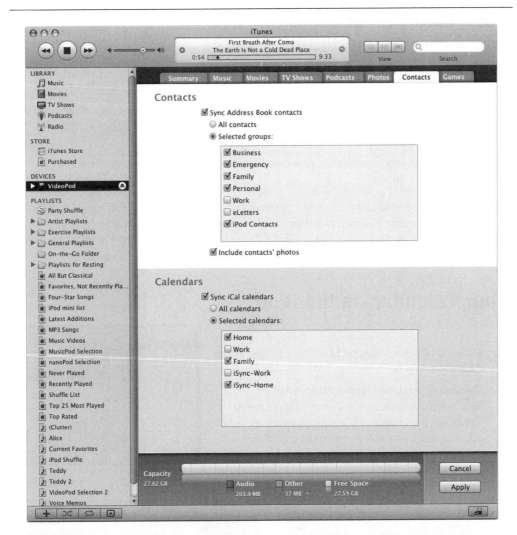

FIGURE 11-2   On the Mac, iTunes can put your Address Book contacts and iCal calendars on the iPod.

7. If you want to put your iCal calendars on the iPod, select the Sync iCal Calendars check box.

8. Select the All Calendars option button if you want to sync all your calendars. To sync only some, click the Selected Calendars option button, and then, in the list box, select the check box for each calendar you want to have on the iPod.

9. Click the Apply button to apply the changes to the iPod. iTunes synchronizes the contacts, calendars, or both with the iPod.

View Your Contacts on the iPod

To view your contacts on the iPod, follow these steps:

1. On the iPod, choose Extras | Contacts from the main menu to display the Contacts submenu (shown on the left in Figure 11-3).

2. Scroll to the contact you want to view and then press the Select button. The iPod displays the contact's information. The right screen in Figure 11-3 shows an example. You may need to scroll down to view all the data about the contact.

3. To display the previous contact, press the Previous button. To display the next contact, press the Next button.

To specify how the iPod should sort and display your contacts' names, scroll to the Sort By item on the Settings screen and then press the Select button to switch between First and Last. First sorts the contacts by first name (for example, "Jane Sixpack" before "Joe Public"), while Last sorts the contacts by last name (for example, "Joe Public" before "Jane Sixpack").

View Your Calendar on the iPod

To view your calendar on the iPod, follow these steps:

1. On the iPod, choose Extras | Calendar to display the Calendars screen.

2. The first Calendars screen contains a list of available calendars, as shown here. Leave the All Calendars item selected if you want to see all your appointments, or scroll down to the calendar you want (or to your To Do list).

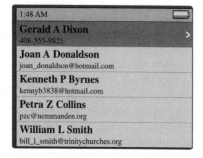
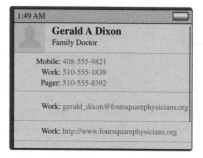

FIGURE 11-3   In the Contacts submenu (left), select the contact you want to view and then press the Select button to display the contact's information (right).

3. Press the Select button to display the calendar you chose, as shown here.

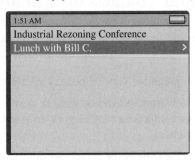

4. Scroll backward or forward to the day you're interested in:

■ To access the next month or the previous month, press the Next button or the Previous button, respectively.

■ If you're happier scrolling, you can scroll back past the beginning of the month to access the previous month, or you can scroll forward past the end of the month to access the next month.

5. Press the Select button to display your schedule for that day.

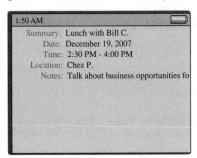

6. To view the details for an appointment, scroll to it and press the Select button. The following illustration shows a sample appointment. From there, you can press the Next button to display the next appointment or press the Previous button to display the previous appointment.

7. Once you've accessed a day, you can press the Next button to access the next day or press the Previous button to access the previous day.

Put Your Contacts and Calendars on the iPod Manually from Windows

If you keep your contacts and calendars in a program that iTunes does not support, you need to transfer them manually to the iPod. This involves four steps:

- Creating vCards from the contacts
- Creating vCalendar or iCalendar files from the calendars
- Enabling disk mode on the iPod
- Transferring the vCards or calendar files

The following sections show you how to perform these steps.

NOTE   *A vCard is a standard format for an electronic business card or contact record. A vCalendar file or iCalendar is a standard format for electronic calendars. Despite its different name, iCalendar is an updated version of vCalendar.*

Create vCards from Your Contacts on Windows

To create vCards, you must find the command for exporting a contact to a vCard. This command varies depending on the program you're using. For example, to create one or more vCards from Palm Desktop (a popular personal-information management program), follow these steps:

1. Click the Contacts button or choose View | Contacts to display the Contacts pane.
2. Select the contact or contacts from which you want to create vCards. If necessary, select the appropriate category of contacts in the Category drop-down list, or choose the All item to display all your contacts.
3. Choose File | Export vCard to display the Export As dialog box.
4. Enter the filename in the File Name text box, specify the destination, and then click the Export button.

Create Calendar Files from Your Calendars on Windows

If you use a calendaring program other than Outlook, you need to create calendar files manually and then put them on the iPod.

Most calendar programs include an Export command or a Save As command that lets you create a calendar file in the iCalendar (.ics) format or the vCalendar (.vcal) format. For example:

- **Windows Calendar on Windows Vista**   Open the calendar, and then choose File | Export.
- **Palm Desktop**   Open the calendar, select the event you want to export, and then choose File | Export vCal.

How to ...   Create vCards from CSV Files

Many address book programs let you create vCards easily. But if the program in which your addresses are stored can't export them as vCards, you need to take a couple of extra steps to get the addresses onto the iPod. For example, if you use the Yahoo! address book, you won't be able to create vCards directly from it.

The first step is to export the addresses from the application into a text file. Most applications can create a CSV file, so that's usually the best format to use. Other applications create tab-separated values (TSV) files, which usually work as well.

Once you've created the CSV or TSV file, import it into an address book that can handle CSV or TSV files *and* can create vCards. On Windows, Contacts (on Windows Vista) and Address Book (on Windows XP) can handle CSV imports. (If you're using Palm Desktop, that program can handle CSV imports too.)

On the Mac, Address Book in Mac OS X can import text files, vCards, and LDAP Interchange Format (LDIF) files. (LDAP is the abbreviation for *Lightweight Directory Access Protocol*, a standard protocol for accessing directory information.) If you have Entourage, you can use that program instead to import a text file.

Once you've found the appropriate Import command (usually File | Import), the tricky part of importing is assigning each field in the CSV or TSV file to the corresponding field in the address book. The following illustration shows examples of the dialog boxes used for mapping data to fields. The Specify Import Fields dialog box (on the left) is from Palm Desktop for Windows; the Import Contacts dialog box (on the right) is from Entourage, which can usually map some of the fields automatically.

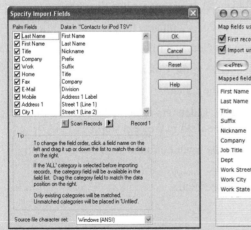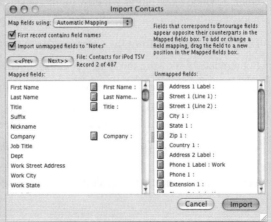

The second step is to export the vCards from the address application, as described earlier in the chapter.

Enable Disk Mode on the iPod on Windows

To enable disk mode, connect the iPod and take the following steps:

1. Open iTunes if it's not already running, or activate it.
2. Click the iPod's entry in the Source pane.
3. If iTunes doesn't display the Summary tab for the iPod, click the Summary tab.
4. Select the Enable Disk Use check box. iTunes displays a dialog box warning you that you need to eject the iPod manually before disconnecting it, as shown here.

5. Select the Do Not Warn Me Again check box if you want to skip this warning in the future.
6. Click the OK button to close the message box.
7. Click the Apply button to apply the change.

Copy the vCards and Calendar Files to the iPod on Windows

Once you've enabled disk mode, you can copy the vCards and calendar files to the iPod using Windows Explorer. Follow these steps:

1. Open a Windows Explorer window to the folder in which you created the vCards.
2. Open another Windows Explorer window to the iPod's Contacts folder.
3. Drag the vCard files from the source folder to the Contacts folder.
4. In the window showing the iPod's contents, change to the Calendars folder.
5. Drag the calendar files from the source folder to the Calendars folder.
6. Close the Windows Explorer window showing the Calendars folder. (If you leave this window open, Windows may be unable to eject the iPod in the next step.)
7. Eject the iPod from iTunes. (For example, click the Eject button next to the iPod's entry in the Source pane.)
8. Verify that the contacts and calendars appear on the iPod.

Put Your Contacts and Calendars on the iPod Manually from the Mac

If you keep your contacts and calendars in a program that iTunes does not support, you need to transfer them manually to the iPod. This involves four steps:

- Creating vCards from the contacts
- Creating vCal or iCalendar files from the calendars
- Enabling disk mode on the iPod
- Transferring the vCards or calendar files

The following sections show you how to perform these steps.

Create vCards from Your Contacts on the Mac

To create vCards, you must find the command for exporting a contact to a vCard. This command varies depending on the program you're using. Here are examples using Microsoft Entourage and Palm Desktop, two programs that are widely used for contacts.

Create a vCard from Entourage

To create a vCard from Entourage, follow these steps:

1. Click the Address button in the upper-left pane to display your address book.
2. Select the contact or contacts from which you want to create vCards.
3. Drag the selected contact or contacts to the folder in which you want to create the vCards, or to the desktop.

Create a vCard from Palm Desktop

You can create a vCard from Palm Desktop by dragging a contact to the folder in which you want to create the vCard. But you can also create vCards by using the Export: Palm Desktop dialog box. To do so, follow these steps:

1. In the Address List window, select the contact from which you want to create a vCard.
2. Choose File | Export to display the Export: Palm Desktop dialog box (shown in Figure 11-4 with settings chosen). The Addresses item will be selected in the Module drop-down list by default.
3. Use the Save As text box to specify the filename and the Where drop-down list to specify the location under which to save the file.

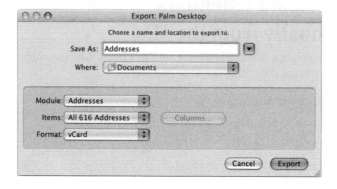

FIGURE 11-4   You can export one or more contacts as vCards easily from Palm Desktop for the Mac.

4. In the Items drop-down list, select the appropriate item—for example, All *NN* Addresses.

5. In the Format drop-down list, select the vCard item.

6. Click the Export button to export the contacts to the specified file.

Create Calendar Files from Your Calendars on the Mac

If you keep your calendars in iCal, you can have iTunes synchronize your calendars automatically with the iPod, as you saw earlier in this chapter. But if you use another calendaring program, you need to create calendar files manually and then put them on the iPod.

Most calendar programs let you export your calendar information to a file in the iCalendar (.ics) format or the vCalendar (.vcal) format. For example:

- **Microsoft Entourage**   Open the calendar, and then drag the appointment or event to the folder in which you want to create the calendar file.

- **Palm Desktop**   Open the calendar, select the event you want to export, and then choose File | Export. In the Format drop-down list, select the vCal item.

Enable Disk Mode on the iPod on the Mac

To enable disk mode, connect the iPod and take the following steps:

1. Open iTunes if it's not already running, or activate it.

2. Click the iPod's entry in the Source pane.

3. If iTunes doesn't display the Summary tab for the iPod, click the Summary tab.

4. Select the Enable Disk Use check box. iTunes displays a dialog box warning you that you need to eject the iPod manually before disconnecting it, as shown here.

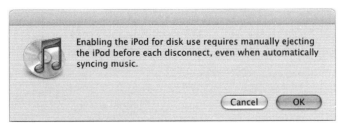

Enabling the iPod for disk use requires manually ejecting the iPod before each disconnect, even when automatically syncing music.

Cancel   OK

5. Click the OK button to close the message box.

6. Click the Apply button to apply the change.

Copy the vCards and Calendar Files to the iPod on the Mac

Once you've enabled disk mode, you can copy the vCards and calendar files to the iPod using the Finder. Follow these steps:

1. Open a Finder window to the folder in which you created the vCards.

2. Open another Finder window to the iPod's Contacts folder.

3. Drag the vCard files from the source folder to the Contacts folder.

4. In the window showing the iPod's contents, change to the Calendars folder.

5. Drag the calendar files from the source folder to the Calendars folder.

6. Close the Finder window showing the Calendars folder. (If you leave this window open, iTunes may be unable to eject the iPod in the next step.)

7. Eject the iPod from iTunes. (For example, click the Eject button next to the iPod's entry in the Source pane.)

8. Verify that the contacts and calendars appear on the iPod.

Chapter 12

Put Text and Books on the iPod

How to . . .

- Understand the basics of putting text on an iPod
- Use the Notes feature to put text on an iPod from a Mac or Windows
- Put text on an iPod from Windows
- Put text on an iPod from a Mac

This chapter discusses how to store other text on an iPod classic or iPod nano so you can display it on the screen. At this writing, you can't store text on an iPod classic or iPod nano in the same way, so what you read in this chapter doesn't apply to the iPod classic or iPod nano. However, the iPhone has a Notes feature that lets you create text notes directly on the iPhone, using its on-screen keyboard. See Chapter 20 for coverage of the iPhone's Notes feature.

By using an iPod as an external drive (as discussed in Chapter 17), you can store any type of file on that iPod. But unless the file is in a text format that the iPod's software can handle, you won't be able to display the file on the iPod's interface—you'll be able to work with the file only when you've connected the iPod to your computer.

The iPod classic and iPod shuffle include a Notes feature that lets you put text files on an iPod so that you can read them on it. How enjoyable reading the text on an iPod is depends on the screen size and resolution, and on your eyesight. But in general, reading text on an iPod with a color screen compares favorably to reading text on a mobile phone. You may not want to read *War and Peace* in its entirety on an iPod, but an iPod is good for shorter texts—and especially for information that you must carry with you, such as driving directions.

> **TIP** *Two great places for finding utilities such as those discussed in this chapter are VersionTracker.com (www.versiontracker.com) and iLounge.com (www.ilounge.com). You'll also find Mac-related utilities at Apple's Mac OS X Downloads page (www.apple.com/macosx/downloads).*

Understand What Text You Can Put on an iPod classic or iPod nano

With the right utilities, you can put on an iPod any text file you have on your computer. That text could be anything from a parts list to part of a novel, from a thesis to a section of a thesaurus. You can store notes of any length on an iPod, but the iPod can display only the first 4KB of a text file. That's roughly 4,000 characters, or about 600–700 words of average length. Various utilities let you split up longer files into iPod-sized bites automatically. An iPod can hold up to 1,000 notes at a time, and the notes can be linked together to make them easy to navigate.

> **NOTE** *The first time you access the Notes category after adding the notes, the iPod has to build an index of the notes it contains. If there are nearly 1,000 notes, building the index takes several minutes. Once the index is built, accessing the notes is quick.*

As you'll see in the following sections, apart from text files, utility designers have concentrated on types of text that are widely useful and can be downloaded easily from sources on the Internet. Here are some examples:

- **News headlines** Various iPod utilities can download news headlines from news sites. Most of these utilities let you choose the sites, whereas other utilities are limited to a single site. Many people find news headlines more or less useless when their accompanying stories aren't available. However, you may find the headlines useful as a means of determining which sites you need to visit and which stories you want to read. But this still pales in comparison to AvantGo on Palms and Pocket PCs, which delivers both the headlines and the full stories.

- **Weather reports** Various iPod utilities can download weather reports from online sites. You specify the city (or ZIP code) and the type of weather reports (for example, today's forecast or a five-day report), and the utility downloads the relevant information.

- **Stock quotes** Several utilities can download stock quotes. You specify the stock symbols and (in some cases) choose the frequency of updates.

- **Lyrics** Some utilities can look up the lyrics to songs you specify.

- **Horoscopes** Some utilities can download horoscopes.

- **Driving directions** Some utilities can download driving directions from mapping services.

- **Gas prices** Now that gas prices have risen, being able to put a list of the latest local prices on an iPod is helpful.

Use the Notes Feature

The main means of putting text on an iPod classic or iPod nano is the Notes feature. This feature works effectively only with plain-text files. You *can* transfer other documents, such as Rich Text Format (RTF) documents or Word documents, by using the Notes feature, but the text displayed on the iPod then includes formatting codes and extended characters. These make the text nearly impossible to read.

To put notes on an iPod, connect the iPod and enable disk mode if it's not currently enabled:

1. Open iTunes if it's not already running, or activate it.

2. Click the iPod's entry in the Source pane.

3. If iTunes doesn't display the Summary tab for the iPod, click the Summary tab.

4. Select the Enable Disk Use check box. iTunes displays a dialog box warning you that you'll need to unmount the iPod manually before disconnecting it, as shown here.

5. Select the Do Not Warn Me Again check box if you want to skip this warning in the future.

6. Click the OK button to close the message box.

7. Click the Apply button to apply the change.

Once disk mode is enabled, you can copy or move the note files to the Notes folder on the iPod using Windows Explorer (Windows) or the Finder (Mac OS X).

> **NOTE** *The Notes folder on the iPod contains a note called Instructions that tells you how to use notes. The first time you open the Notes folder on the iPod, delete this note to prevent it from appearing in your listings.*

On the iPod, you can then read your notes by choosing Extras | Notes, scrolling down to the file, and pressing the Select button.

Use iPod Scripts to Create and Manage Text Notes on the Mac

If you use the Notes feature extensively on the Mac, consider downloading the iPod Scripts collection that Apple provides for creating and managing text notes. These scripts require Mac OS X 10.2 or later.

Learn What the iPod Scripts Do

At this writing, the iPod Scripts collection contains the following scripts:

■ **List Notes**   This script provides an easy way of opening one of the scripts stored on the iPod for editing on your Mac. This script displays a dialog box that lists the notes stored on the iPod. You select the appropriate script and click the Open button to open it:

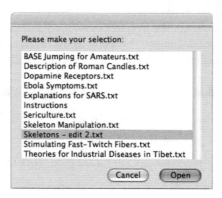

■ **Clear All Notes**   This script deletes all the notes in the Notes folder on the iPod and lets you choose whether to delete subfolders in the Notes folder as well. This script displays these two dialog boxes:

■ **Eject iPod**   This script checks that you want to eject the currently mounted iPod and then ejects it if you click the Continue button. In normal use, you'll find it easier to eject the iPod using either iTunes or the desktop icon (if the iPod is in disk mode) rather than running this script.

■ **Clipboard To Note**   This script creates a note from the current contents of the Clipboard. This script is great for quickly grabbing part of a document or a web page and generating a note from it. Select the text, issue a Copy command, and then run the script. Click the Continue button in the first dialog box (shown on the left in the next illustration), enter the name for the note in the dialog box shown on the right in the next illustration, and click OK. The script then displays a message box telling you that it has created the note.

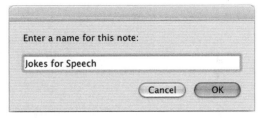

■ **MacCentral and Printer Friendly**   The MacCentral and Printer Friendly scripts appear in the Note From Webpages folder. The MacCentral script is for extracting an article from the MacCentral website from the foremost browser window. The Printer Friendly script follows the same theme but is less specialized, extracting the contents of the foremost browser window to a note. For best effect, set the foremost window ready to print without ads and without other HTML items that will otherwise mess up the text of the note.

Get and Use the iPod Scripts

To use the iPod Scripts collection, follow these steps:

1. Download the iPod Scripts collection from www.apple.com/applescript/ipod/.

2. Mount the disk image (if Mac OS X doesn't automatically mount it for you) and then move its contents to your ~/Library/Scripts folder.

NOTE *If you haven't used any scripts before, you'll need to create the Scripts folder manually under the ~/Library folder.*

3. Connect the iPod to your computer.

4. Use the Script menu to run the script. If you haven't installed the Script menu, do so as described next.

Put the Script Menu on the Mac OS X Menu Bar

You can run the iPod scripts directly from the Scripts folder, but doing so is slower and more awkward than it needs to be. The better way to run scripts is from the Scripts menu that Mac OS X can display on your menu bar.

If you haven't used scripts before, you'll probably need to add the Script menu to the menu bar. To do so, follow these steps:

1. From the Finder, choose Go | Applications to display your Applications folder.

2. Double-click the AppleScript folder to open it in the window.

3. Double-click the AppleScript Utility item to open AppleScript Utility, shown here.

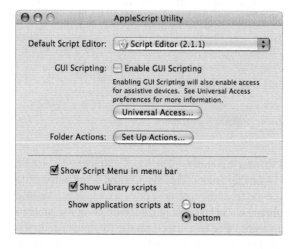

NOTE *In Mac OS X 10.3 (Panther), double-click the Install Script Menu item in the AppleScript folder to install the Script menu rather than running AppleScript Utility.*

4. Select the Show Script Menu In Menu Bar check box and the Show Library Scripts check box.

5. Press ⌘-Q or choose AppleScript Utility | Quit AppleScript Utility to quit AppleScript Utility.

Mac OS X adds an icon that you can click to display the Script menu, shown here with the iPod scripts expanded:

You can then run scripts easily from the desktop by using the Script menu.

Put Information on an iPod from Windows

The Notes feature is great for putting existing text files on an iPod. But if you need to get the text and then put it on an iPod automatically, you can save time by using a custom utility. This section shows you two Windows utilities for putting text on an iPod. The next section shows you several Mac utilities for putting text on an iPod.

iGadget

iGadget ($15; www.ipodsoft.com/site/pmwiki.php?n=IGadget.HomePage) is a powerful utility that can put text, news, weather, Outlook items, and movie listings on an iPod. iGadget (see Figure 12-1) can also back up files from your PC to the iPod and retrieve music files from the iPod's music database. (See Chapter 15 for details on other utilities that can retrieve music files from an iPod.)

NOTE *iGadget was previously named iPod Agent and then PodPlus.*

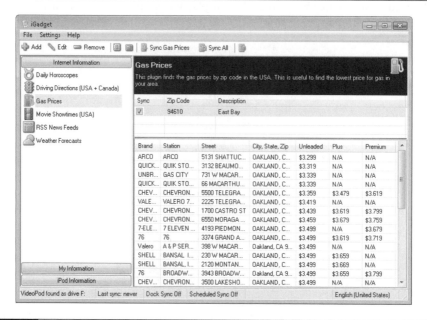

FIGURE 12-1   iGadget's many features include transferring gas prices, news feeds, weather, and text files to an iPod.

How to ... Deal with the COMDLG32.OCX Error on Windows Vista

If iPod Library founders with a message that COMDLG32.OCX is not registered, click the OK button, and then follow these steps to get and register COMDLG32.OCX:

1. In Internet Explorer, go to http://windowsxp.mvps.org/comdlg32.htm.

2. Download the comdlg32.zip file and open it.

3. Copy the COMDLG32.OCX file from the zip file to your computer's %systemroot%\system32 folder.

4. Click the Start button, and then click in the Search field.

5. Type **cmd**, press CTRL-SHIFT-ENTER, and then go through User Account Control for the Windows Command Processor feature. Windows opens a Command Prompt window with Administrator privileges.

6. Type the following command, and then press ENTER:

```
regsvr32 %systemroot%\system32\comdlg32.ocx
```

7. Windows displays a message box to tell you that the DLL-registration operation succeeded:

8. Click the OK button.

9. Click the Close button (the × button) to close the Command Prompt window.

Run iPod Library again. This time, it should work correctly.

iPod Library

iPod Library (freeware; www.sturm.net.nz/website.php?Section=iPod+Programs&Page=iPodLibrary) is a utility for dividing text files, HTML text files, and PDF files into note-sized sections and loading them on an iPod (see Figure 12-2). You may have to download and install extra Windows DLL (dynamic link library) files from the iPod Library website in order to get iPod Library running.

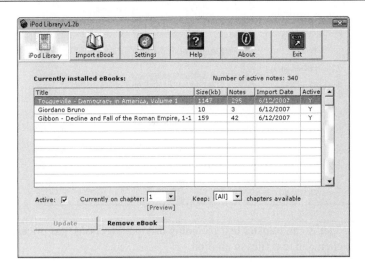

FIGURE 12-2   iPod Library is a freeware tool for managing text notes on an iPod.

Put Information on an iPod from the Mac

This section discusses utilities for putting information on an iPod from a Mac, starting with the most useful.

iGadget X

iGadget X ($15; www.ipodsoft.com/site/pmwiki.php?n=IGadget.HomePage) is a utility that can put many kinds of text onto an iPod, from RSS news feeds and podcasts to horoscope readings and e-books, back up files from your Mac to an iPod, and more. Figure 12-3 shows iGadget X.

iPDA

iPDA ($19.95; www.zapptek.com) is a utility that enables you to copy contacts, notes, tasks, e-mail, and calendar information from Microsoft Entourage, or from Mail, Stickies, Address Book, or iCal, to an iPod (see Figure 12-4). iPDA also supports downloading news headlines from Google, weather forecasts, and directions, and transferring documents in formats including Microsoft Word, Pages, PDF, and RTF.

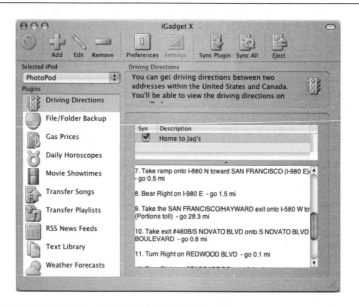

FIGURE 12-3 iGadget X can transfer text including driving directions, gas prices, news feeds, weather, and text files to an iPod.

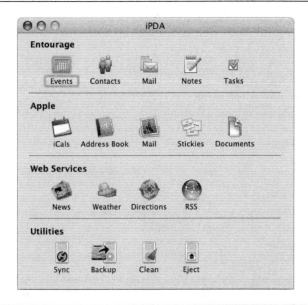

FIGURE 12-4   iPDA can copy a wide variety of text items—including news, weather forecasts, directions, and Entourage items—to an iPod.

Book2Pod

Book2Pod (freeware; www.tomsci.com/book2pod or www.ilounge.com) is a tool for splitting up a text file into pieces the right size for iPod notes (see Figure 12-5). Book2Pod embeds links at the start and end of each note-sized section so that you can navigate to the next section by pressing the Select button. Book2Pod enables you to get around the 1,000-note limitation by letting you load and unload books even after you've split them up into pieces. Book2Pod requires Mac OS X 10.2 or later and iPod firmware 2.0 or higher.

iPodMemo

iPodMemo (freeware; various sites including www.versiontracker.) is a text editor with which you can create memos of up to 1,000 characters and put them on an iPod as contacts (see Figure 12-6). iPodMemo is basic but functional—and the price is right.

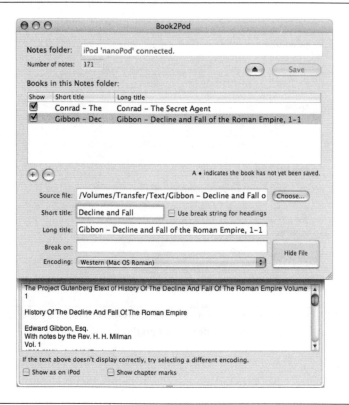

FIGURE 12-5 Book2Pod splits long text documents into note-sized bites and links each note to the previous note and next note.

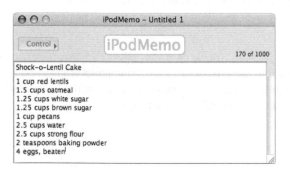

FIGURE 12-6 iPodMemo is a text editor that lets you quickly create memos and put them on an iPod.

Chapter 13

Put Photos and Videos on the iPod or iPhone

How to...

- Configure photo synchronization for the iPod or iPhone
- View photos and slideshows on the iPod
- View photos and slideshows on the iPhone
- Take photos on the iPhone and import them to your computer
- Put videos on the iPod or iPhone
- Create video files suitable for the iPod or iPhone

The iPhone and all iPods except the iPod shuffle can store your photo collection—or part of it—so that you can view your photos on the screen, either one at a time or as slideshows. The iPod lets you play music along with a slideshow, while the iPhone does not.

Even better, the iPod and the iPhone can play back videos. The iPod can play back videos or slideshows either on its built-in screen or on a TV to which you connect it. At this writing, the iPhone can play back videos only on its built-in screen, but a firmware update may enable it to output video as well.

This chapter shows you how to configure photo synchronization for the iPod and iPhone, view photos and slideshows on the devices, and take pictures using the iPhone's built-in camera. After than, you'll learn how to create video files suitable for the iPod or iPhone, transfer them, and play them back.

> **NOTE** *This chapter covers the iPod classic, the third-generation iPod nano, the iPod touch, and the iPhone. However, much of the video-related content also applies to the iPod with video, and much of the photo-related content also applies to the iPod with video, the fourth-generation regular iPods that have color screens, and the first two generations of iPod nano.*

Tell iTunes Which Photos to Put on the iPod or iPhone

First, tell iTunes which photos to put on the iPod or iPhone. You may already have done this. When you first connect the iPod or iPhone to your computer, the iPod Setup Assistant lets you choose whether to copy photos to the iPod or iPhone automatically. If you choose to copy them, you can select the source (more on this in a moment).

You can change your photo-synchronization options at any time. Follow these steps:

1. Connect the iPod or iPhone to your computer. Your computer should launch iTunes (if it's not running) or activate iTunes (if it is running).

2. In iTunes, click the iPod's or iPhone's entry in the Source pane to display the iPod or iPhone screens.

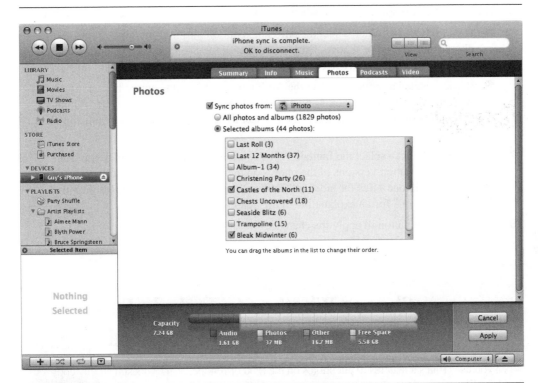

FIGURE 13-1   Configure photo-synchronization options for the iPod or iPhone on the Photos tab in the iPod or iPhone screens.

3. Click the Photos tab to display its contents. Figure 13-1 shows the Photos tab for an iPhone. The Photos tab for most iPods also includes a Include Full-Resolution Photos check box.

4. Select the Sync Photos From check box to make the other controls available.

5. In the drop-down list, select the source of the pictures:

- ■ **Windows Vista**   Your Pictures folder or another folder. If you have Adobe Photoshop Album 2.0 (or a later version) or Adobe Photoshop Elements 3.0 (or a later version), you can sync with the photos in that program instead.

- ■ **Windows XP**   Your My Pictures folder or another folder. If you have Adobe Photoshop Album 2.0 (or a later version) or Adobe Photoshop Elements 3.0 (or a later version), you can sync with the photos in that program instead.

- ■ **Mac OS X**   iPhoto or a folder.

6. After selecting the source, choose whether to include all the pictures or just some of them:

■ If you selected a folder, select the All Photos option button if you want to put all the photos on the iPod or iPhone. Otherwise, choose the Selected Folders option button, and then, in the list box, select the check box for each folder you want to transfer.

■ If you selected a program, select the All Photos And Albums option button if you want to transfer all the photos and albums. Otherwise, choose the Selected Albums option button, and then, in the list box, select the check box for each album you want to transfer.

7. For an iPod, you can select the Include Full-Resolution Photos check box if you want to store full-resolution versions of the photos on the iPod. (You can't put full-resolution photos on the iPhone.) See the sidebar "Choose Whether to Include Full-Resolution Photos on the iPod" for an explanation of this feature.

8. Click the Apply button to apply the changes.

How to ... Choose Whether to Include Full-Resolution Photos on the iPod

When you use iTunes's features to put photos on the iPod or iPhone, iTunes doesn't simply copy the photo files across to the device. Instead, it creates different-sized versions of the photos:

■ A miniature version suitable for viewing in thumbnail mode (where you see a dozen or more pictures at once, allowing you to pick one)

■ A small version suitable for full-screen viewing on the screen

■ A larger version suitable for full-screen viewing on a television (if the device supports external viewing)

These three versions are as small as possible for their purposes and are optimized to look as good as possible at the sizes mentioned. When you synchronize the iPod or iPhone, you'll see iTunes optimizing the various-sized versions of each new photo before it transfers the photos to the device.

Normally, these three sizes of pictures take care of all you're likely to want to do with the iPod or iPhone: view the thumbnails, view the pictures onscreen, or view the pictures on a television. But sometimes you may want to take your actual picture files with you on an iPod—for example, so that you can copy them to another computer, or so that you can manipulate them at work. In this case, select the Include Full-Resolution Photos check box on the Photos tab to make iTunes include the full versions. This feature isn't available on the iPhone or on the iPod touch.

Don't put the full-resolution photos on the iPod unless you need them, because they can take up a large amount of space, especially if you have many photos, a high-resolution digital camera, or both.

You can't display the full-resolution pictures on the iPod's screen or directly on a TV from the iPod. Because of this limitation, you may find it easier to mount the iPod in disk mode and copy the full-resolution versions of photos to the iPod manually. By doing so, you can control the folder in which the photos are stored on the iPod rather than having iTunes create complex folder structures based on the year, month, and day.

On the iPod, iTunes stores the full-resolution photos in the Full Resolution folder inside the Photos folder (Photos\Full Resolution as seen by Windows; Photos/Full Resolution as seen by the Mac). Within this folder, the pictures are divided into subfolders by year, month, and date. For example, pictures you load on December 31, 2007 go into the 2007\12\31 folder (as seen by Windows) or the 2007/12/31 folder (as seen by the Mac). This naming convention ensures that photos are grouped together suitably for sorting by date in either ascending or descending order.

Choose Whether to Display Album Artwork on the iPod

The iPod and iPhone can also display any album artwork associated with the songs you load on the iPod or iPhone. These artwork files take up some space, but not usually a significant amount compared to the songs themselves. This is because the artwork files are relatively compact.

The iPhone automatically loads all available art for the songs you transfer; without the art, Cover Flow view would be a sad thing. The iPod lets you choose whether to transfer the art to the iPod. Unless you're trying to stuff your iPod's last megabyte with music, having the art is usually a good idea. If you transfer the art, the iPod automatically displays it.

To transfer the art, select the Display Album Artwork On Your iPod check box on the Music tab for the iPod, and then click the Apply button to apply the change.

View Photos and Slideshows on the iPod

You can either browse photos on the iPod or create slideshows and play them back.

View Photos on the iPod

To view photos on the iPod, follow these steps:

1. Press the Menu button as many times as necessary to get to the Main menu.
2. Scroll down to highlight Photos, and then press the Select button.

How to ... Delete Unneeded Photo Cache Folders

iTunes caches the photos it puts on the iPod or iPhone in a folder named iPod Photo Cache that it creates in the folder that contains your photos. This folder contains all the photos you put on the iPod or iPhone, so it typically takes up about as much space on your computer's hard disk as on the iPod or iPhone. (Depending on the file systems used, there may be a minor difference in size.) If you put a lot of photos on the iPod or iPhone, the cache can take a fair bite out of your hard disk capacity. If you're short of disk space anyway, this bite may cause problems.

When you set iTunes to synchronize a new folder of photos, you can delete your old iPod Photo Cache folder to reclaim space. (iTunes doesn't delete the cache folder for you.) Open the parent folder and then delete the iPod Photo Cache folder:

- In Windows, click the iPod Photo Cache folder, press the DELETE key, and then click the Yes button in the Confirm Folder Delete dialog box that checks whether you want to move the folder to the Recycle Bin. You'll need to empty the Recycle Bin to actually recover the disk space. (Alternatively, click the iPod Photo Cache folder, hold down the SHIFT key, press the DELETE key, and then click the Yes button in the Confirm Folder Delete dialog box to bypass the Recycle Bin.)

- On the Mac, drag the iPod Photo Cache folder to the Trash. You'll need to empty the Trash to actually get the space back.

3. Scroll down to select your Photo Library or the album you want, and then press the Select button. The iPod displays thumbnails of the photos.

4. Scroll to select the thumbnail of the photo you want (scroll clockwise to go forward; scroll counterclockwise to go backward), and then press the Select button to display it.

5. Navigate from photo to photo:

   - Press the Previous button to move to the previous photo.

   - Press the Next button to move to the next photo.

   - Scroll forward or back to move quickly through the photos.

   - To start playing a slideshow without music from the photo you're currently viewing, press the Play/Pause button. Press the button again to pause the slideshow.

6. To exit the album, press the Menu button.

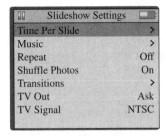

FIGURE 13-2   Use the options on the Slideshow Settings screen to set up your slideshow.

Choose Slideshow Settings on the iPod

Before starting a slideshow, you'll normally want to choose suitable slideshow settings. To do so, follow these steps:

1. Press the Menu button as many times as necessary to get to the Main menu.

2. Scroll down to highlight Photos and then press the Select button.

3. Select the Slideshow Settings item and then press the Select button to display the Slideshow Settings screen (see Figure 13-2). This is the Slideshow Settings screen for a fifth-generation iPod; the iPod nano does not have the TV Out option or the TV Signal option.

4. Scroll to the Time Per Slide item, press the Select button, and use the Next Slide screen (see Figure 13-3) to choose either manual advancing or a specific time interval. Press the Menu button to return to the Slideshow Settings screen.

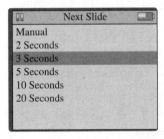

FIGURE 13-3   You can set the iPod to advance the slides automatically or advance them manually yourself.

FIGURE 13-4 Use the Slideshow Music screen to add music to the iPod slideshow. If you don't have a suitable playlist, create an On-the-Go playlist for your slideshow, and then assign it.

5. Scroll to the Music item, press the Select button, and use the Slideshow Music Screen (see Figure 13-4) to select the music you want for the slideshow. (Choose the Off item if you don't want any music.) Press the Menu button to return to the Slideshow Settings screen.

6. Change the Repeat setting if necessary by scrolling to it and then pressing the Select button. Repeat can be either On or Off.

7. Change the Shuffle Photos setting if necessary by scrolling to it and then pressing the Select button. Shuffle Photos can be either On or Off.

8. Scroll to the Transitions item, press the Select button, and use the Transitions screen (see Figure 13-5) to choose the transition to apply between slides. Press the Menu button to return to the Slideshow Settings screen.

9. To choose whether to output the slide show to a TV, scroll to the TV Out setting, and then press the Select button to choose the setting you need: Off to display the slideshow on the iPod's screen, On to send the output via the cable to a TV, or Ask to have the iPod prompt you when you start a slideshow. The On setting is available on only some iPods.

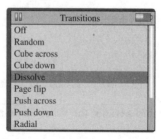

FIGURE 13-5 The iPod offers a modest number of transitions between slides. Avoid the Random setting for formal presentations, because many people find it distracting.

NOTE   *First- and second-generation iPod nanos do not offer TV output.*

10. If you're using a TV, scroll to the TV Signal setting, and then press the Select button to choose the appropriate standard: NTSC (which is used in North America, Japan, and some other countries) or PAL (which is used in most European countries and some others).

11. Press the Menu button to return to the Photos screen.

Play a Slideshow on the iPod

If you want to display the slideshow on a TV, connect the iPod to the TV with an Apple iPod AV Cable (http://store.apple.com; $19) or equivalent. This cable has an overlong miniplug at one end and three RCA plugs at the other. Connect the miniplug to the iPod's headphone socket, and the RCA plugs to the appropriate, color-coded RCA jacks on your TV. The S-video plug is colored yellow, and the two audio plugs are colored white and red.

NOTE   *Apple recommends using the Apple Component AV cable, Apple Composite AV Cable, or Apple AV Connection Kit for connecting an iPod to a TV. All these items are available from the Apple Store. Other cables that are apparently equivalent may work with some iPods but not with others.*

To start a slideshow, navigate to the album that contains the pictures, and then select the picture at which you want the show to start. Press the Select button to start the show running. If you chose Ask for the TV Out setting on an iPod, scroll to select TV Off or TV On from the resulting screen, and then press the Select button.

When the iPod is outputting the slideshow to a TV, on the iPod's screen you see the current slide, together with miniatures of the previous slide and the next slide as well as a countdown of the seconds to the next slide (if you're using automatic advancement).

View Photos and Slideshows on the iPhone or iPod touch

On the iPhone or iPod touch, you can either browse through photos or create slideshows and play them back. On the iPhone, you can also take photos and import them into Windows or iPhoto (see the next section for coverage of this topic).

View Photos on the iPhone or iPod touch

To view photos you've loaded on the iPhone or iPod touch, follow these steps:

1. Press the Home button to go to the Home screen unless you're already there.

2. Touch the Photos icon to display the Photo Albums screen (see Figure 13-6). Here you'll find the following items:

How to ...   Give a Presentation Using an iPod

If you're forced to travel light, you can give a straightforward presentation direct from the iPod. To do so, follow these steps:

1. Create the slides in your presentation software—for example, PowerPoint or Keynote—as usual, and then save the presentation. Don't include transitions, animations, or audio in the slides because they won't be transferred to the iPod. (If you must show a slide that appears one element at a time, create it as a sequence of partial slides: the first slide containing the first element, the second slide adding the second element, and so on until the final slide contains all the elements.)

2. Export the slides as graphics. Here are two examples:

   ■ From PowerPoint, choose File | Save As, select JPEG File Interchange Format in the Save As Type drop-down list, and then click the Save button. When PowerPoint prompts you, click the Every Slide button to export every slide in the presentation.

   ■ From Keynote, choose File | Export, select the Images option button, and then select the JPEG item in the Format drop-down list.

3. Put the slides in a photo album of their own, and then synchronize them with the iPod.

4. Navigate to that album on the iPod, and then play it as a slideshow. You'll have to use the buttons on the iPod to control the slideshow—even if you have a remote control, the iPod's slideshow feature won't recognize it.

■ **Camera Roll**   (iPhone only) Contains the photos on the iPhone's camera. The Camera Roll item lets you view the photos you've taken on the iPhone and not yet transferred to your computer. If the camera contains no photos, this item doesn't appear on the Photo Albums screen.

■ **Photo Library**   Contains all the pictures in all the albums except for Camera Roll.

■ **Albums or folders by name**   These are the albums from the photo application (for example, iPhoto on the Mac) or the folders you've chosen to synchronize.

3. Touch an item to display its contents. The iPhone or iPod touch shows a thumbnail of each picture (see Figure 13-7).

4. Touch the photo you want to view full screen. The iPhone or iPod touch displays the photo together with onscreen controls (see Figure 13-8). The iPhone or iPod touch then fades out the controls if you don't use them within a few seconds. Touch the picture again to bring them back.

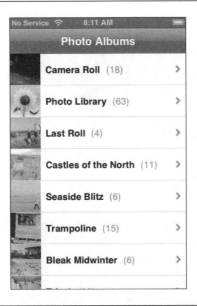

FIGURE 13-6   The Photo Albums screen shows you the various sets of photos on your iPhone or iPod touch.

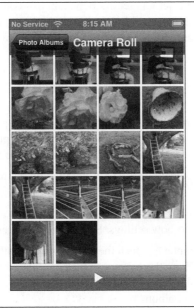

FIGURE 13-7   From the album-contents screen, touch the photo you want to see first.

Album Name

Send

Delete

Previous   Play Slideshow   Next

FIGURE 13-8   The photo controls let you return to the album's contents screen, move from picture to picture, start a slideshow playing, or send the picture. The Delete button appears only for the Camera Roll item on the iPhone.

5. To see the picture in landscape orientation rather than portrait orientation, rotate the iPhone or iPod touch.

6. To move to the next picture, touch the Next button (if it's displayed) or flick your finger across the screen from right to left. To move to the previous picture, touch the Previous button (if it's displayed) or flick your finger across the screen from left to right.

7. To zoom in on a picture, pinch outward or double-tap on the part of the picture you want to see. To zoom back out, pinch inward or double-tap again.

8. To start a slideshow, touch the Play button. (Before you start a slideshow, you may want to check or change the slideshow settings. See the section after next for details.)

9. To return to the album's contents, touch the button with the album's name in the upper-left corner of the screen. From there, you can pick another picture, or touch the Photo Albums button (again in the upper-left corner) to return to the Photo Albums screen, where you can open another album.

Use a Photo as Wallpaper, E-mail It, or Assign It to a Contact

Touching the Send button in the lower-left corner of the photo screen brings up the menu shown in Figure 13-9. You can take the following actions on the iPhone (on the iPod touch, you can only set a photo as wallpaper):

- **Use As Wallpaper** Touch this button to display the picture as it will appear when used for wallpaper. You can move the picture by dragging it with your finger, or zoom it in or out by pinching inward or outward. When the picture is as you want it, touch the Set Wallpaper button.

- **Email Photo** Touch this button to start an e-mail message with the photo attached. You can then address and send the photo as you would any other message (see Chapter 20 for details).

- **Assign To Contact** Touch this button to display the All Contacts screen. Touch the contact to whom you want to assign the photo. The iPhone displays the picture as it will appear. You can move the picture by dragging it with your finger, or zoom it in or out by pinching inward or outward. When the picture is as you want it, touch the Set Photo button. The iPhone saves the photo in the contact record, and then returns you to viewing the photo.

- **Send To Web Gallery** Touch this button to start the process of posting to a Web Gallery you've created using iPhoto 08 on the Mac.

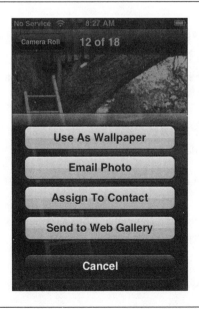

FIGURE 13-9 Touch the Send button to bring up a menu for using a photo as wallpaper, e-mailing it, assigning it to a contact record, or posting it to a Web Gallery.

Choose Slideshow Settings for the iPhone or iPod touch

To choose slideshow settings, such as the length of time to display each slide and whether to repeat the slideshow, follow these steps:

1. Press the Home button to go to the Home screen unless you're already there.

2. Touch the Settings button to display the Settings screen.

3. Scroll down to the bottom of the list, and then touch the Photos item to display the Photos screen.

4. Choose settings as needed:

   - **Play Each Slide For**   Touch this item to change the number of seconds, choose on the Play Each Slide For screen (2, 3, 5, 10, or 20 seconds), and then touch the Photos button to return to the Photos screen.

   - **Transition**   Touch this item to see the Transition screen. Choose the transition you want—Cube, Dissolve, Ripple, Wipe Across, or Wipe Down—and then touch the Photos button to return to the Photos screen.

   - **Repeat**   Touch this item to toggle between Off and On.

   - **Shuffle**   Touch this item to toggle between Off and On.

5. Touch the Settings button to return to the Settings screen, or simply press the Home button to go to the Home screen.

Take Photos on the iPhone and Import Them

The iPhone's built-in camera lets you take pictures any time you're carrying the iPhone. You can then import the pictures from the iPhone into Windows or directly into iPhoto on the Mac, where you can manipulate them if necessary.

Take Photos on the iPhone

To take photos on the iPhone, follow these steps:

1. Press the Home button to go to the Home screen unless you're already there.

2. Touch the Camera icon to display the Camera screen.

3. Aim the lens at your subject and frame the photo. (The lens is at the upper-left corner of the back of the iPhone, seen from the back.)

> TIP
>
> *When you turn the iPhone to landscape orientation, do so with the Camera button at the right end of the screen. That way, your photos will be the right way up rather than upside down.*

4. Press the shutter button at the bottom of the screen.

View the Photos You've Taken on the iPhone

To look through the photos you've taken on the iPhone, follow these steps:

1. On the Camera screen, touch the button in the lower-left corner to display the Camera Roll screen.

> **TIP**   *You can also reach the Camera Roll screen by touching the Camera Roll item on the Photo Albums screen.*

2. Touch the Camera Roll item to display the Camera Roll screen, which shows thumbnails of the photos.

3. Touch a photo to display it full screen. You can then touch the photo to bring up controls that enable you to take the following actions:

   - **Delete the photo**   Touch the Delete button, and then touch the Delete Photo button on the confirmation panel that appears.

   - **Use the photo**   See the section "Use a Photo as Wallpaper, E-mail It, or Assign It to a Contact," earlier in this chapter.

   - **Move from photo to photo**   Touch the Previous button or the Next button, or flick your finger across the screen.

   - **Start a slideshow**   Touch the Play button.

4. When you're ready to return to the camera, touch the Camera button at the bottom of the screen.

Import Photos from the iPhone

Viewing photos on the iPhone lets you quickly cull any duds, but usually what you'll want to do is transfer the photos to your computer so that you can view them at full size and manipulate them as necessary.

Import Photos from the iPhone into Windows Vista

To import photos from the iPhone into Windows Vista, follow these steps:

1. Place the iPhone in its dock.

2. Windows automatically opens the AutoPlay window for the Apple iPhone, as shown here.

3. If you want to import photos automatically each time you dock the iPhone (and it contains photos), select the Always Do This For This Device check box.

4. Click the Import Pictures Using Windows button. The Importing Pictures And Videos dialog box appears, as shown here.

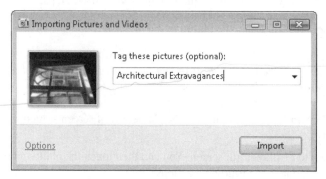

5. In the Tag These Pictures text box, type a tag for the photos if you want to.

NOTE *You can choose further import settings, such as deleting the photos from the camera after importing them, by clicking the Options link, and then working in the Import Settings dialog box.*

6. Click the Import button. Windows imports the pictures, opens Windows Photo Gallery, and then displays the photos in it. The photos are in the Recently Imported category.

NOTE *Instead of clicking the Import Pictures Using Windows button in the AutoPlay window, you can click the Open Device To View Files Using Windows Explorer button. Windows Vista opens a Windows Explorer window showing the folder on the iPhone that contains the photos. You can then copy the pictures manually to a folder of your choice—or simply delete them from the iPhone if you don't like them.*

Import Photos from the iPhone into Windows XP

To import photos from the iPhone into Windows XP, follow these steps:

1. Place the iPhone in its dock.

2. Windows automatically opens the AutoPlay window for the Apple iPhone, as shown here.

3. In the Select The Program To Launch For This Action list box, click the Microsoft Scanner And Camera Wizard item.

4. If you want always to import photos using the Scanner and Camera Wizard (as is usually easiest), select the Always Use This Program For This Action check box.

5. Click the OK button. Windows launches the Scanner and Camera Wizard, which displays its Welcome screen.

6. Click the Next button to reach the Choose Pictures To Copy screen of the Wizard (see Figure 13-10).

7. Clear the check box for each photo you don't want to import. The Scanner and Camera Wizard selects all the check boxes for you automatically, but you can click the Clear All button if you need to clear them all.

8. Click the Next button to reach the Picture Name And Destination screen of the Wizard (see Figure 13-11).

9. In the Type A Name For This Group Of Pictures text box, type the name you want to give the photos. The Wizard appends numbers (01, 02, and so on) to this name to create the filenames.

FIGURE 13-10   The Scanner and Camera Wizard is the easiest way to import photos from an iPhone into Windows XP.

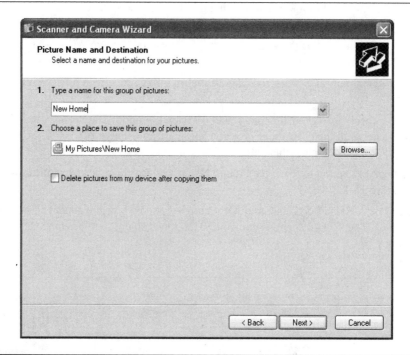

FIGURE 13-11 On the Picture Name And Destination screen of the Scanner and Camera Wizard, type a name for the group of photos.

10. In the Choose A Place To Save This Group Of Pictures box, enter the folder in which to save the pictures. The Wizard suggest a folder with the name you provided in the previous step, located in your Pictures folder.

11. Select the Delete Pictures From My Device After Copying Them check box if you want the Wizard to delete the photos from the iPhone after importing them.

12. Click the Next button. The Wizard copies the photos, and then displays the Other Options screen.

13. Make sure the Nothing. I'm Finished Working With These Pictures option button is selected, and then click the Next button.

14. The final screen of the Wizard provides a link you can click to open the folder to which the Wizard has imported the photos. But you don't need to click the link, because Windows opens the folder anyway when you close the Wizard.

TIP *If you prefer to import photos manually, choose Start | My Computer to open a My Computer window, and then double-click the Apple iPhone item in the Scanners And Cameras area. You can then copy the photos from the iPhone manually (or simply delete them if you don't want to keep them).*

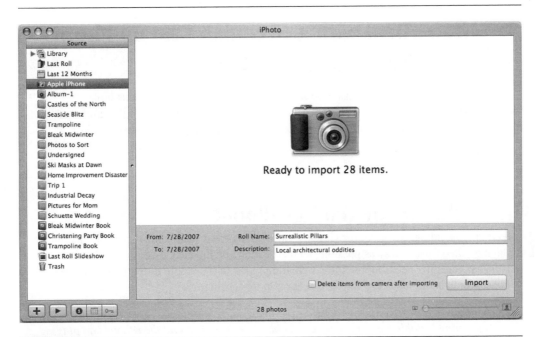

FIGURE 13-12   The easiest way to get your photos from the iPhone to a Mac is to let iPhoto import them.

Import Photos from the iPhone into iPhoto

To import photos from the iPhone into iPhoto, follow these steps:

1. Place the iPhone in its dock.

2. If you've set the iPhone to sync automatically with iPhoto, the program opens automatically. If iPhoto is already running, Mac OS X activates it.

3. iPhoto automatically selects the Apple iPhone item in the Source pane, showing you how many photos there are to import (see Figure 13-12).

4. If you want, type a name for the roll in the Roll Name text box and a description in the Description text box. You can use this text to identify the roll of photos more easily in iPhoto.

5. Select the Delete Items From Camera After Importing check box if you want iPhoto to delete the photos from the iPhone after it imports them. Usually, this is helpful.

6. Click the Import button. iPhoto imports the photos. You can then access them by clicking the Last Roll item in the Source pane.

How to ...   # Deal with a Greenish Cast on Photos Taken with the iPhone

Some iPhones tend to add a greenish cast to each picture they take. The results look disappointing, but you can usually sort out the color balance simply once you've imported the photos. For example, in iPhoto, open a photo for editing, and then simply click the Enhance button.

Put Video Files on the iPod or iPhone

The iPod and the iPhone are great for viewing videos. Apple has made the process of loading and playing video files as easy as possible, so this section and the next cover this topic only briefly. What generally needs more effort is creating video files suitable for putting on the iPod or iPhone, which is the subject of the third section in this chapter.

NOTE   *Video formats are confusing at best—but the iPod, iPhone, and iTunes make the process of getting suitable video files as easy as possible. The iPod and the iPhone can play videos in the MP4 format up to 2.5 Mbps (megabits per second) or the H.264 format up to 1.5 Mbps. Programs designed to create video files suitable for the iPod and iPhone typically give you a choice between the MP4 format and the H.264 format.*

Buy Video Files from the iTunes Store

The easiest way to get suitable video files is to buy them from the iTunes Store. At this writing, the iTunes Store sells movies, music videos, and episodes of TV shows.

When you download videos from the iTunes Store, iTunes adds them to your Purchased playlist. You can play the videos from there, or by browsing to them, and you can add them to other playlists using the same techniques as for song files. As discussed in Chapter 2, you can control which videos iTunes synchronizes with the iPod or iPhone by connecting the device, clicking it in the Source pane, and then using the controls on the Videos screen.

Play Videos on the iPod

To play videos on the iPod, scroll to the Videos entry on the main menu, and then press the Select button to access the Videos screen (see Figure 13-13). Scroll to the appropriate category, and then press the Select button to access it. Scroll to the item you want, and then press the Select button to access it and start it playing.

You can fast-forward through the video file by pressing the Fast Forward button, and rewind by pressing the Rewind button, but these controls are comfortable only for moving short distances.

FIGURE 13-13   The Videos screen gives you access to your video playlists, video files, and the Video Settings screen.

To move farther, press the Select button twice to display the scrub bar, and then scroll to scrub forward or backward. When you reach the point you want, press the Select button to hide the scrub bar again.

To play a video file through a television rather than on the iPod's built-in screen, scroll to the Settings item on the Videos screen, and then press the Select button to display the Settings screen (see Figure 13-14). Set the TV Out setting to On if you want the iPod always to output the video to TV, or to Ask if you want the iPod to prompt you first (Ask is often more convenient). Set the TV Signal setting to NTSC or PAL, as appropriate for your TV. (NTSC is primarily used in North America and Japan, while PAL is used in most European countries.)

For the Fullscreen setting, choose On or Off to suit your TV or your tastes. If you want to see captions, set the Captions setting to On; otherwise, leave it turned off.

Press the Menu button to return to the Videos screen, and then connect the iPod to the TV using a cable such as the Apple Component AV cable or the Apple Composite AV Cable. Connect the miniplug to the iPod's headphone socket, and the RCA plugs to the appropriate, color-coded RCA jacks on your TV. The S-video plug is colored yellow, and the two audio plugs are colored white and red.

Set the video playing, and enjoy.

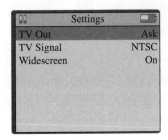

FIGURE 13-14   On the Settings screen, choose whether to output to a TV and, if so, which format to use.

Play Videos on the iPhone or iPod touch

To play videos on the iPhone or iPod touch, follow these steps:

1. On the iPhone, press the Home button to go to the Home screen unless you're already there or in the iPod mode, and then touch the iPod button at the bottom of the screen to switch to iPod mode.

2. Touch the Videos button at the bottom to display the Videos screen.

3. Touch the video you want to play, and then turn the iPhone or iPod touch to landscape orientation.

4. Touch the screen to bring up play controls (see Figure 13-15):

   ■ Use the Previous/Rewind button to move back, or the Next/Fast-Forward button to move forward.

   ■ Drag the Playhead to move to a different point in the video.

   ■ Touch the Zoom button to zoom the picture as large as possible. Touch again to zoom back in.

5. Touch the Done button when you've finished watching the video.

<table>
<tr><td>NOTE</td><td>If you play right to the end of a movie, the iPhone or iPod touch prompts you to delete the movie to conserve space. Touch the Delete button if you want to delete the movie; if not, touch the Keep button.</td></tr>
</table>

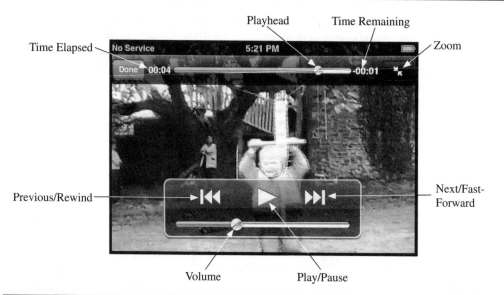

FIGURE 13-15   Use the onscreen controls to rewind, fast-forward, or jump to another part of the video.

Create Video Files Suitable for the iPod or iPhone

Buying video files from the iTunes Store is easy, but you probably already have video content that you'd like to put on the iPod or iPhone.

The first step is to get the video file you plan to convert. Possible sources of video files include your digital video camera, your DVDs, video files you download, and video files that you record from a TV, VCR, or similar source.

Create Video Files from Your Digital Video Camera

If you make your own movies with a digital video camera, you can easily put them on the iPod or iPhone. Use an application such as Windows Movie Maker (Windows) or iMovie (Mac) to capture the video from your digital video camera, and then turn it into a home movie.

Create Video Files Using Windows Movie Maker

At this writing, Windows Movie Maker can't export video files in an iPod- or iPhone-friendly format, so getting video from Windows Movie Maker to the iPod or iPhone is a two-stage process.

First, create the movie, and then export it as DV-AVI:

- **Windows Vista**   Choose File | Publish Movie. Select the This Computer item on the Where Do You Want To Publish Your Movie? screen, and then click the Next button. On the Name The Movie You Are Publishing screen, type the name for the movie, choose the folder in which to store it, and then click the Next button. On the Choose The Settings For Your Movie screen, select the More Settings option button, and then select the DV-AVI item in the drop-down list. Click the Publish button to export the movie in this format.

NOTE   *The DV-AVI item appears as DV-AVI (NTSC) or DV-AVI (PAL), depending on whether you've chosen the NTSC option button or the PAL option button on the Advanced tab of the Options dialog box.*

- **Windows XP**   In Windows Movie Maker, choose File | Save Movie File. Select the My Computer item on the Movie Location screen, and then click the Next button. On the Saved Movie File screen, enter the name and choose the folder for the movie, and then click the Next button. On the Movie Setting screen, click the Show More Choices link (unless you see the Show Fewer Choices link), select the Other Settings option button, and then select the DV-AVI item in the drop-down list. Click the Next button to save the movie in this format.

Second, use an application such as Videora iPod Converter or Videora iPhone Converter (both freeware; www.videora.com) to convert the AVI file to a MOV file.

Create Video Files Using iMovie

To create iPod- or iPhone-friendly video files from iMovie, follow these steps:

1. With the movie open in iMovie, choose File | Share to display the Sharing sheet.
2. Click the QuickTime button to display its tab.
3. In the Compress Movie For drop-down list, choose Expert Settings, and then click the Share button to display the Save Exported File As dialog box.
4. Type the name for the file in the Save As text box, and specify the folder in which to save it.
5. In the Export drop-down list, select the Movie To iPod item or the Movie To iPhone item, as appropriate.
6. Click the Save button, and then wait while iMovie creates the compressed file.

Create Video Files from Your Existing Video Files

There are several ways of converting your existing video files so that they'll work on the iPod or iPhone.

The way that Apple approves and recommends is to use QuickTime Pro, which you can purchase from the Apple Store (http://store.apple.com) for around $30. As you'll see if you read the reviews on the Apple Store page for QuickTime Pro, users have severely polarized reactions to QuickTime Pro: some love it and find it does everything they want (with video files, that is), while others have negative experiences and corresponding opinions.

You can also use third-party software if you prefer. This section shows you how to create iPod- or iPhone-friendly video files using QuickTime and also using the third-party application ViddyUp!, which runs only on the Mac.

Create Video Files Using QuickTime

QuickTime, Apple's multimedia software for Mac OS X and Windows, comes in two versions: QuickTime Player (the free version) and QuickTime Pro, which costs $29.99. On Mac OS X, QuickTime Player is included in a standard installation of the operating system; and if you've somehow managed to uninstall it, it'll automatically install itself again if you install iTunes. Likewise, on the PC, you install QuickTime Player when you install iTunes, because QuickTime provides much of the multimedia functionality for iTunes. The "Player" name isn't entirely accurate, because QuickTime provides encoding services as well as decoding services to iTunes—but QuickTime Player does prevent you from creating most formats of video files until you buy QuickTime Pro.

QuickTime Player is a crippled version of QuickTime Pro, so when you buy QuickTime Pro from the Apple Store, all you get is a registration code to unlock the hidden functionality. To apply the registration code, choose Edit | Preferences | Register in Windows to display the Register tab of the QuickTime Settings dialog box. On the Mac, choose QuickTime Player | Registration to display the Register tab of the QuickTime dialog box.

CAUTION   *When you register QuickTime, you must enter your registration name in the Registered To text box in exactly the same format as Apple has decided to use it. For example, if you've used the name John P. Smith to register QuickTime, and Apple has decided to address the registration to* Mr. John P. Smith, *you must use* **Mr. John P. Smith** *as the registration name. If you try to use* **John P. Smith**, *registration will fail, even if this is exactly the way you gave your name when registering.*

To create an iPod or iPhone video file from QuickTime, follow these steps:

1. Open the file in QuickTime, and then choose File | Export to display the Save Exported File As dialog box.

2. Specify the filename and folder as usual, and then choose Movie To iPod or Movie To iPhone (as appropriate) in the Export drop-down list. Leave the Default Settings item selected in the Use drop-down list.

3. Click the Save button to start exporting the video file.

Create Video Files with ViddyUp! on Mac OS X

ViddyUp! (formerly Podner) from Splasm Software (www.splasm.com; $9.99) is a video-transformation application focused directly at creating files suitable for the iPod and transferring them automatically to iTunes. To transform video files, ViddyUp! uses QuickTime's capabilities, which means that if your video file is in a format that QuickTime Player can play, ViddyUp! should be able to convert it to an iPod- or iPhone-friendly format for you.

Splasm offers an evaluation version of ViddyUp! that's limited to converting the first two-and-a-half minutes of any video file—plenty for you to see whether ViddyUp! will work with your files.

When you run ViddyUp!, you see a window that invites you to drag a file to it. To convert a video file:

1. Drag a movie file to the window. ViddyUp! displays its control panel.

2. Drag the video slider, or simply play the video, to the frame that you want to use as the poster frame, the picture used as the still image for the file's thumbnail.

3. Click the Set Poster Frame button to set the poster frame (see Figure 13-16).

4. In the Encoding drop-down list, choose the appropriate iPod option:

   - **iPod, 320 × 240, MPEG-4**   This format gives fast encoding, moderate picture quality, and a relatively large file size.

   - **iPod, 480 × 480, MPEG-4**   This format gives fast encoding, good picture quality, but has a 1:1 aspect ratio (the other three choices have a 1.5:1 aspect ratio) that uses more pixels. The file size is correspondingly larger.

   - **iPod 320 × 240, H.264**   This format gives better picture quality and a smaller file size than MPEG encoding, but the encoding takes longer.

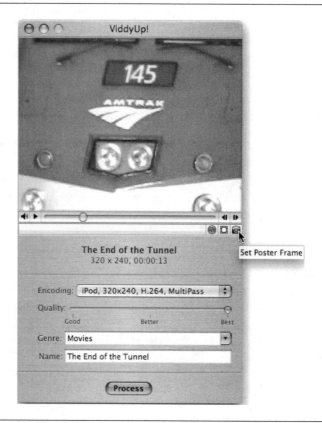

FIGURE 13-16 In ViddyUp!, set the poster frame, and then choose suitable encoding options for the video.

- ■ **iPod 320 × 240, H.264 Multipass** This format gives you the highest-quality movie with the smallest possible file size of the 320 × 240 formats, but it requires much more processing and takes the longest.

- ■ **iPod 640 × 480, H.264** This format gives you a high-quality picture but at the expense of a far larger file.

5. If the Quality slider is available, you can drag it to the Good, Better, or Best position, depending on the results you want. The higher the quality, the longer the processing will take. The slider is not available for some formats.

6. Choose the appropriate genre in the Genre drop-down list: Movies, Music Videos, Sports, or TV Shows.

7. Type the name for the movie in the Name text box. ViddyUp! enters the file's name (minus the extension) by default.

8. Click the Process button to start processing the movie. ViddyUp! displays a Processing readout showing you the elapsed time and remaining time as it works, then displays a Process Complete message that tells you that ViddyUp! has put the video inside the ViddyUp! playlist in iTunes.

9. Click the Go To iTunes button if you want to go directly to iTunes, or click the OK button if you just want to dismiss the Process Complete message so that you can drag another movie file to the ViddyUp! window.

Create Video Files from Your TiVo

If you have a TiVo, chances are that it contains content you'd like to transfer to the iPod or iPhone. To do so:

- On the PC, use DirectShow Dump (http://prish.com/etivo/tbr.htm) to convert the shows from the TiVo format to MPEG. Then use another application (for example, QuickTime, Videora iPod Converter, or Videora iPhone Converter) to convert the MPEG file to iPod or iPhone video format.

- On the Mac, if you have a hacked TiVo, use TivoTool (www.tivotool.com; donationware) to create iPod or iPhone video files from TiVo content.

Create Video Files from Your DVDs

Another possibility is to rip your DVDs to files that you can put on the iPod or iPhone. Ripping DVDs is usually considered to be a violation of copyright unless you have specific permission to do so (or you hold the copyright to the DVD—for example, if it's one you've created yourself).

In Windows, you can use an application such as DVDx (http://sourceforge.net; freeware) or DVD43 (www.dvd43.com, then follow the links) to rip the DVD to an AVI file. You can then use an application such as Videora iPod Converter or Videora iPhone Converter (www.videora.com; freeware) or QuickTime to convert the AVI file to a MOV file.

On the Mac, you can use an application such as HandBrake (http://handbrake.m0k.org; freeware) or MacTheRipper (search at www.versiontracker.com) to rip a DVD to one or more MPEG files that you can then put on the iPod or iPhone.

Part IV

Learn Advanced Techniques and Tricks

Chapter 14

Use Multiple iPods or iPhones, Multiple Computers, or Both

How to...

■ Move an iPod classic or iPod nano from Windows to the Mac or from the Mac to Windows

■ Move an iPhone or iPod touch from Windows to the Mac or from the Mac to Windows

■ Change the computer to which an iPod or iPhone is linked

■ Synchronize several iPods or iPhones with the same computer

■ Load an iPod from two or more computers

This chapter starts by walking you through the processes of moving an iPod classic or iPod nano from a Mac to a PC, and vice versa. After that, it shows you how to do the same with an iPhone or an iPod touch, as these devices behave differently. Then it shows you how to change the computer to which an iPod or iPhone is linked—a useful skill when you upgrade your computer.

The chapter explains the nuances of synchronizing several iPods or iPhones with the same computer, and it walks you through loading an iPod from two or more computers at the same time. At this writing, you can synchronize the iPhone only with one computer at a time. However, you can load non-media items—such as contacts—on the iPhone from different computers if necessary.

Move an iPod from the Mac to Windows—and Back

The first generation of iPod worked only with the Mac. Enough Windows users craved the iPod for the program EphPod (discussed in Chapter 16) to be created, which let Windows users run Mac iPods. Apple then released second-generation iPods in separate versions for the Mac and for Windows; the iPods for the two platforms started off separate, but you could convert them from one platform to the other.

Subsequent iPods, including all the current models and the iPhone, all come in a single version for both the Mac and Windows. But because all iPods except the iPod touch and the iPod shuffle use a different file system when used with Macs than when used with Windows, you may have to "restore" the iPod when moving it between the two operating systems. See the sidebar "Which File System Does the iPod Use" for details of the file systems.

 *If you reformat an iPod, you'll lose all its contents—every file you've stored on it. If the iPod contains valuable files, back them up to your PC or Mac before reformatting the iPod.*

Move an iPod from the Mac to Windows

If you've used an iPod classic or iPod nano only with a Mac, and you move it to Windows, you must reformat the hard disk or flash memory. This permanently removes all the contents of the iPod. Follow the procedure described in the upcoming section "Move a Mac-Formatted iPod to Windows."

Did you know?

Which File System Does the iPod Use?

That bit about iPods coming in a single version for both the Mac and Windows isn't entirely true. At this writing, the iPod classic and the iPod nano ship with their disks or memory partitioned using the Mac OS Extended file system. When you connect a new iPod classic or iPod nano to a Windows PC, iTunes on the PC detects that the iPod needs to be reformatted, and it reformats using the FAT32 file system without notifying you. If the iPod contains files, iTunes warns you before reformatting the iPod. More on this topic later in this chapter.

The Mac OS Extended file system works better for the Mac than FAT32 does, but Windows can't read Mac OS Extended; so the iPod uses FAT32 for Windows instead. FAT32 works with Mac OS X as well as with Windows, so once you've formatted an iPod for Windows, you don't necessarily need to reformat it if you need to use it with a Mac again.

Both generations of the iPod shuffle use the FAT32 file system for both Windows and the Mac, so there's no need to convert an iPod shuffle from one format to another.

The iPhone performs some tricks to stop you from accessing its contents directly via a file-management program (such as Windows Explorer or the Finder) rather than through iTunes. To Windows, the iPhone's accessible storage uses the Design Rule for Camera File System (DCF). To Mac OS X, all the iPhone's storage appears to be inaccessible. You do not need to reformat an iPhone when moving it between Windows and the Mac or vice versa.

Like the iPhone, the iPod touch makes its storage inaccessible to programs other than iTunes. Unlike the iPhone, however, the iPod touch doesn't have a camera, so it doesn't need to make even part of its file system available to Windows Explorer.

If you've used an iPod classic or iPod nano with Windows, and then moved it to the Mac without reformatting it, and you then move it back to Windows, you won't need to reformat the iPod. Follow the procedure described in "Move a FAT32-Formatted iPod from the Mac Back to Windows."

If you have an iPod shuffle or iPod touch, it is formatted with FAT32, so use the procedure described in "Move a FAT32-Formatted iPod from the Mac Back to Windows," even if you've been using the iPod only with a Mac.

Move a Mac-Formatted iPod to Windows

To move an iPod from the Mac to Windows, follow these steps:

1. Make sure the PC has iTunes installed—preferably the latest version. (If in doubt, download the latest version from www.apple.com/itunes/download/ and install it.)

2. If nobody has used iTunes on that computer, run iTunes and complete the iTunes Setup Assistant. Close iTunes again.

3. Connect the iPod to the PC. If the iPod is formatted with the Mac OS Extended file system, the iPod Software tells you that it needs to be reformatted, as shown here. If so, follow Steps 4 and 5. Otherwise, go to Step 6.

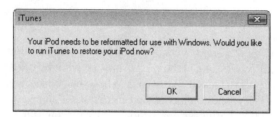

4. Click the OK button to launch iTunes. iTunes tells you that the iPod is Mac-formatted, as shown here.

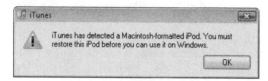

5. Click the OK button to close the message box.

6. Click the Restore button to format the iPod using the FAT32 file system and to reinstall the iPod firmware on it. iTunes displays a confirmation message box, as shown here, to make sure you know that all songs and data will be erased.

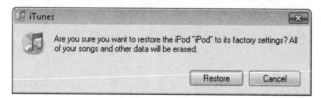

7. Click the Restore button, and then allow the restore process to continue. iTunes downloads the latest version of the iPod Software if necessary, and then installs the software. During the process, iTunes displays the informational message box shown here for 15 seconds. Either click the OK button to dismiss the message box, or allow the countdown to complete, after which iTunes closes the message box automatically.

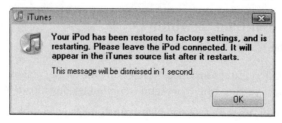

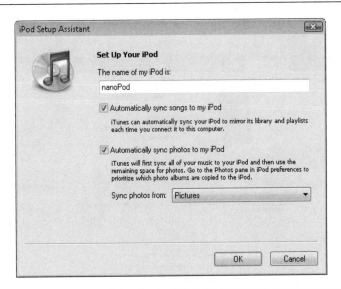

FIGURE 14-1   In the iPod Setup Assistant, specify the name for the iPod, and choose whether
to sync songs and photos with it

8. iTunes displays the iPod Setup Assistant dialog box (see Figure 14-1). Follow through
the steps of assigning the iPod a name and choosing whether to sync songs and photos
with the iPod automatically. The first time you set up an iPod, you can also choose
whether to register it.

9. If you choose to sync songs to the iPod automatically, and the iPod doesn't have enough
space to contain all the songs, iTunes lets you know of the problem, as shown here. Click
the Yes button if you want iTunes to create a playlist for the iPod. Click the No button if
you want to choose songs for the iPod yourself.

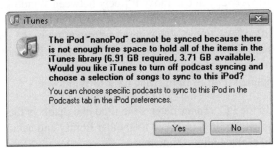

10. When the restore operation (and synchronization, if you chose that option) has
completed, the iPod appears in the Devices list with the name you gave it. Figure 14-2
shows an example.

FIGURE 14-2 The iPod appears in the Devices list when the restore operation is complete.

Move a FAT32-Formatted iPod from the Mac Back to Windows

If an iPod is formatted with FAT32, you can move it freely between Windows and the Mac. The iPod will be formatted with FAT32 if you have formatted it on Windows using the iPod Updater. If you've then moved the iPod back to the Mac without reformatting it, the iPod will still be formatted with FAT32 rather than the Mac OS Extended file system. The same applies if the iPod is an iPod shuffle, because this iPod uses only the FAT32 file system.

To move a FAT32-formatted iPod from the Mac back to Windows:

1. Connect the iPod to the PC. iTunes detects the iPod and displays the dialog box shown here, warning you that the iPod is linked to another library and asking if you want to change the link and replace all its contents.

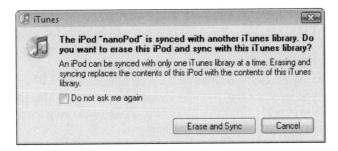

2. Click the Erase And Sync button to associate the iPod with the Windows library and overwrite the Mac library.

Wait while iTunes associates the iPod with the Windows library, and then syncs the songs and other items with the iPod.

Move an iPod from Windows to the Mac

To move an iPod from Windows to the Mac, follow these steps:

1. For best results, update iTunes to the latest version available.

> **TIP**   *The easiest way to check that iTunes is up to date is to choose Apple | Software Update to check for updates. If Software Update identifies any iTunes updates, or other updates that your Mac requires, install them before moving the iPod to your Mac.*

2. Connect the iPod to the Mac. When iTunes detects the iPod, it displays a dialog box such as that shown here, pointing out that the iPod is linked to a different library and asking if you want to replace that library.

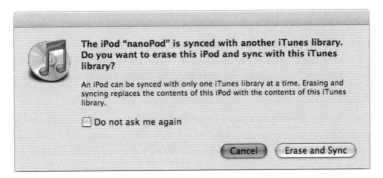

3. Click the Erase And Sync button. iTunes replaces the library on the iPod with the library on the Mac. This may take some time if the library is extensive.

At this point, you've set up the iPod to work with your Mac, but you've left it using the FAT32 file system. FAT32 works fine with Mac OS X but is marginally less efficient than the Mac OS Extended file system, so you won't be able to fit quite as many files on the iPod with FAT32 as with Mac OS Extended.

If you intend to use the iPod with the Mac for the long term, and if the iPod doesn't contain any valuable files that you want to keep, you may choose to convert it to Mac OS X Extended to pack on as many songs as possible. To do so, restore the iPod by following the process described in the section "Restore an iPod on Mac OS X" in Chapter 18.

If you want to boot your Mac from a hard-drive based iPod, you must reformat the iPod with the Mac OS Extended file system. You must also reformat the iPod if you want to update it to the latest version of the iPod software using the Mac.

Move an iPhone or iPod touch Between Windows and the Mac

At this writing, the iPhone or iPod touch use the same file system when connected to either a Windows computer or a Mac. This means that transferring an iPhone from Windows to the Mac, or from the Mac to Windows, is usually painless, because you do not need to restore the iPhone or iPod touch and thus wipe out all its current contents.

However, when you connect the iPhone or iPod touch to another computer, you will still need to decide whether to replace it's songs, videos, information, and so on with the corresponding media file or information from the new computer, as described in the next section.

Change the Computer to Which an iPod or iPhone Is Linked

Apple has designed the iPod and iPhone so that they can synchronize with only one computer at a time. This computer is known as the *home* computer—home to the iPod or iPhone, not necessarily in your home. However, you can use two or more Macs, or two or more Windows PCs, to load files onto the same iPod. See the section "Load an iPod from Two or More Computers at Once," later in this chapter, for details. This doesn't work with the iPhone, which is limited to a single computer at a time for media files.

Linking an iPod or iPhone to another computer replaces all the songs and playlists on the device with the songs and playlists on the other computer. Be sure you want to change the link before you proceed. You can restore your previous library by linking again to the first computer, but, even with USB 2.0 file-transfer speeds, you'll waste a good deal of time if your library is large.

To change an iPod's or iPhone's home computer, follow these steps:

1. Make sure the other computer contains an up-to-date version of iTunes. If necessary, set up iTunes and install any relevant updates.

NOTE *If you're moving an iPod formatted with the Mac OS Extended file system to Windows, you'll need to restore it as described in "Move an iPod from the Mac to Windows," earlier in this chapter. This doesn't apply to the iPhone.*

2. Connect the iPod or iPhone to the other PC or Mac.

3. iTunes displays a dialog box warning you that the iPod or iPhone is synced to another iTunes music library and asking if you want to change the sync to the current computer's iTunes music library. The next dialog box is for an iPhone, but the dialog box for an iPod is similar.

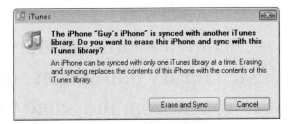

4. If you're sure you want to replace all the songs on the iPod, click the Erase And Sync button.

Because changing the iPod to a different home computer replaces the entire music library, the initial synchronization may take a long time, depending on how big the music library is and whether it's stored on a local drive or a network drive.

Synchronize Several iPods or iPhones with the Same Computer

As you've seen earlier in this book, usually a computer and an iPod (or iPhone) have a mutually faithful relationship—but, as discussed in the previous section, the iPod or iPhone can decide to leave its home computer and set up home with another computer. It can even switch to the other platform as well.

For most people, such fidelity (or serial fidelity) works fine. But if you have several iPods or iPhones and one computer, you can sync all the iPods and iPhones from that computer. Keep the following points in mind:

- Even if your computer has plenty of USB ports, it's best not to plug in more than one iPod or iPhone at once. That way, neither you nor iTunes become confused, and synchronization can take place at full speed.

- Each iPod and iPhone has a unique ID number that it communicates to your computer on connection, so your computer knows which device is connected to it. You can even give two or more devices the same name if doing so amuses you rather than confuses you.

- You can configure different updating for each iPod or iPhone by choosing options on the iPod screens or iPhone screens when the device is connected.

NOTE   *When you use the same user account on Windows or the Mac to synchronize multiple iPods, Apple recommends that you use the same synchronization settings for each. However, this isn't an absolute requirement—which is just as well, because the iPods have such different capacities and capabilities. If you find yourself having problems synchronizing different iPods using different synchronization settings, consider creating a separate user account for synchronizing a particular iPod.*

How to ...

Synchronize a Full—Different—Music Library onto Different iPods or iPhones from the Same Computer

Synchronizing two or more iPods or iPhones with the same computer works well enough provided that each user is happy using the same music library or the same playlists (perhaps a different selection from the set of playlists). But if you want to synchronize the full music library for each iPod or iPhone, yet have a different music library on each, you need to take a different approach.

In most cases, the easiest solution is to have a separate user account for each separate user who uses an iPod or iPhone with the computer. Separate user accounts are best in any case for keeping files and mail separate.

Place the music files that users will share in a folder that each user can access. In iTunes, make sure that the Copy Files To iTunes Music Folder When Adding To Library check box on the General subtab of the Advanced tab of the iTunes dialog box (in Windows) or the Preferences dialog box (on the Mac) is cleared so iTunes doesn't consolidate the files for the music library.

If you have enough free space on your hard disk, users can set up their own music libraries under their own user accounts and store all their music files in them. But unless your hard disk is truly gigantic, sharing most of the files from a central location is almost always preferable.

Another possibility is to start iTunes using a different library from within the same user account. To start iTunes using a different library:

- ■ **Windows** Hold down SHIFT as you click the iTunes icon to start iTunes.
- ■ **Mac** Hold down OPTION as you click the iTunes icon to start iTunes.

See the section "Use Multiple Libraries on the Same Computer" in Chapter 10 for more details on using multiple libraries.

Load an iPod from Two or More Computers at Once

As you read earlier in this chapter, you can synchronize an iPod or iPhone with only one computer at a time—the device's home computer. You can change the home computer from one computer to another, and even from one platform (Mac or PC) to the other, but you can't actively synchronize the iPod or iPhone with more than one computer at once.

But you *can* load songs, videos, or other items onto the iPod from computers other than the home computer. If the iPod is formatted using the FAT32 file system, you can use a mixture of Macs and PCs to load files onto the iPod. If the iPod is formatted using the Mac OS Extended file system, you can use only Macs. You can't load songs onto the iPhone from computers other than the home computer at this writing, but you can load other items, such as photos or contacts. See the following section for details.

All the computers you use must have iTunes installed and configured, and you must configure the iPod for manual updating on each computer involved—on the home computer as well as on each other computer. Otherwise, synchronizing the iPod with the home computer after loading tracks from other computers will remove those tracks because they're not in the home computer's music library.

Configure an iPod for Manual Updating

The first step in loading an iPod from two or more computers is to configure it for manual updating. You'll need to do this on the iPod's home computer first, and then on each of the other computers you plan to use.

To configure the iPod for manual updating, follow these steps:

1. Connect the iPod to your Mac or PC. Allow synchronization to take place. (If you need to override synchronization, see the sidebar "Temporarily Override Automatic Synchronization.")

2. Click the iPod's entry in the Source pane to display the iPod screens.

3. Select the Manually Manage Music check box. iTunes displays a message box warning you that you'll need to eject the iPod manually before disconnecting it, as shown here.

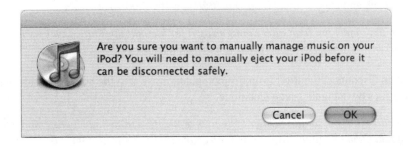

How to ... Temporarily Override Automatic Synchronization

If an iPod is configured for automatic synchronization, you can override this setting by holding down keys when you connect the iPod:

- **Windows**   Hold down CTRL-SHIFT.
- **Mac**   Hold down CTRL-OPTION.

Once the iPod appears in the Source pane in iTunes, you can let go of the keys.

4. Click the OK button to return to the iPod screens. iTunes selects the Enable Disk Use check box (if it wasn't already selected) and makes it unavailable so that you can't clear it manually.

5. Click the Apply button to apply the changes.

Load Files onto an iPod Manually

After you've configured an iPod for manual updating, you can load files onto it manually by following these general steps:

1. Connect the iPod to the computer that contains the files you want to load. The iPod appears in the Source pane in iTunes.

2. Drag song files from your iTunes library, or from a Windows Explorer window or a Finder window, and then drop them on the iPod or on one of its playlists.

3. After loading all the songs you want from this computer, eject the iPod by issuing an Eject command before you disconnect it. For example, right-click the iPod's entry in the Source pane and choose Eject *iPod*, where *iPod* is the iPod's name.

CAUTION   *If you don't eject the iPod after configuring it for manual updating, you may lose data or corrupt the iPod's contents when you disconnect it.*

You can then disconnect the iPod from this computer, move it to the next computer, and then add more song files by using the same technique.

NOTE   *From this point on, to add further song files to the iPod from your home computer, you must add them manually. Don't synchronize the iPod with your home computer, because synchronization will delete from the iPod all the song files that do not appear in your music library.*

Load an iPhone from Two or More Different Computers at Once

At this writing, you can load songs and videos on an iPhone from only one computer at a time—but you can load other items, such as information (contacts, calendars, e-mail, and bookmarks) or photos, from a different computer than the songs.

In general, loading an iPhone this way is a recipe for confusion, but you may occasionally find it useful. In particular, you may want to merge information from two (or more) separate computers onto the iPhone so that you can carry it all with you.

To load an iPhone from two or more computers at once, follow these steps:

1. Connect the iPhone to the home computer—the computer that will supply the iPhone with songs and video files.

2. Sync the iPhone as described earlier in this book. If you want to load only some items from the home computer, select the Only Sync Checked Items on the Summary tab of the iPhone's screens.

3. Disconnect the iPhone from the home computer, and then connect it to the computer that will provide the information or photos.

4. If iTunes prompts you to erase the iPhone and sync it with the library on the second computer, as shown here, click the Cancel button.

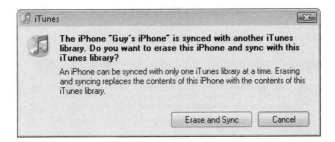

5. On the Summary tab of the iPhone's screens, select the Only Sync Checked Items check box.

6. To sync information, follow these steps:

   ■ Click the Info tab to display its contents.

   ■ To sync contacts, select the Sync Contacts From check box, and then choose the contacts source in the drop-down list. Choose whether to sync all contacts or just selected groups.

■ To sync calendars, select the Sync Calendars From check box, and then choose the Calendars source in the drop-down list. Choose whether to sync all calendars or just those you select.

■ To sync e-mail, select the Sync Selected Mail Accounts From check box, and then choose the program in the drop-down list. Select the check box for each e-mail account you want to sync (you may have only one available).

■ To sync bookmarks, select the Sync Bookmarks From check box, and then choose the browser in the drop-down list.

■ In the Advanced area (shown next), select the Contacts check box, the Calendars check box, the Mail Accounts check box, or the Bookmarks check box if you want to replace the existing information on the iPhone rather than add to it.

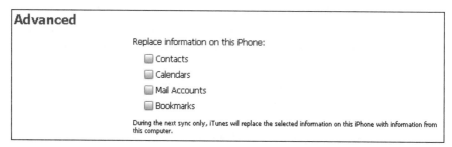

■ Click the Apply button. The iPhone displays the following dialog box, telling you that the iPhone's information is synced with a different user account and asking whether you want to merge the information or replace it.

■ Click the Merge Info button. iTunes merges the information.

7. To add photos from the new computer, follow these steps:

■ Click the Photos tab to display its contents.

■ Select the Sync Photos From check box, and then choose the source folder or program in the drop-down list.

■ Choose whether to sync all photos or just some of them.

■ Click the Apply button. iTunes displays the following dialog box, checking that you want to replace the existing photos on the iPhone with photos from the new computer.

■ Click the Sync Photos button.

8. When you've finished, disconnect the iPod from the second computer.

Chapter 15

Recover Your Songs and Videos from an iPod or iPhone

How to . . .

- ■ Know why the iPod and iPhone hide their song files and video files from you
- ■ Understand how the iPod and iPhone store song files and video files
- ■ Recover your songs and videos from an iPod or iPhone in Windows
- ■ Recover your songs and videos from an iPod or iPhone on the Mac

As you saw in Chapter 2, you can copy all or part of your library onto an iPod or iPhone almost effortlessly by choosing suitable synchronization settings and then synchronizing the device. Normally, any songs and videos on the iPod or iPhone are also in your library, so you don't need to transfer the songs and videos from the player to your computer. But if you have a computer disaster, or if your computer is stolen, you may need to recover the songs and videos from the iPod or iPhone to your new or repaired computer.

This chapter shows you how to recover songs and videos from an iPod or iPhone on both Windows and the Mac. The chapter starts by explaining why the iPod and iPhone hide the song and video files. It then covers where the files are stored on the devices, how you can access them through conventional file-management utilities (such as the Finder or Windows Explorer), and why copying the files using conventional means yields unsatisfactory results. The chapter ends by showing you the best recovery utilities for Windows and the Mac.

Why the iPod and iPhone Hide Their Song and Video Files from You

For copyright reasons, the basic configuration of the iPod and iPhone prevents you from copying music and video files from the player's library to your computer. This restriction prevents you from loading files onto the player on one computer via iTunes and then downloading them onto another computer, which would most likely violate copyright by making unauthorized copies of other people's copyrighted material.

But if you turn on disk mode (discussed in detail in Chapter 17), you can use an iPod as a portable drive. (Disk mode does not work on the iPhone at this writing, although programs such as iPhone Drive offer a workaround.) In disk mode, you can copy music and video files onto an iPod from one computer, connect the iPod to another computer, and copy or move the files from the iPod to that computer. The only limitation is that the files you copy this way aren't added to the iPod's music and video database, so you can't play them on the iPod.

Normally, you shouldn't need to copy songs and videos from an iPod or iPhone to your computer, because your computer will already contain all the songs and videos that the player contains. But there may come a time when you need to get the song files and video files out of the player's library for legitimate reasons. For example, if you dropped your MacBook, or your PC's hard disk died of natural causes, you might need to copy the music files and video files from the iPod or iPhone to a replacement computer or disk. Otherwise, you might risk losing your entire music and video collection.

> **TIP** *To avoid losing data, you should back up all your valuable data, including any songs and videos that you can't easily recover by other means (such as ripping your CDs again), especially the songs and videos you've bought from the iTunes Store or other online stores. However, the amount of data—and, in particular, the size of many people's libraries—makes backup difficult, requiring either an external hard drive (preferably USB 2.0 or FireWire) or multiple DVDs.*

To help you avoid this dreadful possibility, iPod enthusiasts have developed several utilities for transferring files from the player's hidden music and video storage to a computer.

Where—and How—the iPod and iPhone Store Song and Video Files

When you turn on disk mode, you can access the contents of the iPod's hard drive or flash memory by using Windows Explorer (in Windows) or the Finder (on the Mac). Until you create other folders there, though, you'll find only a few folders: Calendar, Contacts, Notes, and Photos (once you've synchronized photos). There's no trace of your song files and video files.

You can't see the song files and video files because the folders in which they are stored are formatted to be hidden in Windows and to be invisible on the Mac. Before you can see the folders or the files they contain, you need to change the Hidden attribute on the Windows folders or the Visible attribute on the Mac folders.

> **TIP** *If you're comfortable with Unix commands, you can open a Terminal window on Mac OS X and use the* `ls` *command to list the folders and files on the iPod, even though they're invisible to the Finder. Navigate to /Volumes/ipodname/iPod_Control/Music, where* ipodname *is the name of the iPod, and then examine the folders named F00, F01, and so on.*

Make the Hidden Folders Visible in Windows Vista

To display hidden files and folders in Windows Vista, follow these steps:

1. Choose Start | Computer to open a Computer window.
2. Click the Organize button on the toolbar, and then choose Folder And Search Options to display the Folder Options dialog box.
3. Click the View tab to display it (see Figure 15-1).

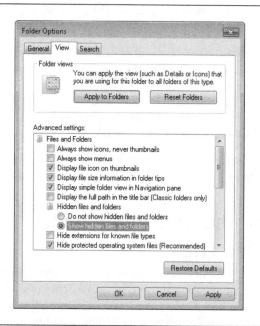

FIGURE 15-1
Use the controls on the View tab of the Folder Options dialog box to make the iPod's hidden folders visible in Windows Vista.

4. Select the Show Hidden Files And Folders option button.

5. Click the OK button to apply the change and to close the Folder Options dialog box. Windows Explorer now displays hidden files and folders as well as normal, unhidden files and folders.

To see the song folders on the iPod, follow these steps:

1. Double-click the icon for the iPod in the Computer window. Windows Explorer displays the contents of the iPod, including an iPod_Control folder that was previously hidden.

2. Double-click the iPod_Control folder to display its contents: a Device folder, an iTunes folder, and a Music folder.

3. Double-click the Music folder to display its contents: a series of folders named F*NN*, where *NN* is a two-digit number (F00, F01, F02, and so on).

4. Double-click one of these F folders to display its contents. Figure 15-2 shows an example. (The Address Bar shows the full path to the folder whose contents are displayed.)

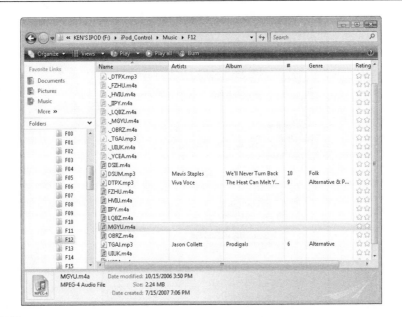

FIGURE 15-2   The iPod stores songs in folders named F00, F01, F02, and subsequent numbers.

Make the Hidden Folders Visible in Windows XP

To display hidden files and folders in Windows XP, follow these steps:

1. Choose Start | My Computer to open a My Computer window.

2. Choose Tools | Folder Options to display the Folder Options dialog box.

3. Click the View tab to display it (see Figure 15-3).

4. Select the Show Hidden Files And Folders option button.

5. Click the OK button to apply the change and to close the Folder Options dialog box. Windows Explorer now displays hidden files and folders as well as normal, unhidden files and folders.

To see the song folders on the iPod, follow these steps:

1. Double-click the icon for the iPod in the My Computer window. Windows Explorer displays the contents of the iPod: the Calendars and Contacts folders, as before, and the Notes folder on a third-generation or later iPod, but also an iPod_Control folder that was previously hidden.

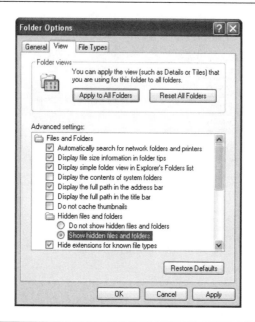

FIGURE 15-3 Use the controls on the View tab of the Folder Options dialog box to make the iPod's hidden folders visible in Windows XP.

2. Double-click the iPod_Control folder to display its contents: an Artwork folder, a Device folder, an iTunes folder, and a Music folder.

3. Double-click the Music folder to display its contents: a series of folders named F*NN,* where *NN* is a two-digit number (F00, F01, F02, and so on).

4. Double-click one of these F folders to display its contents. Figure 15-4 shows an example.

Make the Hidden Folders Visible on the Mac

To make hidden folders visible on Mac OS X, download and install TinkerTool from www .bresink.de/osx/TinkerTool.html. TinkerTool is a free configuration utility that lets you perform a variety of tweaks on Mac OS X, including making hidden folders visible.

After installing TinkerTool, follow these steps to make hidden folders visible:

1. Run TinkerTool from wherever you installed it (for example, your Applications folder).

2. On the Finder tab (see Figure 15-5), select the Show Hidden And System Files check box in the Finder Options area.

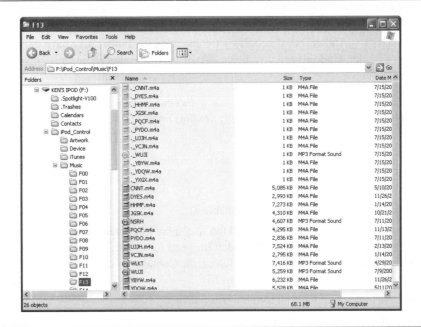

FIGURE 15-4   The iPod stores songs in folders named F00, F01, F02, and subsequent numbers.

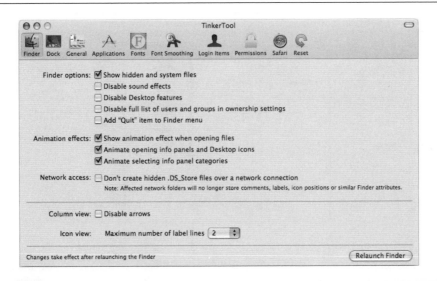

FIGURE 15-5   TinkerTool is the easy way of making hidden folders visible on the Mac.

3. Click the Relaunch Finder button in TinkerTool to relaunch the Finder. (You need to relaunch the Finder to make it read the now-visible folders.)

4. Navigate back to TinkerTool if necessary (relaunching the Finder may have moved the focus to a Finder window) and then press ⌘-Q or choose TinkerTool | Quit TinkerTool to quit TinkerTool.

CAUTION *Turning on the display of hidden and system files makes system files pop out of the woodwork. For example, you'll probably see files named .DS_Store and .localized appear on your desktop.*

After the Finder relaunches, you can examine the song folders. To do so, follow these steps:

1. Connect the iPod to your Mac as usual.

2. If you haven't yet enabled disk mode, enable it.

3. Double-click the iPod's icon on the desktop to display its contents in a Finder window. You'll be able to see the previously hidden files and folders: the Spotlight-V100 folder, the iPod_Control folder, the Calendars folder, the Contacts folder, the Notes folder, the .Trashes folder, and the .VolumeIcon.icns file.

4. Double-click the iPod_Control folder to open it.

5. Double-click the Music folder to open it.

6. Double-click one of the F folders to open it. Figure 15-6 shows an example of the structure of the iPod's music folders in Column view.

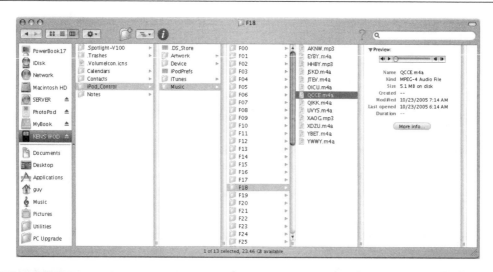

FIGURE 15-6 Turn on the display of hidden and system files to reveal the iPod's song folders and files.

Did you
know?

Why You Shouldn't Transfer Song and Video Files from an iPod Using the Finder or Windows Explorer

If you looked closely at the illustrations of the song files in the previous three sections, you probably noticed that the way in which the iPod stores files isn't immediately useful to most humans, for two reasons:

- First, the iPod lumps files arbitrarily into automatically named folders (F01, F02, and so on) at its convenience. As long as the iPod's internal database knows which folder a particular song or video is in, that's fine. But if you want to find a particular file, you'll need to search for it.

- Second, the iPod doesn't store the actual filenames in the file system. Instead, it uses a cryptic name for each file.

So if you copy or move files from the iPod's library folders to your computer, you'll need to perform some heavy-duty sorting and renaming afterward. If you're facing the loss of your entire library, you may be prepared to do this—but normally you'll be better off using one of the utilities discussed in the next two sections.

Windows Utilities for Transferring Song and Video Files from an iPod to Your PC

At this writing, there are several Windows utilities for transferring song and video files from an iPod to your PC. This section discusses two specialist utilities, iPod Access for Windows and iGadget.

The three heavy-duty iPod-management applications for Windows—EphPod, Anapod Explorer, and XPlay—also enable you to transfer media files to, and generally manage, an iPod, and are discussed in detail in the next chapter. See the sections "Recover Media Files from an iPod with Anapod Explorer," and "Recover Media Files from an iPod with XPlay" for details.

iPod Access for Windows

iPod Access for Windows from Findley Designs (www.findleydesigns.com) lets you transfer files from an iPod to your PC. iPod Access for Windows (see Figure 15-7) costs $19.99, but you can

FIGURE 15-7   iPod Access for Windows can recover files from an iPod to a PC.

download a limited evaluation version to see if the application works for you. You can also use iPod Access to play back songs directly from an iPod.

iGadget

iGadget from iPodSoft (www.ipodsoft.com) lets you transfer files from an iPod to a PC. iGadget (see Figure 15-8) costs $15 and also lets you transfer weather forecasts, driving directions, gas prices, Outlook data, and other text to your iPod.

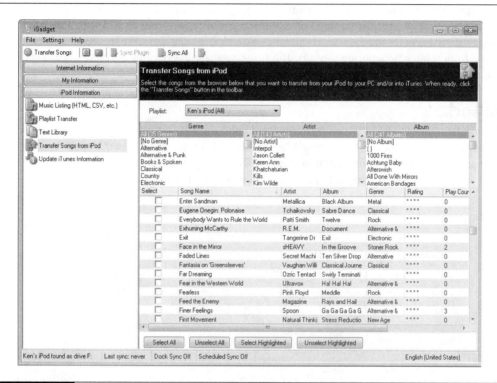

FIGURE 15-8   iGadget lets you recover songs from an iPod to a PC.

Mac OS X Utilities for Transferring Song and Video Files from an iPod to Your Mac

iPod enthusiasts have created an impressive array of utilities for transferring song and video files from an iPod to a Mac. This section discusses some of the leading utilities for doing so.

NOTE   *If you don't like the look (or performance) of these utilities, search sites such as iLounge.com (www.ilounge.com), VersionTracker.com (www.versiontracker.com), MacUpdate (www.macupdate.com), and Apple's Mac OS X Downloads page (www.apple.com/downloads/macosx) for alternatives.*

Different utilities work in different ways. The most basic utilities simply assemble a list of the filenames in the iPod's music folders, which leaves you with cryptic filenames. The best utilities read the database the iPod maintains of the files it holds, whereas other utilities plow painstakingly through each file on the iPod and extract information from its ID3 tags. Reading the iPod's database gives much faster results than assembling what's essentially the same database from scratch by scouring the tags. But if the database has become corrupted, reading the tags is a good recovery technique.

PodWorks

PodWorks from Sci-Fi Hi-Fi ($8; www.scifihifi.com/podworks) is a neat utility for transferring song and video files from an iPod to your Mac. Figure 15-9 shows PodWorks in action. You can download an evaluation version that limits you to 30 days, copying 250 songs, and copying one song at a time—enough limitations to persuade you to buy the full version.

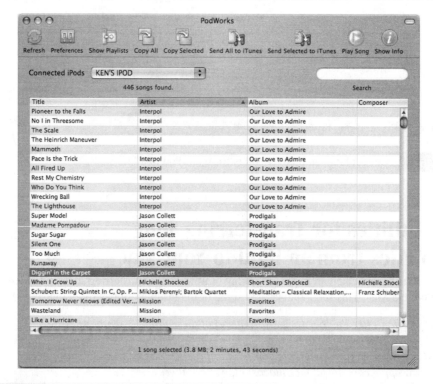

FIGURE 15-9   PodWorks can quickly recover songs from an iPod.

FIGURE 15-10   iPod Access can recover songs from an iPod or simply play them back.

iPod Access

iPod Access from Findley Designs (www.findleydesigns.com) also simplifies the process of transferring song and video files from an iPod to a Mac. iPod Access (see Figure 15-10) costs $19.99, but you can download a limited evaluation version to see if the application works for you. You can also use iPod Access to play back songs directly from the iPod.

iPodRip

iPodRip from The Little App Factory PTY Ltd. ($14.95; www.thelittleappfactory.com) integrates with iTunes and enables you to play back songs from either your library or an iPod. iPodRip (see Figure 15-11; the application's title bar shows the iPod's name) comes in a trial version that you can use ten times before it cripples itself. iPodRip's SmartSync feature enables you to automatically copy to your library songs and videos that you've loaded onto an iPod using a different computer.

FIGURE 15-11 iPodRip is a utility that can recover files from an iPod even if the player's database has been corrupted.

Apart from being able to recover songs using the data in the iPod's database, iPodRip can also perform a "hard recover" when the iPod's database is corrupted or missing. In a hard recover (see the next illustration), iPodRip copies any songs found on the iPod to your desktop. When the database is corrupted or missing, iPodRip may not be able to find and recover all the files.

Chapter 16

Use the iPod with Software Other Than iTunes

How to...

- Understand why to use software other than iTunes to control the iPod
- Manage the iPod with Winamp on Windows
- Manage the iPod with Anapod Explorer on Windows
- Manage the iPod with XPlay on Windows
- Use Clutter to give iTunes a super-graphical interface on the Mac

Apple not only designed iTunes for the iPod and iPhone but also makes iTunes available for free to anyone who wants to download it—so you have a strong incentive to use iTunes to manage the iPod or iPhone. But if you choose not to use iTunes, there are some alternatives, particularly on Windows. This chapter introduces you to those alternatives, starting with the key question: Why use them at all?

At this writing, none of these programs works with the iPhone—but iPhone-compatible versions of the programs are due soon.

Why Use Software Other Than iTunes to Control the iPod?

iTunes is one of the core applications that have made Mac OS X such a powerhouse for multimedia, and both iTunes and Mac OS X have been built to work with iPods and iPhones. As a result, iTunes is by far the best software for managing an iPod or iPhone on the Mac, unless you need features that iTunes cannot or will not provide, such as recovering song files from the iPod or iPhone to the computer (see Chapter 15) or the ability to synchronize large amounts of your Entourage data with the iPod or iPhone.

iTunes for Windows, which was introduced several years after iTunes for Mac OS X, has largely caught up with the Mac version in functionality, even if it is still not as slickly integrated into the operating system. However, over the years of iTunes for Windows' development, third-party developers created other programs for managing iPods, both to allow you to avoid iTunes' teething troubles and to give you features that iTunes for Windows doesn't provide, such as Outlook integration or the ability to recover your music library after your PC has disagreed violently with itself.

NOTE   *Another reason to use other software is if iTunes doesn't run on your operating system. For example, iTunes for Windows requires Windows Vista, Windows XP, or Windows 2000. If you're brave enough to continue using an earlier version of Windows, such as Windows 98 or Windows Me, you'll need to use other software.*

Control the iPod with Other Software on Windows

If you find iTunes for Windows slow or balky, or if iTunes doesn't run on your version of Windows, or you simply don't like iTunes, you have several alternatives. This section discusses the three leading contenders: Anapod Explorer, Winamp, and XPlay.

None of these applications can rip and encode audio from CD or burn CDs (unless you buy the Pro version of Winamp). iTunes will perform both tasks, as will Windows Media Player, which is included with most versions of Windows Vista and Windows XP.

Anapod Explorer

Anapod Explorer is a full-fledged utility for managing iPods on Windows. Anapod Explorer comes in a Trial Edition that's free but has limited features, and a Full Edition that costs between $20 and $30, depending on how many iPods you use and which model or models they are. For example, the iPod shuffle license for Anapod Explorer is less expensive than those for the iPod nano and the iPod with video. (If you're like most iPod users, further iPods probably lie in your future, so the full version is probably the best bet.)

Anapod Explorer runs as a plug-in to Windows Explorer, so you work in a largely familiar interface, and you can use drag-and-drop to perform file transfers.

NOTE *Anapod Explorer works with Windows Vista, Windows XP, Windows 2000, Windows Me, and Windows 98. At this writing, Anapod Explorer does not yet work with the iPhone.*

Get and Install Anapod Explorer

To get Anapod Explorer, go to the Red Chair Software, Inc. website (www.redchairsoftware .com) and either download the Trial Edition or buy one of the paid versions. Double-click the download file to open it.

NOTE *Windows Vista or Windows XP with Service Pack 2 may display an Open File – Security Warning dialog box warning you that the publisher of the Anapod Explorer distribution file cannot be verified. This is because the file is not signed with a digital signature. But if you've just downloaded the file from the Red Chair Software website, you can probably be confident that it contains only trustworthy code.*

Anapod Explorer installs easily using a wizard. You can choose whether to create Desktop shortcuts and a group on the Start menu. Windows Vista or Windows XP with Service Pack 2 may display a Windows Security Alert dialog box at the end of the Anapod Explorer installation asking if you want Windows Firewall to keep blocking the Red Chair Manager from accepting connections from the Internet or a network (see Figure 16-1). You need to click the Unblock button to allow Red Chair Manager to accept connections before Anapod Explorer will work correctly.

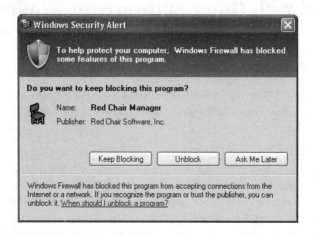

FIGURE 16-1   Windows XP with Service Pack 2 or later automatically blocks Red Chair Manager from accepting connections. You must unblock Red Chair Manager to get Anapod Explorer to work.

Red Chair Manager manifests itself as a controller named Anapod Manager, which is used to establish communication with and control the iPod. Anapod Manager runs by default when you launch Windows and displays an icon in the notification area. You can right-click this icon to launch Anapod Explorer or configure Anapod Manager.

When the installation is complete, connect the iPod, and then open Anapod Explorer in one of the following ways:

- Right-click the Anapod Manager icon in the notification area, and then choose Open Anapod Explorer from the shortcut menu. This is usually the easiest way, and it gives you access to the Anapod Manager's other commands.

- Double-click the Anapod Explorer icon on your Desktop (if you chose to create one).

- Choose Start | All Programs | Red Chair Software | Anapod Explorer | Anapod Explorer.

NOTE   *The first time you run Anapod Explorer, you must activate it for each iPod you will use with it.*

You'll see a Windows Explorer window named Anapod Explorer. You can navigate around the Anapod Explorer window using standard Windows techniques.

NOTE   *If the Open Anapod Explorer command on the Anapod Manager shortcut menu is grayed out, choose the Connect iPod item first to establish the connection with the iPod and then choose the Open Anapod Explorer item.*

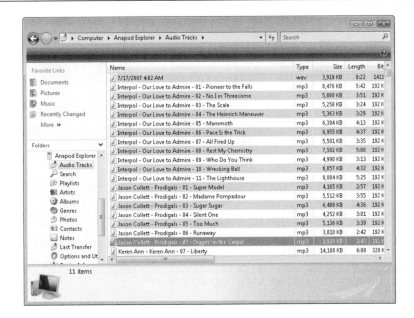

FIGURE 16-2   Anapod Explorer uses Windows Explorer as its interface.

Transfer Songs to the iPod with Anapod Explorer

To see the songs on the iPod, click the Audio Tracks item under the Anapod Explorer heading (see Figure 16-2).

You can then add songs to the iPod by dragging them or by using SpeedSync:

- Drag the song files and drop them on the Audio Tracks item. Anapod Explorer displays the Transferring To Device dialog box (Figure 16-3 shows an example), which not only lets you see which file Anapod Explorer is working on, the overall progress, and the transfer performance, but also lets you compare the transfer performance to that of other users. You can drop further song files on the Transferring To Device dialog box to include them in the transfer, or you can simply wait until the transfer is complete and then click the Close button.

- Designate one or more SpeedSync folders that you want Anapod Explorer to check automatically for new songs. To designate a SpeedSync folder, choose Anapod Explorer | Anapod Options And Utilities | Anapod Options from within the Anapod Explorer window, and then click the SpeedSync item in the iPod category on the left to display the SpeedSync items (see Figure 16-4). Use the Add Folder button and the resulting Browse For Folder dialog box to add one or more folders to the PC Source Folders list. Then use the PC Target Folder drop-down list to select one of the folders as the destination for song files you recover from the iPod to your PC.

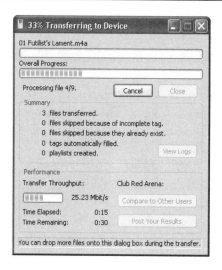

FIGURE 16-3   Transferring song files with Anapod Explorer

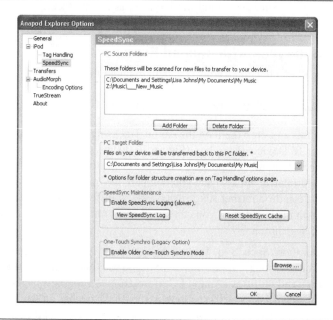

FIGURE 16-4   On the SpeedSync section of the Anapod Explorer Options dialog box, designate one or more PC Source Folders and a PC Target Folder.

Use the AudioMorph Feature to Convert Songs
Automatically when Loading Them on the iPod

Anapod Explorer's AudioMorph feature lets you automatically convert song files in the MP3, WAV, OGG (Ogg Vorbis), and WMA formats to a particular bitrate when loading them on the iPod. For example, you might choose to load all song files on the iPod at the 128 Kbps bitrate if you felt that bitrate delivered the optimum balance of audio quality versus file size. Anapod Explorer then converts song files encoded at other bitrates (usually higher bitrates) to your specified bitrate before transferring them to the iPod.

Here's how to use AudioMorph:

1. Choose Anapod Explorer | Anapod Options And Utilities | Anapod Options from within the Anapod Explorer window to display the Anapod Explorer Options dialog box.

2. Click the AudioMorph item in the left column to display its contents (see Figure 16-5).

3. Select the Enable AudioMorph During Transfers check box to turn AudioMorph on.

4. Check the list boxes at the top of the pane to see which plug-ins are installed. To get further plug-ins, click the Help And More Plugins button and follow the instructions in the resulting browser window to download and install the plug-ins.

FIGURE 16-5   You may need to use the Help And More Plugins button to get Anapod Explorer's AudioMorph feature working for all the audio file types you want Anapod Explorer to convert automatically when loading songs onto the iPod.

NOTE *If you're using Windows Vista or Windows XP with Service Pack 2, when you double-click the distribution file of an Anapod Explorer encoder, you may see an Open File – Security Warning dialog box warning you that the publisher cannot be verified because the file is not signed with a digital signature. But if you've just downloaded the file from the Red Chair Software website, it should be okay.*

5. To change the transfer rule for a file format, right-click the rule in the lower pane, and then choose the rule you want from the shortcut menu.

6. To change the encoding rate for creating or reencoding MP3 or WMA files, click the Encoding Options item in the left list and work with the resulting controls (see Figure 16-6).

Recover Songs from the iPod with Anapod Explorer

Before recovering songs from the iPod with Anapod Explorer, you must designate the PC target folder, as described in the previous section. (If you missed it: Choose Anapod Explorer | Anapod Options And Utilities | Anapod Options from within the Anapod Explorer window to display the Anapod Explorer Options dialog box, click the SpeedSync item in the iPod category on the left, and then select the folder in the PC Target Folder drop-down list.)

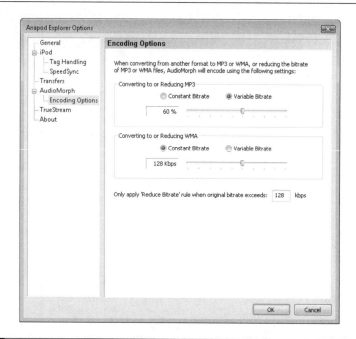

FIGURE 16-6   Anapod Explorer can reduce the bitrate of songs when transferring them to the iPod. This is a great way to maximize the amount of music the iPod can hold.

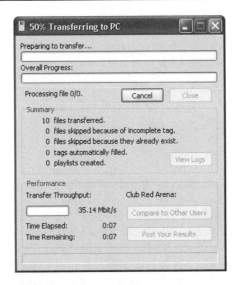

FIGURE 16-7   Anapod Explorer also lets you recover songs from an iPod.

Once you've designated your PC target folder, proceed as follows:

1. Select the songs you want to recover.

2. Right-click the selection, and then choose Copy To Computer from the shortcut menu. Anapod Explorer displays the Browse For Folder dialog box.

3. Navigate to and select the target folder and then click the OK button. Anapod Explorer copies the song files, displaying the Transferring To PC dialog box as it does so (see Figure 16-7).

TIP

Anapod Explorer includes a miniature web server called Anapod Xtreamer that allows you to access the iPod remotely from any computer on the network. You can play songs in formats that your browser's plug-ins can play, or you can download any song to your local hard disk. You can even stream music from the iPod to your own computer. See the Anapod documentation for instructions on this feature.

Disconnect the iPod

Before disconnecting the iPod from your computer, right-click the Anapod Manager icon in the notification area and choose Disconnect iPod from the shortcut menu.

XPlay

XPlay was originally developed to let Windows users synchronize Mac-formatted iPods with their PCs. XPlay now works with Windows-formatted iPods as well as Mac iPods, and runs on Windows XP, Windows 2000, Windows Me, and Windows 98.

NOTE *At this writing, XPlay does not run on Windows Vista—but XPlay version 3, which is due to be released in the first quarter of 2008, will run on Vista.*

Get and Install XPlay

To get XPlay, go to the Mediafour Corporation website (www.mediafour.com). The full version of XPlay costs $29.95, so it's best to start by downloading the 15-day trial version of XPlay to make sure it works for you and that you like it before you pay.

The XPlay installation procedure is straightforward, but you will probably need to restart your PC to enable XPlay fully. After the restart, the XPlay iPod Setup Wizard opens and walks you through the process of setting up the iPod to work with XPlay. The setup procedure also lets you rename the iPod and choose whether to synchronize it automatically using XPlay.

At the end of the setup procedure, start XPlay in one of these ways:

■ Double-click the Explore My iPod With XPlay icon in the notification area.

■ Double-click the Explore My iPod With XPlay icon on your Desktop.

■ Choose Start | All Programs | XPlay | Explore My iPod.

XPlay then opens a Windows Explorer window to the root of the drive that represents the iPod. Double-click the XPlay Music item to view XPlay's representation of the iPod's music database (see Figure 16-8). Within the XPlay Music folder, you can drill down to view playlists, albums, and artists. You can use the Songs item to view all the songs on the iPod.

Transfer Songs to the iPod with XPlay

To copy song files to the iPod, drag them and drop them on the iPod icon.

Recover Songs from the iPod with XPlay

To copy song files from the iPod to your PC using XPlay, drill down to the appropriate song or folder on the iPod. Then either drag the song or folder to a folder on your PC or click the Copy This Item link in the XPlay Music Tasks pane, use the resulting Browse For Folder dialog box to specify the destination, and then click the OK button.

Prepare the iPod for Disconnection

Before disconnecting the iPod, click the Stop My iPod button (the button with the Eject icon) on the toolbar in the XPlay window.

FIGURE 16-8   The XPlay Music item lets you access your music by playlists, albums, artists, genres, composers, or songs.

Winamp

Winamp has been a favorite MP3 player for many music addicts since shortly after the MP3 revolution. Recent versions of Winamp can also interface with an iPod—which is great news if you're one of those addicts.

Get and Install Winamp

To get started, download the latest version of Winamp from the Winamp website (www.winamp .com). Double-click the distribution file to run the installation, or simply accept Windows' offer to run the program.

NOTE   *Winamp comes in a free version called Basic and a paid version called Pro. Start with the Basic version and see how you like it. You can upgrade easily to the Pro version if you want.*

Installation is straightforward, but pay attention on the Choose Install Options screen:

■ **Icons**   Most people find the System Tray Icon/Agent the most useful, as it allows you to launch or control Winamp from the notification area. You probably do not need all three of the Start Menu Group, Desktop Icon, and the Quick Launch Icon.

■ **Associations** If you plan to use Winamp as your primary music and video player, accept its offer to associate itself with audio files, video files, audio CDs, and playlist files. Otherwise, clear these check boxes.

Winamp launches itself at the end of the installation. Winamp then prompts you to add media files to its library so that it knows which songs you have. Figure 16-9 shows Winamp in a typical configuration, with the main window at the upper-left corner, the Playlist Editor window next to it, and the Media Library window below them both.

Choose How to Synchronize the iPod with Winamp

Next, connect your iPod to your computer, and tell Winamp how to synchronize it. Follow these steps:

1. In the Media Library window, expand the Portables category in the left pane, and then select the item for the iPod. You may need to collapse any expanded categories, or simply scroll down, to reach the Portables category.

2. Press CTRL-P or, on the main Winamp window, choose Options | Preferences to display the Winamp Preferences dialog box.

3. Under the Media Library category, locate the Portables category, and then click the entry for the iPod (see Figure 16-10).

FIGURE 16-9   Winamp uses several windows, which you can position (or close) as you please.

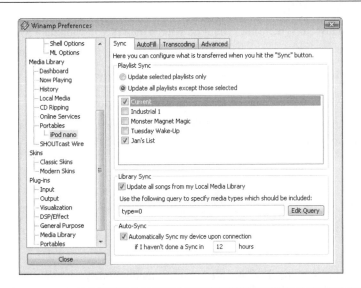

FIGURE 16-10   You'll find the iPod's settings in the Portables subcategory of the Media
Library category.

4. Choose synchronization settings:

■ **Sync tab**   Choose whether to update selected playlists, all playlists *except* those you
select, or your entire media library. You can also choose to automatically sync the
iPod if you haven't synced it during the specified number of hours (for example,
12 or 24).

■ **AutoFill tab**   Choose whether to have Winamp automatically fill the iPod with
songs. Winamp lets you choose how full to stuff the iPod—for example, 90 percent
full.

■ **Transcoding tab**   Choose whether to transcode incompatible tracks—for example,
to create MP3 files of tracks the iPod otherwise wouldn't be able to play. Click the
Advanced button if you want to force transcoding of high-bitrate compatible tracks
as well. This setting lets you put more music on your iPod, but the transcoding
makes syncs take longer.

■ **Advanced tab**   Choose whether to use Gapless Playback if your iPod supports it.

5. When you've finished choosing synchronization options, click the Close button to close
the Winamp Preferences dialog box.

Load the iPod from Winamp

Once you've chosen how to synchronize the iPod with Winamp, you can either sync it or AutoFill it.

Sync the iPod with Winamp   To sync the iPod with Winamp, follow these steps:

1. Select the iPod in the left pane in the Media Library window.

2. Click the Sync button at the bottom of the Media Library window. Winamp displays the Sync dialog box, as shown here.

3. If there are songs on the iPod that are not in the media library, choose the appropriate option button: Leave Them, Delete Them, or Copy Them To The Local Media Library.

4. If you want to sync the iPod automatically when you connect it, select the Automatically Sync Upon Connection check box.

5. If you want to see the songs that Winamp will put on the iPod or remove from it, click the More button to expand the dialog box, as shown here. You can choose to remove songs from the selection.

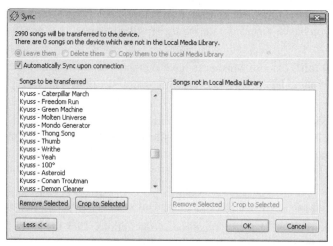

6. When you've finished choosing options, click the OK button. Winamp syncs the songs with the iPod.

AutoFill the iPod from Winamp   To AutoFill the iPod from Winamp, follow these steps:

1. Select the iPod in the left pane of the Media Library window.

2. Click the AutoFill button at the bottom of the Media Library window. Winamp displays the AutoFill dialog box, as shown here.

3. If you want to AutoFill the iPod automatically when you connect it, select the AutoFill My Device Immediately Upon Connection check box.

4. To see the details of which songs Winamp will put on the iPod and remove from it, click the More button to expand the dialog box, as shown here.

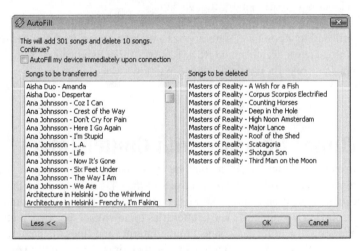

5. When you're ready to fill your iPod, click the OK button.

Eject the iPod

Before you disconnect the iPod, eject it. Select the iPod in the left pane of the Media Library window, and then click the Eject button in the lower-right corner of the Media Library window.

Did you
know?

EphPod—a Great Utility for Older iPods

EphPod (pronounced *eef*pod rather than *eff*pod, and downloadable from www.ephpod .com and other sites) is a free and very full-featured application for managing iPods on Windows. Technically, EphPod is donationware rather than freeware—the author invites you to contribute to his beer fund, and even allows you to request that a donation be spent on something better than beer.

EphPod was originally built, in the days when the iPod worked only with the Mac, to enable you to use Mac iPods with Windows PCs. Since then, Apple's release of iTunes for Windows has greatly reduced the need for EphPod.

These days, EphPod works with Windows iPods as well as Mac iPods—but at this writing, EphPod does not work with the latest iPods, making it primarily useful for owners of older iPods. However, it is worth checking the EphPod website (www.ephpod.com) to see if EphPod's developer has created an updated version.

If you do have an older iPod, EphPod is great not only for managing it, but also for recovering song files if your computer's library has a disaster. Apart from this feature, EphPod can download news, weather, and RSS (Really Simple Syndication) web feeds to the iPod. EphPod also works on Windows 98 and Windows Me.

Improve the iTunes Interface with Clutter (Mac)

Sleek and effective as iTunes' interface is, it could be more visually compelling. If you'd like to be able to navigate your music collection by the covers of the CDs rather than by their names, download the freeware application Clutter (see Figure 16-11) from www.sprote.com/clutter.

When you start playing a song in iTunes, Clutter tries to download the cover picture for the CD that contains the song. If Clutter can connect to the Internet and finds the picture at Amazon .com, it displays it in the Now Playing window. You can then drag the picture to your desktop and position it wherever you want it. Each CD cover is a separate window, so you can overlap the covers however you want.

If you started a song playing while your Mac wasn't connected to the Internet, after connecting, you can force Clutter to search Amazon.com for the CD cover by pressing ⌘-F or choosing File | Find Cover On Amazon. If Amazon.com doesn't have the cover, you can search Google by pressing ⌘-G or choosing File | Search Google. Alternatively, you can drag a graphic to the Now Playing window from a browser window or a Finder window, so you can apply any graphic that you have or that you can find.

FIGURE 16-11   Clutter is a free application that enables you to spread your music collection across your desktop and select music by its CD cover.

The main Clutter window shows the details of the song that's currently playing, and it provides a Play/Pause button, a Previous button, and a Next button. You can start the first available song on any CD playing by double-clicking that CD's cover on your desktop.

To get your desktop back again, quit Clutter (press ⌘-Q). The next time you start Clutter, it places the CD covers across the desktop in the same arrangement as you left them.

Chapter 17

Use an iPod as an External Drive or Backup Device

How to ...

- Decide whether or not to use an iPod as an external drive
- Enable disk mode on an iPod using Windows
- Enable disk mode on an iPod using a Mac
- Transfer files to and from an iPod
- Use iPhone Drive to turn an iPhone into a drive (Mac only)
- Start up your Mac from an iPod
- Back up an iPod so you don't lose your music or data

Apple sells the iPod primarily as a portable music and video player—and, as you know by now, it's arguably the best portable player around. But, as you also know by now, the iPod is essentially an external USB drive with sophisticated audio and video features. This chapter shows you how to use an iPod as an external drive for backup and portable storage. If your computer is a Mac, you can even boot from an iPod for security or to recover from disaster.

NOTE   *One external-drive feature this chapter doesn't show you is how to transfer files from an iPod's library onto your computer. Chapter 15 covers this subject.*

At this writing, Apple does not let you use an iPhone as a drive, so most of the coverage in this chapter does not apply to the iPhone—or at least not yet. However, you can use the third-party program iPhone Drive to store data on an iPhone from a Mac.

Decide Whether to Use an iPod as an External Drive

If all you want from an iPod is huge amounts of music and video to go, you may never want to use an iPod as an external drive. Even so, briefly consider why you might want to do so:

- *A regular iPod provides a great combination of portability and high capacity.* You can get smaller portable-storage devices (for example, USB keys, CompactFlash drives, SmartMedia cards, and Memory Sticks), but they're expensive and generally have much lower capacities. Even an iPod nano has enough space to carry a fair amount of data with you along with your songs. On an iPod shuffle, you'll feel the pinch a bit more—but you can take your essential files with you.

- *You can take all your documents with you.* For example, you could take home that large PowerPoint presentation you need to get ready for tomorrow. You could even put several gigabytes of video files on an iPod if you needed to take them with you (for example, to a studio for editing) or transfer them to another computer.

- *You can use an iPod for backup.* If you keep your vital documents down to a size you can easily fit on an iPod (and still have plenty of room left for songs, videos, and other files), you can quickly back up the documents and take the backup with you wherever you go.

■ *You can use an iPod for security.* By keeping your documents on an iPod rather than on your computer, and by keeping the iPod with you, you can prevent other people from accessing your documents. If your computer is a Mac, you can even boot it from a regular iPod, thus preventing anyone else from using your computer at all.

The disadvantages to using an iPod as an external disk are straightforward:

■ Whatever space you use on the iPod for storing other files isn't available for music and video.

■ If you lose or break the iPod, any files stored only on it will be gone forever.

Enable Disk Mode

To use an iPod as an external drive, you must first enable disk mode. In disk mode, your computer uses an iPod as an external disk. You can copy to the iPod any files and folders that will fit on it.

NOTE   *You can copy song files, video files, and playlists to an iPod in disk mode, but you won't be able to play them on the iPod. This is because when you copy the files, their information isn't added to the iPod's database the way it's added by iTunes and other applications designed to work with the iPod, such as Anapod Explorer or XPlay. So the iPod's interface doesn't know the files are there, and you can't play them.*

From the computer's point of view, an external disk connected via USB works in essentially the same way as any other disk. Here are the differences:

■ The disk is external.

■ The disk may draw power across the USB connection (as iPods do) rather than being powered itself (as high-capacity and high-performance external disks tend to be).

■ If the iPod uses a USB connection, the USB controller and the USB cable or connection must supply enough power to feed the iPod. All USB connections supply power, but some don't supply enough for an iPod. (Other devices, such as USB keyboards and mice, require much less power than an iPod.) Apple refers to USB ports as "high-powered" (giving enough power for an iPod) and "low-powered" (not giving enough power).

CAUTION   *Using an iPod as an external disk with a connection that can't supply power may run down the battery quickly. Part of the problem is that the iPod can't use its caching capabilities when you use it as an external disk. (Caching works only for playlists and albums, when the iPod knows which files are needed next and thus can read them into the cache.) If the iPod isn't receiving power, check the battery status periodically to make sure the iPod doesn't suddenly run out of power.*

Enable Disk Mode on an iPod Using Windows

To use an iPod as an external disk on a PC, enable disk mode. Follow these steps:

1. Connect the iPod to your PC as usual.

2. Launch iTunes if it doesn't launch automatically.

3. In the Source pane, click the iPod's icon to display the iPod screens.

4. For a regular iPod or an iPod nano, click the Summary tab if it isn't already displayed (see Figure 17-1). For an iPod shuffle, click the Settings tab if it isn't already displayed.

5. Select the Enable Disk Use check box. iTunes displays the following warning dialog box, telling you that using disk mode requires you to manually unmount the iPod before each disconnect, even when you're automatically updating music:

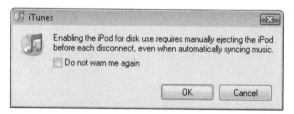

6. Select the Do Not Warn Me Again check box if you want to suppress this warning in the future, and then click the OK button. iTunes returns you to the Summary tab or Settings tab.

7. For an iPod shuffle, drag the slider along the More Songs–More Data continuum to specify how much space you want to devote to data and how much to songs:

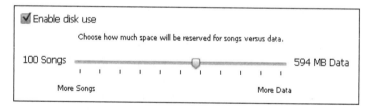

8. Click the Apply button to apply the changes.

Once you've enabled disk mode, the iPod appears to Windows Explorer as a removable drive. Windows Explorer automatically assigns a drive letter to the drive, so you can access it as you would any other drive connected to your computer.

To eject the iPod, take any of the following actions:

- In the Source pane in iTunes, click the Eject icon next to the iPod's name. (This is the easiest means of ejection.)

- In the Source pane in iTunes, right-click the icon for the iPod and then choose Eject.

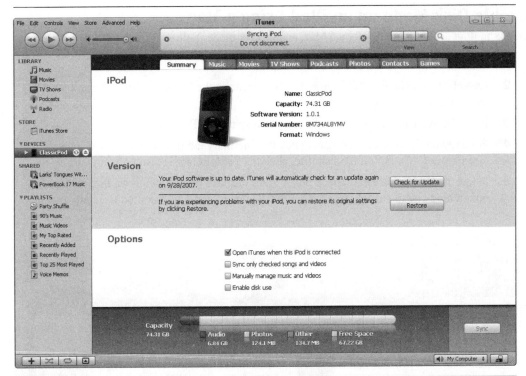

FIGURE 17-1   Select the Enable Disk Use check box on the Summary tab to enable disk mode
on an iPod in Windows. For an iPod shuffle, this setting is on the Settings tab.

■ In the Source pane in iTunes, select the icon for the iPod and then click the Eject iPod
button in the lower-right corner of the iTunes window.

■ In Windows Vista, choose Start | Computer to open the Computer window. In Windows
XP, choose Start | My Computer to open the My Computer window. Right-click the icon
for the iPod and then choose Eject from the shortcut menu.

When the iPod displays the "OK to disconnect" message, you can safely disconnect it. On an
iPod shuffle, make sure the iPod is showing a green light or a steady orange light rather than a
flashing orange light before you disconnect it.

CAUTION   *Don't just disconnect the iPod without ejecting it. You might damage files or lose data.*

Enable Disk Mode on an iPod Using a Mac

To use an iPod as an external disk on a Mac, enable disk mode. Follow these steps:

1. Connect the iPod to the Mac as usual.

2. Launch iTunes (for example, click the iTunes icon in the Dock) if iTunes doesn't launch automatically.

3. In the Source pane, click the iPod's entry to display the iPod's screens.

4. For a regular iPod or an iPod nano, click the Summary tab if it isn't already displayed (see Figure 17-2). For an iPod shuffle, click the Settings tab if it isn't already displayed.

5. Select the Enable Disk Use check box. iTunes displays the following warning dialog box, telling you that using disk mode requires you to unmount the iPod manually before

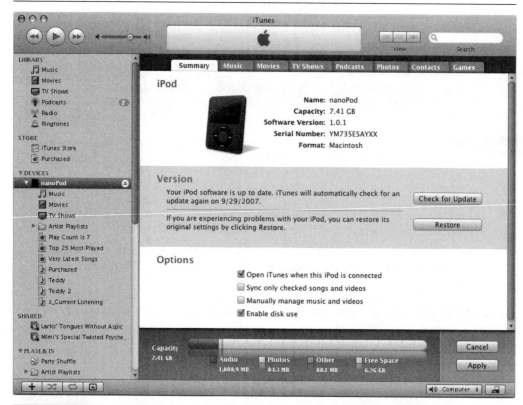

FIGURE 17-2   Select the Enable Disk Use check box on the Summary tab to enable disk mode on an iPod on the Mac. For an iPod shuffle, this setting is on the Settings tab.

each disconnect, even when synchronizing songs (instead of being able to have iTunes unmount the iPod automatically):

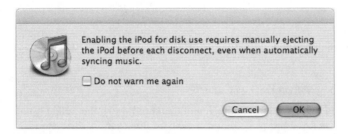

6. Select the Do Not Warn Me Again check box if you want to suppress this warning in the future, and then click the OK button. iTunes returns you to the Summary tab or Settings tab.

7. For an iPod shuffle, drag the slider along the More Songs–More Data continuum to specify how much space you want to devote to data and how much to songs:

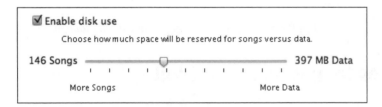

8. Click the Apply button to apply the changes.

Once you've enabled disk mode, you'll need to eject the iPod manually after each connection. To eject the iPod, take any of the following actions:

- In the Source pane in iTunes, click the Eject icon next to the iPod's name. (This is the easiest means of ejection.)
- In the Source pane in iTunes, select the icon for the iPod and then click the Eject iPod button in the lower-right corner of the iTunes window.
- In the Source pane in iTunes, right-click the icon for the iPod and then choose Eject from the shortcut menu.
- Select the icon for the iPod on the desktop and then issue an Eject command from the File menu or the shortcut menu. (Alternatively, press ⌘-E.)
- Drag the desktop icon for the iPod to the Trash.

When an iPod displays the "OK to disconnect" message, you can safely disconnect it. On an iPod shuffle, make sure the iPod is showing a green light rather than an orange light before you disconnect it.

How to ... **Force Disk Mode**

If your USB port is underpowered, you may need to force an iPod to enter disk mode. To do so for a regular iPod or iPod nano, follow these steps:

1. Connect the iPod via USB as usual.

2. Toggle the Hold switch on and off, and then hold down the Select button and the Menu button for about five seconds to reboot the iPod.

3. When the iPod displays the Apple logo, hold down the Select button and Play button briefly. The iPod sends the computer an electronic prod that forces the computer to recognize it.

CAUTION   *Don't just disconnect the iPod without ejecting it. You might damage files or lose data.*

Transfer Files to and from the iPod

When the iPod is in disk mode, you can transfer files to it by using the Finder (on the Mac), Windows Explorer (in Windows), or another file-management application of your choice. (You can transfer files by using the command prompt, if you so choose.)

CAUTION   *If the iPod appears in the Computer window (on Windows Vista) or My Computer window (on Windows XP) as a drive named Removable Drive, and Windows Explorer claims the disk isn't formatted, chances are you've connected a Mac-formatted iPod to your PC. Windows Explorer can't read the HFS Plus disk format that Mac-formatted iPods use, so the iPod appears to be unformatted. (HFS Plus is one of the disk formats Mac OS X can use and is also called the Mac OS Extended format.)*

You can create and delete folders on the iPod as you would any other drive. But be sure you don't mess with the iPod's system folders, such as the Calendars folder, the Contacts folder, the Notes folder, and the iPod_Control folder. The iPod_Control folder is a hidden folder, so it does not appear unless you have set Windows or Mac OS X to display hidden files.

NOTE   *As mentioned earlier, don't transfer music or video files to an iPod by using file-management software if you want to be able to play the files on the iPod. Unless you transfer the files by using iTunes or another application designed to access the iPod's database, the details about the files won't be added to the iPod. You won't be able to play those files on the iPod because their data hasn't been added to its database of contents.*

The exception to transferring files from an iPod is transferring files that you've put on the iPod by using iTunes or another application that can access the iPod's database. The section "Transfer Song Files from an iPod's Library to Your Computer," in Chapter 16, shows you how to do this.

Put Files on an iPhone Using iPhone Drive

At this writing, Apple doesn't provide a way to put an iPhone into disk mode so that you can transfer files to it. However, you can do so by using a program such as iPhone Drive (www .ecamm.com/mac/iphonedrive/; $9.99). Start with the trial edition, which is fully functional until it expires after seven days.

Once you've installed iPhone Drive, run the program. iPhone Drive, shown next, has an easy-to-use interface:

- **Copy Items to the iPhone** Drag files or folders from a Finder window to the iPhone Drive window.

- **Copy Items from the iPhone** Drag files or folders from the iPhone Drive window to the Desktop or to a Finder window.

- **Create a Folder on the iPhone** Click the New Folder button in the iPhone Drive window, and then type the name for the folder.

- **Delete an Item from the iPhone** Click the item, click the Delete button, and then confirm the deletion.

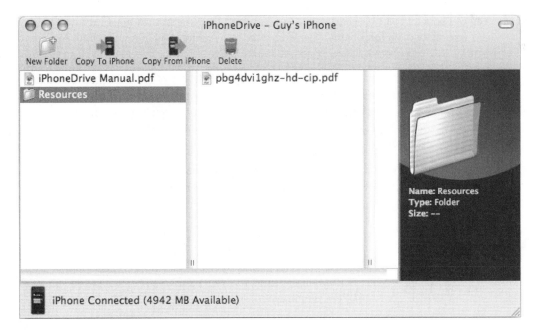

Start Up Your Mac from a Regular iPod

One special trick of the regular iPod is that you can *boot* (start up) your Mac from the iPod instead of from the Mac's hard disk. To do so, you install Mac OS X on the iPod's hard disk and then tell the Mac to use the iPod as its startup disk instead of using the hard disk as usual.

Booting your Mac from an iPod can be useful in several situations, such as these:

- If you've got an old iPod, you can prepare it as an emergency boot device in case your Mac's hard disk fails. Having an extra hard disk is particularly comforting when you're on the road.

- You can use an iPod to create daily backups of your hard disk. The backups are bootable, so if your Mac's hard disk suffers corruption or fails, you can use the iPod to recover.

- If you need to maintain tight security, you can make an iPod the only bootable disk for your Mac. By taking the iPod with you wherever you go, you can prevent other people from booting your Mac.

Make Sure You've Got a Suitable iPod and Mac

Booting your Mac from an iPod can be helpful when things go wrong. But it works only with Macs (not with PCs) and only with some iPods. Here's what you need to know:

- You must use a regular iPod, one of the full-sized iPods that have hard disks. The iPod mini (which has a tiny hard disk) and the iPod touch and the iPod nano (which uses flash memory) do not support booting.

- You can boot a Power-based Mac that has a built-in FireWire port from a FireWire iPod, and you can boot an Intel-based Mac from either a FireWire iPod or a USB iPod. At this writing, you can't boot a Power-based Mac from a USB iPod.

NOTE *A Power-based Mac is one with a Power processor, such as a G3, G4, or G5 processor. An Intel-based Mac is one with an Intel processor in it. Apple switched from Power processors to Intel processors in 2005–2006. If you're not sure which processor your Mac has, choose Apple | About This Mac and look at the Processor readout in the About This Mac dialog box.*

- After booting from the iPod, you must keep the iPod connected until you shut down the Mac. Removing the boot disk almost always makes Mac OS X crash.

- Apple doesn't support booting as a feature.

CAUTION *Even though FireWire and USB are fast connections, booting from an iPod will take much longer than booting from the hard disk, and your Mac will run more slowly than usual. The iPod will usually get hot because it is working much harder than usual. Booting from the iPod may shorten the iPod's life. Make sure the iPod is charging along the FireWire or USB cable, because otherwise running your Mac from the iPod will run the battery down quickly.*

Install Mac OS X on an iPod

The next step is to install Mac OS X on the iPod. How you do this depends on whether the iPod uses FireWire or USB.

If the iPod uses FireWire, you can install Mac OS X on it in either of two ways:

- **Install Mac OS X directly on the iPod** This method gives you a clean installation of Mac OS X, which you should update (via Software Update) to make sure that it contains all the latest patches. To install Mac OS X directly on the iPod, you need to have an install DVD (rather than install CDs—the install process usually fails when switching from the first CD to the second CD). See the next section for instructions.

- **Clone an existing installation of Mac OS X** This method lets you copy your existing installation of Mac OS X—fully up to date and with all your applications and settings— onto the iPod. The easiest way to clone your existing installation is to use a utility such as the freeware Carbon Copy Cloner. See the upcoming section "Clone Your Existing Mac OS X Installation onto an iPod" for instructions.

If the iPod uses USB, you need to use a different technique. See "Install Mac OS X on a USB iPod," later in this chapter, for details.

Install Mac OS X Directly on a FireWire iPod

To install Mac OS X directly on a FireWire iPod, you run the installation routine from your Mac OS X installation DVD exactly as you would to install the operating system on your Mac, but you specify the iPod, rather than your Mac's hard disk, as the destination disk for the install.

To install Mac OS X on an iPod, follow these steps:

1. Make sure the iPod has plenty of free space. You need between 2GB and 4.8GB for Tiger, depending on which files you choose to install, and around 6GB minimum for Leopard.

2. Connect the iPod to your Mac via FireWire.

3. Enable disk mode on the iPod if it isn't already enabled (see the section "Enable Disk Mode," earlier in this chapter, for instructions).

4. If you're not certain that the iPod is formatted with the Mac OS Extended file system rather than the FAT32 file system, click the iPod's icon in the Source pane in iTunes. On the Summary tab, verify that the Format readout says Macintosh. If this readout says Windows, you must restore the iPod to Mac OS Extended before you can boot from it. Restoring the iPod loses all the songs and other data it contains, so back up the iPod before taking this drastic step.

5. Insert the Mac OS DVD in your Mac's optical drive. If Mac OS X doesn't automatically open a window showing the DVD's contents, double-click the DVD's icon on your desktop or in a Finder window.

6. Double-click the Install Mac OS X application icon to display the Install Mac OS X window.

NOTE *Launching the Mac OS X installation may feel like you're going to wipe your Mac's hard drive, but you get to specify the iPod as the destination drive after your Mac restarts.*

7. Click the Restart button. Mac OS X displays the Authenticate dialog box (shown here).

8. Type your username and password and then click the OK button. (You must have administrator-level privileges to install the operating system, even on the iPod rather than on your Mac.) Your Mac restarts and displays the installation screen on which you select the language to use.

9. Choose the language—for example, select the Use English As The Main Language item—and then click the arrow button. The Install Mac OS X window appears.

10. Continue with the installation procedure until you reach the Select Destination screen.

11. Click the iPod's icon to set it as the destination for the installation, and then click the Continue button.

CAUTION *The Mac OS X installation routine offers you the option of erasing your hard drive and formatting it using either Mac OS Extended (HFS Plus) or Unix File System. Don't use this option. Erasing the disk will do more harm than good.*

12. When installing Mac OS X, it's a good idea to customize the installation to reduce the amount of space it takes up. On the Installation Type screen, click the Customize button instead of accepting the default Easy Install option. On the resulting Custom Install screen, clear the check boxes for the items you don't want to install. Keep these points in mind:

■ You must install the Essential System Software item, so the Installer doesn't let you clear its check boxes.

■ Consider installing only some printer drivers rather than all of them and not installing the Additional Fonts (for Chinese, Korean, Arabic, and other eastern languages), the Language Translations, or X11.

13. Click the Install button to start the installation, and then let it run. At the end of the installation, your Mac automatically boots from the iPod, and you see the Welcome screen for Mac OS X. You'll then need to go through the Mac OS X setup routine of selecting your country, choosing a keyboard layout, registering Mac OS X, and setting up a user account.

Clone Your Existing Mac OS X Installation onto an iPod

The second way to make an iPod bootable is to clone your existing Mac OS X installation onto it. This method gives you an iPod with an up-to-date and fully patched installation—and all your files and settings.

This section shows you how to clone Mac OS X using Carbon Copy Cloner (CCC), which you can download from Mike Bombich's website (www.bombich.com/software/ccc.html). Carbon Copy Cloner is donationware: if you like it, you can make a donation to the author.

> **TIP** *Another powerful cloning utility for the Mac is SuperDuper!, which you can buy from Shirt Pocket Software (www.shirt-pocket.com/SuperDuper/SuperDuperDescription.html). Shirt Pocket offers a trial edition that you'll probably want to test before buying the full version.*

To clone your installation of Mac OS X, follow these steps:

1. Prepare your installation of Mac OS X for cloning:

   a. Run Software Update and apply any new patches or updates.

   b. Install any applications that you want to have on the iPod when you boot from it. For example, you might want to install troubleshooting tools.

   c. If you've been meaning to clear out old files, now is a good time to do so.

   d. Empty the Trash.

2. Connect the iPod to your Mac via FireWire.

3. Enable disk mode on the iPod if it isn't already enabled (see the section "Enable Disk Mode," earlier in this chapter, for instructions).

4. Make sure the iPod has enough free space for the installation of Mac OS X that you want to clone.

5. Run CCC. It displays the Cloning Console (shown in Figure 17-3 with the source disk and target disk selected).

6. In the Source Disk drop-down list, choose the disk that contains the installation of Mac OS X that you want to clone. CCC displays a list of the disk's contents in the Items To Be Copied list box.

7. By default, CCC clones everything on your disk. To remove an item, select it in the Items To Be Copied list box and then click the Delete button (the button bearing a red circle with a line through it above the Items To Be Copied list box).

8. In the Target Disk drop-down list, select the iPod.

9. Click the lock button in the lower-left corner of the Cloning Console to display the Enter Your Administrative Password pane.

10. Type your password, and then click the OK button. CCC closes the pane and activates the Clone button.

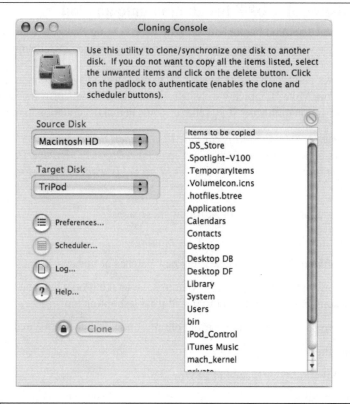

FIGURE 17-3 Select the source disk and target disk in the Cloning Console.

11. Click the Clone button to start the cloning operation. CCC displays a progress readout (in the bottom-left corner of the Cloning Console) as it works (see Figure 17-4).

12. CCC displays a message box to tell you when it has finished cloning your Mac OS X installation:

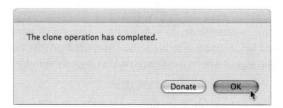

13. Click the OK button to close the message box. Then press ⌘-Q or choose Carbon Copy Cloner | Quit Carbon Copy Cloner to quit CCC.

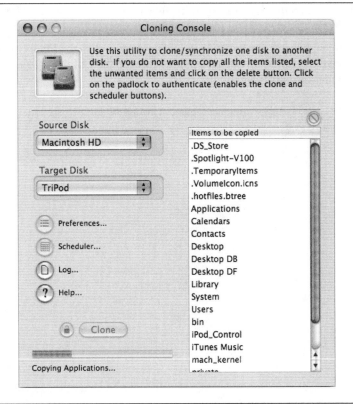

FIGURE 17-4   Carbon Copy Cloner shows its progress as it clones your disk to the iPod.

Install Mac OS X on a USB iPod

To install Mac OS X on a USB iPod so that you can boot an Intel-based Mac from it, follow these steps:

1. Connect the iPod to your Mac. If it's set to synchronize automatically, allow it to do so.

2. Check that the iPod is formatted with the Mac OS Extended file system. Right-click the iPod's icon on the desktop and then choose Get Info from the shortcut menu. In the Info window, check the Format readout. If the iPod is formatted with FAT32, you must use the iPod Updater to restore the iPod to Mac OS Extended before you can boot from it. (Use the technique described in the section "Restore the iPod" in Chapter 18.) Restoring the iPod loses all the songs and other data it contains, so back up the iPod before taking this drastic step.

3. Enable disk mode on the iPod if it isn't already enabled (see the section "Enable Disk Mode," earlier in this chapter, for instructions).

4. Open a Terminal window (as shown here). For example, click the Finder button on the Dock, choose Go | Utilities to open a window showing the Utilities folder, and then double-click the Terminal item.

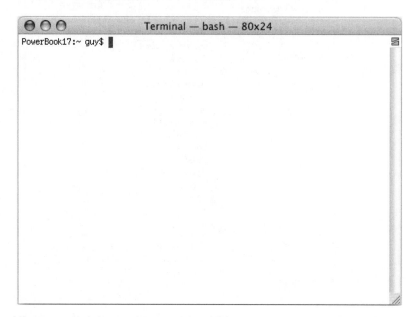

5. Make sure you know what your Mac's hard disk and the iPod are called. Issue the **ls /Volumes** command and press RETURN to list the volumes mounted on your Mac. You'll see something like the following, which indicates that Mac OS X knows the Mac's hard disk as "Macintosh HD" and the iPod by the name "VideoPod":

```
PowerBook17:~ guy$ ls /Volumes
Macintosh HD    VideoPod
```

6. Use the following **sudo** command (sudo is "do as super-user") and press RETURN to tell Apple Software Restore (**asr**) to copy the Mac's hard disk to the iPod. Substitute the name of your hard disk for "Macintosh HD" and the name of the iPod for "VideoPod" in the following command. If either name includes a space, put it within double quotation marks (as with "Macintosh HD" here).

```
sudo asr -source /Volumes/"Macintosh HD" -target /Volumes/VideoPod
```

7. When you press RETURN, Terminal prompts you for your password. Type it, and then press RETURN. You'll see messages as Terminal validates the target, the source, and sizes, and then copies your Mac's hard disk to the iPod.

8. When Terminal has finished copying the files, it displays a message about the target not being "blessed"—not being recognized as a bootable drive:

```
asr: did not copy blessed information to target, which may have
missing or out-of-date blessed folder information.
```

9. To bless the folder, use the following **sudo** command, substituting the name of the iPod for VideoPod, and press RETURN at the end of the command:

```
sudo bless -folder /Volumes/VideoPod/System/Library/CoreServices
```

10. Press ⌘-Q or choose Terminal | Quit Terminal to close the Terminal window.

Boot from the iPod

The next step is to set the Mac to boot from the iPod. To do this, you tell the Mac to use the iPod as its startup disk.

NOTE   *If you've installed Mac OS X from scratch on the iPod, you don't need to take this step, as your Mac will already have booted from the iPod at the end of the installation.*

To designate the iPod as the startup disk, follow these steps:

1. Choose Apple | System Preferences to display the System Preferences window.

2. Click the Startup Disk icon in the System area to display the Startup Disk sheet (shown here).

3. Select the item that represents the iPod.

4. To restart immediately and check that your bootable iPod works, click the Restart button. Mac OS X displays this confirmation dialog box:

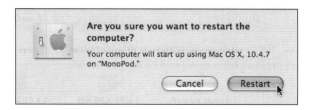

5. Click the Restart button. Your Mac restarts and boots the operating system from the iPod.

If you don't want to restart your Mac immediately, press ⌘-Q or choose System Preferences | Quit System Preferences to quit System Preferences. Then restart your Mac as normal, whenever.

Set Your Mac to Boot from Its Hard Disk Again

To make your Mac boot from its hard disk again instead of from the iPod, follow these steps:

1. Choose Apple | System Preferences to open System Preferences.

2. Click the Startup Disk item to display the Startup Disk sheet.

3. Select the entry for your hard disk, and then click the Restart button. Mac OS X displays a confirmation dialog box.

4. Click the Restart button in the dialog box. Mac OS X restarts from your hard disk.

 **Display All Available Startup Disks**

If your Mac fails to boot from the iPod, you may wonder whether you've wrecked the Mac for ever—or your Mac may give up on looking for the iPod and decide to boot from its hard disk anyway. If it *doesn't* boot at all, and you find yourself looking at a blank screen, take the following steps:

1. Press ⌘-CONTROL-POWER to force a restart.

2. When your Mac plays the system sound, hold down OPTION to display a graphical screen of the available startup disks.

3. Click the disk from which you want to start the computer.

4. Click the arrow button on the screen to start your Mac using that startup disk.

Back Up an iPod So You Don't Lose Your Music or Data

If you synchronize your complete library with an iPod, and perhaps load your contacts, calendar information, and photos on the iPod as well, you shouldn't need to worry about backing up the iPod. That's because your computer contains all the data that's on the iPod. (Effectively, the iPod is a backup of part of your hard disk.) So if you lose the iPod, or it stops functioning, you won't lose any data you don't have on your computer.

If your computer's hard disk stops working, you might need to recover your library, contacts, calendar data, and photos from the iPod onto another computer or a new hard disk. You can transfer contacts, calendars, and full-resolution photos by enabling disk mode and using the Finder (Mac) or Windows Explorer (PC) to access the contents of the Contacts folder, the Calendars folder, and the Photos/Full Resolution folder. For instructions on recovering song and video files from an iPod, see Chapter 15.

So, normally, an iPod will be the vulnerable member of the tag team. But if you store files directly on an iPod, you should back them up to your computer to make sure you don't lose them if the iPod vanishes or its hard disk gives up the ghost.

To back up files, either use a file-management utility (for example, the Finder or Windows Explorer) to simply copy the files or folders to your computer, or use custom backup software to create a more formal backup. For example:

- ■ **Windows Vista**   Backup and Restore Center (Start | All Programs | Maintenance | Backup And Restore Center)

- ■ **Windows XP**   Backup Utility (Start | All Programs | Accessories | System Tools | Backup)

- ■ **Mac OS X**   Backup application to .Mac iDisk (which you can access via any Internet connection)

For Mac OS X, other options are to use iDisk Utility to mount your .Mac iDisk via WebDAV (a protocol for transferring information to web servers), or use a commercial alternative such as EMC Retrospect (www.emcinsignia.com).

Chapter 18

Troubleshoot the iPod, iPhone, and iTunes

How to...

- ■ Understand what's in the iPod
- ■ Understand what's in the iPhone
- ■ Avoid things that may harm the iPod or iPhone
- ■ Keep the iPod's or iPhone's operating system up to date
- ■ Carry, clean, and look after the iPod or iPhone—and avoid voiding the warranty
- ■ Troubleshoot the iPod classic, iPod nano, and iPod shuffle
- ■ Troubleshoot the iPhone and iPod touch
- ■ Troubleshoot iTunes problems on Windows
- ■ Troubleshoot iTunes problems on the Mac
- ■ Recover from iTunes running you out of disk space on Windows or the Mac

Apple designs and builds the iPods and iPhone to be as reliable as possible—after all, Apple would like to sell at least one iPod or iPhone to everyone in the world who has a computer, and they'd much prefer to be thwarted in this aim by economics or competition than by negative feedback. But even so, iPods and iPhones go wrong sometimes. Other times, iTunes has problems, either in communicating with the iPod or iPhone or in other ways.

This chapter shows you how to deal with problems with the iPod, the iPhone, and iTunes. The chapter focuses on the models that are current at this writing—the iPod classic, the third-generation iPod nano, the second-generation iPod shuffle, the iPod touch, and the iPhone—but also provides some information about troubleshooting other models (such as the first two generations of iPod nano and the first-generation iPod shuffle) that are still widely used.

Know What's in the iPod

The iPod classic is based around a hard drive that takes up the bulk of the space inside the case. The hard drive is similar to those used in the smaller portable PCs.

NOTE   *The iPod nano and iPod shuffle use flash memory chips rather than a hard disk, which makes them more or less immune to shock. Besides the flash memory, the iPod nano and iPod shuffle contain a battery, a controller chip, and audio-processing circuits.*

Some of the remaining space is occupied by a rechargeable battery that provides between 8 and 20 hours of playback. The length of time the battery provides depends on the model of iPod and on how you use it. Like all rechargeable batteries, the iPod's battery gradually loses its capacity—but if your music collection grows, or if you find the iPod's nonmusic capabilities useful, you'll probably want to upgrade to a higher-capacity model in a couple of years anyway.

CAUTION *The iPod isn't user-upgradeable—in fact, it's designed to be opened only by trained technicians. If you're not such a technician, don't try to open the iPod if the iPod is still under warranty, because opening it voids the warranty. Open the iPod only if it's out of warranty and there's a problem you can fix, such as replacing the battery. See* iPod Repair QuickSteps, *also published by McGraw-Hill, for detailed instructions on replacing the battery and other components of iPods.*

The iPod classic includes a 32MB memory chip that's used for running the iPod's operating system and for caching music from the hard drive. The cache reads up to 20 minutes of data ahead from the hard drive for two purposes:

- Once the cache has read the data, the iPod plays back the music from the cache rather than from the hard disk. This lets the hard disk *spin down* (stop running) until it's needed again. Because hard disks consume relatively large amounts of power, the caching spares the battery on the iPod and prolongs battery life.

NOTE *After the hard disk has spun down, it takes a second or so to spin up again—so when you suddenly change the music during a playlist, there's a small delay while the iPod spins the disk up and then accesses the song you've demanded. If you listen closely (put the iPod to your ear), you can hear the disk spin up (there's a "whee" sound) and search (you'll hear the heads clicking).*

- The hard disk can skip if you joggle or shake the iPod hard enough. Modern hard drives can handle G loads that would finish off elite fighter pilots, so take this on trust rather than trying it out. If the iPod were playing back audio directly from the hard disk, such skipping would interrupt audio playback, much like bumping the needle on a turntable (or bumping a CD player, if you've tried that). But because the memory chip is solid state and has no moving parts, it's immune to skipping.

The length of time for which the caching provides audio depends on the compression ratio you're using and whether you're playing a playlist (or album) or individual songs. If you're playing a list of songs, the iPod can cache as many of the upcoming songs as it has available memory. But when you switch to another song beyond those cached, or to another playlist, the iPod has to start caching once again. This caching involves spinning the hard disk up again and reading from it, which consumes battery power.

NOTE *The iPod classic caches video as well, but because video files are much larger than audio files, playing them makes the hard disk work more than does playing songs.*

Know What's in the iPhone and iPod touch

Much of the space behind the iPhone's touch screen is taken up by a large battery that can hold enough power for several days' standby, a day's worth of phone calls, or around 24 hours of audio playback. The iPod touch is slimmer and needs less power, because it doesn't need to keep tracking the telephone network, but it still needs a fair amount of energy to play back videos and music.

Then there's the storage (for example, 4GB, 8GB, or 16GB of flash memory); the processor, wireless chips, and assorted circuitry; an amplifier, microphone, speaker, and a camera lens and sensor (in the iPhone only). Compared to the touch screen and the battery, these items are surprisingly small.

Apart from these items, the iPhone also contains the following:

- **Antenna**   The iPhone uses the antenna for connecting to cell networks.
- **Ambient light sensor**   The iPhone automatically changes the brightness of the screen to make it visible in current light conditions. You can turn off the light sensor and adjust the brightness manually.
- **Accelerometer**   The accelerometer detects when you turn the iPhone and changes the display of supported programs to match the orientation. For example, when browsing in Safari, when you turn the iPhone to landscape orientation, Safari changes the display of the current webpage to landscape (which is normally better for browsing).
- **SIM card**   The SIM card lives in the slot at the top of the iPhone. You can take it out, but there's little reason to do so beyond curiosity unless you're planning to hack your iPhone with another SIM. (To open the SIM slot, push a blunt object such as the end of a straightened paperclip into the little hole.)

The iPod touch contains the accelerometer and ambient light sensor, but not the cell-phone antenna or SIM card.

Avoid Things That May Harm the iPod or iPhone

This section discusses four items that are likely to make the iPod or iPhone unhappy: unexpected disconnections, fire and water (discussed together), and punishment. None of these should come as a surprise, and you should be able to avoid all of them most of the time.

Avoid Disconnecting the iPod or iPhone at the Wrong Time

When you synchronize the iPod or iPhone, always wait until synchronization is complete before disconnecting the player. The easiest way to be sure synchronization is complete is to watch the readout in iTunes. Alternatively:

- **iPod classic or iPod nano**   Make sure the iPod is showing the "OK to disconnect" message.
- **iPod shuffle**   Make sure the green light or amber light stays on steadily.
- **iPhone or iPod touch**   Make sure that the Sync screen is not showing. If the screen is blank, you're fine.

NOTE   *If you have turned on disk mode for the iPod, you must eject the iPod manually after each sync.*

Disconnecting at the wrong time may interrupt data transfer and corrupt files. In the worst case, you may need to restore the iPod or iPhone, losing any data on the player that wasn't already on your computer (for example, photos on an iPhone).

If you disconnect the iPod from your Mac at the wrong time, your Mac displays the Device Removal dialog box, shown in Figure 18-1, telling you that you should have ejected it properly and that data may have been lost or damaged. If iTunes was transferring data to the iPod when you disconnected it, you may also see another dialog box such as the one that appears at the bottom of Figure 18-1.

At this writing, iTunes for Windows tends not to notice if you disconnect an iPod when it's telling you not to. If you find that the iPod's entry is showing up in the Source pane in iTunes for Windows long after the iPod has bolted, shut the stable door by right-clicking the iPod's entry in the Source pane and choosing Eject iPod from the shortcut menu.

After an unexpected disconnection, the iPod simply figures out there's a problem, dusts itself down, and then displays its main screen.

Avoid Fire and Water

The iPods and iPhone have a wider range of operating temperatures than most humans, so if you keep the iPod or iPhone in your pocket, it will generally be at least as comfortable as you are.

Where an iPod or iPhone may run into trouble is if you leave it running in a confined space, such as the glove box of a car parked in the sun, that might reach searing temperatures. If you live somewhere sunny, take the iPod or iPhone with you when you get out of the car.

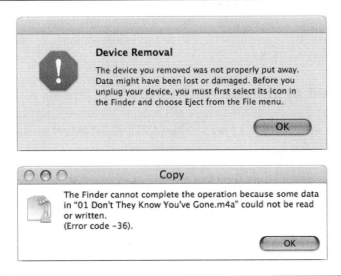

Device Removal

The device you removed was not properly put away. Data might have been lost or damaged. Before you unplug your device, you must first select its icon in the Finder and choose Eject from the File menu.

OK

Copy

The Finder cannot complete the operation because some data in "01 Don't They Know You've Gone.m4a" could not be read or written.
(Error code –36).

OK

FIGURE 18-1   Mac OS X objects when you disconnect the iPod at the wrong time.

If the iPod or iPhone gets much too hot or much too cold, don't use it. Give it time to return to a more normal temperature before trying to find out if it still works.

Further, the iPod and iPhone aren't waterproof, so don't expect to use them for swimming or in the bath unless you get a fully waterproof case (see Chapter 4).

Avoid Physically Abusing the iPod or iPhone

Apple has built the iPod and iPhone to be tough, so they will survive an impressive amount of rough handling. If you're interested in finding out how tough a particular model is without funding the experiment yourself, check out sites such as these:

- Ars Technica (http://arstechnica.com) performs real-world tests to destruction, such as dropping devices.
- Will It Blend (www.willitblend.com) tests devices in a blender, which is entertaining if less practical.

TIP   *Use a case to protect the iPod or iPhone. Chapter 4 outlines some of the many options available.*

Keep the iPod's or iPhone's Operating System Up to Date

To get the best performance from the iPod or iPhone, it's a good idea to keep its operating system (or *firmware*) up to date. To do so, follow the instructions in this section to update the iPod or iPhone on Windows or Mac OS X.

Update the iPod or iPhone on Windows

iTunes is set to check automatically for updates, and it displays a message box such as that shown here if it finds an update. Click the Download And Install button to download the update and install it immediately.

NOTE   *If you don't want iTunes to check for updates automatically, clear the Check For Updates Automatically check box on the General tab of the iTunes dialog box.*

Alternatively, you can check for updates manually. Follow these steps:

1. Connect the iPod or iPhone to your computer. The computer starts iTunes (if it's not running) or activates it (if it is running).

2. In iTunes, click the iPod's or iPhone's entry in the Source pane to display the iPod or iPhone screens.

3. Click the Summary tab if it's not automatically displayed. (For an iPod shuffle, click the Settings tab.)

4. Click the Check For Update button.

When the update is complete, the iPod or iPhone appears in the Source pane in iTunes.

Update the iPod or iPhone on Mac OS X

You can get iPod or iPhone updates on Mac OS X in three ways:

- **iTunes**   iTunes checks periodically for updates. When it finds an update, iTunes displays a dialog box such as the one shown here. Click the Download And Install button to download the update and install it immediately.

NOTE   *If you don't want iTunes to check for updates automatically, clear the Check For Updates Automatically check box on the General tab of the Preferences dialog box for iTunes.*

- **Software Update**   Choose Apple | Software Update to check for updates to Mac OS X and all Apple software. Mac OS X presents all updates to you in the Software Update dialog box. Click the Install button, and then enter your administrative password in the Authenticate dialog box. Mac OS X downloads the updates and installs them.

Alternatively, you can check for updates manually. Follow these steps:

1. Connect the iPod or iPhone to your computer. The computer starts iTunes (if it's not running) or activates it (if it is running).

How to ... Clean the iPod or iPhone

The iPhone and iPod touch come with a soft cloth for wiping smudges off the screen, which is made of scratch-resistant, optical-quality glass. Unless you do anything horrible to your iPhone or iPod touch, the cloth should be all you need.

To keep an iPod looking its best, you'll probably need to clean it from time to time. Before doing so, unplug it to reduce the chance of short disagreements with the basic principles of electricity. Treat the Dock Connector port and headphone port with due care; neither is waterproof.

Various people recommend different cleaning products for cleaning iPods. You'll find assorted recommendations on the Web—but unless you're sure the people know what they're talking about, proceed with great care. In particular, avoid any abrasive cleaner that may mar an iPod's acrylic faceplate or its polished back and sides.

Unless you've dipped the iPod in anything very unpleasant, you'll do best to start with Apple's recommendation: Simply dampen a soft, lint-free cloth (such as an eyeglass or camera-lens cloth) and wipe the iPod gently with it.

But if you've scratched the iPod, you may need to resort to heavier-duty cleaners. Sites such as everythingiPod.com (www.everythingipod.com) and iKaput (www.ikaput.com) offer scratch removers such as iCleaner, iCleaner Pro, and iFresh iPod Scratch Remover.

2. In iTunes, click the iPod's or iPhone's entry in the Source pane to display the iPod or iPhone screens.

3. Click the Summary tab if it's not automatically displayed. (For an iPod shuffle, click the Settings tab.)

4. Click the Check For Update button.

When the update is complete, the iPod or iPhone appears in the Source pane in iTunes.

Carry and Store the iPod or iPhone Safely

Carrying and storing the iPod or iPhone safely is largely a matter of common sense:

- Use a case to protect the iPod or iPhone from scratches, dings, and falls. A wide variety of cases are available, from svelte-and-stretchy little numbers designed to hug your body during vigorous exercise, to armored cases apparently intended to survive *Die Hard* movies, to waterproof cases good enough to take sailing or even swimming. See Chapter 4 for details.

■ If the iPod or iPhone spends time on your desk or another surface open to children, animals, or moving objects, use a dock or stand to keep it in place. A dock or stand should also make the iPod or iPhone easier to control with one hand. For example, if you patch the iPod or iPhone in to your stereo, use a dock or stand to keep it upright so you can push its buttons with one hand. See Chapter 4 for more information on docks and stands.

Understand Your Warranty and Know Which Actions Void It

Like most electronics goods, your iPod or iPhone almost certainly came with a warranty. Unlike with most other electronics goods, your chances of needing to use that warranty are relatively high. This is because you're likely to use the iPod or iPhone extensively and carry it with you. After all, that's what it's designed for.

Even if you don't sit on the iPod or iPhone, rain or other water doesn't creep into it, and gravity doesn't dash it sharply against something unforgiving (such as the sidewalk), the iPod or iPhone may suffer from other problems—anything from critters or debris jamming the Dock Connector port, to its hard drive getting corrupted or its flash memory becoming faulty, or its operating system getting scrambled. Perhaps most likely of all is that the battery will lose its potency, either gradually or dramatically. If any of these misfortunes befalls your iPod or iPhone, you'll probably want to get it repaired under warranty—provided you haven't voided the warranty by treating the iPod or iPhone in a way that breaches its terms.

The first iPods carried a 90-day warranty, which inspired little confidence in their durability. However, Apple then moved to a one-year warranty both for newer iPods and for those already sold. The iPhone also has a one-year warranty.

To find details of whether an iPod or iPhone is under warranty, use these sites:

■ **iPod Service Page (http://depot.info.apple.com/ipod/index.html)**   For all iPods except the iPod shuffle. Lets you see which iPods are still under warranty and the prices you'll pay for repairs on an iPod that's out of warranty.

■ **iPod shuffle Service Page (http://depot.info.apple.com/ipodshuffle/)**   For the iPod shuffle only. Lets you see whether an iPod shuffle is still under warranty and the prices you'll pay for repairs if it's out of warranty.

■ **iPhone Service FAQ (www.apple.com/support/iphone/service/faq/)**   Contains answers to various iPhone service questions, including the prices for repairs after the warranty has expired.

Most of the warranty is pretty straightforward, but the following points are worth noting:

■ You have to make your claim within the warranty period, so if the iPod or iPhone fails a day short of a year after you bought it, you'll need to make your claim instantly. Do you know where your receipt is?

■ If the iPod or iPhone is currently under warranty, you can buy an AppleCare package for it to extend its warranty to two years. Most extended warranties on electrical products are a waste of money, because the extended warranties largely duplicate your existing rights as a consumer to be sold a product that's functional and of merchantable quality. But given the attrition rate among hard-used iPods and iPhones, AppleCare may be a good idea.

■ Apple can choose whether to repair the iPod or iPhone using either new or refurbished parts, exchange it for another device that's at least functionally equivalent but may be either new or rebuilt (and may contain used parts), or refund you the purchase price. Unless you have valuable data on the iPod or iPhone, the refund is a great option, because you'll be able to get a new iPod or iPhone—perhaps even a higher-capacity one.

■ Apple takes no responsibility for getting back any data on the iPod or iPhone. This isn't surprising because Apple may need to reformat the hard drive or memory or replace the player altogether. But this means that you must back up the iPod or iPhone if it contains data you value that you don't have copies of elsewhere.

■ If you send your iPhone in for repairs, you can rent an AppleCare Service phone for $29 for the duration of the repair. You remove the SIM card from your iPhone before sending it for repair, insert the SIM in the Service phone, and then sync the Service phone with iTunes to transfer your data to it.

You can void your warranty more or less effortlessly in any of the following easily avoidable ways:

■ Damage the iPod or iPhone deliberately.

■ Open the iPod or iPhone or have someone other than Apple open it for you. The iPod and iPhone are designed to be opened only by trained technicians. The only reason to open an iPod or iPhone is to replace its battery or replace a component—and you shouldn't do that yourself unless the iPod or iPhone is out of warranty (and out of AppleCare, if you bought AppleCare for it). If you're tempted to replace a battery, make sure you know what it involves: Replacing the battery in the iPhone and in some iPods requires a delicate touch with a soldering iron. See *iPod Repair QuickSteps* for the gory details.

■ Modify the iPod or iPhone. Modifications such as installing a higher-capacity drive in an iPod would necessarily involve opening it anyway, but external modifications can void your warranty, too. For example, if you choose to trepan an iPhone so as to screw a holder directly onto it, you would void your warranty. (You'd also stand a great chance of drilling into something sensitive inside the case.)

Troubleshoot the iPod

When something goes wrong with the iPod, take three deep breaths before you do anything. Then take another three deep breaths if you need them. Then try to work out what's wrong.

Remember that a calm and rational approach will always get you further than blind panic. This is easy to say (and if you're reading this when the iPod is running smoothly, easy to nod your head at). But if you've just dropped the iPod onto a hard surface from a great enough height for gravity to give it some acceleration, left it on the roof of your car so it fell off and landed in the perfect position for you to reverse over it, or gotten caught in an unexpectedly heavy rainfall, you'll probably be desperate to find out if the iPod is alive or dead.

So take those three deep breaths. You may well *not* have ruined the iPod forever—but if you take some heavy-duty troubleshooting actions without making sure they're necessary, you might lose some data that wasn't already lost or do some damage you'll have trouble repairing.

Things can go wrong with any of the following:

- The iPod's hardware—anything from the Dock Connector port or headphone port to the battery, the hard disk, or the flash memory
- The iPod's software
- The iPod's power adapter (if it has one)
- The cable you're using to connect the iPod to your computer
- Your computer's USB port or USB controller
- iTunes or the other software you're using to control the iPod

Given all these possibilities, be prepared to spend some time troubleshooting any problem.

Learn Troubleshooting Maneuvers for the iPod

This section discusses several maneuvers you may need to use to troubleshoot the iPod: resetting the iPod, draining its battery, restoring its operating system on either Windows or Mac OS X, and running a disk scan.

NOTE *See the Special Project for instructions on using the built-in diagnostic tools to pinpoint problems in the iPod classic and the third-generation iPod nano.*

Reset the iPod

If the iPod freezes so it doesn't respond to the controls, you can reset it:

1. Connect it to a power source—either a computer that's not sleeping or the iPod Power Adapter plugged into an electrical socket. (The iPod Power Adapter, or a generic equivalent, is a great weapon to have in your troubleshooting arsenal.)

2. Reset the iPod: Move the Hold switch to the On position, and then move it back to the Off position. Hold down the Menu button and the Select button for about six seconds, until the iPod displays the Apple logo.

3. After you release the buttons, give the iPod a few seconds to finish booting.

If the iPod freezes when you don't have a power source available, try resetting it by using the preceding technique without the power source. Sometimes it works; other times it doesn't. But you've nothing to lose by trying.

To reset a second-generation iPod shuffle, move the switch on the bottom to the Off position, and then move it back to the On position. To reset a first-generation iPod shuffle, move the switch on the back to the Off position, and then move it to one of the other two positions.

Drain the iPod's Battery

If you can't reset the iPod, its battery might have gotten into such a low state that it needs draining. This supposedly seldom happens—but the planets might have decided that you're due a bad day.

To drain the battery, disconnect the iPod from its power source and leave it for 24 hours. Then try plugging the iPod into a power source. After the iPod has received power for a few seconds, reset the iPod: Move the Hold switch to the On position, and then move it back to the Off position. Hold down the Menu button and the Select button for about six seconds, until the iPod displays the Apple logo.

If draining the battery and recharging it revives the iPod, update the iPod's software with the latest version to try to prevent the problem from occurring again. See the section "Keep the iPod's or iPhone's Operating System Up to Date," earlier in this chapter, for details on how to update the operating system.

Restore the iPod

If the iPod is having severe difficulties, you may need to restore it. Restoring the iPod replaces its operating system with a new copy of the operating system that has Apple's factory settings.

Restoring the iPod deletes all the data on the iPod's hard disk or flash memory—the operating system and all your songs, photos, videos, contacts, calendar information, and notes—and returns the iPod to its original factory settings. So restoring the iPod is usually a last resort when troubleshooting. Unless the iPod is so messed up that you cannot access its contents, back up all the data you care about that's stored on the iPod before restoring it.

Restore the iPod on Windows

To restore the iPod on Windows, follow these steps:

1. Connect the iPod to your PC via USB as usual. Allow iTunes to synchronize with the iPod if it's set to do so.

2. In iTunes, click the iPod's entry in the Source pane to display the iPod screens.

3. Click the Summary tab if it's not already displayed. For an iPod shuffle, click the Settings tab.

4. Click the Restore button. iTunes warns you that you will lose all the songs and data currently stored on the iPod, as shown here:

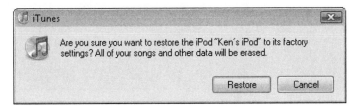

5. Click the Restore button. iTunes formats the iPod's hard disk or flash storage, and then restores the iPod's operating system.

6. iTunes displays a message box on a 15-second countdown telling you (as shown here) that the iPod is restarting and that it will appear in the iTunes Source pane after that. Either click the OK button to dismiss this message box, or wait for the timer to close it automatically.

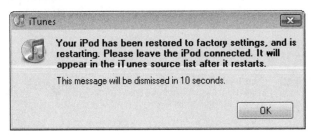

7. When iTunes notices the iPod after it restarts, iTunes starts the iPod Setup Assistant, which walks you through the process of naming the iPod and choosing how to load it.

After you disconnect the iPod, set the language it uses.

Restore the iPod on Mac OS X

To restore the iPod on Mac OS X, follow these steps:

1. Connect the iPod to your computer as usual. If the iPod is set to synchronize automatically with iTunes, allow it to do so.

2. In iTunes, click the iPod's entry in the Source pane.

3. Click the Summary tab if it's not already displayed. For an iPod shuffle, click the Settings tab.

4. Click the Restore button to start the restore process. iTunes warns you that you will lose all the songs and data currently stored on the iPod, as shown here:

5. Click the Restore button if you want to proceed. Mac OS X displays the Authenticate dialog box to check that you have administrative rights.

6. Type your password in the Password text box, and then click the OK button. iTunes formats the iPod's hard disk or flash storage, and then restores the iPod's operating system.

7. iTunes displays a message box on a 15-second countdown telling you (as shown here) that the iPod is restarting and that it will appear in the iTunes Source pane after that. Either click the OK button to dismiss this message box, or wait for the timer to close it automatically.

8. When iTunes notices the iPod after it restarts, iTunes starts the iPod Setup Assistant, which walks you through the process of naming the iPod and choosing how to load it.

After you disconnect the iPod, set the language it uses.

Troubleshoot Specific Problems with iPods

This section discusses how to troubleshoot specific problems with the iPod, starting with the more common problems and moving gradually toward the esoteric end of the spectrum.

How to ...   Recover from a Disk Insertion Error on the Mac

If something goes wrong while you're restoring the iPod, Mac OS X may display a Disk Insertion error message box such as the one shown here.

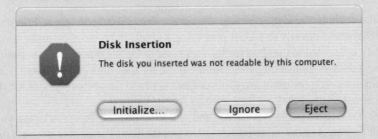

The large red exclamation icon makes the problem seem severe, but click the Ignore button rather than the Initialize button. (Clicking the Initialize button launches Disk Utility, the tool used for partitioning, repairing, and initializing regular hard disks, as opposed to the iPod.) Then try the Restore operation again. Usually, you'll be able to make it work after an attempt or two.

The iPod Won't Respond to Keypresses

If the iPod won't respond to keypresses, follow as many of these steps, in order, as are necessary to revive it:

1. Check that the Hold switch on the iPod isn't on. If you're using a remote control that has a Hold switch, check that too.

2. Check that the battery is charged. When the battery is too low to run the iPod (for example, for playing back music), the iPod displays a low-battery symbol—a battery icon with an exclamation point—for a few seconds when you press a key. (You may miss this icon if you're using a remote or you're pressing the iPod's buttons without looking at the screen.) Connect the iPod to a power source (either a computer that's not asleep or the iPod Power Adapter, if you have one), give it a few minutes to recharge a little, disconnect it again, and then try turning it on.

3. Reset the iPod (see the section "Reset the iPod," earlier in this chapter).

4. Enter diagnostic mode and run the Key test (see the section "Check the iPod's Buttons" in the Special Project).

Your Computer Doesn't React when You Plug in the iPod

If your computer (Mac or PC) doesn't react when you plug in the iPod, any of several things might have gone wrong. Try the actions described in the following subsections.

Unplug Any Other Devices in the USB Chain   If there's another device plugged into your computer's USB controller, try unplugging it. The problem may be that the controller can't supply power to another unpowered device as well as to the iPod.

If the connection uses a hub, disconnect the hub and try a direct connection.

Check That the Cable Is Working   For any iPod other than a first-generation iPod shuffle (which you normally connect directly to a USB port using its built-in connector), make sure that the cable is firmly connected to the iPod (or its dock) and to the USB port on your computer. If you normally use a dock or connecting stand for the iPod, try the connection without it in case the dock or stand is causing the problem. (This doesn't apply to the second-generation iPod shuffle, which you cannot connect without its dock or a special cable.)

If you're not sure the cable is working, and you have an iPod Power Adapter, you can run a partial check by plugging the cable into the iPod and the iPod Power Adapter, and then plugging the iPod Power Adapter into an electrical socket. If the iPod starts charging, you'll know that at least the power-carrying wires on the cable are working. It's likely that the data-carrying wires are working as well.

Check That the USB Port on the Computer Is Working   Check that the USB port on the computer is working. In most cases, the easiest way to check is by plugging in another device that you know is working. For example, you might plug in a USB scanner or external CD-ROM drive.

The iPod Says "Do Not Disconnect" for Ages when Connected to Your Computer

When you connect the iPod to your PC or Mac, the iPod displays the "Do not disconnect" message while it synchronizes with iTunes. When synchronization is complete, the iPod should display the charging indicator for as long as it's taking on power via the USB cable.

But sometimes it doesn't. If the iPod displays the "Do not disconnect" message for long after synchronization should have finished, first try to remember if you've enabled disk mode on the iPod. If so, you always need to eject the iPod manually, so this message doesn't mean that there's a problem. You can eject the iPod in one of these ways:

■ Click the Eject button next to the iPod's entry in the Source pane in iTunes.

■ Right-click the iPod in the Source pane, and then choose Eject from the shortcut menu.

■ Right-click the iPod's drive icon in a Computer window (Vista) or My Computer window (Windows XP), or CTRL-click the iPod's icon on your Mac desktop, and then choose Eject from the shortcut menu.

■ On the Mac, from the Finder, drag the iPod to the Trash, or select it and press ⌘-E.

The iPod should then display the "OK to disconnect" message.

If you haven't enabled disk mode on a hard drive–based iPod (such as the iPod classic), the iPod's hard drive may have gotten stuck spinning. If you pick up the iPod to scrutinize it further, you'll notice it's much hotter than usual if the drive has been spinning for a while. Try unmounting it anyway using one of the methods described in the preceding list. The iPod should then display the "OK to disconnect" message, and you can disconnect it safely.

If that doesn't work, you may need to reset the iPod (see "Reset the iPod," earlier in this chapter). After the iPod reboots, you should be able to eject it by taking one of the actions listed previously.

TIP   *If you experience this problem frequently, try updating the iPod to the latest software version available. If there's no newer software version, or if an update doesn't help, use the AC adapter to recharge the iPod rather than recharging it from your computer.*

The iPod Displays a Disk Icon with Magnifying Glass, Arrow, Check Mark, X, or Exclamation Point

If the iPod displays a disk icon on startup, as shown here, it suspects there's a problem with its hard disk. See the section "Run a Disk Scan" in the Special Project for details.

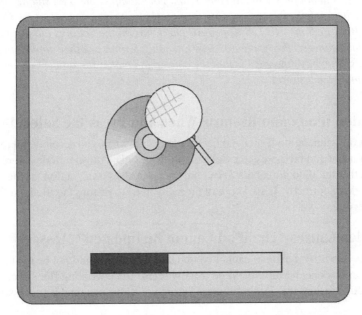

The iPod Displays Only the Apple Logo When You Turn It On

If, when you turn on the iPod, it displays the Apple logo as usual but goes no further, there's most likely a problem with the iPod software. Try resetting the iPod first to see if that clears the problem. (See "Reset the iPod," earlier in this chapter.)

If resetting doesn't work, usually you'll need to restore the iPod as described in "Restore the iPod," earlier in this chapter. Restoring the iPod loses all data stored on it, so try several resets first.

Songs in Your Library Aren't Transferred to the iPod

If songs you've added to your library aren't transferred to the iPod even though you've synchronized successfully since adding the songs, there are two possibilities:

- First, check that you haven't configured the iPod for partial synchronization or manual synchronization. For example, if you've chosen to synchronize only selected playlists, the iPod won't synchronize new music files not included on those playlists.

- Second, check that the songs' tags include the artist's name and song name. Without these two items of information, iTunes won't transfer the songs to the iPod, because the iPod's interface won't be able to display the songs to you. You can force iTunes to transfer song files that lack artist and song name tags by adding the song files to a playlist, but in the long run, you'll benefit from tagging all your song files correctly.

NOTE   *For an iPod shuffle, there's another possibility: The songs may be in a format that the iPod shuffle cannot play without conversion. For example, the iPod shuffle cannot play songs in the Apple Lossless Encoding format. However, you can select the Convert Higher Bit Rate Songs To 128 Kbps AAC check box on the Settings tab for the iPod. iTunes then converts the Apple Lossless Encoding format or other unplayable files to AAC files. The only downside is that the conversion makes the process of loading the iPod shuffle much slower.*

First-Generation iPod nano Restarts When You Press the Select Button

If you find that a first-generation iPod nano decides to restart when you scroll down to the Music item on the main menu and then press the Select button, go to Diagnostic mode and run the Key test to check whether the iPod thinks the Select button (or the "Action" button, as the firmware refers to it) is working correctly. If so, you will probably need to restore the iPod's software to restore normal service.

iPod with Video Causes "The iPod Cannot Be Updated" Message

The message "The iPod 'iPod_Name' cannot be updated. The disk could not be read from or written to." is a curious one, because the iPod usually seems to be working fine. Even so, you will probably need to restore the iPod's software before your Mac can read it successfully again.

Troubleshoot the iPhone and the iPod touch

Unlike the iPods, which run their own operating systems, the iPhone and iPod touch actually run a version of Mac OS X. As a result, troubleshooting the iPhone and iPod touch sometimes is more like dealing with problems in Mac OS X than troubleshooting the other iPods.

Deal with Program Crashes

Normally, the programs in the iPhone and iPod touch just keep running: When you use the Home screen to switch to a different program, the program you were using before keeps running in the background, where you can't see it. When you go back to that program, you'll find it doing what it was doing before.

If a program stops responding, you can close it by "force-quitting" it—in other words, forcing it to quit. To force-quit a program, hold down the Home button for six seconds. Release the Home button when the iPhone or iPod touch displays the Home screen. In the background, the iPhone or iPod touch restarts the program, so if you touch its icon on the Home screen, you'll find it running again.

Restart, Reset, or Erase the iPhone or iPod touch

Usually, you'll keep the iPhone running all the time so that you can receive incoming calls even when you're not using any of its other functions. Similarly, you'll keep the iPod touch running so that you can play songs or videos, or access wireless networks. But if your iPhone or iPod touch gets seriously hung, so that it stops responding to the touch screen, you may need to restart it. If restarting doesn't work, you will need to reset it.

Restart the iPhone or iPod touch

To restart the iPhone or iPod touch, follow these steps:

1. Hold down the Sleep/Wake button until the screen shows the message Slide To Power Off.
2. Slide your finger across the screen. The iPhone or iPod touch shuts down.
3. Wait a few seconds, and then press the Sleep/Wake button again. The Apple logo appears, and the iPhone or iPod touch then starts.

Perform a Hardware Reset

If you're not able to restart the iPhone or iPod touch as described in the previous section, escalate the problem to the next level and perform a hardware reset. Hold down the Sleep/Wake button and the Home button together until the Apple logo appears on the screen.

Perform a Software Reset

If performing a hardware reset (as described above) doesn't clear the problem, you may need to perform a software reset. This action resets the iPhone's or iPod touch's settings but doesn't erase your data from the device.

To perform a software reset, follow these steps:

1. Press the Home button to go to the Home screen unless you're already there.
2. Touch the Settings icon to reach the Settings screen.

3. Touch the General item to reach the General screen.

4. Touch the Reset item to reach the Reset screen.

5. Touch the Reset All Settings button, and then touch the Reset All Settings button on the confirmation screen.

Erase the Content and Settings on the iPhone or iPod touch

If even the software reset doesn't fix the problem, try erasing all content and settings. Before you do so, remove any content you have created on the iPhone or iPod touch—assuming the device is working well enough for you to do so. For example, if you have an iPhone, send any notes that you have written on it to yourself via e-mail, or sync the iPhone to transfer any photos you have taken with its camera to your computer.

To erase the content and settings, follow these steps:

1. Press the Home button to go to the Home screen unless you're already there.

2. Touch the Settings icon to reach the Settings screen.

3. Touch the General item to reach the General screen.

4. Touch the Reset item to reach the Reset screen.

5. Touch the Erase All Content And Settings button, and then touch the Erase iPhone button or Erase iPod button on the confirmation screen.

After erasing all content and settings, sync the iPhone or iPod touch to load the content and settings back onto it.

Restore the iPhone or iPod touch

If you've tried all the other troubleshooting actions described earlier in this section, and your iPhone or iPod touch is still acting hinky, you need to restore it. The process is the same for Windows and the Mac; this section shows screens from Windows with an iPhone.

Restoring the iPhone or iPod touch wipes all the data off the device, resets the hardware, and reinstalls the software. For an iPhone, restoring essentially returns the iPhone to the condition in which you bought it, except that the SIM remains activated. After restoring the iPhone, you sync it with iTunes again, and it picks up all the data from iTunes (and other programs, such as your address book) that it had before. For an iPod touch, which doesn't have a SIM, restoration is more comparable with restoration of one of the other iPod models.

Before restoring the iPhone, remove any content that you've created on the iPhone—for example, notes or photos. Again, this assumes that your iPhone is functioning well enough for you to remove the content.

To restore the iPhone or iPod touch, follow these steps:

1. Connect the iPhone or iPod touch to your computer, and wait for it to appear in the Source pane in iTunes.

2. Click the iPhone's or iPod touch's entry in the Source pane to display the iPhone screens or iPod screens.

3. Click the Summary tab if it's not already displayed.

4. Click the Restore button. iTunes displays a confirmation message box, as shown here, to make sure you know that you're about to erase all the data from the device.

5. Click the Restore button to close the message box. iTunes wipes the device's contents, and then restores the software, showing you its progress (as in the next illustration) while it works.

6. At the end of the restore process, iTunes restarts the iPhone or iPod touch. iTunes displays an information message box, shown next, for 15 seconds while it does so. Either click the OK button, or allow the countdown timer to close the message box automatically.

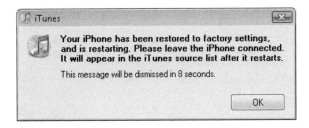

7. After the iPhone or iPod touch restarts, it appears in the Source pane in iTunes. For an iPhone, instead of the iPhone's regular tabbed screens, the Set Up Your iPhone screen appears (see Figure 18-2).

FIGURE 18-2 After restoring the iPhone's system software, you will normally want to restore your data from backup. The alternative is to set up the iPhone as a new iPhone.

8. To restore your data, make sure the Restore From The Backup Of option button is selected, and verify that the correct iPhone appears in the drop-down list. Unless you have two or more iPhones, the setting should be correct.

9. Click the Continue button. iTunes restores your data and then restarts the iPhone, displaying another countdown message box while it does so, as shown here. Either click the OK button, or allow the countdown timer to close the message box automatically.

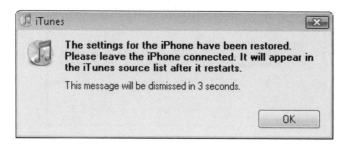

10. After the iPhone appears in the Source pane in iTunes following the restart, you can use it as normal.

How to ...   Resolve the "SIM Card Is Not Installed" Error on an iPhone

If the iPhone shows you the message "The iPhone cannot be used with iTunes because the SIM card is not installed," as shown next, have a look at the SIM slot on top of the iPhone to make sure that it hasn't been popped out. Normally, opening the SIM slot requires human intervention, though not necessarily your own—for example, the iPhone seems to have an even greater attraction for children than for adults.

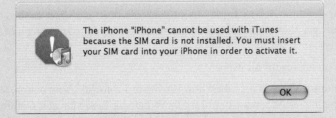

If the SIM slot is open, make sure the SIM is correctly aligned, and then push it back in. If the SIM slot seems fine, check the connection between the iPhone and the computer. This error can occur when the connection between the two is broken while iTunes is trying to access the iPhone—for example, if you bump the iPhone shortly after you dock it.

Troubleshoot iTunes on Windows

This section shows you how to troubleshoot the problems you're most likely to encounter when running iTunes on Windows.

iTunes Won't Start on Windows

If iTunes displays this Cannot Open iTunes dialog box saying that you can't open iTunes because another user currently has it open, it means that Windows is using Fast Switching and that someone else is logged on under another account and has iTunes open. The following illustration shows the Cannot Open iTunes dialog box on Windows Vista, but this dialog box also appears on Windows XP.

Click the OK button to dismiss the dialog box. If you know the other user's password, or if you know they have no password, switch to their account, close iTunes, and then switch back to your own account.

If you don't know the other user's password and you have a Standard user account (Windows Vista) or a Limited user account (Windows XP), you'll need to get them to log on and close iTunes for you.

If you have an Administrator account, you can use Task Manager to close iTunes. Follow these steps:

1. Right-click the taskbar, and then choose Task Manager from the shortcut menu to open Task Manager.

2. Click the Processes tab to display its contents. At first, as shown on the left in Figure 18-3, Task Manager shows only the processes running for your user session of Windows, not for other users' sessions.

3. Display processes for all users:

■ **Windows Vista**   Click the Show Processes From All Users button, and then go through User Account Control for the Windows Task Manager feature. Task Manager replaces the Show Processes From All Users button with the Show Processes From All Users check box (which it selects), and then adds the other users' processes to the list.

■ **Windows XP**   Select the Show Processes From All Users check box.

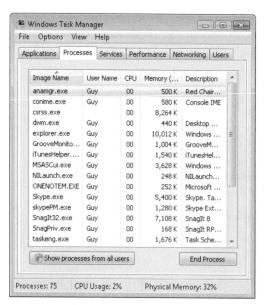 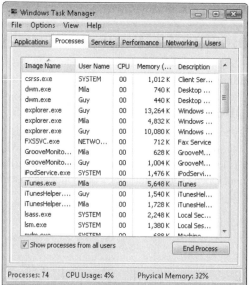

FIGURE 18-3   If someone else is running iTunes on a Windows Vista computer that uses Fast User Switching, you may need to use Task Manager to close iTunes before you can use it.

4. Select the iTunes.exe process in the Image Name column, as shown on the right in Figure 18-3. (If the list isn't sorted by the Image Name column, click the Image Name header to sort it that way.)

5. Click the End Process button. Task Manager displays the dialog box shown next, confirming that you want to end the process.

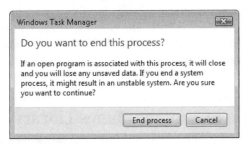

6. Click the End Process button. Task Manager closes the instance of iTunes in the other user's session.

7. Click the Close button (the × button) to close Task Manager.

You can now start iTunes as normal.

iTunes Doesn't Recognize the iPod

If the iPod doesn't appear in the Source pane in iTunes, take as many of the following steps as necessary to make it appear there:

1. Check that the iPod is okay. If you find it's displaying an exclamation point or the Sad iPod symbol, you'll know iTunes isn't guilty this time.

2. Check that the iPod knows it's connected to your PC. The iPod should be displaying the Do Not Disconnect message. If it's not, fix the connection so that it does display this message.

3. Toggle the Hold switch on the iPod, and then restart the iPod by holding down the Play button and the Menu button together for several seconds. See if the iPod appears in the Source pane in iTunes.

4. If restarting the iPod doesn't make it appear in iTunes, repeat the process for restarting it. This time, when the iPod displays the Apple symbol, hold down the Select button and the Play button for a moment to force disk mode. Forcing disk mode sends a request to the computer to mount the iPod as a drive.

5. Restart iTunes, and see if it notices the iPod this time.

6. If restarting iTunes doesn't make it recognize the iPod, restart Windows, and then restart iTunes.

iTunes Won't Play Some AAC Files

iTunes and AAC go together like bacon and eggs, but you may find that iTunes can't play some AAC files. This can happen for either of two reasons:

- You're trying to play a protected AAC file in a shared library or playlist, and your computer isn't authorized to play the file. In this case, iTunes skips the protected file.

- The AAC file was created by an application other than iTunes that uses a different AAC standard. The AAC file then isn't compatible with iTunes. To play the file, use the application that created the file, or another application that can play the file, to convert the file to another format that iTunes supports—for example, MP3 or WAV.

"The iPod Is Linked to Another iTunes Library" Message

If, when you connect the iPod to your computer, iTunes displays the message "The iPod 'iPod_name' is linked to another iTunes library," chances are that you've plugged the wrong iPod into your computer. The message box also offers to change this iPod's allegiance from its current computer to this PC. Click the No button and check which iPod this is before synchronizing it.

NOTE *For details about moving the iPod from one computer to another, see "Change the Computer to Which an iPod or iPhone Is Linked," in Chapter 14.*

iTunes Runs You Out of Hard-Disk Space on Windows

As you saw earlier in the book, iTunes lets you choose between copying to your library folder all the files you add to your library and leaving the files in other locations. Adding all the files to your library means you have all the files available in one place. This can be good, especially if your computer is a laptop and you want to be able to access your music and videos when it's not connected to your external drives or network drives. But if you have a large library, it may not all fit on your laptop's hard disk.

If your files are stored on your hard drive in folders other than your library folder, you have three choices:

- You can issue the Advanced | Consolidate Library command to make iTunes copy the files to your library folder, doubling the amount of space they take up. In almost all cases, this is the worst possible choice to make. (Rarely, you might want redundant copies of your files in your library so you can experiment with them.)

- You can have iTunes store references to the files rather than copies of them. If you also have files in your library folder, this is the easiest solution. To do this, clear the Copy Files To iTunes Music Folder When Adding To Library check box on the General subtab of the Advanced tab in the iTunes dialog box in Windows.

- You can move your library to the folder that contains your files. This is the easiest solution if your library is empty.

If you choose to consolidate your library, and there's not enough space on your hard disk, you'll see the following message box. "IBM_PRELOAD" is the name of the hard disk on the computer.

Clearly, this *isn't* okay, but iTunes doesn't let you cancel the operation. Don't let iTunes pack your hard disk as full of files as it can, because that may make Windows crash. Quit iTunes by pressing ALT-F4 or choosing File | Exit. If iTunes doesn't respond, right-click the taskbar and choose Task Manager to display Windows Task Manager. On the Applications tab, select the iTunes entry, and then click the End Task button. If Windows double-checks that you want to end the task, confirm the decision.

Once you've done this, you may need to remove the files you've just copied to your library from the folder. You can do this by using the Date Created information about the files and folders, because Windows treats the copy made by the consolidation as a new file.

To find the files and folders, search for them. The process differs on Windows Vista and Windows XP, so follow the instructions in the next sections for the OS you're using.

Search for the New Files and Folders on Windows Vista

To search for the new files and folders on Windows Vista, follow these steps:

1. Choose Start | Search to display a Search Results window.

2. Click the Advanced Search link at the right end of the toolbar to display the Advanced Search options.

3. In the Location drop-down list, click the Choose Search Location item to display the Choose Search Locations dialog box.

4. In the Change Selected Locations box, navigate to the folder that contains your iTunes Music folder. For example, if your iTunes Music folder is in its default location, follow these steps:

    ■ Click the triangle next to your username to expand its contents.

    NOTE   *If you're not sure where your iTunes Music folder is, switch to iTunes, press CTRL-COMMA, and look at the iTunes Music Folder Location box on the General subtab of the Advanced tab in the iTunes dialog box.*

    ■ Click the triangle next to the Music folder to expand its contents.

    ■ Click the triangle next to the iTunes folder to expand its contents.

    ■ Click the iTunes Music folder to select its check box. Windows adds the folder to the Summary Of Selected Locations list box.

5. Click the OK button to close the Choose Search Locations dialog box and enter the folder you chose in the Location drop-down list in the Search Results window.

6. On the line below the Location drop-down list, set up the condition Date Created (in the first drop-down list), Is (in the second drop-down list), and today's date (in the third drop-down list).

7. Click the Search button. Windows searches and returns a list of the files and folders created.

8. If the Search Results window is using any view other than Details view, choose Views | Details to switch to Details view.

9. Display the Date Created column by taking the following steps:

- Right-click an existing column heading, and then choose More from the shortcut menu to display the Choose Details dialog box.

- Select the Date Created check box.

- Click the OK button to close the Choose Details dialog box.

10. Click the Date Created column heading twice to make Windows Explorer sort the files by reverse date. This way, the files created most recently appear at the top of the list.

11. Check the Date Created column to identify the files created during the consolidation and then delete them without putting them in the Recycle Bin. (For example, select the files and press SHIFT-DELETE.)

12. Click the Close button (the × button) to close the Search Results window.

After deleting the files (or as many of them as possible), you'll need to remove the references from iTunes and add them again from their preconsolidating location before iTunes can play them. When iTunes discovers that it can't find a file where it's supposed to be, it displays an exclamation point in the first column. Delete the entries with exclamation points and then add them to your library again.

Search for the New Files and Folders on Windows XP

To search for the new files and folders on Windows XP, follow these steps:

1. Choose Start | Search to display a Search Results window.

2. On the What Do You Want To Search For? screen, click the Pictures, Music, Or Video link. (If Search Companion displays the Search By Any Or All Of The Criteria Below screen instead of the What Do You Want To Search For? screen, click the Other Search Options link to display the What Do You Want To Search For? screen. Then click the Pictures, Music, or Video link.)

3. On the resulting screen, select the Music check box and the Video check box in the Search For All Files Of A Certain Type, Or Search By Type And Name area.

4. Click the Use Advanced Search Options link to display the remainder of the Search Companion pane.

5. Display the Look In drop-down list, select the Browse item to display the Browse For Folder dialog box, select your iTunes Music folder, and then click the OK button.

NOTE *If you're not sure where your iTunes Music folder is, switch to iTunes, press CTRL-COMMA, and look at the iTunes Music Folder Location box on the General subtab of the Advanced tab in the iTunes dialog box.*

6. Click the When Was It Modified? heading to display its controls and then select the Specify Dates option button. Select the Created Date item in the drop-down list and then specify today's date in the From drop-down list and the To drop-down list. (The easiest way to specify the date is to open the From drop-down list and select the Today item. Windows XP then enters it in the To text box as well.)

7. Click the Search button to start the search for files created in the specified time frame.

8. If the Search Results window is using any view other than Details view, choose View | Details to switch to Details view.

9. Click the Date Created column heading twice to make Windows Explorer sort the files by reverse date. This way, the files created most recently appear at the top of the list.

10. Check the Date Created column to identify the files created during the consolidation and then delete them without putting them in the Recycle Bin. (For example, select the files and press SHIFT-DELETE.)

After deleting the files (or as many of them as possible), you'll need to remove the references from iTunes and add them again from their preconsolidating location before iTunes can play them. When iTunes discovers that it can't find a file where it's supposed to be, it displays an exclamation point in the first column. Delete the entries with exclamation points and then add them to your library again.

"iTunes Has Detected That It Is Not the Default Player" Message on Startup

When you start iTunes, you may see the message box shown next, telling you that "iTunes has detected that it is not the default player for audio files" and inviting you to go to the Default Programs control panel to fix the problem.

This message box doesn't indicate a problem as most people understand the word, but having it appear each time you start iTunes grows old fast, so you'll probably either want to suppress the message box or deal with the problem.

What's happened is that some other audio player has grabbed the associations for one or more of the audio file types that iTunes can play. For example, Windows Media Player may have taken the association for the MP3 file type. In this case, if you double-click an MP3 file in a Windows Explorer window, the file will play in Windows Media Player rather than in iTunes.

If you've set up your file associations deliberately to use different programs, simply select the Do Not Show This Message Again check box, and then click the No button. iTunes will drop the matter and not bug you again.

If you want to reassign the file associations to iTunes, click the Yes button. iTunes opens the Set Program Associations window (see Figure 18-4), which shows you the available associations and the programs to which they are assigned.

Select the check box for each file type you want to associate with iTunes, and then click the Save button.

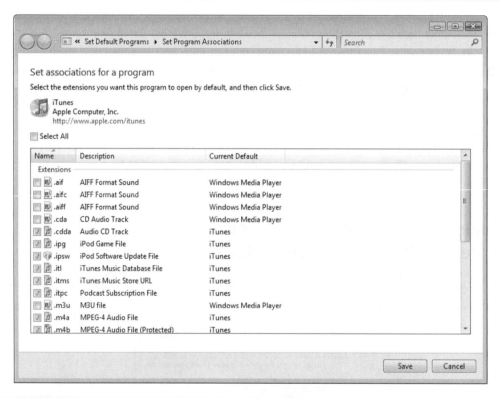

FIGURE 18-4 You can use the Set Program Associations window to reassign audio file associations to iTunes after other programs have grabbed them.

Troubleshoot iTunes on the Mac

This section shows you how to troubleshoot a handful of problems that you may run into when running iTunes on the Mac.

"The iPod Is Linked to Another iTunes Library" Message

If, when you connect the iPod to your computer, iTunes displays the message "The iPod '*iPod_name*' is linked to another iTunes library," chances are that you've plugged the wrong iPod into your computer. The message box also offers to change this iPod's allegiance from its current computer to this Mac. Click the No button and check which iPod this is before synchronizing it.

> **NOTE** *For details about moving an iPod from one computer to another, see "Change the Computer to Which the iPod Is Linked," in Chapter 14.*

Eject a "Lost" CD

Sometimes Mac OS X seems to lose track of a CD (or DVD) after attempting to eject it. It's as if the eject mechanism fails to get a grip on the CD and push it out, but the commands get executed anyway, so that Mac OS X believes it has ejected the CD even though the CD is still in the drive.

When this happens, you probably won't be able to eject the disc by issuing another Eject command from iTunes, but it's worth trying that first. If that doesn't work, use Disk Utility to eject the disc. Follow these steps:

1. Press ⌘-SHIFT-U or choose Go | Utilities from the Finder menu to display the Utilities folder.
2. Double-click the Disk Utility item to run it.
3. Select the icon for the CD drive or the CD itself in the list box.
4. Click the Eject button.
5. Press ⌘-Q or choose Disk Utility | Quit Disk Utility to quit Disk Utility.

If that doesn't work, you may need to force your Mac to recognize the drive. If it's a hot-pluggable external drive (for example, FireWire or USB), try unplugging the drive, waiting a minute, and then plugging it back in. If the drive is an internal drive, you may need to restart your Mac to force it to recognize the drive.

> **TIP** *See also the sidebar "Eject Stuck Audio Discs" in Chapter 6 for instructions on ejecting an optical disc using the Mac's Open Firmware mode.*

"You Do Not Have Enough Access Privileges" when Importing Songs

The following error occurs when you've moved the iTunes music folder to a shared location and the user doesn't have Write permission to it:

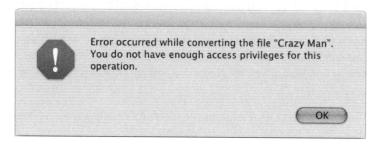

To fix this problem, an administrator needs to assign Write permission for the music folder to whoever received this error.

iTunes Runs You Out of Hard-Disk Space on the Mac

As you saw earlier in the book, iTunes can copy to your library folder all the files you add to your library. Adding all the files to your library means you have all the files available in one place. This can be good when (for example) you want your 'Book's hard disk to contain copies of all the song and video files stored on network drives so you can enjoy them when your computer isn't connected to the network. But it can take more disk space than you have.

If your files are stored on your hard drive in folders other than your library folder, you have three choices:

- You can use the Advanced | Consolidate Library command to cause iTunes to copy the files to your library. This doubles the amount of space the files take up and is usually the worst choice. (Rarely, you might want redundant copies of your files in your library so you can experiment with them.)

- You can have iTunes store references to the files rather than copies of them. If you also have files in your library folder, this is the easiest solution. To do this, clear the Copy Files To iTunes Music Folder When Adding To Library check box on the General subtab of the Advanced tab in the Preferences dialog box.

- You can move your library to the folder that contains your files. This is the easiest solution if your library is empty.

If you choose to consolidate your library, and your Mac doesn't have enough disk space, iTunes displays this message box to alert you to the problem:

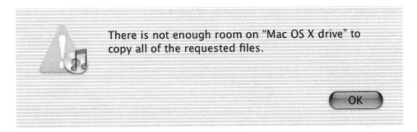

There is not enough room on "Mac OS X drive" to copy all of the requested files.

OK

Click the OK button to dismiss this message box—iTunes gives you no other choice. Worse, when you click the OK button, iTunes goes ahead and tries to copy all the files anyway.

This is a bad idea, so stop the copying process as soon as you can. To do so, quit iTunes by pressing ⌘-Q or choosing iTunes | Quit iTunes. If you can't quit iTunes gently, force quit it: OPTION-click the iTunes icon in the Dock, and then choose Force Quit from the shortcut menu. (Failing that, press ⌘-OPTION-ESC to display the Force Quit dialog box, select the entry for iTunes, and then click the Force Quit button.)

Once you've done this, remove the files you've just copied to your library from the folder. Unfortunately, Mac OS X maintains the Date Created information from the original files on the copies made by the consolidation, so you can't search for the files by date created on the Mac the way you can on Windows.

Your best bet is to search by date created to identify the folders that iTunes has just created in your library folder so that you can delete them and their contents. This approach will get all of the consolidated songs and videos that iTunes put into new folders, but it will miss any songs and videos that were consolidated into folders that already existed in your library.

For example, if the song file The Pretender.m4a is already stored in your library with correct tags, your library will contain a Foo Fighters/Echoes, Silence, Patience & Grace folder. If you then consolidate your library so that other songs from that album are copied, the files will go straight into the existing folder, and your search will miss it. The date-modified attribute of the Echoes, Silence, Patience & Grace folder will change to the date of the consolidation, but you'll need to drill down into each modified folder to find the song files that were added.

To search for the new folders, follow these steps:

1. Press ⌘-F or choose File | Find from the Finder to open a New Search window.

2. In the Search bar, click the Others button to open the Search In dialog box.

3. Click the Add button (the + button), and then use the resulting Choose A Folder dialog box to specify your iTunes Music folder. (If you're not sure where your iTunes Music folder is, check on the General subtab of the Advanced tab in the Preferences dialog box in iTunes.) After selecting the folder, click the Choose button to return to the Search In dialog box.

4. In the list box, make sure the check box for your iTunes Music folder is selected. Clear the check box for each other location you don't want to search. Click the OK button to return to the New Search window.

5. In the top search line, set up this condition: Kind: Folders.

6. In the second search line, set up this condition: Created: Today. Mac OS X searches for folders created today and displays a list of them.

7. Sort the folders by date created, identify those created during the consolidation by the time on the date, and then delete them.

8. Verify that the Trash contains no other files you care about, and then empty the Trash to get rid of the surplus files.

After deleting the files (or as many of them as possible), you'll need to remove the references from iTunes and add them again from their preconsolidating location before iTunes can play them. When iTunes discovers that it can't find a file where it's supposed to be, it displays an exclamation point in the first column. Delete the files with exclamation points and then add them to your library again.

Chapter 19

Make Phone Calls with the iPhone

How to…

- Make phone calls with the iPhone
- Receive phone calls on the iPhone
- Make conference calls with the iPhone
- Get your messages with Visual Voicemail
- Put your contacts on the iPhone and the iPod touch

Music, videos, photos, even file storage—so far in this book, you've learned how to get a wide variety of both entertainment and practical uses out of the iPhone. But what you haven't seen yet is how to make phone calls with it.

This chapter shows you how to make and receive phone calls on the iPhone—including conference calls, which the iPhone makes almost as easy as breaking an egg. You'll also learn how to set up Visual Voicemail and use it to retrieve your messages, and how to put your contacts on the iPhone so that you almost never need to dial a number manually.

The information about contacts applies to the iPod touch as well, even though you can't use the contact information directly on the iPod touch. The rest of the chapter does not apply to the iPod touch.

Make and Receive Phone Calls

Making phone calls is about as easy as it could be—provided that you've got a signal. First, look at the signal-strength icon in the upper-left corner of the display. As long as there's at least one bar, you should be good to go.

Make a Phone Call

To make a phone call, follow these steps:

1. If you're planning to use the headphones and their microphone rather than the iPhone's built-in speaker and microphone, plug in the headphones and plant them in your ears. Or if you're using a Bluetooth headset, make sure it's connected and in place.

2. Press the Home button to go to the Home screen unless you're already there.

3. Touch the Phone button at the bottom of the screen to display whichever of the five Phone screens you were using last:

   - **Keypad**   Displays a keypad so that you can dial a call.
   - **Favorites**   Displays a list of up to 20 favorite numbers you designate. This is handy for making quick calls to those numbers.

How to ... Create Your Favorites List

If you have a small group of people you telephone most frequently, you can save a lot of time by putting them on your Favorites list.

To add a number to the Favorites list, follow these steps:

1. Go to the Contacts list.
2. Touch the name of the contact you want to add to the Favorites list. The iPhone displays the Information screen for the contact.

> **NOTE** *See the section "Put Your Contacts on the iPhone or the iPod touch," later in this chapter, for a discussion of how to put contacts on the iPhone or iPod touch or create new contacts directly on either device.*

3. Touch the Add To Favorites button.
4. Touch the All Contacts button to return to the Contacts list.

To change the order of the Favorites list, follow these steps:

1. Touch the Favorites button to display the Favorites screen.
2. Touch the Edit button in the upper-left corner to switch the Favorites list into editing mode.
3. Touch the three bars at the right end of the contact you want to move, and then drag the contact up or down the screen.
4. When you've finished changing the order, touch the Done button.

To remove a favorite from the Favorites list, follow these steps:

1. Touch the Favorites button to display the Favorites screen.
2. Touch the Edit button in the upper-left corner to switch the Favorites list into editing mode.
3. Touch the favorite you want to remove. The iPhone adds a Remove button to it.
4. Touch the Remove button.
5. When you've finished removing favorites, touch the Done button.

■ **Recents** Shows a list of calls you've made, received, and missed. The missed calls appear in red. Touch the Missed button at the top of the screen to see the list of missed calls so that you can easily return them. Touch the All button at the top of the screen to restore the full list. Touch the Clear button if you want to get rid of all the recents (for example, because you've dealt with all the missed calls).

■ **Contacts** Shows a list of your contacts, as on the right in Figure 19-1. You can display either all your contacts or just a group, such as your personal contacts. To choose a group, touch the Groups button at the upper-left corner of the Contacts screen, and then touch the group on the Groups screen.

■ **Voicemail** Touch the message to which you want to reply, and then touch the Call Back button.

4. Choose the number you want to dial, either from the Phone screen you're on, or by touching the button for the Phone screen you want to access.

FIGURE 19-1 You can simply dial a number by using the keypad (left), but often it's more convenient to call a contact by choosing their entry on the Contacts screen (right).

How to ...   **Control How the iPhone and iPod touch Sort Your Contacts List**

The iPhone and iPod touch can sort your Contacts list into either "first, last" order (for example, "Jan, Weiss") or "last, first" order (for example, "Weiss, Jan"). And the iPhone and iPod touch can also display the contacts in the same order as the sort order or in the other order.

To choose the sort order, follow these steps:

1. Press the Home button to go to the Home screen unless you're already there.

2. Touch the Settings icon to display the Settings screen.

3. On the iPhone, touch the Phone button to display the Phone screen. On the iPod touch, touch the Contacts button to display the Contacts screen.

4. In the Contacts area, look at the Sort Order readout. It'll say either "Last, First" or "First, Last." To change the order, touch the Sort Order item, touch the other item on the Sort Order screen, and then touch the Phone button to return to the Phone screen.

5. Still in the Contacts area, look at the Display Order readout. This too will say either "Last, First" or "First, Last." To change the order, touch the Display Order item, touch the other item on the Display Order screen, and then touch the Phone button to return to the Phone screen on the iPhone or the Contacts button to return to the Contacts screen on the iPod touch.

Receive a Phone Call

Receiving a phone call is almost as easy as picking up the phone. Follow these steps:

1. When a call comes in, the iPhone rings—as you'd expect. The iPhone also switches to Phone mode and displays information on the call—the number (if it's available) and details of the caller. If you're listening to music, the iPhone fades the music, and then pauses it.

NOTE   *If you've set the iPhone to vibrate, it vibrates as well. To turn vibration on or off, press the Home button, touch the Settings icon, and then touch the Sounds button. On the Sounds screen, touch the opposite setting on the Vibrate bar—for example, if it's set to On, touch the Off setting.*

2. Touch the Answer button if you want to take the call. If you're using the iPhone's headset, click the button on the cord. If you want to send the call to voicemail, touch the Decline button, hold down the clicker on the headset cord, or simply don't answer for the set number of rings (the default is four rings).

TIP   *You can press either volume key or the Sleep/Wake button on the top of the iPhone to turn off the ringing before you answer the call—for example, because the phone ringing will disturb other people while you're trying to put your headset on. You can also turn the iPhone's ringer off completely by moving the Silencer switch on the left side of the iPhone toward the back, so that the orange dot appears.*

3. During the call, you can use the iPhone's other features freely, except for playing music or video. For example, if you need to take a note during the call, press the Home button, touch the Notes icon, and work on the Notes screen as usual.

4. To end the call, touch the End Call button. If you're using the iPhone's headset, click the button on the cord. If you were listening to music, the iPhone restarts the music.

Use the Onscreen Icons During Calls

When you make a call, the iPhone displays the icons shown in Figure 19-2. Here's what you can do with them:

- **Mute**   Touch this icon to mute the iPhone's microphone—for example, so that you can confer with someone near you without the person at the other end of the phone call being able to hear. Touch this icon again to remove the muting. You can still hear the person at the other end when your microphone is muted.

- **Hold**   Touch this icon to put the whole call on hold. Hold is like muting on steroids: It interrupts the entire call, so neither end hears anything from the other. Touch the Hold icon again to remove the hold.

- **Keypad**   Touch this icon to bring up the iPhone's keypad—for example, so that you can navigate your way through the voicemail hell that pretends to be customer service for all too many companies these days. Touch the Hide Keypad button when you've finished with the keypad. (Alternatively, touch the End Call button to end the call.)

- **Speaker**   Touch this icon to switch from the earpiece to the speaker at the bottom of the iPhone. The speaker works only when you don't have the headset connected. Touch the Speaker icon again if you want to stop using the speaker.

- **Contacts**   Touch this icon to display the Contacts list.

- **Add Call**   Touch this icon to make a conference call or to make another call while putting the current call on hold. See the next two sections for details.

FIGURE 19-2   The onscreen icons let you easily mute a call, pop up the keypad to communicate with touch-tone systems, or switch to using the speaker.

Put the Current Call on Hold and Make Another Call

If you make many calls, you probably use call waiting to let you interrupt an existing call to take an incoming call. If so, you'll love the iPhone's Add Call feature, as it not only lets you do this (see the next section) but also lets you make an outgoing call while putting the current call on hold.

To put the current call on hold and make another call, follow these steps:

1. In your current call, touch the Add Call button. The iPhone puts the current call on hold and displays whichever Phone screen you were using last—for example, Contacts.

2. Dial the second call as usual. For example, touch the Favorites icon, and then touch the favorite you want to call.

3. Make the call as usual. The only difference is that the name or number of the first call appears at the top of the screen, and two icons change, as shown here.

4. To switch to the caller who's on hold, touch the Swap button. You can also touch the caller's name or number at the top of the screen.

5. Touch the End Call button when you want to hang up the current call.

Receive an Incoming Call During an Existing Call

If you receive an incoming call during an existing call, you have three choices (see Figure 19-3):

- ■ **Send the call to voicemail** Touch the Ignore button.
- ■ **Put the current call on hold, and take the call** Touch the Hold Call + Answer button.
- ■ **End the current call, and take the call** Touch the End Call + Answer button.

Make Conference Calls

One of the iPhone's great features is that it enables you to make conference calls easily. Here's all you need to do to establish a conference call to two people:

1. Call the first person.

2. Put the first person on hold.

3. Call the second person, as described in the section "Put the Current Call on Hold and Make Another Call," earlier in this chapter.

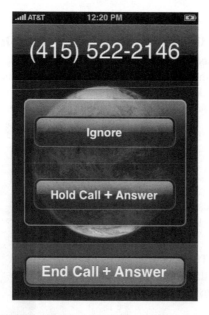

FIGURE 19-3 You can put an existing call on hold to take an incoming call.

4. Touch the Merge Calls button. You're then speaking to both the other people.

5. To add another person to the conference call, you can dial another number, and then touch the Merge Calls button to add that person to the conference call.

6. To hang up one of the participants, touch the blue button with the white arrow to display the Conference screen, and then touch the red button next to the participant's name.

7. To speak privately to one of the participants, touch the blue button with the white arrow to display the Conference screen, and then touch the Private button to the right of the participant's name.

Use Visual Voicemail

When you send a message to voicemail, the iPhone records it directly on the phone, so you can access it at any time.

First, though, you must set up your outgoing message. Follow these steps:

1. Press the Home button to go to the Home screen unless you're already there.

2. Touch the Phone button to display whichever Phone screen you were using last.

3. Touch the Voicemail button. The iPhone displays the Set Your Outgoing Message screen, shown on the left in Figure 19-4.

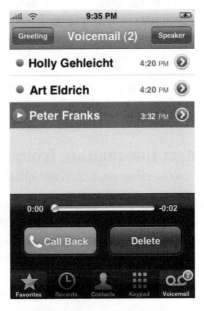

FIGURE 19-4   After you set your outgoing message, you can access your voicemail messages in an easy-to-browse list.

4. If you want to use the iPhone's automatic message (which gives your number in a female voice), touch the Default button. Otherwise, touch the Custom button, touch the Record button, and then record the outgoing message you want.

5. Touch the Play button to play the message, and verify that it's what you want. Then click the Save button.

To listen to your messages, follow these steps:

1. Press the Home button to go to the Home screen unless you're already there.

2. Touch the Phone button to display whichever Phone screen you were using last.

3. Touch the Voicemail button. The iPhone displays the Voicemail screen, shown on the right in Figure 19-4. The blue dots show the messages you haven't listened to yet.

4. Connect the headset or touch the Speaker button to switch the speaker on.

5. To listen to a message, touch it twice in quick succession.

6. To delete the current message, touch the Delete button. The iPhone doesn't ask you to confirm the deletion.

7. To call the person who left a message, touch the message, and then touch the Call Back button.

Put Your Contacts on the iPhone or iPod touch

If you make many phone calls on an iPhone, make sure you've got all the contact information you need on it. You can create new contacts on the iPhone by using its keyboard or by adding people who call you, but the main way of getting contact information is by using iTunes to sync it from your PC or Mac.

The iPod touch also lets you synchronize your contact information so that you can view it (for example, so that you can dial a call on a separate phone). The iPod touch also lets you create contacts directly.

Sync Contact Information from the PC or Mac

You can sync contact information from the following sources on the PC:

- **Windows Contacts**   This is Windows Vista's built-in program for storing contacts. If you create contacts from Windows Mail, you'll find them in Windows Contacts.

- **Windows Address Book**   This is Windows XP's built-in program for storing contacts. If you create contacts from Outlook Express, you'll find them in Windows Address Book.

- **Yahoo! Address Book**   If you have Yahoo! Mail, this is where your contacts are stored. Yahoo! Address Book is stored online rather than on your computer.

■ **Outlook 2007 or Outlook 2003**   If you use either of these versions of Outlook, the iPhone can pick up either all contacts or just the groups you choose.

You can sync contact information from the following sources on the Mac:

■ **Address Book**   This is the program built into Mac OS X for storing contacts. Mac OS X shares these contacts with Mail.

■ **Entourage**   If you use Entourage 2004, the iPhone can pick up either all contacts or just the groups you choose.

To set up contact synchronization, follow these steps:

1. Connect the iPhone or iPod touch to your computer. The computer starts iTunes (if it wasn't running) or activates iTunes (if it was running). Allow synchronization to take place.

2. In iTunes, click the iPhone's entry in the Source pane to display the iPhone screens. For an iPod touch, click its entry to display the related screens.

3. Click the Info tab to display its contents.

4. Select the Sync Contacts From check box, and then choose the program in the drop-down list.

5. If you want to put all the contacts on the iPhone, select the All Contacts option button. Otherwise, click the Selected Groups option button, and then, in the list box, select the check box for each group you want to put on the iPhone.

6. Click the Apply button to apply the changes.

Create a Contact on the iPhone or iPod touch

Sometimes, you may want to create a contact directly on the iPhone or iPod touch—or perhaps edit a contact record when you learn a juicy new detail about the contact. You can do so easily enough, but the process of entering full contact details on the on-screen keyboard tends to be daunting.

To add a contact, follow these steps:

1. On the iPhone, in Phone mode, touch the Contacts button to display the Contacts screen. On the iPod touch, press the Home button, and then touch the Contacts icon on the Home screen to display the Contacts screen.

2. Touch the + button in the upper-right corner of the Contacts screen to display the New Contact screen, shown on the left in Figure 19-5.

3. To enter the contact's name, touch the First Last button. The iPhone or iPod touch displays the Edit Name screen, shown on the right in Figure 19-5.

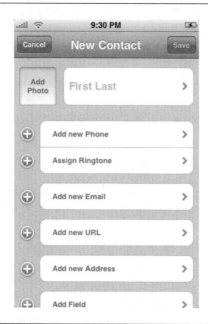

FIGURE 19-5   Creating a new contact on the iPhone or iPod touch is easy enough, but it can mean a whole bunch of one-fingered typing.

4. Type the contact's first name, last name, and company (if appropriate), and then click the Save button. The iPhone or iPod touch displays the New Contact screen, now with the name in place, as shown on the left in Figure 19-6.

5. Touch the next item of information you want to add. For example, touch the Add New Phone button to display the Edit Phone screen, shown on the left in Figure 19-6, on which you can enter the phone number and choose the phone type (mobile, home, work, and so on).

6. When you've finished adding the contact's details, touch the Save button. The iPhone or iPod touch displays the Info screen for the contact.

7. Touch the All Contacts button to return to the All Contacts screen. If you started adding the contact from within a group, touch the button to return to that group instead.

Add Data to an Existing Contact

Rather than add a whole new contact on the iPhone or iPod touch, you may want to add data to an existing contact. To do so, touch the contact's name on the All Contacts screen or the screen for a group, and then touch the Edit button on the Info screen for the contact.

 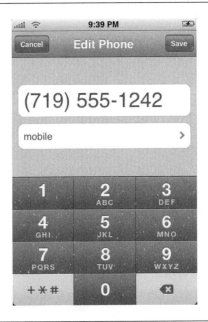

FIGURE 19-6   From the New Contact screen, touch the item of information you want to add, and then use the resulting screen to fill in the details.

TIP

When you meet with a contact in person, and you have your iPhone to hand, you'll have a great opportunity to add a new photo for the contact if the contact record doesn't have one yet. Touch the contact's name to display the Info screen, touch the Edit button, and then touch the Add Photo button. On the panel that pops up, touch the Take Photo button, line the contact up against some attractive scenery, and then press the shutter button. On the Move And Scale screen, move or scale the photo as needed, and then touch the Set Photo button to apply it to the contact.

Delete a Contact

In business as in love, not all relationships work out—and you may sometimes need to delete a contact from the iPhone or iPod touch. To do so, follow these steps:

1. On the Contacts screen or a group screen, touch the contact's name to display the Info screen.

2. Touch the Edit button to start editing the record.

3. Scroll down to the bottom of the screen, touch the Delete Contact button, and then touch the Delete Contact button on the confirmation screen that appears.

Chapter 20

Connect the iPhone or iPod touch to Wireless Networks, Send E-mail, and Surf the Web

How to...

- Connect the iPhone or iPod touch to a wireless network
- Set up an e-mail account
- Send and receive e-mail and attachments
- Surf the Web with Safari
- Create text notes

In the previous chapter, you saw how easy the iPhone makes it to import contact data from your computer and set up (and possibly even enjoy) conference calls with several other people at once. And earlier in the book, you've read about many of the iPhone's other features, from playing songs and videos to snapping digital photos with its built-in camera.

This chapter discusses the main features of the iPhone that have not been discussed so far in this book. The chapter starts by explaining how to connect the iPhone to a wireless network, since you will almost certainly want to do this so that you can enjoy high-speed Internet access with the iPhone. The chapter then shows you how to set up your e-mail accounts on the iPhone, send and receive e-mail and attachments, and surf the Web with Safari. Finally, it shows you how to create text notes—and how to transfer them to your computer.

About half of this chapter applies to the iPod touch as well as to the iPhone. Like the iPhone, the iPod touch can connect to wireless networks and surf the Web—but unlike the iPhone, the iPod touch has neither the Mail program nor the Notes program at this writing, although iPod touch owners are hoping that Apple may add these programs in a revision of the device's firmware.

Connect the iPhone or iPod touch to a Wireless Network

Most likely, you'll want to connect the iPhone to a wireless network whenever possible so that you can send and receive e-mail and browse the Web without suffering the EDGE network's slow data rates. For example, you can connect to a wireless hotspot at an Internet café or an airport. Or you can connect to your home wireless network and use the iPhone's Internet features freely throughout your home.

Given that a wireless network is the iPod touch's only means of connectivity, you'll almost certainly want to connect the iPod touch to a wireless network if one is available.

Set Up a Wireless Network Connection

To connect to a wireless network, you need to know its name, which is called a *service set identifier*, or SSID. If the wireless network has a password, as most do, you need to know that as well. You may also need to know the security type used for the network, which will be one of these three types:

- **WEP**   Wired Equivalent Privacy is the weakest form of protection used on wireless networks. WEP contains systemic errors that make it easy for malefactors to crack. Avoid using WEP if you have the choice. However, because many Wi-Fi hotspots still use WEP, you may find yourself forced to use it.

- **WPA**   WPA is the first level of Wi-Fi Protected Access (the second is WPA2, discussed next). WPA is far more secure than WEP—some experts compare WPA to a decent safe and WEP to a brown envelope—and is a good choice for home use.

- **WPA2**   WPA2 is the strongest level of wireless security in widespread use. Some wireless access points do not support WPA2, but if yours does, you might as well use WPA2, because the iPhone supports it as well. There *is* such a thing as too much wireless network security, but this isn't it.

Armed with this information, you're ready to set up your wireless network connection. Follow these steps:

1. Press the Home button on the iPhone or iPod touch to go to the Home screen unless you're already there.

2. Touch the Settings icon to display the Settings screen.

3. Touch the Wi-Fi Networks icon to display the Wi-Fi Networks screen (shown on the left in Figure 20-1). This screen shows the open wireless networks that the iPhone or iPod touch can detect. *Open* means that a wireless network is broadcasting its network name.

4. Touch the button for the network you want to join. The iPhone or iPod touch displays the Enter Password screen for the network, as shown on the right in Figure 20-1.

> **NOTE**   *If the network you want to join doesn't appear in the list on the Wi-Fi Networks screen, it's probably* closed *(not broadcasting its SSID) rather than open. See the next section for instructions. If the network is* open, *most likely it's out of range of the iPhone or iPod touch.*

5. Type the password. Passwords are usually case sensitive, which can be awkward when the iPhone or iPod touch is being security-conscious and displaying dots rather than the characters you type.

6. Touch the Join button. The iPhone or iPod touch joins the network.

> **TIP**   *Wi-Fi network connections make the iPhone and iPod touch far more useful—but they use a lot of battery power. If you don't use Wi-Fi network connections, or use them only occasionally, turn Wi-Fi off to save battery life. On the Wi-Fi Networks screen, touch the right half of the Wi-Fi slider to turn Wi-Fi off. When you need to join a Wi-Fi network, revisit this screen, and touch the left half of the Wi-Fi slider.*

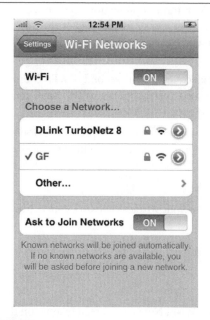 

FIGURE 20-1   Use the Wi-Fi Networks screen (left) to choose a network. The check mark
shows the current connection (if there is one). Type the network password on
the Enter Password screen.

Add a Wireless Network That's Not Listed

Closed wireless networks—ones configured not to broadcast their SSIDs, usually to deter casual
attempts to connect—do not appear in the Choose A Network list on the Wi-Fi Networks screen.
To join a closed wireless network, follow these steps from the Wi-Fi Networks screen:

1. Touch the Other button to display the Other Network screen (shown on the left in
    Figure 20-2).

2. In the Name box, type the name of the wireless network.

3. If the wireless network uses security (as most do), touch the Security button to display
    the Security screen (shown on the right in Figure 20-2).

4. Touch the WEP button, the WPA button, or the WPA2 button, as appropriate. (If you
    don't know which type of security the network uses, consult the network administrator.)
    The iPhone displays the Other Network screen again, which shows the security type you
    chose on the Security line and displays a Password box under it.

5. Type the password, and then touch the Join button. The iPhone or iPod touch joins the
    network.

FIGURE 20-2   Use the Other Network screen (left) to join a closed wireless network. Choose
the security type on the Security screen.

How to ...

Turn Off the "Ask to Join Networks" Feature When in Busy Areas

The Join Networks feature is useful when you want the iPhone or iPod touch to alert you to
a wireless network you might need to join, but it can be a menace when you're somewhere
there are many wireless networks. For example, if you wander down a business street or
even a residential street, the iPhone or iPod touch may find dozens of wireless networks.

In this case, the iPhone or iPod touch is just wasting its battery power keeping track of
the networks around. To stop it from doing so, go to the Wi-Fi Networks screen, and then
touch the right half of the Ask To Join Networks slider.

Make the iPhone or iPod touch Forget a Wireless Network

When you no longer want to use a particular wireless network, tell the iPhone or iPod touch to forget it. To do so, open the wireless network's configuration screen, and then touch the Forget This Network button.

If you find you need to join the wireless network again, join it as described earlier in this chapter. You will need to type the password for the network.

Did you know?

Why You Should Never Use a Wireless Access Point's Default Name

Normally, when you buy a wireless access point, it comes with a default network name, administrator name, and password that the manufacturer has programmed into it.

The idea is that you can get your wireless network up and running in short order, and then change the network name and password (and perhaps the administrator name) for security.

Most people don't change the network name. Or the password.

As you can imagine, this is bad for security, because any attacker who knows the password for one of the default network names (and they're widely published on the Web) can access the network. But it's doubly bad for the iPhone and iPod touch, because Apple set them up in a user-friendly but insecure way. Once you've connected to a wireless network successfully, the iPhone or iPod touch remembers the network, and automatically connects to it again when it's within range—but without making sure that the network is the same network. So a malefactor can create a wireless network that has the same name (SSID) and password as a network you've used before, and the iPhone or iPod touch will happily connect to the malefactor's network. The malefactor can then attempt to grab your data off the iPhone or iPod touch.

For this reason, it's a good idea not to use the manufacturer's default name (SSID) for any wireless network you set up. Using a unique network name will make it harder for a casual attacker to target your iPhone or iPod touch. However, a determined attacker who wants to target you specifically can use a packet sniffer program to detect the wireless network settings you're using, after which they can implement this attack.

If you connect to a wireless network at a hotspot, you won't have the chance to change its network name or password—so be on your guard for anything unusual when connected. For example, if the iPhone or iPod touch can establish the connection to the wireless network, but you cannot access your e-mail as usual, you may have connected to the wrong network.

Apple may change the iPhone's and iPod touch's firmware or software to get around this problem. But even if it does, you're better off creating a unique name for your wireless network.

Send and Receive E-mail on the iPhone

The iPhone can send and receive not only e-mail but also attachments, so you can receive files while out and about with your iPhone, and view them immediately.

The iPhone supports various widely used file formats for attachments, including:

- **Word documents**   Word 2007 format (DOCX) or Word 97–2003 format (DOC).
- **Excel workbooks**   Excel 2007 format (XLSX) or Excel 97–2003 format (XLS).
- **Portable Document Format**   PDF files, such as those produced by Adobe Acrobat or any program running on Mac OS X.
- **Text files**   Plain text files, in the TXT format. The iPhone can't display Rich Text Files (RTF format).

First, you need to set up the iPhone to use your e-mail account. Then you can start sending and receiving.

Set Up an E-mail Account

As you'll know if you've set up an e-mail account manually on a computer (for example, in Windows Mail or Mac Mail), you need to know a handful of details and enter them accurately and in the right places. The process is tedious and can be frustrating.

Apple has largely bypassed this problem by teaching iTunes to grab the settings for your existing e-mail account and load them on the iPhone for you. So if you use one of the mail programs that iTunes supports, you won't actually need to type your username, password, mail servers, and so forth on the iPhone.

These are the Windows mail programs that iTunes supports at this writing:

- **Outlook**   Either Outlook 2007 or Outlook 2003.
- **Outlook Express**   The free e-mail program included with Windows XP and other versions of Windows before Windows Vista.
- **Windows Mail**   The free e-mail program included with Windows Vista. (Windows Mail is an updated and renamed version of Outlook Express.)

These are the Mac mail programs that iTunes supports at this writing:

- **Mail**   The mail program included with Mac OS X.
- **Entourage**   The e-mail (and much more) program included in Office for the Mac—the Mac version of Outlook, if you will.

If you have another type of e-mail account, you can set it up manually on the iPhone. The iPhone provides help for setting up widely used web-mail accounts, such as Gmail and Yahoo! Mail. If you have another type of account, you can set it up the hard way.

Set Up an E-mail Account from Your Computer

To set up an e-mail account from your computer, follow these steps:

1. Connect the iPhone to your computer, and allow synchronization to take place.
2. In iTunes, click the iPhone's entry in the Source pane to display the iPhone screens.
3. Click the Info tab, and then scroll down to the Mail Accounts area.
4. Select the Sync Selected Mail Accounts check box, and then choose the program in the drop-down list. If the program doesn't appear there, chances are that iTunes doesn't support it.
5. Click the Apply button. iTunes passes the details of the account to the iPhone.

Set Up an E-mail Account Manually on the iPhone

If iTunes can't grab the details of the e-mail account you want to use with the iPhone, you'll need to set it up manually on the iPhone. Follow these steps:

1. Press the Home button to go to the Home screen unless you're already there.
2. Touch the Settings button to display the Settings screen.
3. Scroll down, and then touch the Mail button to display the Mail screen, shown on the left in Figure 20-3.

FIGURE 20-3   From the Mail screen, touch the Add Account button to reach the Add Mail screen. If your e-mail provider is listed here, touch it; if not, touch the Other button.

4. Touch the Add Account button to display the Add Mail screen, shown on the right in Figure 20-3.

5. If the Add Mail screen shows your e-mail provider, touch its button, enter the details on the resulting screen, and then touch the Save button. The adjacent illustration shows the Gmail screen. Otherwise, touch the Other button, and then follow through the remaining steps in this list.

6. On the Other screen (as shown in Figure 20-4), touch the button for the type of incoming e-mail server your e-mail provider uses: IMAP, POP, or Exchange. (If in doubt, ask the administrator for this and the other details you need.)

7. Touch the Save button. The iPhone verifies the account information, and then adds the account to the Mail screen.

You're now ready to send and receive e-mail using this e-mail account. But while you're at the Mail screen, let's look quickly at some of the configuration options you may want to set.

FIGURE 20-4   On the Other screen, choose the incoming e-mail server type, and then enter the details of the account. Scroll down to the bottom to reach the more deeply buried settings.

Configure Mail Settings

When you set up an e-mail account, the iPhone automatically applies standard settings to it. These settings work well for many people—well, presumably—but you may want to change some of them. These settings apply to all the e-mail accounts you've set up on the iPhone: You can't apply them to one account but not to another.

These settings appear on the Mail screen. The left half of Figure 20-5 shows the top part of the Mail screen, and the right half shows the bottom part.

Here's what you need to know about the settings:

- **Auto-Check**   Controls whether Mail automatically checks for new messages. Your choices are Manual (in other words, don't check automatically), Every 15 Minutes, Every 30 Minutes, or Every Hour.

- **Show**   Controls how many recent messages Mail shows. Your choices are 25, 50, 75, 100, or 200 recent messages.

- **Preview**   Controls how many lines of the message Mail shows as a preview. Your choices are None, 1 Line, 2 Lines, 3 Lines, 4 Lines, or 5 Lines.

- **Minimum Font Size**   Controls the smallest font size used. Your choices are Small, Medium (the default), Large, Extra Large, or Giant.

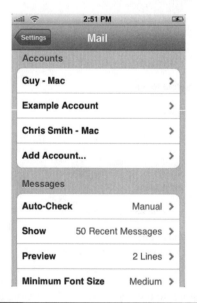
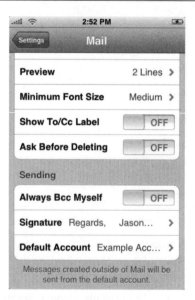

FIGURE 20-5   It's worth spending a few minutes examining the settings on the Mail screen in case the defaults cause you grief.

- **Show To/Cc Label**   Controls whether Mail automatically shows the To label for a message (and the Cc label, if there is one) when you open the message. You can display these labels manually by touching the Details button. Hiding the labels lets you see more of the message onscreen at once.

- **Ask Before Deleting**   Controls whether Mail prompts you to confirm each deletion of an e-mail message. Some people find the confirmation handy, while others find it irritating.

NOTE *If you delete a message and then wish you hadn't, you can usually retrieve it from the Trash and move it back to your Inbox or another folder.*

- **Always Bcc Myself**   Controls whether Mail automatically sends a blind carbon copy (one that the other recipients of the message can't see) to your e-mail address. On some e-mail systems, this is a convenient way of keeping copies of messages you send. Other e-mail systems provide a more convenient way of keeping copies, such as a Sent Items folder.

- **Signature**   Lets you set up text that Mail adds automatically to each new message you create. The iPhone's default signature is "Sent from my iPhone," which is cute for the first couple of messages but not great for long-term use. (For example, you may not want your colleagues to know that you're actually working from the beach today.) To change the signature, touch the Signature bar, and then use the Signature screen (shown next) to compose a signature; alternatively, simply touch the Clear button to clear the current signature. Touch the Mail button when you've finished.

■ **Default Account**   Controls which e-mail account Mail uses when you send a photo or a note (both discussed later in this chapter). If you've set up only one account, that will be the default account. If you've set up two or more, check the readout. If it shows the wrong account, touch the Default Account bar to display the Default Account screen (shown next), touch the account you want to use as the default, and then touch the Mail button.

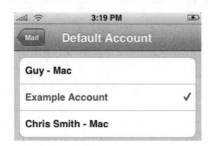

When you've finished choosing mail settings, touch the Settings button to return to the Settings screen.

Send E-mail

To send e-mail, follow these steps:

1. Press the Home button to go to the Home screen unless you're already there.

2. Touch the Mail button to go to Mail.

3. If Mail displays the Accounts screen, touch the account you want to use.

4. Touch the Write Message button in the lower-right corner of the window (see Figure 20-6).

5. Address the message:

■ If the recipient is in your Contacts list, touch the + button at the right end of the To line to display the Contacts screen. Touch the contact to add them to the To line.

■ Otherwise, type the e-mail address.

> TIP   *To remove one of the recipients you've added, backspace over the name. The first backspace selects the address, and the second deletes it.*

6. If you need to add Cc recipients, touch the Cc field, and then add the address or addresses using the same techniques as in the previous step.

7. Add the subject line. Touch the Subject field, and then type the text.

8. Add the message content. Touch in the text area, and then type the text.

9. Touch the Send button.

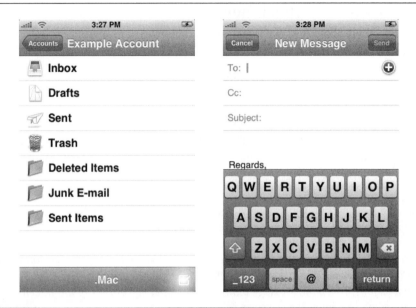

FIGURE 20-6   Touch the Write Message button (left screen, lower-right corner) to start a new message (right) from the e-mail account you've selected.

Send Photographs via E-mail

You can send a photo that you've either taken on the iPhone or loaded onto it. Follow these steps:

1. Press the Home button to go to the Home screen unless you're already there.

2. Touch the Photos icon to display the Photo Albums screen.

> **NOTE** *If you're taking photos with the camera, you can start directly from there. Open the Camera Roll album, and then open the photo.*

3. Touch the album that contains the photo, and then touch the photo to open it.

4. Touch the Send button in the lower-left corner of the screen, and then touch the Email Photo button on the pop-up screen. Mail starts a new message including the photo.

5. Address the message, type the subject line, type any text that's needed, and then touch the Send button.

The iPhone also lets you send notes via e-mail. See the section "Send Notes via E-mail," later in this chapter, for details.

Receive E-mails and Attachments

Sending e-mail is only half the fun. You'll almost certainly receive it as well. To check, review, and deal with e-mail, follow these steps:

1. Press the Home button to go to the Home screen unless you're already there.

2. Touch the Mail button to go to Mail.

3. If Mail displays the Accounts screen, touch the account you want to view. You can see at a glance how many new messages are in each Inbox, as shown on the left in Figure 20-7.

4. On the screen for the account (see the example on the right in Figure 20-7), touch the Inbox to display its contents. The left screen in Figure 20-8 shows an example of an Inbox.

5. Touch the message you want to view. The iPhone displays its contents. The right screen in Figure 20-8 shows an example of a message with an attachment.

NOTE   *If an attachment appears as a button, you can touch the button to view the attachment. At this writing, the iPhone can display only some attachments, such as PDF files or graphics files. Touch the Message button in the upper-left corner of the screen to return from the attachment to the message.*

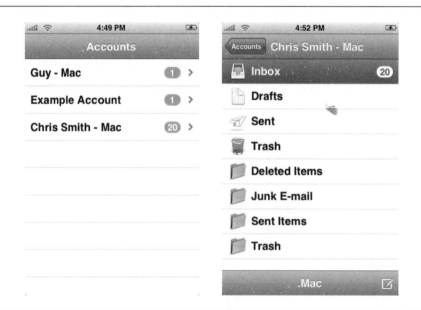

FIGURE 20-7   Mail lets you see at a glance how many messages are in each account.

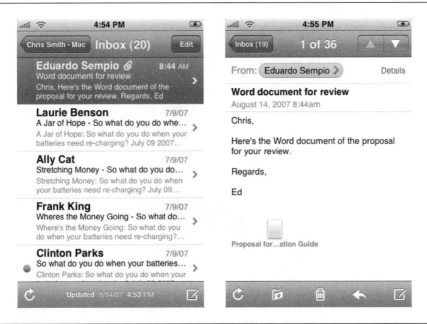

FIGURE 20-8 Touch the Inbox (left) to display its contents, and then touch the message you want to open to display it. Touch the button in the lower-left corner of the Inbox to check for new messages.

6. To reply to the message or forward it, touch the button with the left-pointing arrow at the bottom of the screen, and then touch the Reply button or the Forward button on the panel that appears. Write the required text, address the message if you're forwarding it, and then touch the Send button.

7. To delete the message, touch the Delete button in the middle of the row at the bottom of the screen.

8. To file the message, touch the Move button, the button with the folder on it. Mail displays the list of folders for the mail account, as shown in Figure 20-9. Touch the destination folder. Mail moves the message there, and then displays the next message in the Inbox (if there is one).

9. To move through the messages, touch the Up button or the Down button in the upper-right corner of the screen.

10. To return to your Inbox, touch the Inbox button in the upper-left corner of the screen.

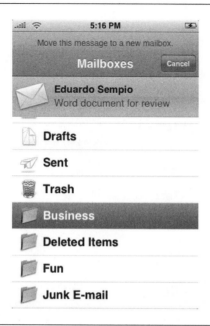

FIGURE 20-9 To remove a message from your inbox without deleting it, file it in one of the folders for the mail account.

Browse the Web with Safari on the iPhone and iPod touch

If you're used to browsing the Web on a big screen, you'll know how vital it is to have plenty of space so that you can see what's on each page. That may make you think that browsing the Web on the iPhone must be a nonstarter.

All credit to Apple, Safari on the iPhone and iPod touch is a marvel of miniaturization and makes browsing quite viable—even though you'll have to do plenty of zooming and scrolling to navigate most web pages:

- **Zoom** Either pinch out with your fingers (or a finger and thumb) on the area you want to zoom in on, or double-touch a point to zoom in quickly on it. Pinch back in or double-touch again to zoom back out.

- **Scroll** Flick your finger in the direction in which you want to move the page—up, down, left, right, or diagonally.

For best results, you'll usually want to turn the iPhone or iPod touch to landscape orientation almost immediately after switching to Safari.

Switch to Safari

First, switch to Safari. Follow these steps:

1. Press the Home button to go to the Home screen unless you're already there.

2. Touch the Safari icon at the bottom of the screen.

Get Your Bookmarks into Safari

Typing URLs into a web browser is a chore even on a full-sized keyboard. Typing URLs on the onscreen keyboard is pretty tedious, even though the iPhone or iPod touch does its best to help by putting essential keys such as /, ., and .COM on the keyboard in Safari, as shown here.

If you browse extensively, you'll need to type some URLs on the onscreen keyboard sooner or later. But what you should do instead is create a bookmark in your web browser for each website you'll want to access using your iPhone or iPod touch, and then synchronize those bookmarks with the iPhone or iPod touch.

To synchronize your bookmarks, follow these steps:

1. Connect the iPhone or iPod touch to your computer, and allow synchronization to take place.

2. Click the iPhone's or iPod touch's entry in the Source pane to display the screens for the device.

3. Click the Info tab, and then scroll down to the Web Browser area.

4. Select the Sync Bookmarks From check box, and then choose the browser in the drop-down list. If the browser doesn't appear there, chances are that iTunes doesn't support it.

TIP *If iTunes can't import the bookmarks from your favorite browser, there is a workaround—even if it's an ugly one. Export the bookmarks from the browser, import them into Internet Explorer or Safari, and then synchronize the iPhone or iPod touch with Internet Explorer or Safari. You will not be able to keep your bookmarks synchronized with your preferred browser, but at least this gives you a way of getting your bookmarks from that browser onto the iPhone or iPod touch.*

5. Click the Apply button. iTunes copies the bookmarks to the iPhone or iPod touch.

Go to a Bookmark

To go to a bookmark on the iPhone or iPod touch, follow these steps:

1. Touch the Bookmarks button at the bottom of the screen, as shown on the left in Figure 20-10.

2. The iPhone or iPod touch displays the Bookmarks screen you were using last. The first time, you will usually see the main Bookmarks screen, as shown on the right in Figure 20-10.

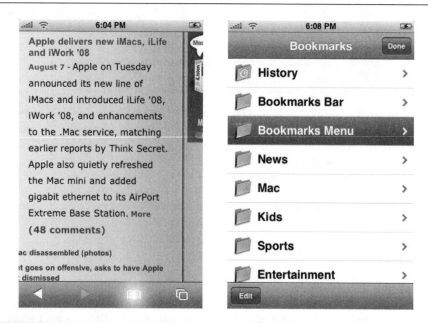

FIGURE 20-10 The easiest way of getting to a website on the iPhone or iPod touch is to use a bookmark.

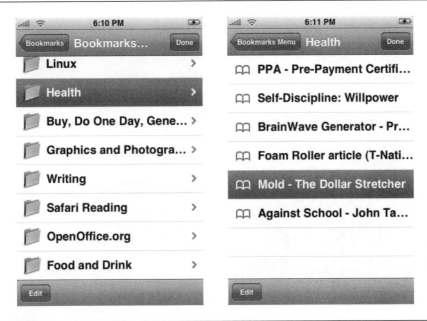

FIGURE 20-11   Touch the bookmark category you want (left), and then touch the bookmark to display the page it marks (right).

3. Touch the category of bookmarks you want to view. For example, touch the Bookmarks Menu button to display the Bookmarks Menu screen, as shown on the left in Figure 20-11.

4. Touch the bookmark for the webpage you want to display, as shown on the right in Figure 20-11. Safari opens the webpage.

Add a Bookmark on the iPhone or iPod touch

If you browse on the iPhone or iPod touch, you'll probably run into webpages that you want to bookmark for later reference. The good news is that not only can you do this, but iTunes syncs your bookmarks back to your browser, so you can use the bookmark on your computer as well.

To add a bookmark, follow these steps:

1. On the iPhone or iPod touch, browse to a webpage that deserves a bookmark. (At this writing, this step is often tougher than it should be.)

2. Touch the Add Bookmark button (the + button) near the upper-left corner of the screen. (If you've scrolled down the webpage, you'll need to scroll back up to the top to reach the button.) The iPhone or iPod touch displays the Add Bookmark screen, shown on the left in Figure 20-12.

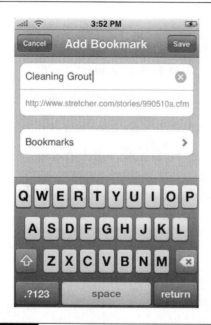
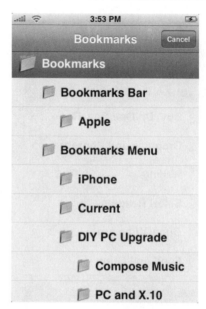

FIGURE 20-12   You can add a bookmark on the iPhone or iPod touch and have it be synchronized back to your computer.

3. The Add Bookmark screen displays the page's title in the top text box. You can either accept this as the name for the bookmark, edit it by using the keyboard, or clear the name (touch the × button) and then type a new name.

4. To change the location in which the iPhone or iPod touch stores the bookmark, touch the bar indicating the current location (in the example, this is Bookmarks). On the resulting screen, shown on the right in Figure 20-12, touch the location you want. The iPhone or iPod touch displays the Add Bookmark screen again, with the bar now showing the location you chose.

5. Touch the Save button to save the bookmark. The iPhone or iPod touch then returns you to the webpage from which you started the bookmarking process.

Go to Webpages You've Visited Before

To navigate among the webpages you've visited before in this session, touch the Back button or the Forward button at the lower-left corner of the screen.

The Back button is available as soon as you've navigated from one webpage to another. The Forward button becomes available when you use the Back button to go back to a webpage you've visited earlier.

Open Multiple Pages at the Same Time

Safari lets you open multiple pages at the same time, and then switch among them. This is handy when you want to view another webpage without closing the webpage you're currently viewing.

To open a new page in Safari, follow these steps:

1. Touch the button in the lower-right corner of the screen. Safari shrinks the current page and displays a New Page button and a Done button, as shown here.

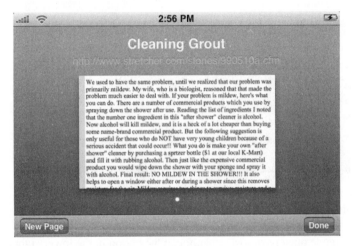

2. Touch the New Page button. Safari displays a blank new page, as shown here. The button in the lower-right corner of the screen shows the number of pages you have open.

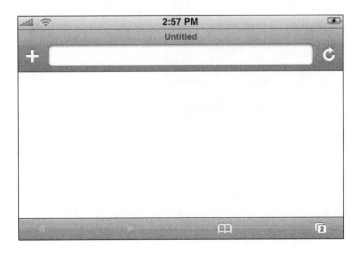

3. Go to a URL in one of the usual ways:

■ Touch the Address box to display the keyboard, type the URL, and then touch the Go button, as shown here.

■ Touch the Bookmarks button to display your list of bookmarks, and then choose the bookmark you want.

To navigate from one open page to another, touch the button in the lower-right corner of the screen to shrink the current page and display the control buttons, as shown here.

Scroll left or right to reach the page you want to view, and then touch it to display it. To close a page, touch the × button that appears in its upper-left corner.

Create Text Notes on the iPhone

The iPhone includes a Notes program that lets you jot down text notes using the onscreen keyboard. You can then e-mail the notes to yourself on your computer.

TIP *The iPod touch does not have a Notes program at this writing, which many iPod touch owners consider a sad loss. The only way around this limitation is to create a contact record for the note, touch the Add Field button, scroll down to the bottom of the Add Field screen, and then touch the Note button. You can enter a good amount of text in the Note field for a contact—but you will then have to retrieve the text from the contact record on your computer after you synchronize the iPod touch.*

Create a Note

To create a note, follow these steps:

1. Press the Home button to go to the Home screen unless you're already there.
2. Touch the Notes icon to display the Notes screen, shown on the left in Figure 20-13 with several notes created already.

FIGURE 20-13   From the Notes screen (left), touch the New button (+) to start a new note (right).

3. To start a new note (as shown on the right in Figure 20-13), touch the New button at the upper-right corner of the screen. To open an existing note, touch it in the list.

4. If you created a new note, type it using the keyboard. The first line becomes the title of the note.

5. Type the body of the note. If you make a typo for which the iPhone suggest a correction, you can accept the correction by pressing SPACEBAR, as shown here. To refuse the correction, touch the word on the screen, and then continue typing.

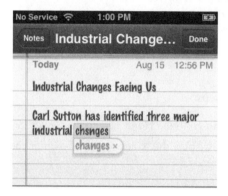

6. If you need to zoom in on the text to see it larger, touch (and hold) on the word you want to see, as shown here. Move your finger to move the magnifier.

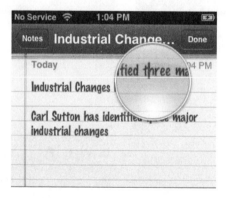

7. If you want to hide the keyboard so that you can read more of the note, touch the Done button.

8. When you've finished working on the note, touch the Notes button to return to the Notes screen.

Delete a Note

To delete a note, open it, touch the Delete button at the bottom of the screen, and then touch the Delete Note button on the pop-up panel. If the keyboard is displayed, touch the Done button to close it first. You can then see the Delete button.

Send a Note via E-mail

At this writing, iTunes and the iPhone don't provide a convenient way of getting your text notes onto your computer. iTunes does back up the text notes along with the iPhone's other data, but there's no easy way for you to get at them.

So the standard way of getting a note off your iPhone onto your computer is to e-mail the note to yourself. And to get a note to somebody else, of course, you e-mail the note to that person instead.

To send a note, follow these steps:

1. Create the note as usual, and open it.

2. If the keyboard is displayed, touch the Done button to close it.

3. With the note open, touch the Send button at the bottom of the screen, as shown on the left in Figure 20-14. The iPhone creates a new message in Mail, using your default e-mail account, with the note's subject as the subject line and the note's text as the body text, as shown on the right in Figure 20-14.

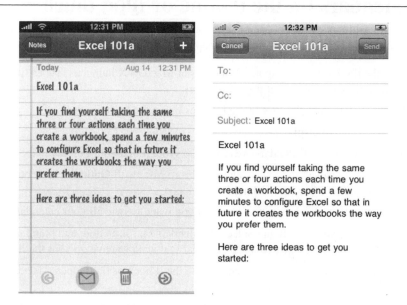

FIGURE 20-14   Touch the Send button (left) to create a message containing the current note (right). You can then address it and send it in moments.

How to ... **Read Documents on the iPhone**

At this writing, one of the iPhone's big omissions is a reader program that lets you put e-books on the iPhone and read them on its clear, bright screen. Sooner or later, Apple will presumably provide such a program. But in the meantime, you can use Mail's ability to display attachments as a cheap-and-cheerful reader program. Simply get the document in a suitable format—for example, a text file, a Word document, or a PDF file—and then e-mail it to yourself, open it up in Mail on the iPhone, and you're reading.

4. Touch the To field to display the keyboard and the address button, and then address the message as usual. (The address button is the blue circle containing a plus sign.) For example, touch the address button, and then select the recipient from your Contacts list.

5. Touch the Send button to send the message.

Put Your Calendars on the iPhone or iPod touch

You can put your calendars on the iPhone or iPod touch by using much the same technique described for the iPod classic and iPod nano in Chapter 11. To recap, follow these steps:

1. Connect the iPod to your computer. Windows or Mac OS X launches iTunes (if it wasn't running) or activates iTunes (if it was running).

2. In iTunes, click the iPod's entry in the Devices list in the Source pane.

3. Click the Info tab to display its contents.

4. Use the controls in the Calendars area to set up synchronization. For example:

   ■ On Windows, select the Sync Calendars From Microsoft Outlook check box. On the Mac, select the Sync iCal Calendars check box.

   ■ Select the All Calendars option button if you want to sync all your calendars.

   ■ To sync only some, click the Selected Calendars option button, and then, in the list box, select the check box for each calendar you want to have on your the iPod.

5. Click the Apply button to apply the changes to the iPhone or iPod touch. iTunes synchronizes the calendars with it.

6. After the synchronization, disconnect the iPhone or iPod touch.

To view your calendars on the iPhone or iPod touch, follow these steps:

1. Press the Home button to go to the Home screen unless you're already there.

2. Touch the Calendar icon to display the Calendar.

3. To switch view, touch the List button, the Day button, or the Month button. The left screen in Figure 20-15 shows the Day view, which many people find most useful for getting an overview of what's on their plate.

4. To view the details of an appointment, touch its entry. On the Event screen (the right screen in Figure 20-15 shows an example), you can touch the Edit button to edit the event.

5. Touch the button in the upper-left corner of the screen when you want to return to the previous view.

On the iPhone, you can add a new event by touching the + button in the upper-right corner of the Calendar screen and then working on the Add Event screen (shown on the left in Figure 20-16). Touch one of the buttons on the Add Event screen to display a screen on which you can enter the

FIGURE 20-15   Day view (left) in the Calendar shows you a scrollable list of appointments and times. Touch an appointment to see its details (right).

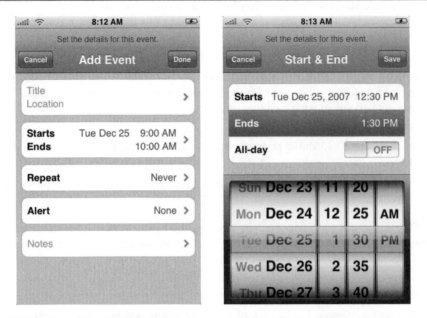

FIGURE 20-16   The iPhone lets you create events directly; the iPod touch does not.

details for that item. For example, touch the Starts/Ends button to display the Start & End screen (shown on the right in Figure 20-16), on which you can choose the start time and end time for an event. Touch the Done button when you've finished creating the event.

Index

B